The Political Economy of Development and Environment in Korea

This book examines the economic, social and spatial development of (South) Korea from the early modernisation period until the seismic events of the 1997 economic crisis.

The book focuses on two main areas: first, on the political and ideological control of the state during the developmental era, and second, on the environmental problems in Korea in order to examine how society and environment have been used as a means to rapid accumulation. The main characteristics of Korean economic growth and social control reveal why the financial crisis of the late 1990s was an unavoidable event waiting to happen.

The Political Economy of Development and Environment in Korea explores the process of capital accumulation, population concentration and environmental degradation in circumstances in which the state has played a highly particular role. The interventionist Korean state has always striven to maintain the capital accumulation process, mediating between national interests and global forces, whilst at the same time attempting to establish the basis for its own legitimation.

With its breadth of coverage, including an extensive range of statistical data drawn from both official and NGO sources, the book develops a succinct theorisation of the political–economic and spatial history of Korea from the era of Japanese colonialism to the present. Overall, this study of the environmental consequences of Korea's economic and spatial development offers an indispensable resource. As such it will also be of interest to the general researcher in contemporary political and human geography, development economics and environmental issues.

Jae-Yong Chung is a lecturer at the Department of Architecture, Chungnam National University in Korea. His special interests are Korean economic and environmental problems as well as sustainable urban development issues. He is currently involved in various urban planning projects in Seoul and Daejeon, Korea.

Richard J.R. Kirkby is an independent consultant on East Asian affairs. His special interest is the urbanisation process in the People's Republic of China, where he has lived and worked since 1974. He has also worked as a consultant for major academic and development projects in East and Southeast Asia.

Routledge Studies in the Growth Economies of Asia

The Political Economy of Development and Environment in Korea

Jae-Yong Chung and
Richard J.R. Kirkby

London and New York

First published 2002
by Routledge
11 New Fetter Lane, London EC4P 4EE

Simultaneously published in the USA and Canada
by Routledge
29 West 35th Street, New York, NY 10001

Routledge is an imprint of the Taylor & Francis Group

© 2002 Jae-Yong Chung and Richard J.R. Kirkby

Typeset in Baskerville by
Florence Production Ltd, Stoodleigh, Devon
Printed and bound in Great Britain by
MPG Books Ltd, Bodmin, Cornwall

British Library Cataloguing in Publication Data
A catalogue record for this book is available from the British
Library

Library of Congress Cataloging-in-Publication data
Chung, Jae-Yong.
  The political economy of development and environment in
  Korea/Jae-Yong Chung and Richard J. Kirkby.
     p. cm. — (Routledge studies in the growth economies of Asia)
  Includes bibliographical references and index.
  1. Korea (South)—Economic policy—1960–   2. Sustainable
  development—Korea (South)   3. Environmental degradation—
  Korea (South)   I. Kirkby, R. J. R. (Richard J. R.)
  II. Title.   III. Series.
  HC467.C587 2001
  338.95195—dc21   2001031729

ISBN 0–415–20536–0

Contents

Tables

Figures

Appendices

Tables

Figures

Acknowledgements

The authors are grateful to the many individuals and organisations who have materially supported this project and to the many whose thoughts and writings have given depth and richness to this book. Professor Peter Dicken who prompted us to publish this work deserves a special mention.

We extend our special thanks to our families for their many years of support and especially to Mr. I. K. Chung for his encouragement. So we dedicate this book to them.

The authors and publishers would like to thank the following for granting permission to reproduce material in this work: Chang, S-M. for the reproduction of a table on p.158 from 'Republic of Korea' in Asian Development Bank and Economic Development Institute (eds) *The Urban Poor and Basic Infrastructure Services in Asia and the Pacific*, A Regional Seminar, 22–28 January 1991, with permission from Asia Development Bank. Park, S-O. and F.E.I. Hamilton, for the reproduction of an illustration from *Industrialisation in Developing and Peripheral Regions*, 1986, with permission from Taylor and Francis. Mason E.S. for the reproduction of tables on pp.48 and 101 from *The Economic and Social Modernization of the Republic of Korea*, 1980, with permission from Harvard University Asia Center. A. Tickell and I. Peck for the reproduction of a table on p.45 from 'Accumulation, Regulation and the Geographies of Post-Fordism: Missing Links in Regulationist Research' in *Progress in Human Geography*, 16(2) 1992, reproduced with permission from Arnold Publishers. All the Korean publishers for granting permission to use material from their respective sources.

Every effort has been made to contact copyright holders for their permission to reprint material in this book. The publishers would be grateful to hear from any copyright holder who is not here acknowledged and will undertake to rectify any errors or omissions in future editions of this book.

Jae-Yong Chung, Ph.D.
Richard Kirkby, Ph.D.

Glossary of abbreviations

ACHR	Asian Coalition for Housing Rights
CCZ	Core consumption zone
CISJD	Christian Institute for Study of Justice and Development
EOI	Export-Oriented Industrialisation
EPB	Economic Planning Bureau
FEER	*Far Eastern Economic Review*
FYEDP	Five Year Economic Development Plan
IDL	Industrial Distribution Law
IRD	Integrated Rural Development
KAAPRI	Korea Anti-Nuclear Anti-Pollution Peace Research Institute
KCFA	Korea Catholic Farmers Association
KRIHS	Korea Research Institute for Housing and Settlement
LIDL	Local Industrial Development Law
MoC	Ministry of Construction
MoE	Ministry of Environment
MoTI	Ministry of Trade and Industry
MSR	Mode of social regulation
NIC	Newly industrialising country
NIDL	New International Division of Labour
NSO	National Statistical Office
OoE	Office of Environment
PRZ	Peripheral rural zone
SCG	Seoul City Government
SIZ	Semi-peripheral industrial zone
SMA	Seoul Metropolitan Area
SMG	Seoul Metropolitan Government
SMR	Seoul Metropolitan Region
UN	United Nations
WCED	World Conference on Environment and Development

Introduction

The year 1997 proved a turning point in Korea's modern history. The unprecedented financial crash and ensuing crisis led to a currency collapse and, by November, chain bankruptcies had left the Korean government little alternative but to appeal to the International Monetary Fund. After thirty years of spectacular but often turbulent growth, Korea's peculiar state-orchestrated economy had finally run up against the buffers. The pundits of globalisation had completely failed to prepare us for the debacle of Korea, Thailand and Indonesia in 1997, and, naturally, the impact of economic collapse was felt far beyond Asia. In the poorer regions of the UK, for instance, much heralded Korean electronics factories such as the Lucky Goldstar (LG) plant in Wales, and Hyundai in Scotland, were immediately put on hold.

Korea's meteoric economic transformation from war-devastation in the 1950s to prosperous industrial nationhood had not been without considerable internal tension. The causes lie deep within the nation's body politic. The newly industrialising country (NIC) literature is wide-ranging; until recently, however, it was the protagonists of the free market who were dominant in explication (Chen 1979, Balassa 1981). Interpretations from the left were marginalised largely because dependency theory was unable to account for the NIC phenomenon. But in the 1990s there was a reassessment from all sides of the political divide regarding the contribution of state institutions, and of external political-economic pressures in shaping the development of late industrialising nations such as Taiwan, Singapore and Korea (Henderson and Appelbaum 1992, Henderson 1993a, 1993b, Amsden 1989, Luedde-Neurath 1988, 1993). Analysis has dwelt on the distortion of 'free markets'; as Amsden states for the Korean case, the state wilfully 'got the prices wrong' in order to stimulate growth (Amsden 1989, p.14).

A division in approach has emerged within the growing body of dissident thinking on supra-national political economy. There are on the one hand those of the 'world systems' and 'globalist' persuasion who place emphasis on the larger, extra-national forces at play (Cumings 1988, Dicken 1993, Lipietz 1987). On the other hand, often conversely, there are those who emphasise the central position of government – the 'statist' approach (Luedde-Neurath 1988, Amsden 1989). While the former group is often said to underplay internal factors in the development process, the latter may fall into the trap of functional reductionism: their proposition of a 'developmental state' takes insufficient account of global capitalist development. In reality, a synthesis of both contending theses is essential to a mature understanding. In our own terms, the post-1997 crisis in Korea and other East and Southeast nations arises directly from mode of development – exposure to global forces alongside state manipulation of the economy.

This book investigates the link between capitalist development processes and the environment in Korea. It gives due weight to both global and internal forces. Although the national state has played and continues to play a pivotal role in economic management, the setting is unequivocally a capitalist accumulation system of global dimensions. State strategies are devised to promote the growth of domestic capital and defuse internal political pressures; moreover, they also guide industries towards niche markets in the global arena while shielding them from foreign competition. The state is a central agent for development, but global flows and markets play an equally important role in the realisation of accumulation. The state is not an institution which is monolithic and unshifting: it is itself subject to transformation, and never more so than during a crisis. The authors feel that while all theoretical approaches are mere aids to understanding, it is the framework known as regulation theory which offers the widest scope for incorporating both statist and globalist tendencies.

The term 'regulation' was introduced by Destanne de Bernis and the Research Group on the Regulation of the Capitalist Economy in the 1970s. The regulation approach emerged to study the crisis of Fordism and its restructuring into the post-Fordism (Tickell and Peck 1992b). The theoretical advances were carried on by Michel Aglietta, particularly in his work *A Theory of Capitalist Regulation* (1979).[1] This was followed by Alain Lipietz (1986, 1987) and Robert Boyer (1990a) to mention but a few.

The regulationist approach defines meta-theoretical tools by which to examine the nature of the accumulation system across contiguous time and space. Periodisation of Korea's economic history illuminates the changing character of both mode of development and state intervention. Korea's development trajectory has seen a succession of often discontinuous stages, each of which endeavours to resolve the contradictions of the one preceding. The post-1997 crisis period is exceptional merely in its degree of adjustment.

Our investigation starts from the premise that the 1997 crisis was deep-rooted within Korea's political-economy fabric – that is, in the interaction of state power with monopoly capital, and in the nature of regulation of the finance sector. Conventional wisdom, which we broadly share, regards the root problem as being the nexuses of Korea's 'developmentalist' state.

These have long rested on an alliance between the state bureaucracy and Korea's dominant form of private sector conglomerate – the chaebol. It might be thought that the authoritarian state and concentrated economic power went hand in hand. However, the form of economic regulation exercised by the state upon the chaebol conglomerates registered few real changes after the democratisation of late 1988.

Rather than moving towards the specialisation and higher productivity demanded by external conditions, the chaebol continued on their old path of continual diversification aimed at opportunistic profits. For its part, the state was unable to relinquish direct and indirect controls. The outcome was that the structurally uncompetitive monopolies continued to dominate Korea's domestic market while smaller non-chaebol enterprises were starved of capital.

Liberal economists customarily present the latest crisis of the Korean economy as being the outcome of a form of state management which stifled the natural flow of market forces. Our own position locates the causes as deeper, and presents the notion of the mode of social regulation as key. Broadly, the three factors which led to Korea's exchange rate crisis were internationalisation, the relaxation of rules governing off-shore investment, and the rigidity of domestic labour relations. With the post-democratisation consolidation of collective bargaining, worker militancy made flexiblisation of labour a fraught process which even the mid-1990s recession failed to shift in a direction more favourable to capital. This prompted the chaebol to seek offshore locations for major new production lines. At this point, even the UK had lower labour costs and higher unit productivity than did Korea. Loan capital and indeed national foreign currency reserves were increasingly redirected offshore in this sudden bid to internationalise Korean production. Under domestic political pressure, Korea's banks continued to make the greater part of their loans to the chaebol despite the latters' already high level of leverage. As the banks started to default on their repayments to international lending institutions, particularly after the collapse of one major company – Kia Motors – credit ratings were lowered and loan conditions tightened. The value of the Korean won against the dollar spiralled downwards, this in turn making loan repayments across the board far more burdensome.

The 1997 crisis, coming not coincidentally at the end of a presidential term, also coincided with the withering of a particular mode of social regulation, and the appearance of more rigid labour relations. The manner in which the post-1997 crisis is resolved and the nature of the emerging accumulation regime and mode of social regulation depend upon the type of compromise forged between political and economic blocs, including the labour unions. It also depends on the receptiveness of society at large to accept a Korean 'new deal'. These issues will be examined (in Chapter 2) as we traverse the path towards explanations of Korea's environmental problems.

The central concern of this book is environment and development. Human beings have forever been in precarious balance with nature.

But it is the industrial revolutions of the past two centuries which have brought a far sharper edge to this conflict. And only in the last few decades have mass consumption patterns which often have a global character brought the intensification of resource exploitation – particularly of global commons – and of general pollution of ecosystems. The depletion of renewable and non-renewable resources, including the precious ozone layer, the loss of biodiversity, atmospheric contamination by greenhouse gases cumulatively sufficient to usher in climate change – these are now well rehearsed (World Bank 1992). This book, however, presents essentially a country study: global environmental problems are rooted in specific human practices which relate to specific places.

The later industrialising countries, as well as the underdeveloped regions which remain essentially resource providers, have been subjected in the last decades to new forces as the spiral of capital penetration has deepened. As transnationals shifted their production to the space of hitherto unindustrialised regions, so did they implant the environmental depredations associated with the manufacture of world market consumption goods. A large part of rural and urban populations have not merely remained or become economically marginalised: their living and working environments have seen significant deterioration (Redclift, M. 1984, Drakakis-Smith, D. 1987, WCED 1987, Hardoy and Satterthwaite 1989, Goodman and Redclift 1991, Gilbert and Gugler 1992, Hasan and Azam Ali 1992). It is clear that contemporary environmental conditions must be understood in the context of the historical development process. Second, emerging states of environment and ecology are differentiated by level of development and attitude within the global economy.

While we shall not be centrally concerned with charting the emergence of a global environmental consciousness, it should be recalled that the first major step towards an international structure came only recently. In 1972, incipient popular pressure in mainly Western Europe and North America culminated in the UN Economic and Social Council's first international forum, the Stockholm Conference.[2] This brought together representatives of 113 countries – to great astonishment China was amongst them; additionally 400 inter-governmental and non-governmental organisations were present. From this key event came the Stockholm Declaration on the Human Environment as well as the Action Plan for the Human Environment which dealt with issues such as education and science, social and economic development and pollution (Grubb *et al.* 1993, p.5). Though the linkages between environment and development were formally recognised in several principles of the Declaration, in terms of detailed commitments under the Action Plan, 'development' was largely ignored. The exception was in the discussion of human settlement policies (Grubb *et al.* 1993). An important legacy of Stockholm was the United Nations Environment Programme (UNEP).[3]

The momentum of Stockholm carried through in the 1970s and 1980s to specific environmental protocols – the London Dumping Convention, the Basle Convention on the Protection of the Ozone Layer (and its Montreal Protocol), together with regional initiatives such as the Mediterranean Action Plan under the UNEP. These common environmental concerns created the conditions for further UN action – the Brandt Commission on North–South relations and the Palme Commission on security and disarmament. Both brought development issues to the fore (Grubb *et al.* 1993, p.6).

The debt crises of the early 1980s and the obvious undermining of the resource bases of many non-industrialised nations added further weight to the idea that 'development' and 'environment' are inextricable. It is not surprising, therefore, that the subsequent move of the UN on this front was to form in 1983 the World Commission on Environment and Development (WCED). Led by Norwegian prime minister Gro Harlem Brundtland, the WCED's task was to critically re-examine 'issues of environment and development and to formulate innovative, concrete and realistic proposals to deal with them, and to strengthen international co-operation on environment and development' (WCED 1987, pp.356–357). The Brundtland report identified the following interrelated requirements:

- a political system that secures effective citizen participation in decision making;
- an economic system that is able to generate surplus and technical knowledge on a self-reliant and sustainable basis;
- a social system that provides for solutions to the tensions arising from disharmonious development;
- a production system that respects the obligation to preserve the ecological base for development;
- a technical system that can search continuously for new solutions;
- an international system that fosters sustainable pattern of trade and finance;
- an administrative system that is flexible and has the capacity for self-correction.

This wish-list was expressed in the catch-phrase 'sustainable development', the familiarity of which is probably the chief legacy of the 1992 UN Conference on Environment and Development. The Rio 'Earth Summit' fully acknowledged the need to reverse environmental degradation, the linkage of environmental and developmental issues, the importance of international co-operation and the developmental priorities of the developing countries.

The reality, however, is that the Rio process was limited by the vested economic interests of private capital, particularly that which spanned an increasingly globalised economy. As Pepper (1993) remarks, '. . . Western leaders staunchly defended the "right" of multinational capital to continue operating in the same old way and resurrect old Malthusian third world [sic] "overpopulation" canards for their explanations of causes' (p.2). The powerful nations signed up to a host of accords which, even if they had some vague intention of respecting, they lacked both the will and the means to enforce upon the transnationals that they have spawned. Hindsight on Rio provides a sad verdict: the 'developed' countries have by default at least preserved their economic dominance and energy intensive development strategies. The elites of the 'developing' nations have largely been motivated by a desire to minimise the impact of environmental and trade restrictions, while maximising financial and technological aid (Kim, B-W. 1994, p.152–153).

Environmental issues do not merely encompass the problems of natural environment such as resource depletion and pollution: social and economic justice are conceptually integral. Access to environmental 'goods' is clearly another area of inequality (means of reproduction such as housing) and unequal shouldering of environmental 'bads'. It is not surprising that scholarly interpretations of the sustainable development idea have little to say about the broader dynamics and have been unable to go beyond abstract musing (Archibugi and Nijkamp 1989, Adams 1990, Carley and Christie 1992, Meadows *et al.* 1992, Holmberg 1991, Pearce *et al.* 1990, 1991, Redclift 1987).

The present study holds that uneven development at the sub-national scale is reflected in the differentiation of environmental conditions (O'Connor 1989, Tickell and Peck 1992a). The research thus commences by seeking a suitable framework within which to locate and understand the mass of empirical material which any country study excavates. The demands placed upon such a framework are broad: it must be capable of incorporating political-economic and cultural-social variables over time, at both 'global' and 'local' levels of resolution; it must also provide a means of seeing differentiated space and the 'environment'. The analysis aims to be holistic and yet conducted at the level of concrete detail. Our present efforts rest on an attempt to synthesise diverse economic, spatial and state theses. They borrow and build upon the traditions of regulation theory, rehearsed in Chapter 1. Regulation theory is broadly helpful as a 'geographical, historical materialist' thesis which can locate issues and developments at the level of the nation-state within a wider system of capital accumulation, while not losing sight of the particularist milieu of the local. The 'development and environment' dichotomy invokes numerous political, economic, cultural, social, ideological and spatial processes. The manner in which these interact in a specific territory, particularly at the level of the nation-state, has not been thoroughly explored in prior research literature.

The primary objective is to identify the causal mechanisms of environmental degradation in a nation-state which has experienced extremely rapid industrialisation and consequent social change.[4] The analysis in Chapter 2 of Korea's historical process of development aims to cast light upon the mechanisms underlying the contemporary 'economic miracle' and its associated problems, including those of an environmental character. Attention is given to the influence of extra-national forces and their impact on accumulation strategy within the nation-state. The impact of capital accumulation on social development is examined, as is the system of regulation of labour. An analysis of the 1997 economic crisis and its aftermath is integrated into Chapter 2, as a commentary on previous state strategies and an indicator of possible future outcomes.

The manner in which Korea's developing economy has played out territorially – including its environmental impacts – is the subject of Chapter 3. The analysis attempts to relate economic development and differentiated environmental conditions through an examination of the uneven spatial development process. Attention is aimed at the character of state intervention, particularly in terms of Korea's economic and spatial transformation.

The following two Chapters (4 and 5) home in on the environmental. A historical review of issues analyses Korea's environmental problems within three fairly clear spatial divisions. Finally, Chapter 6 concerns itself with questions of regulation of the environment in the context of accumulation regimes. The examination of the mode of environmental regulation invokes both state regulatory mechanisms and the broader means of control implicit in the notions of hegemonic ideology. The socio-ecological strategies of the state provide a measure of issues which can be broadly termed 'environmental justice'. Prevailing social attitudes towards the environment are assessed as part of a wider mode of social regulation.

Several decades of ruthless economic expansion have denied the social and environmental needs of South Korea's population at large. According to our understanding, it is likely that the 1997 crisis will provide the trigger for a further transformation of Korea's mode of development. While the problems of environment and society will intensify, within the resolution of the crisis there are also the seeds of solutions in a more sustainable direction. Chapter 7 examines the contradictions between Korea's export-oriented industrialisation regime and the ideal prescriptions for sustainable development. It provides some tentative pointers for a more equitable and environmentally appropriate development of Korea. The Korean state's impulses of the 1990s to dissolve barriers with the external economy has transformed the regime of accumulation; this, we assert, presses in the direction of greater socio-ecological problems. The final chapter also revisits the question of regulation theory's utility to socio-environmental analysis. It is obviously our belief that the choice of this framework is one which illuminates rather than obscures. We hope that application and indeed development of the general approach might suggest itself to further case studies of the political economy of the environment.

1 A new framework for environmental analysis

The vast new literature concerning the environment is marked by its empiricism and its lack of broader conceptualisation. Few studies start from political economy, from the position of the state. The present work aims to avoid this fundamental shortcoming, and in this chapter we will set out our framework for so doing: regulation theory. In recent times, three distinct ecopolitical perspectives have evolved: environmental problems as problems of 'participation' came to the fore in the 1960s, of 'survival' in the 1970s and as opportunities for 'emancipation' in the late 1980s. This at least is the plausible view of Eckersley:

> the last three decades have seen a general broadening of ecopolitical dialogue as a result of the gradual interpenetration of these themes or phases of inquiry. That is, the participatory, survivalist and emancipatory phases may be seen as representing the thesis, antithesis and higher synthesis respectively in the ecopolitical dialogue of the last three decades.
>
> (Eckersley 1992, p.7)

Each phase of ecopolitical development has widened the spectrum of the environmental debate, rendering environmentalism[1] a commonplace of the 1990s (O'Riordan 1981, 1989, Dobson 1990). If we can summarise the cleavage within environmentalism, there are three main strands: techno-centrism, anthropocentrism and ecocentrism, within which lie further divisions. Explanatory frameworks stemming from Marxism, eco-anarchism and Gaianism span this spectrum. These both prescribe the manner of resolution of environmental problems and take particular stances towards their causes.

Theories of development–environmental analysis: a review

The liberal and the neo-classical approaches which represent the techno-centrist perspective are the least critical of the underlying political-economic order, blaming technical processes for environmental problems whether these be the failure of the free market or the inefficiency of state intervention. The problem is not seen to lie at the heart of the economic and political system itself. The prescribed solutions are improvements in technology, the application of measures such as taxes on carbon emissions and fines for pollution, and the like. Moreover, nature preservation is viewed in terms of resource conservation, where natural goods have instrumental value to the society. This has spawned a significant literature centering on environmental economics (Hufsmidt 1983, Nijkamp 1977, Pearce 1993). The solutions are anthropocentric and limited within the existing mode of development. In addition, such market approaches can be used to justify protectionist strategies, for example, advanced industrialised countries may levy environmental taxes on products from countries with lower environmental standards. The market-liberal betrays a partial, narrow understanding of both the causes of, and solution to, the environmental morass.

It is the green movement of the last three decades of the twentieth century which of course is the dominant voice of the environmental movement. The anti-technocentrism of mainstream greens disposes them to regard environmental problems as the consequences of 'industrialisation' per se (Porritt 1984). The moralising and voluntarist tenor of the greens would elevate attitudes and personal values to prime place. They would thus take issue with the societal assumptions of post-enlightenment science; the Judeo-Christian tradition, patriarchy, invoking 'greed, hubris and original sin' are all to be blamed (White 1967, Capra 1982, Pepper 1991, pp.116–118). Human beings in general and the *self* in particular come to be seen as the 'seventh enemy' (Higgins 1980). 'We have met the enemy and it is us' (Parsons 1977): this is rightfully characterised as 'a self-accusing and self-moralising abstraction' typical of ecocentrists and arising out of their strong neo-Malthusian tradition (Pepper 1993, pp.90–91). The greens' consensus holds that 'limits to growth' must underlie all human activity, and this translates directly into 'Gaian' desires to fashion societies that mirror the rest of nature and are subject to its self-limiting laws.

Atkinson's (1992) prescription of bioregionalism perfectly encapsulates the desire for living within the means of ecological limits. Bioregionalism entails a return to a network of small decentralised 'democratic' communities based on ecological planning concepts – for example the carrying capacity of a river basin in constraining future settlement (Atkinson 1992). There is more than a hint of authoritarianism, a conviction that all decentralised societies will necessarily construct themselves upon the values of democracy, liberty, freedom and justice (Sale 1985, Dobson 1990, p.122).

The approach of the 'bioregionalists' fails to consider how economic linkage with other communities can be squared with the maintenance of local autarky. Nor does it explain how freedom of the individual is compatible with the exclusion that a localised system implies (Harvey 1993, p.45). Pepper (1993) criticises the ecological movement for its inherent strain of liberal economics, to 'subjective preference' and cost of production theories (p.43).[2] The lack of close analysis of the socio-economic conditions underlying environmental problems has been the fundamental weakness of the greens.

In contrast to the greens and liberal approaches, Marxism posits a view of the society–nature relationship which is complex and dialectical (Pepper 1993). Further, the historical materialist approach holds that it is not just individual 'greedy' monopolists or consumers who are to blame for environmental problems, but rather the mode of production itself – the productive forces and relations which constitute capitalism. Marxists hold that it is the specific interface of capitalism with nature which creates environmental degradation and human misery on the scale we have witnessed in the second half of the twentieth century. The polarisation of consumption, an inseparable feature of capitalism, is also a fundamental cause of environmental degradation (Seabrook 1985, p.37, Pepper 1993, p.91). It is this school of thought that provides the most insightful perspectives on the environmental question. We must, however, distinguish between the prognostications of socialist thinkers within the Western capitalist democracies and the practice of state planning in those national formations which in the twentieth century have characterised themselves as 'socialist' or 'peoples' republics. Here, technocratic and anthropocentric approaches to nature have generally been very much to the fore. 'Scientific' determinism has brought numerous promethean projects in which domination of nature is essential and even 'heroic' (Harvey 1993, pp.3–4). The proponents of a human-dominated nature are not confined to 'socialist' states such as the former Soviet Union, or present day China with its mammoth Three Gorges project: while liberal marketeers pay lip service to the environmental programme, the essence of their approach is to promote economic 'growth' through an uncritical reliance upon technical means. There are few who dare to be so explicit in their advocacy of the complete domination of nature as Grundmann (1991).

In many postwar Western societies there is a further complication. As the working classes were incorporated through the welfare statism of postwar Western economies, the transformational potential of class revolution was called into question. Working class communities have often regarded environmental movements as a threat to their livelihoods. The curtailment of hazardous industrial activities in sectors such as in the chemical industry suggests loss of jobs. These considerations in the advanced industrialised countries brought the new variant of Marxism seen in the Frankfurt school of critical theory. Its adherents concern themselves with the whole process of capitalist accumulation and its social and political context, including conflicts within civil society and the state. This has broadened the traditional Marxist debate centred around social relations of production to a more comprehensive political-economic approach encompassing the economic base, civil society and the state. The emphasis of the Frankfurt school is not so much on the conflict within the workplace, but rather on the conditions of reproduction, that is the struggles in the arena of welfare and collective consumption. Since the responsibility of redistribution of wealth and provision of collective consumption falls on the state, the neo-Marxists' contribution is particularly important in theorising its functions.

The dominant structuralist approach within radical state theory isolates three tiers: the economic base, civil society and the state as the superstructure. There are various schools of thought within leftist state theory, including the instrumentalist, the neo-Gramscian and the neo-Ricardian. While instrumentalists focus upon the state's manipulation by capital, neo-Gramscians emphasise the importance of ideology. Neo-Ricardians dwell upon the economic constraints governing state actions. The arguments are further discussed in due course.

An important and more recent contribution has come in the form of ecosocialism. This approach builds on the neo-Marxists' themes and tries to overcome the human-nature dualism, while incorporating environmental problems into the Marxist theory of production. Much of the ecosocialist literature has risen above anthropocentrism, in that both labour and nature are taken as objects of exploitation, as means of production in the capitalist accumulation process (O'Connor 1988, Enzensberger 1974). Ecosocialism maintains that the domination of labour and nature by the capitalist accumulation process lies at the root of social and environmental problems. Thus, it incorporates both environmental problems and social justice issues, suggesting a new concept of 'environmental justice' (Harvey 1994). There is a clear influence from the approaches of Marxist geographers which link the mode of production/accumulation process to the 'production of nature', production of space and uneven development (Smith 1984, O'Connor 1989). David Harvey, for many the epitome of critical thought regarding space and society, steps into the arena of environmental concerns by asserting the heterogeneous nature of the desired socio-ecological landscape, the indispensable function of socio-ecological projects to the resolution of alienation and to the 'opening up (of) diverse possibilities of self-realisation' in some socialist future (Harvey 1993, pp.44–45). Harvey postulates a 'geographical historical materialism' in which 'socio-ecological' struggles are the fulcrum of societal transformation (1993, p.44).

While such approaches offer a good starting point, we must also recognise that there remain epistemological shortcomings. Meta-approaches are bound to lack the methodological means whereby global and national/local economic phenomena are linked to environmental issues. They tend to deal with environmental problems in abstract form under universal forces of capitalism, providing no framework by which concrete analysis may incorporate those political and ideological projects which regulate societal behaviour. Existing theories of the state and space require synthesis if the causal mechanisms of environmental problems are to be illuminated.

The subsequent sections endeavour to set out a conceptual framework for the study of environmental degradation, taking account of the complex mechanisms of capitalist accumulation and the forces which control the interaction between socio-economic developments and the environment. The theses concerning the interrelationship between the dynamics of capitalism and 'nature' and space touch on the mode of production, the contradictions inherent in the capitalist accumulation process and the dynamics of accumulation.

Capitalism, production of space and the environment

The mechanisms which bring about environmental degradation are considered here through an examination of various constructs and theses which focus on the interrelationship between the capitalist mode of development and environment.

Production of nature thesis

This thesis focuses upon the historical relationship between humankind and nature through the mode of production, from primitive to capitalist. It tries to overcome the dualistic conception of nature in both bourgeois and Marxist literature,[3] of external nature, first nature, and man-made nature, second nature,[4] and tries to see the totality of the transformation of nature through the changing human/nature relationship, which is primarily affected by the development of the mode of production (Marx 1959, Grundmann 1991, Smith and O'Keefe 1980, Smith 1984, O'Connor 1988).

According to Marx:

> Labour is, first of all, a process between man and nature, a process which man, through his own actions, mediates, regulates, and controls the metabolism between himself and nature. He confronts the materials of nature as a force of nature. He sets in motion natural forces which belong to his own body, his arms, legs, head, and hands, in order to appropriate the materials of nature in a form adapted to his own needs. Through this movement he acts upon external nature and changes it, and this way he simultaneously changes his own nature. He develops the potentialities slumbering within nature, and subjects the play of its forces to his own sovereign power.
>
> (Marx 1959, p.283)

This statement asserts that the interaction between 'man' and nature is through the labour process: the labourer does not only transform nature, but in the process he also changes his own nature.[5] As divisions of labour increase, social relations become central to the interaction between human-kind and nature. The division of labour is systematised in the production of subsistence goods as well as a social surplus, the latter becoming a necessity for the reproduction of the society as a whole. In short, this led to the division of society into classes and the control of the means of production and the exploitation of the majority by a specific class.

The differential ability to control people and nature, which affect productivity, has profound implications for consciousness, politics and socio-cultural life as a whole. Entire modes of production came into being as a certain way of enhancing productivity, and directed by particular social relations. So '. . . the totality of these relations of production constitutes the economic structure of society, the real foundation, on which arises a legal and political superstructure and to which correspond definite forms of social consciousness' (Marx 1893, pp.20–21). The development of social institutions such as the state and organised religion not only dictates the direction of surplus production, it also intervenes in the way in which human beings interact with nature. Social development splits the harmonious balance of nature. No longer does the abstract natural individual 'man' fit simply into an equally natural environment, since the relation with nature is mediated through social institutions. Thus, the production of a permanent social surplus allows humankind to begin the long process of emancipating itself from the constraints of nature. But at the same time, the increased social control, which a more complex society necessitates, enslaves a large part of the population (Smith 1984, p.39).

The transformation of mode of production through history has thus changed the relationship between man and nature: from use-value production to production for exchange, to capitalist production for surplus value. Throughout history, each mode of production – and the social relations which pertain to it – has been displaced by the ensuing one, a process precipitated by the developments of the productive forces (Peet 1991, p.63, Smith 1984). As this process intensified, so did the exploitation of nature, the alienation of humankind from nature as an ever greater surplus was extracted as a means of emancipating from nature's constraints. The progressive nature of the capitalist mode of production not only sought means of production and markets on a world scale for the first time, but also – as it developed internationally – dissolved all other modes of production under it (Smith and O'Keefe 1980, p.35).

In a capitalist society, it is the 'production of nature' that unifies the previously separate social and natural realms, but it does so without the loss of their separate identity:

> it is not just this 'second nature' that is increasingly produced as part of the capitalist mode of production. The 'first nature' is also produced. Indeed the 'second nature' is no longer produced out of the first nature, but rather the first is produced by and within the confines of the

second. Whether we are talking about the laborious conversion of iron ore into steel and eventually into auto-mobiles or the professional packaging of Yosemite National Park, nature is produced. In quite concrete sense, this process of production transcends the ideal distinction between a first and a second nature. The form of all nature has been altered by human activity, and today production is accomplished not for the fulfilment of needs in general but for the fulfilment of one particular 'need': profit.

(Smith and O'Keefe 1980, p.35)

Smith and O'Keefe (1980) claim that the idea of production of nature offers a superior framework within which to view natural disasters. The concept emphasises not nature or society as such, but primarily the relation that is responsible for shaping both nature and society in the process of production. Thus, vulnerability to disasters is a function of class relations in which differential access to nature is fundamental (p.37). Environmental disasters are products of a structural process, rather than mere human greed, technology, industrialism or enlightenment philosophy. The development of the productive forces brings a greater exploitation of nature; it also brings alienation from nature. The limitation of this approach is its abstractness. Though Smith constructs a sophisticated framework for understanding the human/nature relationship, its generality offers little insight into the actual mechanisms at work.

Second contradiction thesis

Competition between capital and antagonistic class relations represent the fundamental contradictions of the capitalist order. There exists, however, another contradiction: that between capitalism and nature. This has been termed the 'Second Contradiction' (O'Connor 1988). Harvey (1985a) sees this as arising inevitably from the interaction between capital accumulation and the 'natural resource' (p.3). Nature is turned by capitalism into the 'universal means of production'. Nature is exploited for its raw materials while it becomes the repository of waste in its 'commons'. Exploitation of resources – stripping of assets with no concern for the effects on future production – is an intrinsic tendency which increases exponentially.[6] Costs are externalised and discounted to the future (Pearce *et al.* 1989). Johnston (1989) calls these effects 'ecological imperialism'. Externalisation of costs results in atmospheric, water and land pollution. The social costs of the resultant environmental and social problems are charged to society as a whole, both human and natural resources being treated as 'commons' (Pepper 1993, p.93).

O'Connor's (1988) interpretation of the 'second contradiction' of the capitalist mode of production is one of 'underproduction of the (pre-) conditions of production'.[7] This approach comprehensively encompasses all the environmental issues. O'Connor finds three kinds of production conditions in Marx: the 'external physical conditions', the labour power of workers, and 'the communal, general conditions of social production'. The external physical conditions are natural environmental conditions such as the quality of the biosphere, the resource endowment and ecology of the immediate environment; the reproduction of labour power of the workers includes elements such as living and working conditions; and the communal, general conditions of social production denotes the man-made environment – cities, social, cultural and environmental goods, and means of communication (O'Connor 1988, p.16). He broadens the general scope of 'environment' beyond the issues of nature, pollution and resources, to the 'personal condition for production and reproduction' of the labour force. This would include a diverse range: the physical and mental well-being of workers, the degree of socialisation, intensity of work relations, and the 'social and communal conditions' which include fixed capital for production and consumption. Implicit, therefore, in the concept of 'conditions of production' are 'urban space' and 'social environment', that is, human beings and urban capitalised nature.

O'Connor (1988) notes the tendency of capitalist production relations towards self-destruction. Three contradictory processes are identified: that of exploitation of labour and the valorisation of capital, state regulation of the provision of production conditions, and social struggle organised around capital's use and abuse of these conditions. His ecological Marxist perspective is, thus, not dissimilar to that of the Frankfurt school in which Marcuse and Habermas saw the struggle over the conditions of reproduction as the essence of modern society. O'Connor concludes that the conditions of production are impaired by capital itself due to the valorisation process and capital's universalising tendencies, the negation of site specificity and the lack of ownership of labour power, external nature and space (p.25). The contradiction of capital with nature originates from the inherent characteristics of exploitation and the continuous drive for profits under competition. The three contradictions are seen to be very much linked together, and manifestation of any one or combinations of the three would create a crisis of *over-accumulation*.[8]

Although these identify the economic mechanisms underlying environmental problems, they are limited because they overlook the spatial dynamics of capital accumulation processes. Thus, they are not able to explain the differentiation of environmental problems. The degree of environmental degradation in a particular place depends on the level of development, and the type and distribution of production and consumption in space. Thus we move to an examination of the spatial development of capitalism in order to explain the creation of the differentiated environmental conditions under a particular predominant accumulation process.

Production of space and uneven development

The notion of the production of space was utilised by David Harvey (1973) in his examination of *'created space* ... as the overriding principle of geographic organisation' (p.309); similar ideas were put forward by Castells (1977).[9] However, it was Henri Lefèbvre (1970) who coined the phrase 'the production of space'. Lefèbvre focuses on the reproduction of the social relations of production which, he says, 'constitutes the central and hidden process' of capitalist society. This process is inherently spatial, occurring not only in the factory or even in society as a whole, 'but in space as a whole'. Further, it is 'dialecticised conflictive space that produces reproduction, by introducing into it its multiple contradictions.' Thus, Lefèbvre concludes:

> Capitalism has found itself able to attenuate (if not resolve) its internal contradictions for a century, and consequently, in the hundred years since the writing of Capital, it has succeeded in achieving 'growth'. We cannot calculate at what price, but we do know the means: by occupying space, by producing space
>
> (Lefèbvre 1970, cited in Smith 1984, p.91)

The 'uneven development' thesis argues that capital tries to overcome the inherent contradictions in its mode of production by displacing crisis tendencies through spatial expansion and mobility. To overcome crises of over-accumulation, capital is forced to expand in space in search of new markets and cheaper sources of raw material and labour. The extension of the market in space leads to greater costs and greater time of circulation. This leads to technical improvements in transportation and communication. Increases in fixed investment, particularly in transport infrastructure, enable capital to overcome spatial barriers, dissolving space through time, thus achieving both spatial expansion and concentration. Thus, the mobility of capital is dependent upon the spatial fixity of capital in the form of transport and communication infrastructure (Harvey 1985a, pp.35–37, 1985b, pp.26–29, Smith 1984, pp.97–130, 149–154).

The differentiation of world space is a direct result of the contradictory need for capital to immobilise itself in the landscape while maintaining its mobility. Capital must be fixed for long periods of time in the production process in the form of machinery, factory buildings, transport facilities and other direct and indirect means of production (Smith, 1984, pp.88–89). Technological innovation causes enhanced differentiation through greater clustering in those sectors and areas in which a higher than average rate of profit is possible. There is a tendency, therefore, for concentration of productive activities as well as ancillary services in the urban centres where centralised investment of fixed capital has taken place (Harvey 1985a, p.40, Smith 1984, pp.121–124). Improvements in the means of transportation tend in the direction of already existing markets, centres of production and population, and towards exporting ports. This disposition of production in space is crucial to the reduction of turnover time (and costs) within the circulation process of capital. Here, then, is a depiction of the cumulative forces shaping urbanisation under capitalism (Harvey 1985a, p.40).

However, the tendency towards agglomeration is partially offset by an increasingly specialised territorial division of labour which locates particular branches of production in certain areas of national territory. The attenuation of the international division of labour is also a moderating factor (Harvey 1985a, p.42, Massey 1979). Smith (1984) looks at the separation of *departments, sectors* and *individuals* of capital in space that leads to international and regional differentiations (pp.112–113, 145). It is the switching from one location to another that leads to differentiated conditions. The development of technology, especially means of transportation, not only allows for greater concentration as mentioned above, but also liberates industry from close dependence upon localised raw materials and organic (topological) conditions in general. This results in a shifting and relocation of places of production and of markets with changes in their relative positions in the global market (Smith 1984, p.145, Harvey 1985a).

The other opposing dynamic of the capitalist accumulation process is the tendency toward equalisation. This tendency originates from the universalisation of wage-labour brought about by the displacement of precapitalist modes of production. As we have seen, the need for mobility of capital, and the development of means of transportation and communication lead to the continual drive to overcome all spatial barriers and to the annihilation of space by time. The 'universalising tendency of capital' represents an inherent drive toward spacelessness, in other words, toward an equalisation of conditions and levels of production: thus 'a shrinking world'. Spatial development is treated by Marx as an integral moment of overall societal development rather than simply as an spurious effect. One writer goes even further: the shrinking world is 'not merely an effect of generalised progress of modernisation but the specific necessity of the capitalist mode of production' (Smith 1984, pp.93–94).

For Smith (1984), equalisation reduces the individual worker to a 'crippled monstrosity' and an 'appendage of the machine', dragging workers towards a common denominator. A parallel degradation results from the capitalist pursuit of raw materials at the world scale. The equalisation process is manifested in the common scarcity of objects of labour. From timber to whales to petroleum, the 'scarcity' of these materials is a social creation, not an act of nature. In qualitative terms, capital engages in a relentless search for the primary inputs – old and new – which fuel the accumulation process. Therefore, the capitalist mode of production brings about an equalisation in the relation with nature: 'first, nature is made the universal appendage of capital; second, the quality of nature is levelled downward at the hands of capital' (Smith 1984, p.115).

The geographical fixation of use-value and the fluidity of exchange-value translate into tendencies toward differentiation and equalisation which produce geographical pattern of uneven development. The universalisation tendency of capital reduces the whole globe to source for surplus value, thus equalising the conditions and level of production over space. Yet the division between developed and underdeveloped countries and regions is produced by the inherent tendency of capital to differentiate space. The differentiation of space is the result of capital's displacement of crisis into space. As differentiation becomes an increasing necessity in order to stave off crisis, 'uneven spatial development is both a product and the spatial premise of capitalist development' (Smith 1984, p.153).

The spatial dimension receives acknowledgement in the discussion of issues such as centralisation and decentralisation of industry, the selective industrialisation of the Third World, regional decline, de-industrialisation, urban redevelopment and gentrification, and the more general issues of spatial restructuring during crisis. These geographical processes are the product of contradictory dynamics: the more society strives to emancipate itself from space, the more important does spatial fixity become; second, the displacement of capitalist crises leads to continuing mobility of capital. As this contradictory dynamic unfolds, it results in the production of space according to a very particular pattern. Space is neither levelled out into a single entity nor infinitely differentiated. Rather, the pattern which results is one of *uneven development*. This constitutes the concrete manifestation of the production of space under capitalism (Smith 1984, pp.89–90).

O'Connor (1989) examines the environmental impact of uneven development through the transfer of commodities between developed and underdeveloped regions; he sees environmental problems as resulting from the universal process of capital valorisation. For him, uneven development produces two distinct but related environmental effects: on the one hand there is pollution of the developed areas; on the other, depletion of natural resources occurs in the underdeveloped zones. O'Connor observes that as uneven development of capital is intensified, the greater will be the spatial concentration of industry and population, increasing the pollution in the developed areas to often unsupportable levels, while the exploitation of natural resources will occur at an ever increasing rate in the underdeveloped regions (O'Connor 1989, pp.3–4).

> What has happened, historically, and is still happening, is that the soils and resources of the Third World and raw material zones of the First World were and are, in part, exported through the vehicle of commodity production and exchange and capital accumulation, only to make their appearance in the industrial zones in the form of waste and pollution. It is interesting to speculate about the possibility that industrial pollution is indirectly or directly a form of physical matter which once assumed the form of rich soils, fossil fuels, minerals, forests

and so on, in the raw material zones. In this way, soil exhaustion, the depletion of forests, etc. and pollution and mass Third World poverty constitute a single historical process – 'one big fact'.

(O'Connor 1989, p.8)

Uneven capitalist development, we may then say, is characterised by widespread environmental pollution in the industrial zones and a mass assault on the environments and living standards in the raw material zones. In the context of the world economy as a whole, this process intensifies during boom periods in order to meet demand, while during recessionary periods both export agriculture and subsistence production attempt to maintain incomes through expansion, hence pushing nature further towards its ecological limits. The uneven development thesis conceptualises the link between the environmental problems in the 'North' and the 'South'. Thus, the modes of production and consumption in the industrialised countries have a direct impact on the natural resources of the developing countries. In addition, transnational companies ensure that natural resources are kept at the cheapest possible prices, thus, keeping the population of the developing countries in relative poverty.

'Combined development' is a more extreme form. Here, capital seeks to combine social and economic spheres in the most profitable way – for example, twenty-first century First World technology is conjoined with nineteenth-century labour/political conditions. Combined development[10] is driven by the intensification of the capital valorisation process. This is the combining of a modern industrial sector with a raw material production sector within a national space; the growth in the modern sector is at the expense of the raw material/agricultural production zone. Such a process exacerbates uneven spatial development within the national boundary; often leading to greater concentration of capital and population in large urban centres, and a greater environmental degradation in the underdeveloped regions. There occurs greater exploitation of labour as well as of nature (O'Connor 1989). Cheaper labour is drawn into the older industrial zones; average wages tend to fall, work conditions deteriorate, unions are weakened, occupational health and safety problems grow and environmental conditions worsen. Meanwhile, rural zones are deprived of their prime workforce, male and female, leading to a deteriorating agricultural environment. The out-migration of capital creates new zones of industry in labour surplus regions, or it may capitalise agriculture. At a world scale, pollution of the core is 'exported' to the periphery. Dangerous chemicals banned in the industrialised countries find their way into industrial and agricultural production in the LDCs. Here, more naked forms of labour discipline are applied. In both cases, urban-industrial zones expand uncontrollably, creating all the pathologies of urban life (O'Connor 1989, pp.8–9). Thus, when advanced production systems come face to face with traditional modes, what results is uneven development with all its attendant ecological mal-effects. The 'green revolution' – the capitalisation of underdeveloped countries' agriculture – has been characterised as follows:

> farmers pick the 'best' seeds, plant uniformly over the largest area possible, and douse with chemical fertilisers – the reduction of agriculture to this simple formula – not only leaves crops open to attack by diseases and soils highly vulnerable to deterioration, but also ties the farmer into the vicious cycle of debt repayment. Such reductionist agriculture turns chemical fertilisers and pesticides into necessities to cover for its built-in vulnerabilities, and hence higher production costs and higher and higher debt.
>
> (Moore Lappe 1977, p.164)

In sum, what is transferred from the centre to the periphery is not just technology but also social and environmental costs. If the world is viewed as an arena of capital accumulation in which both forms of combined development occur within the context of uneven development:

> First, low-wage, unorganised, state-controlled labour in the Third World and weakened labour organisations in the First World are unable to resist environmental destruction and harm to workers' and others' health. Second, the combination of high technology with cheap labour increases 'social costs' and externalities and the rate of exploitation globally, hence the rate of profit, hence the speed at which resources are used and destroyed and also the rate of pollution in all its forms. The result is a self-perpetuating spiral of ecological and human destruction.
>
> (O'Connor 1989, p.10)

When uneven and combined development of capital come together, super-pollution in industrial zones may be a natural accompaniment to 'super-ecodestruction' of land and resources in raw material zones.

The above arguments suggest the generalised workings of the capitalist mode of production and its inter-linkage with the environment. A number of significant elements are unveiled. First, our definition of 'environment' includes the reproduction of nature, labour and the 'social environment'. Second, the interaction between the environment and the capitalist mode of production is mediated by social institutions, particularly by the state. Third, as capital tries to reconcile its internal contradictions through the utilisation of space, there is a tendency towards uneven development, this producing differentiated environmental problems. Such a model of development with its associated problems closely fits the Korean situation and corresponds, too, to the conditions in other newly industrialising nations.

These are conceptualisations which help our understanding of the linkage between capitalist development processes and environmental problems; they are not, however without shortcomings. First, they do not properly incorporate the political dimension, especially the capacity of the state to intervene and the impact of class conflict: these exert considerable influence on the direction of economic and spatial development. Second, such efforts to account for spatial environmental effects may not always acknowledge the specificities of national accumulation strategies. These lacunae suggest that the theoretical premises outlined so far require further validation and refinement based on empirical study.

A review of some state theories

The dynamics of the accumulation process give rise to a geographic pattern of uneven development, and its associated differentiation in terms of environmental problems. Capitalist accumulation in itself is mediated through the workings of the set of social institutions encapsulated in the notion of 'the state'. With the inherent tendency towards crisis, the state's bearing on the regulation of accumulation becomes more pronounced. The analysis of environmental problems does not, habitually, consider the precise role of state institutions. Thus, the complex relation of economic, social, spatial and environmental policy – as well as official responses to environmental movements – demand close reference to state theory.

Theories of the state deriving from Marxist origins divide into two main approaches: those which stress the political and those which stress the economic. In the former, the instrumentalist, the structuralist and Gramscian or neo-Gramscian approaches are fairly clearly differentiated. The latter can be divided into two groupings: the Neo-Ricardian and the state monopoly capitalist. In recent years, the 'capital' theories of the state have been proposed in order to remedy the shortcomings of the existing approaches.

The instrumentalist approach sees the state as a tool of the capitalist class whereby it achieves political domination over the labouring classes. This perspective is in direct line of descent from Marx and Engels.[11] Instrumentalists are concerned with who governs, focusing on the character of ruling classes, the mechanism which they exert over state institutions, and the set of interdependencies between the state and capitalist accumulation. They regard the economic base as a constraint, but not as a determinant of state intervention; such a view separates the instrumentalist account from the main body of state theories (Gold *et al.* 1975).

The structuralist approach on the other hand considers class conflicts arising from the contradictions of capital accumulation as the determining force of state intervention. Structuralists regard the state as a superstructural element which is relatively autonomous from the economic base, from civil society and indeed from the class of capitalist. The state thus enjoys 'relative autonomy' from the latter's mandate; however, it is argued that the state has an objective function in maintaining social cohesion so that capital accumulation can proceed unhindered. At the same time, the mission of the state includes fragmentation of the working class, the undermining of its solidarity via expedient short-run class compromises and reforms (Jessop 1990b).

The Gramscian and neo-Gramscian enrich the analysis by introducing the concept of political and ideological hegemony. Their 'class-theoretical', rather than 'capital-theoretical', approach plays down the constraints on the state by capital while emphasising the autonomy of politics and ideology. For them, the state is not merely a simple instrument manipulated by a unitary bourgeois class; rather, it plays a vital role in unifying the bourgeoisie and organising its political and ideological domination, while dissipating working class opposition through various, often short-term concessions. The most important problematic for the state is securing the conditions for these practices to be implemented. This becomes an imperative because competition between capitals threatens the unity of the ruling class, while capital's involvement in class struggle threatens to unify the working class (Poulantzas 1968, pp.188–189, 256–257). Therefore, the form of the state and its ideological hegemony become crucial to counteract the tendencies inherent in capitalism.

As Gramsci argues, consciousness and ideology play a paramount role in the determination of economic structures, and civil society is controlled by consent rather than plain force. Bourgeois hegemony represents a subtle form of cultural domination (Vincent 1987). The state is a means by which the ruling class not only justifies and maintains its dominance, but also manages to win the active consent of those over whom it rules (Gramsci 1971, p.244). Thus, the state is conceived as 'a mystification, a concrete institution which serves the interests of the dominant class, but which seeks to portray itself as serving the nation as a whole, thereby obscuring the basic lines of class antagonism' (Gold *et al.* 1975, p.40). The neo-Gramscians place great emphasis on ideological hegemony, false consciousness and legitimacy and the role of popular-democratic institutions. Elements derived from Gramsci's notion of 'hegemony' are further developed in Poulantzas' concept: 'power bloc' and the 'governing class': ideological hegemony is for both the pivot of capitalist society. The institutions of the state are thus indispensable to the maintenance of social cohesion, and to securing the conditions necessary for continuing capital accumulation.

By contrast, state theories of the economic category pay little attention to the relative autonomy of the state. They emphasise the role of the state in societal regulation as mainly a response to the requirements of capital accumulation.

Neo-Ricardian theorists are explicitly concerned with the economic dimensions of the state. They focus on its influence in the distribution of income between classes, and attempt to show how the state intervenes in the economy to maintain or restore corporate profits at the expenses of wages. Such action is traced back to the pressure on profitability that stems from trade union struggles and/or international competition, and is dependent upon the specific form of the profit squeeze and the balance of class forces. Capital will generally attempt to manipulate business cycles to discipline labour and reduce wage costs in the interests of corporate profit maximisation (Boddy and Crotty 1974, 1975), and to redistribute income to the private sector through fiscal changes, subsidies, nationalisation, deval-uation, wage control and legal restrictions on trade union activities (Glyn and Sutcliffe 1972). Furthermore, it will try to counter the inflationary effects of tax increases and public borrowing through reduction in the 'social wage' (Gough 1975). The dominant position of capital in the state machin-ery means that it determines the nature of solutions to successive economic crises (Boddy and Crotty 1975).

At the heart of the neo-Ricardian analysis is the distributional struggle rather than conflicts at the point of production, and this is reflected in the tendency to discuss state intervention in terms of income distribution while neglecting the state's fundamental role in the accumulation process. The analysis underplays the significance of the social relations of produc-tion and the characteristic form of capitalist exploitation through the creation and appropriation of surplus value; thus it ignores the complex class character of the state. The neo-Ricardians imply that wage restraint and/or public spending cuts are sufficient to resolve crises. They also fail to explain the causes, nature and limitations of growing state involvement in production itself (Jessop 1990b, p.31).

State monopoly capitalism[12] theories are grounded in Marxist economics, and the laws of motion of capitalism occupy a central place. These theo-ries share certain assumptions concerning the periodisation of capitalism and the nature of its latest stage. Thus it is argued that the process of competition during the period of *laissez-faire* capitalism leads inevitably to the concentration (and valorisation) of capital and hence to a new stage in which monopolies dominate the whole economy. Moreover, whereas the preceding stage of liberal competition was marked by the self-regulation of market forces and the progressive self-development of the forces of production, the stage of monopoly capitalism is characterised by the increasing tendency of the rate of profit to fall and thus of production to stagnate. To offset this tendency and thereby maintain the dynamism of capital accumulation requires ever-expanding state intervention in the economy. Such intervention takes numerous forms, which may include the nationalisation of basic industries, provision of essential services, centralised control over credit and money, state subsidies to private investment, the creation of a large state market for commodities, state sponsored research and development at the frontiers of technology, control of wages – in short, general programming of the economy and the creation of international economic agencies.[13] With the growth of such interventions, monopoly capitalism is transformed into 'state monopoly capitalism'. This is alleged to be the final stage of capitalism and the enormous weight of the state is attributed to the general crisis of capitalism that characterises this stage (Jessop 1990b, pp.32–33). Theorists of this school argue that the state and monopolies have 'fused' into a single mechanism which acts on behalf of monopoly capital (Dunleavy and O'Leary 1987). The concept of state monopoly capitalism, in its crudest form, holds that the state is the instrument of monopoly capital in the era of imperialism, and so the means by which the domination of capital over civil society is maintained. This approach obviously does not acknowledge the concept of relative autonomy of the state stemming from class struggle.

The most obvious faults of this theoretical category come from evolutionism and economic reductionism, while political approaches fail to consider the economic sphere and deal with just the surface phenomena in the political sphere. Neither the political nor the economic category of state theory, therefore, is able to grasp the limits of interventionism inherent in the character of a capitalist state, and thus the constraints on the state, both politically and economically (Holloway and Picciotto 1978). Both types of state theories unduly emphasise the relations between the economic and political as discrete forms of capitalist social relations, ignoring the historical development of the state apparatus. A number of state theories under the 'capital' school have tried to overcome such shortcomings.

The state as the ideal collective capitalist – The capital-logic school (originating in West Berlin in the 1970s) has tried to derive the general form and principal functions of a capitalist state from the pure capitalist mode of production and its conditions of existence. For those within this school of thought, the starting point has been the separation of the state, capital and civil society, so that the state (which is not immediately subordinate to market forces) is required to provide those general preconditions of capital accumulation as a whole, such as infrastructure, legal conditions and wage relations. The state is also required to safeguard national capital in the capitalist world market.[14] Thus, to the extent that it is not a unit of capital but a distinct political institution corresponding to the common needs of capital, the state is an ideal collective capitalist (Altvater 1973). Due to the tendency of the rate of profit to fall, the state is required to intervene in order to mobilise counter-tendencies through the restructuring of capital and the reorganisation of the labour process.

The capital-logic school qualifies this view of the ideal collective capitalist by considering the state's continued subordination to the laws of motion of capitalism. It argues that, whilst the state intervenes more and more to maintain demand and reorganise production, it cannot transcend market forces nor eliminate the tendency of the rate of profit to fall. The power of the capitalist state in this respect is necessarily limited, because it cannot directly determine the decision-making of private capital. For state intervention is always mediated through the monetary and legal conditions affecting the operation of market forces and the organization of production in the private sector – this constraint is reinforced by the contradictions inherent in capital accumulation.

The capital-logic school represents a fundamental theoretical advance through the demonstration that the state cannot be conceived as a mere political instrument set up and controlled by capital. Its proponents hold that the capitalist state is an essential element in the social reproduction of capital – a political force that complements the economic force of competition between individual capitals, assuring the immanent necessities that cannot be secured through the latter. This requires, among other things, that the state intervenes against capital as well as the working class, especially when individual capitals or fractions of capital threaten the interests of capital in general. However, the difficulty remains that the 'needs of capital' still provide the only explanation, rather than becoming the point of reference for a more developed theory (Jessop 1990b, pp.37–38). Thus, it commits the reductionist fallacy which argues that the political forms and functions of state intervention are determined by the economic base.

Historical-materialist state – It is in response to some of these difficulties with the capital-logic approach that a more recent school of Marxists, centred this time at Frankfurt (but not to be confused with the Frankfurt school of 'critical social science') has attempted to introduce a greater degree of historical specificity and a sharper awareness of the role of class struggle into the study of the capitalist state. Thus, although this school accepts the basic arguments concerning the need for a separate political institution to secure certain preconditions of capitalism, it rejects an emphasis on the needs of competing capitals considered in isolation from their antagonistic relations with wage labour. This school insists that the state can be understood only in terms of its changing functions in the class struggle over the organisation of the labour process and the appropriation of surplus value (Holloway and Picciotto 1977).

The approach not only introduces some historical specificity into the analysis of the capitalist state; it also develops some significant ideas about the nature and effects of class struggle. It holds that crisis is the result of failure to maintain the domination of capital over labour, rather than as the result of the inexorable logic of accumulation. This means that state intervention is rarely directed towards the actual needs of capital and generally reflects a response to the political repercussions of accumulation. Since there is no necessary correspondence between state intervention and the needs of capital, crises play a role in reshaping its form and redirecting its thrust. For it is in crisis that the immanent necessities of capitalism are most likely to become apparent. So crises are steering mechanisms of state intervention. However, since crises are the complex effects of various contradictory factors and affect different classes in contradictory ways, there will be continuing conflict over their interpretation and resolution (Jessop 1990b, pp.39–40).

Offe argues that the political mechanisms required to reproduce these conditions change with the nature of capitalism. As the state is increasingly forced to secure the provision of specific inputs such as productive infrastructure as well as general social conditions for accumulation, it establishes 'planning' and encourages 'participation' as well as centralising the existing administrative system. However, as participation intensifies the class struggle within the state apparatus, the balance of forces required to implement capitalist policies is threatened (Offe 1975). 'The state will continually oscillate between these different mechanisms as the state comes up against their different limitations' (Jessop 1990b, p.40).

The theories of the state considered here involve heterogeneous explanations of the principles of state intervention in capitalist development. Every thesis has its limits in conceptualising the relations between the state and capitalist development. However, a most common shortcoming lies in the lack of a comprehensive economic development theory that incorporates the explanation of state reformation within the political, economic and social changes of the long-term restructuring of capitalism. In an attempt to make up for these shortcomings, a further development lies in the theory of regulation, which has in recent years been applied to the state (Hirsch 1983, Bonefield 1987, Clark 1988, Jessop 1988, 1990b, Bertramsen *et al.* 1991, Florida and Jonas 1991).

We have examined various theories which aim to shed light on the causal mechanism of environmental degradation. The economic dynamics of environmental problems has been outlined above; they remain general and offer no meso-theoretical tools for analysis. This they share in common with the state theories discussed above. It is to regulation theory which we now turn, for it provides a means of synthesising a great number of the theoretical strands while having the capacity to accommodate flexibly the empirical data.

The approaches of regulation theory

So far we have reviewed the implications of modern capitalism for the spatial structure of accumulation, and touched on the environmental consequences. We have also reviewed the main state theories of a broadly Marxist persuasion. The shortcomings of these theories can be characterised thus: the economistic approach neglects the political, while the political approach shows limited understanding of the economic dimensions of capitalism. These issues demand to be brought together in order to analyse the cause of environmental problems in their entire political, social and economic entirety. We need to move towards a theorisation capable of analysing the interdependent relationship of society at large. We thus come to regulation theory as an improved means of achieving this goal. The main features of this quite cogent explanatory paradigm, and its capacity to analyse the social forces which cause the environmental transformation, will now be laid out.

Capitalist society consists of various social relations, wage relations being central. In theories of regulation, the concern is with the concrete expression of these fundamental social relations. The major focus of regulation theory is an explanation of the phenomena of stable and continued reproduction of the capitalist accumulation system despite the contradictions and the intermittent emergence of crises. The regulationist position is the rejection of the functionalist idea that, in the long run, the reforms of a capitalist system result from a self-regulating realm through a sort of 'long-term invisible hand', which plays a role similar to that of the market forces in the short-range regulation of the micro-economic forces, thus resolving macro-economic and social contradictions (Lipietz 1989, p.60, Aglietta 1979). Instead, the theory replaces the functionalist notion of 'capitalist reproduction' with a conjunctural analysis of 'capitalist regulation'. This regulation is seen as an ensemble of practices to adjust and modify short term fluctuations and discontinuous evolutions in the social system through specific institutional forms, societal norms and networks of accumulation strategies (Torfing 1991, p.72).

Regulation theory's advantage over other Marxist derived meta-theories is that it analyses capitalist development over time and space. On the one hand, it periodises capitalist restructuring into successive regimes of accumulation and, on the other, it is concerned with the relationship between global economic forces and national accumulation systems, which makes it explicitly spatial. Its premise is that, first, the nature of the 'coupling' between the accumulation regime and the mode of social regulation varies from nation to nation; and second, for a regime of accumulation to stabilise, this coupling must be functional at the level of the nation-state (Tickell and Peck 1992b). The regulationists identify for each nation-state a succession of regimes of accumulation. Their approach thus overcomes the general and 'universalist' tendency of conventional Marxist discourse.

The mode of development is the primary concept for the historical transformation of the accumulation system. It is defined as 'the articulation at the national level of the structural forms of a regime of accumulation with the institutional features of a mode of regulation into a regulatory ensemble capable of generating growth, prosperity and social peace in the context of the international division of labour' (Torfing 1991, p.77). Regulation is characterised by a synthesis of up to four elements: (i) industrial paradigm, (ii) regime of accumulation, (iii) mode of social regulation and (iv) hegemonic structure.

Regime of accumulation and mode of social regulation (MSR)

Among the above four elements, the twin conceptual pillars of regulation theory are the regime of accumulation and mode of social regulation. A regime of accumulation is a systematic organisation of production, income distribution, exchange of the social product and consumption. With the emergence of a regime of accumulation, economic development is relatively stable: changes in the amount of capital invested, its distribution between sectors and departments and trends in productivity are co-ordinated with changes in the distributions of income and in the field of consumption. A regime of accumulation emerges in accordance with the conditions inherited from the past and the expectations that earlier trends in the norms of production and consumption will continue to be the foundations of a 'social mould' (Dunford 1990).

The regime of accumulation is generally seen to cover the production and consumption processes. It is thus defined in the words of Alain Lipietz as:

> a way of dividing and systematically reallocating the social product. Over an extended period of time, there is a certain convergence between the transformation of production (amount of capital invested, distribution among the branches, norms of production) and transformations in the conditions of final consumption (habits of consumption of wage earners and social groups, collective expenditure etc.)
>
> (Lipietz 1988, p.31)

The mode of social regulation (MSR) is used to denote a specific local and historical collection of structural forms or institutional arrangements within which individual and collective behaviour unfolds. It denotes a particular configuration of market adjustment through which privately made decisions are co-ordinated and which give rise to elements of regularity in economic life. It has two main functions: first, it expresses and serves to reproduce fundamental social relations, and second, it is through these structural forms that multiple, dispersed individual and collective rationalities with their limited horizons result in a regular overall process of economic reproduction. A mode of social regulation, therefore, allows a dynamic adaptation of production and social demands and guides and stabilises the process of accumulation (Dunford 1990, p.306).

The MSR is a collection of political and social strategies which impinge upon economic and extra-economic activities. The MSR, therefore, includes many social compromises between capital, state and civil society (labourer/consumer) such as the allocation of capital, wage settlements, provision of welfare or basic infrastructure and integration in the global economy.

Two distinct types of regulation are identified: competitive and monopolistic. A competitive mode of regulation does not necessarily imply that the economy is a model of free marketism. Nor does monopolistic regulation mean that the economy is dominated by monopolistic behaviour. A competitive MSR is one in which basic welfare and amenities are the responsibility of the individual, wage bargaining is at the level of the firm, and allocation of capital is on a competitive basis. In sum, individual competition in all manner of private and collective consumption underlies competitive MSR. On the other hand, a monopolistic MSR is one in which there is social provision of welfare, collective bargaining procedures and state management of effective demand. The distinction between the two forms of regulation is important to the understanding of the particular characteristics of the regime of accumulation.

This approach identifies several schematic regimes of accumulation and modes of social regulation in the development of capitalist economies. In Western Europe of the nineteenth century, a regime of extensive[15] accumulation gave way to one involving a combination of extensive and intensive[16] accumulation in which the investment of constant capital, including investment in iron and steel, railway construction and shipbuilding itself validated the growth of Department I.[17] In the 1930s, and after World War II in particular, Western Europe and North America saw the establishment of a regime of intensive accumulation in which the conditions of existence of the wage earning class were transformed through the articulation of mass production and mass consumption. The MSR underwent a corresponding transformation. Indeed, in this century MSR has assumed very different forms: a Taylorist or competitive regulation in which intensive working systems were introduced without a commensurate change in working class earnings, and a Fordist[18] or monopolistic regulation in which new norms of production and consumption were established (Dunford 1990, pp.310–314, Tickell and Peck 1992a, pp.6–11). The framework for successive regimes of accumulation and modes of social regulation is outlined in Table 1.1.

Regulationists accept the Marxists' tenets of the contradictions inherent in the capitalist mode of production to produce crises as part of the normal capitalist development process. Crises occur due to failures in the regime of accumulation and/or mode of regulation. Regulation theory identifies three types of crisis (Boyer 1990a, Lipietz 1987, DeVroey 1984, Moulaert and Swyngedouw 1989, Tickell and Peck 1992a): *micro-crises* affect individual units or fractions of capital which fail to adjust to changes in consumption patterns or to transformations in the production process. They exist during stable periods of regime of accumulation and their effects are limited at the level of the firm or sector. *Conjunctural crises* reflect a cyclical downturn in the economy. Such crises may be resolved within the given 'coupling' between accumulation regime and the MSR, requiring 'minor' adjustments,

Table 1.1 Regimes of accumulation and associated modes of social regulation in Western industrialised countries*

Era	Regime of accumulation	Mode of social regulation
19th century	Extensive	Competitive
Early 20th century	Extensive and intensive	Modified competitive
1947–76	Intensive	Monopolistic
1976–present	Flexible	Neo-competitive

Source: Based on Dunford (1990) and Clark (1988).

Note:
*Including Japan.

that is, a change in the spatial division of labour or small-scale institutional changes. Conjunctural crises are important for the stability of regime of accumulation because they force minor changes to take place which are capable of preserving the 'unity of the circuit' (Lipietz 1987, p.34).

Structural crises, on the other hand, involve crises in the mode of regulation, signifying exhaustion of a model of development. These types of crises are also associated with changes in the forces of production.

Structural crises do not, in the view of most writers in this tradition, have regular causes. In 1929, a cumulative collapse was a result of the limits to accumulation in Department I and obstacles to the growth of demand in Department II, whereas the crisis of the 1970s was rooted in a fall in the rate of profit and the exhaustion of an industrial paradigm. The resolution of structural crisis can only occur when a new regime of accumulation is linked to a complementary MSR. Such linkage is of crucial importance. However, this is not to argue that a given accumulation system has but one corresponding MSR; there are a number of possible solutions to the crisis and outcomes are contingent upon the historical formation of social and spatial organisations and the dominant hegemony at the time. The particular coupling is a 'chance discovery' (Dunford 1990, Jessop 1990a, Lipietz 1987, Peck and Tickell 1992a).

Hegemonic structures

In the moments of change in the direction of human social development, there is not one but a whole range of different possibilities: which ones succeed depends in part on the economic success of different models and in part on the strength of different strategic concepts, the influence of the social groups that support them, the construction of coalitions and the actions of the state. The hegemonic structure is a complex political, ideological and cultural formation which is propagated by the dominant social group or institution such as the state, and whose domain is the civil society. The overall direction of social development is determined by 'hegemonic projects' of the dominant societal groupings (Jessop 1983).

Jessop (1983) has suggested that state action is related to accumulation strategies on the one hand, and hegemonic projects and associated alliance strategies on the other. An accumulation strategy is said to be a specific economic growth model complete with its various extra-economic preconditions and the general strategy appropriate to its realisation (Jessop 1983). Thus, economic policies implemented by the state are usually accompanied by a particular propagation of political and ideological strategy. It is also possible to say that under a dominant hegemonic ideology pervasive in civil society, the state is also restricted in the type of socio-economic policies it adopts.

A hegemonic project is a political, institutional and ideological strategy which is economically conditioned but whose domain is civil society as a whole and not just the economic sphere. Through a programme that has a material as well as an ideological content, the construction and reproduction of wider social and electoral blocs is accordingly facilitated. The hegemonic project is vital to the determination of the direction of class compromises as well as the propagation of the dominant ideology. For the Fordist state, it aims at the incorporation of the working class for the advancement of industrial capital's interests: social reform, individual consumption, equal opportunities and steady economic advancement are the characteristic promises (Dunford 1990). Of particular relevance to this study, the hegemonic project also aims to determine which environmental perspective wins the public consensus, for it is important to marginalise any ideological tendencies damaging to the interests of dominant capital.

Technological paradigm and industrial trajectories

In regulationist terms, a sub-component of the regime of accumulation is the 'technological paradigm'. This encompasses the developments in labour processes and in the productive forces. With each development of the labour process, a crisis in the accumulation system can be identified.

The development of labour processes in the Western industrialised countries has been punctuated by several transformations. A phase of *manufacturing* was superceded by mechanisation. Mechanisation was given a new impetus by the development of scientific management of Taylorism which divided the production into simple tasks, thus reducing the skill level of each individual and raising productivity. In the 1920s the introduction of Ford's semi-automatic assembly line resulted in a mechanisation of transfer and a rationalisation of the flow of work. In the 1970s and 1980s, with advances in electronics, computers and communications technologies, automation or *systemofacture* emerged as new principles of work organisation. This also brought the vertical disintegration of the Fordist production processes and hastened a new international division of labour.

Successive waves of industrialisation have been associated not merely with changes in the organisation of work, in the skills and capabilities of workers and with the development of new machines, but also with the development of new materials, a sequence of new products and a succession of leading sectors. After World War II, for example, growth was centred on the spectacular development of the durable consumer goods and the construction industries. This stimulated the demand for investment goods and for energy and intermediate goods such as steel and plastics (see Dunford 1988, Freeman 1987). To explain the waves of accumulation and investment, attention must be paid to the development of the forces of production which include the development of industries, technologies and human skills.

Institutional forms

The interrelationship between the regime of accumulation, the MSR and the hegemonic bloc produces structural forms which crystallise institutionalised compromises. These 'institutional forms' are characterised by the dominant mode of production (Dunford 1990, p.307). They 'enable the transition between constraints associated with an accumulation regime and collective strategies' (Boyer 1990b, p.332). The institutional forms are an intermediate level of constructs which allow concrete analysis of the economic formations to shed light on the character of the regime of accumulation and the mode of social regulation (Torfing 1991, Boyer 1990a, p.37).

Figure 1.1 shows the regulationists' conceptual structure of capitalist economic formation, and the institutional forms that are identified as central to the capitalist mode of production (Boyer 1990a, 1990b):

1   forms of monetary constraint;
2   configurations of the wage relation;
3   mode of competition;
4   position within the international regime;
5   the character and role of the state.

Figure 1.1 also shows a sixth institutional form, the structuration of spatial form and the crises arising from environmental problems. These newly identified elements are the culmination of the review of spatial and environmental theses. The incorporation into regulation theory will be discussed at a later point.

The most important institutional form is the role and character of the state. The state plays a nodal role in bringing about the coherence of a mode of social regulation, and serves as the ultimate guarantor of the other institutional forms (Dunford 1988, p.355, Jessop 1990b, p.202). It is both an object and an agent of regulation since it not only ensures stabilisation of the regime of accumulation through the articulation of accumulation strategies and hegemonic projects but, because of its ability to effect change

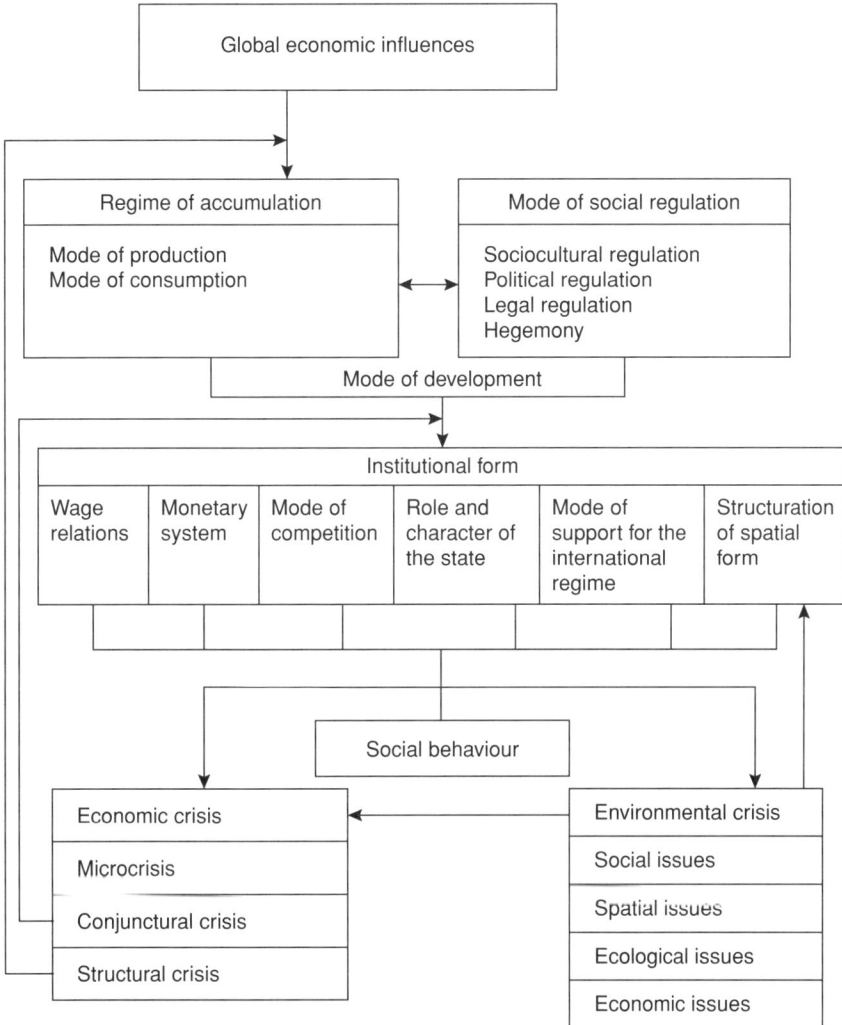

Figure 1.1 Capitalist mode of development in regulation theory.

in the regime of accumulation and mode of social regulation, it is itself an object for transformation (Jessop 1990b, p.200).

The inadequacies of the state theories reviewed in the previous section lie in over-simplification and dualism of their approaches: the state theses of an essentially political category such as the instrumentalist and structuralist only emphasise the state-mode of regulation relationship, while the Gramscian and neo-Gramscian theories stress the state-hegemony relationship. The economic category focuses on the interrelationship between the state and accumulation processes. The regulationist approach has introduced some new advancement in state theories (Bonefield 1987, Clark 1988, Jessop 1988, Bonefield and Holloway 1991). The German school of thought, of which Hirsch is the most prominent exponent, emphasises the dimension of political and economic regulation (regime of accumulation), whereas Jessop (1982 and 1983) is principally concerned with hegemony and politics through the concepts of accumulation strategies and hegemonic projects. Chou, however, synthesises Hirsch (1983) and Jessop's conceptualisation of the state, in order to achieve 'a relatively balanced comprehension of the state transformation in dynamic terms' (Chou 1994, p.38). He achieves the synthesis by stressing the dual importance of falling rate of profit and intensifying class struggle, whereby the accumulation regime is restructured not only through the re-articulation of the mode of social regulation but also through the propagation of hegemonic projects, which shifts the existing historical bloc to a new one (Chou 1994, pp.38–42).

Although regulation theory has successfully conceptualised diverse social forces and relations of capitalist development under an encompassing interpretative framework, it has nonetheless attracted many criticisms. First, it is accused of over-generalisation in the periodisation into two distinct phases of 'binary opposition': the rigid or collective Fordist period on the one hand, and flexible or fragmented post-Fordist period on the other (Williams *et al.* 1987, Sayer 1989a, Thrift 1989, Sayer and Walker 1992). It is challenged on the grounds of both its historical accuracy concerning the nature and breakdown of Fordism and its claim that flexible accumulation is replacing mass production (Brenner and Glick 1992, Sayer 1989a, b). Thus, Amin (1994) maintains that theories of transition,[19] of which the regulationist approach is merely one, should be seen as part of a debate rather than as universalist theory (Amin 1994, p.3). Second, it is argued that the 'productionist' bias of regulation theory tends to overlook the importance of non-Fordist production processes, service industries and non-Taylorist work organisation in the accumulation regime and MSR (Martin 1994, Clark 1988, Foster 1988, Williams and Haslam 1991). Third, due to the above mentioned flaws, it is also argued that regulation theory ascribes and imposes a façade of coherence upon what is a much more confused and unstructured reality, and its exponents fall into the functionalist trap (Amin 1994, p.11, Martin 1994, p.32). Many critics stress the open nature of change that depend upon the outcome of conflicting social relations as well as the mixture of continuity and change from one period to another (Meegan 1988, Rustin 1989, Bonefield and Holloway 1991, Lovering 1991, Graham 1992, Bonefield 1993). Fourth, it is clear that, despite the importance attached to the institutional forms in linking together production and consumption, these forms have not been examined in detail. In particular, the nature of the state has not been adequately theorised (Martin 1994, p.32). Lastly, due to the macro-economic orientation of regulation theory, it is clear that the national economy, as the key unit of analysis, has been prioritised over both local and global economic and regulatory processes. Thus, the integration of accumulation and regulation at different spatial scales remains untheorised (Martin 1994, Tickell and Peck 1992b).

The conceptual framework set out below attempts to address some of the criticisms and shortcomings of the regulation approach.

The synthesis of space, state and environment

We have already suggested that regulation theory has the capacity to incorporate factors explicitly spatial. However, due to its main focus on the economic transformation, there exist some limitations in dealing with spatial problems. Tickell and Peck (1992a) note that the theory contains no explicit conception of uneven spatial development, either at the subnational or supra-national scales, and that there exist several methodological problems. A number of people have concerned themselves with these issues, namely Scott and Storper (1990), Florida and Jonas (1991), Moulaert and Swyngedouw (1992), and Tickell and Peck (1992b). It is Lipietz, however, who has broken new ground in spatialising regulation theory. Lipietz (1992) came up with a conceptual framework which aims to integrate space into regulation theory by referring to and developing the Marxist geographers' conception of space. Rather than being some empty container in which events occur, it is produced out of social relations. Space and society do not simply 'interact': a specific logic (that of capital accumulation) guides the historical dialectic of space and society.

In Lipietz's words:

> The structuring of space is one of the material dimensions of this stabilization of relations which structures social practices. In this regard, it is at first sight the result of this stabilization. The 'choreography' of Hagerstrand illustrates this aspect quite well: because it is human nature to assemble regularly under conditions, and for humankind to continually circulate close to those same places, human beings quite naturally wind up forming places and networks, much the same way one crushes a path into a lawn by always crossing it in the same places. But this structuration of space is at the same time the material base of this social stabilization: once the social places and networks are defined, the infinite plasticity of social practices, as Marx has noted, is framed or reified. In this sense, human space is already a mode of regulation.
>
> (Lipietz 1992, pp.103–104)

If we were to investigate the structuration of space into its component parts, we would find a concrete interaction between people, society and the environment, where the action of one will affect others and their environment:

> Each individual human action is embedded in a preexistent space, an always already given space, and participates in the creation of material conditions of all other human activities (in cities, traffic, production, waste). Each human activity occurs within an 'environment', but also is an integral part of all other human activities and their environments. In turn, each activity can transform (for better or worse) every other environment (e.g. the construction of an apartment building or the disposal of garbage).
>
> (Lipietz 1992, p.104)

These interdependent activities are what Lipietz calls 'structure' (skeleton) and 'agency' (flesh and blood), which simultaneously authorise self-reproduction, crisis and transformation. Thus, the economic activities are embedded in space by their physical fix in the environment, which in turn means that spatial development is a change in human and environmental conditions through the accumulation system.

Tickell and Peck (1992b) pose questions regarding the linkage between the national MSR and sub-national spatial development, and the interaction between national and global spatial scales. In the discussion of the former, they suggest the possibility of the national MSR being hegemonic to support conditions for the reproduction of accumulation in 'core' areas at the expense of the 'peripheral' accumulation system, thus conceiving a geographically expressed 'two nations' MSR (Tickell and Peck 1992b, p.210). Though this raises the question of the linkage between accumulation regime–MSR coupling and different forms of uneven development, such linkage has not been properly theorised at either sub-national or international scales. In the latter, according to Tickell and Peck, the division of the world into a series of national regimes of accumulation also requires reassessment. They stress the need to consider both the historical balance of power within the nation-state (for example, between finance and industrial capital) and the pressures arising from the global regime of accumulation (Tickell and Peck 1992b, p.210). These questions need further explanation: they do, though, show the capacity for regulation theories to address spatial problems.

Lipietz (1992) examines the spatial and environmental consequences of a changing mode of development. He claims that two paradigmatic axes emerged to resolve the crisis of Fordism, stemming from the exhaustion of Taylorist production processes and from the rigidity of the national MSR. These are identified by him as the neo-Fordist regime, which aims to re-establish the flexibility of market relations as well as capital–labour relations, and the post-Fordist regime, which aims to overcome the limitation of Taylorist model of mass production by job qualification, 'just in time' organisation and strategic co-operation between companies.

The spatial forms of these two regimes are quite different: the neo-Fordist model implies a return to urban concentration since proximity of social and economic interactions becomes ever more important in a social regulation that takes direct marketing as its universal form. The result is megalopolisation, bringing with it urban diseconomies as well as widespread environmental problems. This is quite different to the Fordist 'hierarchy', where everything was dispersed over a topography, although controlled within the hierarchies. However, the post-Fordist model produces a network of smaller and highly articulated production systems with 'organised mobilisation of territories' at its base. Instead of a Fordist hierarchy, this model depends on 'negotiated collective and a contractually stabilised interaction, with all the corresponding institutions (professional associations, research and development departments, arbitration boards and union locals)' (Lipietz 1992, p.106). Megalopolisation and all its social and ecological consequences in both the North and the South[20] are the greatest menace that the neo-Fordist models can impose on the future. Just as Fordism of the 1960s tightly steered the direction taken by different countries through the decades after the collapse of Fordism, likewise the urban space bequeathed by the 1990s will impose ever more rigid limits on our choices in the twenty-first century.

In the above discussion, it is emphasised that spatial form is actively created and recreated through the social activities between people and their environments. Space is not simply an outcome of the current accumulation regime, but is marked by the pre-existing configuration, thus helping to form the accumulation strategies of the ensuing period.

Summary

In this chapter we have reviewed economic, spatial and state theories which lay the foundations for the understanding of the causes of environmental problems. These are taken as the starting point for our investigations of the environment. As we have seen in the examination of the theses above, the capitalist mode of production is the process by which the interaction between capital, labour and the environment are brought together as essential elements in the accumulation process. Production, whether capitalist in form or not, is the process where human beings turn the environment and its resources into use values or commodities for exchange. In the capitalist mode of production, capital mobilises labour as well as raw materials from nature, producing commodities to be consumed by the society in the reproduction of labour. Thus, nature is transformed into commodities by capital and consumed by society in the production and reproduction process. As capital tries to overcome the inherent contradictions in the system by displacing crisis tendencies in space, a landscape of exploitation is created. The production of space in the image of capitalism is characterised by uneven development with all its problems of over- and underdevelopment. The concept of uneven development unifies environmental conditions in different places. In the era of global capitalism, uneven spatial development between and within nations is the manifestation of the interaction between capital, labour and environment in specific places which themselves are connected by a web of commodity exchanges and flow of capital.

The state which defends the interest of capital in general as well as implementing social compromises and reforms working to achieve a degree of social cohesion, plays an important part in both the capital accumulation process and the moderation of the tendencies of capital to exploit labour and environment to the limit and then to move on to a 'greener pasture'. Within the political and economic constraints in which the state operates, it actively intervenes in the provision of the preconditions for capital accumulation and for the reproduction of labour, for it is uneconomical for capital to provide these by itself. In the latter half of the twentieth century, many national states increasingly regulated natural resources and the environment. Policies relating to land-use, housing, safety at work and home, water supply and waste management, timber production, nuclear energy, and emission standards for automobiles – these have become a commonplace.

Figure 1.2 demonstrates the integration of economy, civil society, state and the environment. This diagram also indicates how the state (and other social, hegemonic institutions) regulates the interactions between capital, civil society and environment. We can divide the regulation of the state into three categories. The first is the regulation in the production and consumption relationship between capital and labour through various social and economic measures (as represented by triangle A in Figure 1.2). Setting interest rates to curb inflation, managing the capital–labour nexus, and setting of minimum wages are just some of the state's actions aimed at ensuring continued capital accumulation. Second is the regulation of the interaction between capital and the environment, which involves securing of the physical preconditions for capital accumulation such as industrial location, construction of infrastructure and raw materials (as seen in Figure 1.2 as triangle B). The third regulation involves the balance between the environmental needs of the population and the conservation of nature (triangle C in Figure 1.2). The state, therefore, must balance the three spheres of regulation to obtain the best possible conditions for the continued reproduction of the accumulation regime. The emphasis has long been upon the production and reproduction of capital (and to a lesser extent, labour) at the expense of 'environment'. With environmental consciousness awakened in the last two decades of the century, nature has assumed an ever greater importance as a 'resource' for ever more efficient reproduction of capital. In many nations, national parks which were intended

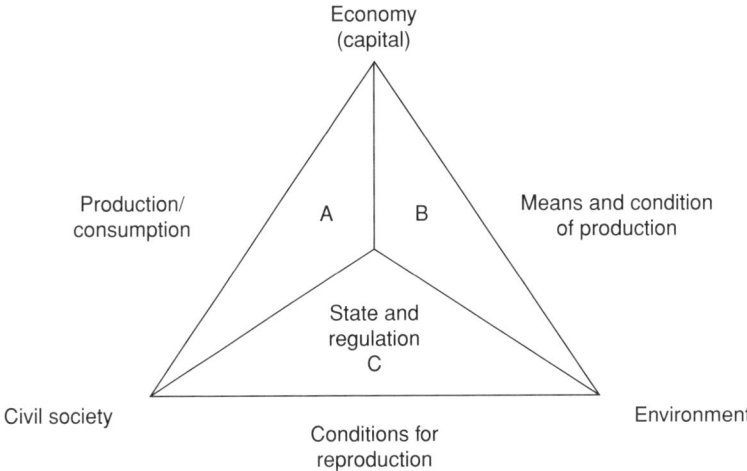

Figure 1.2 Economy, civil society, environment and the state: a conceptual framework.

Source: Chung (1997), p.48.

Notes:

Segment A: social regulation in the production/consumption relations such as intervention in union activity, consumption behaviour, education and training, fertility, working conditions etc.

Segment B: social regulation and state provision of physical infrastructure from production and the enabling of obtaining raw materials for production, and the protection of nature from overuse and abuse; spatial regulation.

Segment C: social regulation of consumption of nature and environmental goods, that state regulation in the provision of public consumption goods such as clean water, roads, low cost housing and general living conditions.

to preserve natural wildernesses have become themed packages for tourist consumption.

The above model (Figure 1.2) shows that crisis could be produced by the dysfunction in any of the interactions between capital, labour and the environment, and that any adjustment may involve a change in all the other relationships. The formation of crisis in the accumulation regime gives new directions to state policies as well as new relationships between economy, space and the environment. The conjunctural and structural crisis would necessitate some sort of adjustment within the existing regime of accumulation, or a new accumulation with a new mode of regulation. Both of these forms of restructuring of the accumulation system would have a degree of social and spatial impact which depended on the adjustment required. They may also require a 'spatial strategy' in order to help the restabilisation of the accumulation system. However, the new spatial arrangement would be constrained by the spatial structure of the previous regime.

The changing interaction of accumulation regimes and the physical environment lies at the basis of spatial transformation. Changing spatial configurations bring about changing environmental conditions. As new industrial space is formed and old ones go into decline, there is a qualitative change in the environmental conditions of both. Uneven spatial development results in differentiated environmental qualities. Environmental degradation stems not only from the economic system, that is, the mode of production and consumption and capital concentration, but also from its spatial configuration, the social regulation of production, consumption and the disposal of wastes.

So as to overcome the generality of the existing theories and to introduce intermediate analytical concepts, it is hoped that our resort to regulation theory will provide greater insights into the causal relationships of environmental degradation, and do so in a comprehensive and yet concrete way. The periodisation of capitalist development and the concepts of institutional forms are the elements which promote the utility of regulation theory in the analysis of economic, spatial and environmental processes.

To conclude, using the regulationist conceptual framework, we view the dynamics of environmental degradation as arising from the crisis-ridden capitalist mode of production which is sustained through the continual restructuring of the accumulation regime stabilised by concurrent changes in the mode of social regulation. At the same time, space is restructured in order to remove the barriers to the capital valorisation process, creating a new configuration which reflects the new accumulation regime and mode of regulation. However, the new spatial form constrained by the past spatial structure may intensify socio-environmental problems, due to the intensifying accumulation regime and the mode of regulation.

Thus:

1 The environmental degradation of a nation-state reflects the spatial form that arises out of the dialectical relationship between spatial legacy and accumulation strategy. The latter is promoted by the state in the process of restructuring of the failing regime of accumulation and mode of social regulation stemming from the changing global economic order and/or industrial paradigm.

2 Successive, intensifying regimes of accumulation and their MSRs exacerbate the topography of uneven spatial development, resulting in differentiated environmental conditions in spatial zones of differing levels of development.

3 The stance towards environmental problems is dependent on the mode of social regulation (the hegemonic ideology, the regulation of industrial and domestic wastes, the provision of social and environmental amenities), as well as the 'industrial trajectory'.

2 Economic development, state strategies and social change in Korea

The investigation of the causes of environmental problems in Korea must begin with the examination of that country's mode of development in its historical articulation. Successive regimes of accumulation and modes of social regulation will be explored to illustrate the way in which economic, social and political changes have affected spatial structure and environmental conditions.

The introductory section will examine the changing international economic environment in which Korean economic development has taken place. The development of world economy will be reviewed through the lens of regulation theory. This will not only provide a global perspective, but also a reference point from which Korean development can be compared. The internal dynamics and mechanisms of the development process are crucial factors of environmental change, these cannot be separated from economic factors at the global scale.

Regulation theory's approach to global economy is well established, but its application to the analysis of Korean economy, spatial or social development is somewhat novel. This theory not only provides greater understanding of the causes of crises; through its periodisation it allows us to distinguish different accumulation strategies adopted at the various phases of development. Therefore, it is hoped that the interpretation which it provides will shed new light on the development process in postwar Korea (see Figure 2.1).

After a brief discussion of the colonial legacy which was to play an important role in the immediate postwar development process, the chapter will focus on political, economic and social changes after 1950. Post-independence Korean economic development can be divided into five phases which are distinguished by the changes in the regime of accumulation and/or MSR: the 'Import Substitution Industrialisation (ISI) period'; the 'Taylorist Export-Oriented Industrialisation (EOI) period'; the '*Yusin*[1] EOI period'; the 'Peripheral Fordist EOI period'[2]; and the 'Neo-Fordist period'[3]. These different modes of development have had specific impacts on space and the environment through changes in industrial, social and institutional

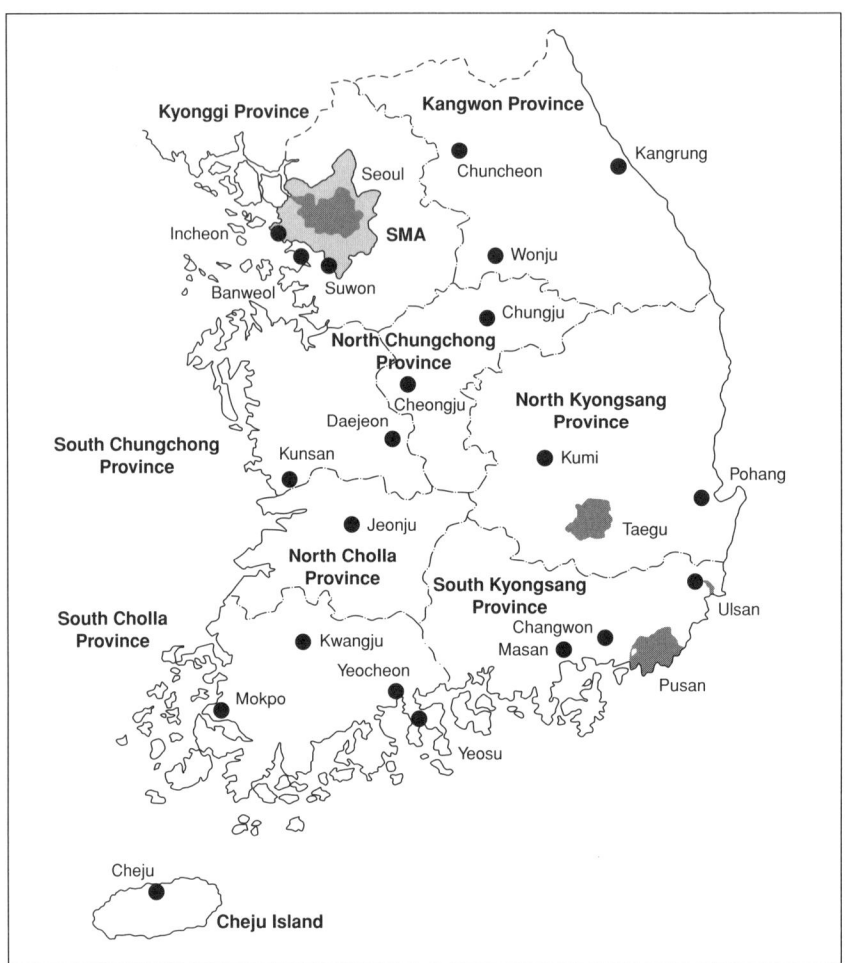

Figure 2.1 Korea: provinces and major cities.

structure. In this process the industrial relations, social norms and political systems which affect the use and abuse of the environment will also be identified.

The Fordist regime of accumulation, crisis and the rise of the NIDL

Since the genesis of capitalism, the world economy, upon which Korea has been very much dependent, has been dominated by the advanced

Western industrialised countries. The industrialisation of the core countries in the eighteenth and the nineteenth centuries drew more and more peripheral regions and nations into the capitalist development process. Much of the indigenous mode of production was swept aside to be replaced by capitalist social relations. In the core industrialised countries, there have been many transformations of the regime of accumulation since the late nineteenth century. The *laissez-faire* era of the nineteenth and early twentieth centuries was characterised by extensive regimes of accumulation and competitive regulation. During this time, growth was achieved incrementally, through the insertion of additional productive factors into the capitalist circuit. Accumulation occurred as a result of the expansion of capitalist relations into new industrial sectors, new areas within the core countries (of Europe and North America) and new peripheral countries. The major problem for individual units of capital was meeting rapidly growing demand for their goods in expanding markets. It was because of this that the leading industrial sectors were capital goods industries such as coal, steel and chemical industries, and technical progress was largely limited to these Department I industries, not affecting Department II (consumer goods) to any significant extent (DeVroey 1984, Lipietz 1987). At the level of the nation-state the MSR was economically liberal and non-interventionist. Wages, for example, were negotiated at the level of the individual firm and subject to market fluctuations. At the international level, on the other hand, competitive regulation was characterised by the hegemony of the UK, and also by the gold standard.

After World War I, technical progress began to spread to Department II industries, altering the structure of the regime of accumulation. However, there was insufficient consumer power to create effective demand for increased production in Department II. This mode of development was exhausted in the 1930s and manifested itself in a crisis of overproduction. The core of the problem was that the competitive MSR was unable to form a social framework where wages could be raised in line with productivity growth. In order for the crisis of the 1930s to be resolved, it was essential that a new coupling between the accumulation system and the MSR be established (Tickell and Peck 1992b). Between the two World Wars, there took place a 'long transition' from an extensive regime to the phase of intensive accumulation or Fordism. Technical changes, often involving de-skilling, brought about significant increases in labour productivity in both Departments I and II. This led to a massive rise in real wages, which in turn formed a basis for mass markets for consumer goods.

After World War II, a new mode of development was established, based on mass production with mass consumption on the part of the labouring class. This new regime of accumulation was coupled with a monopolistic mode of social regulation. In the US, the roots of this MSR lay in Roosevelt's New Deal, and in the growing militancy of trade unions (Aglietta 1979).

In Britain, the 'hungry thirties' ended with a transformed political climate, more open to state intervention and underpinned by the consensual nature of politics in the wake of World War II. The monopolistic MSR was characterised by the interventionist state which developed welfare and social programmes designed to maintain the levels of total consumption, and by the collectively determined wage levels through increased bargaining powers of the workers, which again stimulated growth in consumer demand (Tickell and Peck 1992a).

The Fordist regime based on intensive accumulation and a monopolistic MSR began to dysfunction from the late 1960s, although the structural crisis did not manifest itself until the mid-1970s. In the late 1960s, there was a slow-down in productivity growth in the core Fordist countries as the leading industrial branches reached their technical limits in the context of rising real wages. At the same time investment and capital intensification in Department II diminished (although the effects of this were mitigated in the short term by rising exports). Finally, resistance to the Taylorist labour process grew within the workplace and industrial strife exploded. All these factors resulted in falling rates of profit and de-valorisation (Tickell and Peck 1992b). Aglietta (1982) has suggested that the crisis of Fordism was exacerbated by 'exogenous' shocks to the system. The development of contemporary Fordism in the core countries had brought about an increased competition between the three economic poles in the world economy – Western Europe, the US and Japan – in response to the dramatic expansion of global trade. The emergence of Japan as an economic power in the 1960s began to present a considerable threat to the established Fordist economies of Europe and North America, eating into tight consumer markets (Lipietz 1987, Hirsch 1978, Tickell and Peck 1992a, b). The oil shocks in 1973 also contributed to the crisis by inducing acute inflationary consequences (Roddick 1988, Lipietz 1985, 1989).

The unfolding structural crisis triggered further internationalisation of production, in part to offset the rising cost of labour brought about by increased charges on welfare states as a result of increased unemployment. All this led to a reduction in aggregate demand, which in turn caused problems of over-capacity and difficulties in company debt repayment. The internationalisation of production and the growth of the export sector meant that wages were increasingly seen as a burden on economic competitiveness rather than as a contributor to consumption. Consequently, real wages began to slow and then decline, compounding the problems of stagnating consumer demand. The virtuous cycle of Fordism had turned vicious (Tickell and Peck 1992b).

The internationalisation of production (and thus capital) to those peripheral countries with low labour costs and weak labour unions gave rise to a far more articulated international division of labour – characterised in the 1980s as 'New International Division of Labour' (NIDL) (Froebel *et al.* 1980). The Fordist principles of labour organisation were marked by the division of production activities into three levels: (i) conception, organisation/methods, and engineering, all of which became autonomous; (ii) manufacturing, which requires a relatively skilled labour force; and (iii) assembly and execution, which in theory requires few skills (Lipietz 1987). These three vertically integrated tiers of the labour process, essential to the maximisation economies of scale during the Fordist period, were dismantled in order to overcome the crisis. The pressures exerted on industrial capital, combined with the developments in production, transport and communication technology, and growing labour militancy, impelled more and more Fordist assembly lines to go offshore. This triggered a substantial growth in sub-contracting production in peripheral countries in an attempt to restore profitability and control over the production process. The new division of international labour had accordingly been formulated in response to the vertical disintegration or putting-out of the unskilled and labour intensive part from the Fordist production lines. Through the development of an NIDL, central capitalism integrated peripheral countries into the world economy as 'sweatshops' committed to the production of Fordist goods (Lipietz 1985, 1987). Labour intensive industries started to locate to peripheral countries such as Mexico, Brazil, Taiwan, Singapore and Korea. This was to expand markets by gaining a foothold in ISI countries protected by high tariff barriers, and to raise competitiveness in the international market by exploiting an almost inexhaustible reservoir of cheap labour in the developing countries through initiating a transnational and subcontracting reorganisation of production (Lipietz 1987). See Table 2.1.

Under such global economic restructuring, Korea emerged in the late 1960s as a newly industrialised country along with Taiwan, Singapore and Hong Kong. The 'four tigers' or sometimes 'dragons' industrialised within this external economic environment. Although the globalisation of capital and production helped their industrialisation process, the accompanying

Table 2.1 Phases of regulation and accumulation of the industrialised countries in the twentieth century

	To 1914	*1918–39*	*1945–73*	*1974–present*
Accumulation system	Extensive	Emerging intensive	Intensive (Fordist regime)	Emerging flexible? Protracted crisis?
Mode of social regulation	Competitive	Crisis of competitive	Monopolistic (Fordist-Keynsian mode)	Crisis of monopolistic Emerging neo-competitive? neo-conservative? neo-corporatist?

Source: Tickell and Peck (1992b), p.194.

intensification of competition for markets posed a constraint to exports and increased transformational forces in their accumulation regime. As we will see in the following sections, the emergence and collapse of Fordism in the core industrialised countries had a significant effect on the Korean EOI development. However, it will also be clear that Korean economic development was not so dependent upon the transnational subcontracting or foreign direct investment as was the case in other Asian NICs.

Colonial development and the transformation of Korea (1910–45)

The significance of imperialism carries weight in the explanation of economic development in Korea, as it did in the case of Japan a century earlier when that nation articulated Western technological and institutional contacts with its own cultural forms (Morishima 1982). The foundation of Korean economic growth from the 1950s onwards could be attributed to the industrial, social and institutional infrastructure laid down during the Japanese colonial period (Mason *et al.* 1980, p.75).

For Korea, the Japanese annexation signalled the beginning of the modernisation period. The colonial regime brought many social, economic, infrastructural, institutional and political changes. Before that time, modernisation had been slow, and was hampered by the conservative Confucian regime centred around the monarchy. The traditional Confucian social norms were replaced almost overnight by modern social institutions: commercial and financial institution, transportation infrastructure, a judiciary, education and other forms of state administration (Amsden 1989, p.32).

Export-oriented agricultural modernisation and industrialisation

The thrust of the Japanese state into Korea in 1909 coincided with Japan's first wave of industrialisation. The initial material context of Japan's expansion into Korea was its drive to secure sufficient supplies of agricultural commodities for its growing urban and industrial population. During the period of colonial rule, agricultural productivity increased greatly due to the implementation of modern practices and the removal of absentee landlords in favour of smallholder cultivation (Ho 1978, Mason *et al.* 1980, Henderson and Appelbaum 1992, p.7). Although the agricultural system imposed by the Japanese colonial state was not in some senses much different from the traditional Korean one it replaced, the socio-economic impact was considerable. The landlord-tenant system still persisted. However, under the new system the peasants had no rights to their land without a tenant's lease. The introduction of market prices stimulated productivity, but it also intensified the exploitation of the tenants to the maximum. As rents continued to escalate due to increased competition for land, and with few employment opportunities elsewhere along with rising population pressures, the agricultural squeeze was at the tenants' expense (Amsden 1989, pp.53–54). Amsden shows that while output rose,[4] the welfare of the masses declined, in particular for tenant farmers; income distribution deteriorated. The index of rice consumption in Korea fell from 100 in 1915–19 to only 56 in 1934–38, with a similar trend in the consumption of millet, barley and beans (Amsden 1989, p.54). Due to increased production in agricultural commodities for export, the colonial administration was able to expand its tax base, and its food supply to the homeland.

In the 1920s and 1930s, rising wages in Japan and military imperatives for the conquest of Manchuria meant that Japanese companies were encouraged to invest in mining and manufacturing facilities in Korea (Amsden 1989, Henderson and Appelbaum 1993). The 1920s saw much growth in these areas, exploiting cheap labour and raw materials. Jones and Sakong (1980) summarised this period as 'a rather typical colonial dualism with the periphery providing raw material to the center' (p.23).

A small group of Korean entrepreneurs was deliberately nurtured during this early colonial industrialisation period (Amsden 1989, p.33). The number of wholly Korean owned firms increased from 27 in 1911 to 362 in 1929 (Jones and Sakong 1980, p.24). Compared to the number of Japanese companies, this was small; it is nonetheless the beginnings of the modern Korean capitalist enterprise, the chaebol.[5] Jones and Sakong (1980) demonstrate how a present day chaebol, the Sam Yang Group, began in this period – first as a textile company and later diversifying into other areas. It established a newspaper (*Dong-A Ilbo*) and even a university (Korea University) (p.24). They also suggest that the joint venture companies (of which there were 165 in 1929) played a major role in the critical learning process of the period (Jones and Sakong 1980).

In preparation for the war in China and Southeast Asia in the 1930s, the second wave of industrialisation in Korea was led by the heavy and chemical industries based on *zaibatsu*[6] capital (Amsden 1989, p.34, Jones and Sakong 1980, p.24). Most of the heavy and mining industries were located in the north in order to be near the source of mineral resources and hydroelectric power plants, whilst the new, modern, large-scale light industries like food processing and textile industries were situated in the south (see Table 2.2). Their output was to supply the Japanese economy, the share of exports in total manufacturing increasing from roughly one third in 1930 to two thirds in 1940. Foreign ownership of the modern industrial sector was particularly dominant in the 1940s, with 59 per cent of manufacturing firms owned by the Japanese – representing 91 per cent of paid-in capital. Virtually all the large-scale factories were Japanese-owned while small-scale production was in Korean hands (Jones and Sakong 1980, p.25). Although manufacturing averaged an annual growth

Table 2.2 Manufacturing production, South and North Korea, 1939

	(Current million yen)			Share of the South in all Korea (%)
	All Korea	South	North	
Textiles	201.4	171.0 (24.1)	30.4 (3.9)	84.9
Metallurgical	136.1	13.6 (1.9)	122.5 (15.5)	10.0
Machinery	53.2	38.4 (5.4)	14.8 (1.9)	72.2
Ceramics	43.3	12.1 (1.7)	31.2 (4.0)	27.9
Chemicals	501.8	91.2 (12.9)	410.6 (52.0)	18.2
Wood products	21.1	13.7 (1.9)	7.4 (0.9)	64.9
Printing and publishing	19.4	17.2 (2.4)	2.2 (0.3)	89.0
Processed foods	328.4	213.6 (30.1)	114.8 (14.5)	65.1
Gas and elec. production	30.5	11.1 (1.6)	19.4 (2.5)	36.4
Miscellaneous	163.3	127.5 (18.0)	35.8 (4.5)	78.1
Total	1,498.5	709.4 (100.0)	789.1 (100.0)	47.4

Source: Zenku Keizai Chosa Kikan Rengokai, Chosen Keizai Nenpo (1942), cited in Mason (1980), p.89.

rate of over 10 per cent throughout the three decades (Henderson and Appelbaum 1992, Mason *et al.* 1980, p.75), with forward and backward linkages weak, the spread effects of economic growth were minimal (Jones and Sakong 1980, pp.24–25). The early colonial dualism was extended and intensified in all sectors.

Between 1910 and 1945, the above mentioned developments saw the creation of an industrial working class. A large number of Koreans gained experience in factories and in other modern institutions, and became familiar with a modern urban existence. There was a considerable expansion in the size of the Korean factory labour force, from 12,000 in 1912 to nearly 440,000 in 1940 (Mason *et al.* 1980, p.77, Jones and Sakong 1980, p.28). Although there were more than 7,000 Korean managers and 28,000 professional and technical workers,[7] in these skilled categories Koreans were discriminated against: in 1943, Japanese held 81 per cent of the 'technician and engineer' positions in manufacturing (Jones and Sakong 1980, p.26). Although the formation of an industrial working class became the foundation for post-independence development, the lack of skilled workers such as technicians and engineers was also to prove one of the reasons for a low rate of utilisation of factory capacity during the ISI period. Also, as Table 2.2 shows, the industrialisation had a regional bias: the North was dominated by heavy and chemical industries, whereas the South had a higher concentration of light industries. This unbalanced distribution of industries was due to the locational requirements vis-à-vis raw materials.

To facilitate industrialisation and export (to Japan) of agricultural produce and manufactured commodities, a considerable number of infrastructural projects were implemented – the building of railroads, roads and ports, and the provision of electricity, sewerage and piped water to most large urban settlements. All had a great impact on the traditionally rural society (Henderson and Appelbaum 1992, p.7). As will be seen in Chapter 3, the infrastructural network, particularly the rail system, was extensively developed. The latter covered the whole country, allowing the Japanese to appropriate agricultural and industrial goods from Korea as well as Manchuria. The legacy of Japanese colonial industrialisation was the foundation for postwar industrial capitalism in Korea.

Colonial administration, regulation and social change

It is not generally acknowledged that the social and institutional changes that took place during this early period laid down the model for later methods of social control as well as setting the direction for the postwar economy. Establishment of a modern system of education, administration and finance, the abolition of the monarchy and the *yangban* social elite – these had a profound effect on society as a whole. Feudal and Confucian traditions and their institutions were pushed back by 'modern' institutions.

It was probably the militaristic colonial administrative and education systems which were the most significant in the transformation of Korean society (Henderson and Appelbaum 1992, p.7). The former provided the preconditions for Japanese accumulation and expropriation. 'Japanisation' of Korean society penetrated to every sphere. The hierarchical military order with its attendant disciplinary codes was transmitted through the incorporation of Koreans into the educational, military and civil services. Of course, the colonial Japanese were not averse to coercive means. The authoritarian structure later utilised by Park Chung Hee and the subsequent regimes could be traced to the Japanese administration of this time (Cumings 1988). Park Chung Hee himself had served as an officer in the Japanese Imperial Army.

The new education system of the colonialists had no use for the long-standing practices which limited learning to the aristocracy and landed gentry. The opening of educational opportunity to the lower orders was intended to produce a well-educated industrial proletariat to suit the changing economy. Thus, as Amsden remarks, 'Investments in education, even at the university level, were unusually high by colonial standards, but they were motivated by policies designed to assimilate Koreans into Japanese society as the lower elements'. Literacy, discipline and social homogeneity became the guiding precepts of the Korean education system. 'Group-cooperative'[8] norms became deeply rooted; they were enthusiastically imposed, especially in the conglomerates as a means of enforcing hierarchy and discipline. Amsden's view is that the new social system created by Japanese colonialism was 'far more successful in smashing old foundations than establishing new ones'. He asserts that 'colonialism removed the old blockages to industrialisation but created new ones in its wake' (Amsden 1989, p.33). Whether or not this view can be substantiated, the fact remains that the social institutions and cultural norms that were created by the Japanese provided the Korean state with a powerful tool for economic and social regulation.

The import substitution industrialisation period (1953–61)

The Japanese defeat released Korea from colonial rule, only to be locked into a Soviet–American ideological confrontation, which divided the peninsula into two halves at the 38th parallel, north and south. Each faction of occupying forces set about establishing a state in its own image; in 1948, there took place separate elections, which installed a Soviet-oriented regime in the north and a free-market regime in the south. The period between 1945 and 1953 was a time of economic turmoil, contention in ideological and power blocs, eventually leading to the Korean War (1950–53). The political events of the interim period shaped the political and social forces that continue to play upon the Korean peninsula.

American occupation and prelude to import substitution industrialisation

Korea's first years following liberation from the Japanese were strongly influenced by the anti-communism of the American occupation forces and corruption in domestic politics. The chaos of this period curtailed the aspirations of Korea's people to create an independent country founded on justice and equality.

During the early post-colonial years the economy experienced utter dislocation in the wake of the collapse of Japan's 'Greater East Asia Co-Prosperity Sphere' (Mason *et al.* 1980, p.92) as well as by the arbitrary division of the peninsula into Soviet and American occupation zones. The ensuing war between the two Koreas destroyed much of the urban housing stock, infrastructure and productive facilities; rural areas were equally devastated. The Japanese policy of discriminating against Koreans in technical and managerial spheres meant a lack of key skills in the industrial sector, which became unsustainable. By 1948, the number of manufacturing and construction firms in South Korea had fallen to 4,500 from over 10,000 in 1943; employment had declined by 41 per cent in these sectors, and manufacturing output was only 15 per cent of the 1939 level. The division of the country at the 38th parallel had deprived South Korea of a heavy and chemical industries sector, and most of its mineral and energy sources. Three quarters of the mining industry was in the north.[9] At the signing of the Armistice in 1953, the level of production of the Korean economy was far below that of the early 1940s (Mason *et al.* 1980, p.92).

Many analysts lay the blame for the deterioration of the economy upon mismanagement by the American occupation forces as much as upon the political conflicts between the myriad Korean political groups (Jones and Sakong 1980, pp.31–32). The American Military Government in Korea refused to recognise the People's Republic, also set up in the South, and in 1946 suppressed the National Council of Korean Labour Unions, *Chon Pyeong*,[10] since this organisation was said to have had communist tendencies and Soviet support. Instead, the American occupiers chose to govern South Korea through the most conservative political faction, the Korean Democratic Party (KDP), which had very little grassroots support[11] (Cumings 1981). Though this party soon lost power, this partnership safeguarded the survival of the *yangban* class, the civil service, police and capitalists who had collaborated with the Japanese. Although the landlord class was dissolved by the end of the 1950s with the implementation of land reform, a part of the *yangban* became privileged politicians, government bureaucrats, educators and industrialists. This lent continuity to postwar Korea (Amsden 1989, pp.36–37). The Liberal Party which assumed power during the ISI period relied on much of the same class base.

Land reform

During the Japanese colonial period, the social composition of the agricultural population shifted towards landlessness. Tenants accounted for 38 per cent of the agricultural population in 1918 but for as much as 54 per cent in 1932. By the late 1930s, fewer than three per cent of farm households owned two thirds of the cultivated land area (Amsden 1989, p.54). Farm households dispossessed of their land during the Japanese colonial period regarded the land-owning classes as mere Japanese collaborators. As liberation drew closer, expectations of a more just society were raised. Following independence and division of the country, the American and South Korean regime was confronted by increasing political sensitivity on the subject of land and wealth redistribution, which had been conclusive in the Soviet controlled North:

> landlordism had disappeared, the land had been redistributed, major industries had been nationalised, radical reform had eliminated the worst abuses of the colonial factory system and had established formal equality for women.
>
> (Cumings 1981, p.382)

Land reform was implemented for several reasons. First, it was implemented to compete with the North, for socialist and democratic traditions remained strong and the Rhee government needed to establish its legitimacy. Second, the political power of an unproductive land-owning class was a barrier to industrialisation and modernisation. The old *yangban* class favoured land investment rather than industry and commerce. With restrictions on land ownership, the landlord class would be obliged to seek other avenues for investment.

Tenant farming was formally abolished by the *Land Reform Law* of 1950. In June 1949, a land reform Bill was passed by the general assembly but was vetoed by President Rhee. An Act more favourable to landlords was passed in March 1950, providing for the distribution of both land purchased from Korean landlords as well as that confiscated from the Japanese. Nevertheless, by 1964 tenant farmers comprised just 5.2 per cent of rural households, compared with 42.1 per cent in 1947 (Suh 1992, p.10). In addition to abolishing tenant farming, the Act also imposed a three hectare limit on land holding for each farm household (Boyer and Ahn 1991, p.74).

The land-to-the-tiller programme neither enriched the peasantry, nor did it fill out the state coffers. But its impact in the long term was major. Reform redirected idle capital away from land speculation to manufacturing, and uprooted a class that had been unproductive and insulated. It also relieved bottlenecks in food supply; this in turn dampened inflationary pressures, and in the 1960s when labour intensive industries were promoted, rural underdevelopment, especially amongst young females, was absorbed through the first wave of industrialisation. Amsden's view is that the land reform 'cleared the field for strong centralised state power . . .' through the removal of a landed gentry class, which wielded formidable political power (Amsden 1989, p.37).

US aid and the Korean economy

In 1953 South Korea possessed a backward economy in which agriculture, forestry and fishing accounted for 47 per cent of GNP and manufacturing less than 9 per cent. Total fixed investment was only 7 per cent of GNP, barely enough to cover the depreciation on the existing capital stock (Mason *et al.* 1980, p.93). Furthermore, South Korea depended upon aid from the US for its reconstruction and survival. Between 1953 and 1961, US aid financed over 70 per cent of total imports and 75 per cent of total fixed capital formation (Cole 1980, Mason *et al.* 1980, Steinberg 1989, Haggard *et al.* 1991, p.852), the average annual inflow of US aid excluding military spending amounting to $270 million (Amsden 1989, p.39). Since South Korea's independence in 1948, the US had sought to link its foreign assistance to close monitoring of foreign exchange, and to conservative fiscal policies. Integral also to US policy was the privatisation of Japanese properties, land reform and the creation of democratic political institutions. While the US was primarily concerned with stabilisation, the Korean government sought economic self-sufficiency through a rationalised programme of infrastructure development, and through import-substitution. Conflicts developed between client and donor over reconstruction and development strategies, as well as over political issues such as normalisation of relations with Tokyo. The Korean government was dissatisfied with the speed of aid deliveries, the lack of attention given to building industrial infrastructure, and the emphasis on imports of consumer goods such as foodstuffs, and raw materials for light industry (e.g. cotton). These two categories accounted for about three-quarters of all economic aid between 1953 and 1960: only 16.5 per cent of aid went directly to manufacturing during this period (Haggard *et al.* 1991, p.852).

To maximise aid inflow, the Rhee government introduced macro-economic policies which featured low interest rates, overvalued exchange rates, a deficit budget financed by borrowing from the Central Bank when taxes and aid-generated revenues were insufficient, and Central Bank financing of commercial bank credit to the private sector. Such policies inevitably produced an internal financial gap between government and private transactions, and an external financial gap between import demand and foreign exchange supply. The Rhee regime then allocated aid entitlements in exchange for political campaign contributions. The declining political fortunes of the Liberal Party encouraged Rhee to maximise his dependence on aid, to limit the domain of coherent planning, and to maintain discretionary controls over a variety of policy instruments (Haggard *et al.* 1991, p.850).

The windfall gains from aid provided a basis for the emergence of an altogether new entrepreneurial element, which was far more growth-oriented than the conservative class of small-scale industrialists. During this period of pervasive patronage, political cronyism led to an uneven distribution of the spoils from the below-market sale of Japanese property. Favoured firms were also allocated hard currency to import scarce materials – grain and fertilisers – which they then resold on the domestic market at monopoly prices. They were given loans at subsidised interest rates, granted tax exemptions, and awarded preferential contracts for large-scale government projects. In Amsden's words:

> The magnitude of fraud is indicated by the size of the loans that the most favoured firms received, 'loans' on which they paid neither interest nor principal. A Government Audit Report, prepared in 1961 after the First Republic's fall, suggested that the total outstanding equalled about $140 million.
>
> (Amsden 1989, p.39)

Despite the impression of sluggish growth under the import substitution regime, industrial expansion was rapid, albeit from a low base (Suh 1992). Although GDP growth only averaged 3.9 per cent from 1953–55 to 1960–62, this can be attributed largely to the poor performance of agriculture and services. Industry grew at 11.2 per cent a year (Amsden 1989, Cole and Lyman 1971, pp.192–193, Haggard *et al.* 1991, p.852). However, economic performance failed to bring economic improvements to the mass of Korean people; neither did it meet the expectations of aid donors. Annual rates of inflation dropped from over 500 per cent in 1951 to 25–28 per cent in 1953–54, only to rise again in 1955 to 82 per cent (Mason *et al.* 1980, p.94).

Under American pressure, stabilisation measures were adopted from 1956, these focusing on inflation control and on reduction of the large government deficit; pursuit of economic growth through a cohesive plan remained of secondary importance (Haggard *et al.* 1991, Mason *et al.* 1980, p.94). The stabilisation programmes were successful at slowing inflation, but positive effects on investment and development were not forthcoming.

Exhaustion of the ISI paradigm

South Korea's economic growth rate was evidently not sustainable, and 1958 marked the exhaustion of the import substitution phase. GNP growth peaked at 7.7 per cent in 1957, declining to 5.2 per cent in 1958, 3.9 per cent in 1959 and 1.9 per cent in 1960 (Haggard *et al.* 1991, p.853). This trend reflected the demise of the easy import-substitution stage and the simultaneous falling away of American aid. The prevailing political structure that was distorting the allocation of resources, hampering a more rational planning process, undermining investor confidence and cultivating a class of speculation-driven Korean entrepreneurs (Haggard *et al.* 1991, Amsden 1989).

As Rhee's political power waned in the late 1950s the regime became more autocratic and defensive; long-term economic planning was absent. A complex mix of economic policies including allocation of foreign exchange, bank credit, import licences and the distribution of state-owned enterprises continued to play a major role in buttressing a waning political base. The provision of windfall profits to a selected group of industrialists in exchange for political kick-backs and loyalty eroded confidence in the state's ability to manage the economy. This distrust extended to a large section of the capitalist class. The new breed of entrepreneur was generalist and aimed to make money in whatever sector appeared most opportune. This was the genesis of Korea's now massive, diversified business groups, the chaebol (Amsden 1989).

The legitimacy of the state rested on Rhee's credentials in the anti-colonial struggle; his hegemonic ideology was rooted in anti-Japanese nationalism and anti-communism. However, this hegemony started to falter as economic growth failed to materialise, and as government favouritism and patronage towards certain segments of the private sector became evident. Labour and civil unrest became widespread, and student-led demonstrations of 19 April 1960 ended with the downfall of the Rhee regime and the beginnings of a parliamentary period. This new democratic era, however, was also marked by political chaos and continued civil and labour unrest. Improvements in economic performance and institutional reform failed to match the transformation in the political regime. Popular demand failed to be met by the Second Republic (1960–61), mainly because of a stagnant economy. Former Japanese collaborators and the new rich, beneficiaries of the corrupt Rhee regime provoked strong social resentment. Strikes and demonstrations paralysed the economy and inhibited further political liberalisation. The first economic plan under the Second Republic was also import-substituting in nature, with exports largely devoted to primary products. The crisis in the accumulation regime and MSR remained unresolved. The political disorder and economic backwardness could not provide an adequate basis for continued accumulation, and social and political polarisation during this period prevented any consensus for an effective MSR to be implemented (Haggard *et al.* 1991, Steinberg 1989).

Historically, Korea had experienced two forms of state structure, both authoritarian but nevertheless quite different from each other: the Yi dynastic state and the modern Japanese state. The Yi state had an ostensibly strong central cast to it, but it was, in fact, a weak formation, competing with, and hamstrung by, a powerful landed aristocracy which used state power to perpetuate privilege. It was this tradition that permeated the Rhee regime (1948–60), and which helped to account for the revolutionary ferment of the early postwar period as the landed elite sought to maintain its control of land and its access to bureaucratic power. What distinguished the Rhee regime from the succeeding Park regime was that it could not conceive of using the state to stimulate the economic growth. Its energy was directed towards plundering existing surpluses rather than creating greater ones. Most of that surplus arrived in the alluring form of US aid for war reconstruction (Amsden 1989, pp.38–39). It was actually the Japanese colonial regime with its clear conception of the role of the state in economic development that provided a model for the post-1960 Export-Oriented Industrialisation (EOI) phase in Korea (Cumings 1988).

The Taylorist EOI period (1962–70)

Korea's regime of accumulation between 1962 and 1979 was of extensive form. There is a division between the Taylorist-type regime of the 1960s based on labour intensive industries, and the 'Yusin regime' of the 1970s which relied on capital and technology intensive industries to deepen its industrial structure and escape its dependency upon the core industrialised countries. Increases in accumulation were achieved through an expanding basis of labour, land and/or capital. The 1960s are distinguished from the 1970s by their different industrial trajectory and mode of social regulation.

Political change and emergence of the EOI regime

Economic stagnation and social discontent continued during the Second Republic under President Chang Myon. The military regarded the manipulation of political and economic advantage by sections of the social elite as an impediment to national development and a threat to Korea's security. Thus, on 16 May 1961, the Chang government fell to a coup d'état led by General Park Chung Hee. The new rulers saw themselves as puritanical progressives, advancing the same reformist causes as the 19 April student revolution (Haggard *et al.* 1991, p.857). The junta's weak social and political connections with the dominant elite meant that it had few reservations in pushing through reform (Steinberg 1989): government institutions were reorganised, the National Assembly suspended and bureaucrats, politicians and capitalists were prosecuted for illicit accumulation of wealth (Haggard *et al.* 1991). The concentration of political and economic power achieved during this period allowed Park and his successors the power to implement drastic economic measures at times of crisis. The nationalisation of Korea's commercial banks straight after the coup furnished the state with considerable powers to actuate penalty and reward. Thus the junta was able to co-opt that part of the business community which was vulnerable to charges of corruption (Haggard *et al.* 1991).

Despite objections within the junta, American pressure obliged Park to call a general election in 1963, though without giving up the concentrated power of the executive (Haggard *et al.* 1991, Ogle 1990, Steinberg 1989). Some superficial political concessions were introduced (for example, a relatively free press). But at base, the regime maintained authoritarian controls in all spheres.

The new government was able to consolidate its power in the 1960s because competing social classes were weak. Industrial workers constituted a small percentage of the population, capitalists were dependent on state largesse, the aristocracy was dissolved by land reform and the peasantry was atomised into smallholders (Amsden 1989). In addition to economic controls through the nationalised banks, the formation of the Economic Planning Board and control of private industries through the Federation of Korean Industries, Park was able to manipulate the professional elite – teachers, doctors, entertainers and, of course, journalists. The formation of a single, umbrella labour union, monitored by the Korean Central Intelligence Agency, provided the state with huge powers; these failed, however, to extend to Korea's student population (Steinberg 1989). Such was the social regulatory system which was the essential backcloth to the pursuit of export-oriented industrialisation.

The Park period (1961–79) saw a very different type of authoritarianism from that of the Rhee period. There were no more overt protests from the workers and farmers, no more the hitherto common spectacle of youth groups marching and fighting in the streets. Park calculated that economic development might legitimise his regime politically (Steinberg 1989, Haggard *et al.* 1991). Therefore, the state depended upon the success of its EOI policies and it placed itself in control of the economic essentials. Such state intervention has been described as 'developmentalism' (Amsden 1989, Luedde-Neurath 1988).[12]

When the Park junta took over power, the 'easy' phase of ISI was over, but the need then to begin substitution for consumer durables and machinery ran up against the limitations of the Korean economy. These included the small size of the domestic market, limited resource endowment, and lack of large-scale capital required for any new import-substitution phase. Furthermore, a more capital intensive phase would simply exacerbate the prime structural problem in the economy – surplus labour (Kuznets 1977, pp.151–152). The US, which pursued a vision of an international division of labour on the one hand and aid reduction on the other, was hostile to deepening import-substitution. Park's need for external legitimacy meant that South Korea, like Taiwan, pursued an export-led programme emphasising light industries. These states also pursued a policy of diversification of overseas aid (Cumings 1988, pp.261–262).

Pressure from the US obliged the Park regime to normalise relations with Japan, provoking an outcry at all levels of Korean society. This decision sacrificed legitimacy at home for legitimacy abroad. But it was one based upon economic considerations: first, Korea was dependent on American markets; second, normalisation with Japan brought $800 million in grants, loans and commercial credits over a ten year period, and was a precursor to a further $1.4 billion worth of investment by 1985. Additionally, Japanese economic assistance through to 1982 reached $4.4 billion (Steinberg 1989, p.131).

Accumulation, dependence and labour struggle in the 1960s

Under the Park administration (1961–79) industrial policies were aimed at growth maximisation (Kim and Park 1985). They tended to be sectoral, with the emphasis shifting periodically (Linge and Hamilton 1981, pp.32–34). It was the liberal external economic environment and the globalisation of capital in the 1960s that provided Korea with the opportunity to pursue export-oriented industrialisation. Under the First Five

Year Economic Development Plan (1962–66), industrialisation strategy was to promote expansion of export-oriented labour intensive sectors, such as textiles, clothing and footwear. Here Korea had a comparative advantage, derived in part from low wages. The strategy was also aimed at reducing the surplus labour force which was a source of serious social unrest in previous regimes (Park, S-O. 1991).

Vital to the EOI regime were the monetary arrangements of central-ised economic planning. These controlled the direction and rate of indus-trial development while rendering the state the most important institution for directing the mode of social (and economic) regulation. Economic control functions were consolidated institutionally. The budgetary, regula-tory, statistical and planning functions, which were previously under various different ministries, were brought together under a 'super-ministry', the Economic Planning Board (EPB) (Suh 1992, Haggard *et al.* 1991). This was responsible for the preparation of the Five Year Economic Develop-ment Plans (FYEDP), which set the strategies and targets for economic growth. This 'super-ministry' monitored and controlled all subsidiary minis-tries through the EPB's budgetary functions. A further vehicle for the consolidation of economic power in the executive was the Export Pro-motion Council, over which President Park personally exercised command (Amsden 1989). To enhance the effectiveness of the policy planning func-tion, in 1970 the government also established various research institutes covering a range of economic and social areas.[13]

The First FYEDP (1962–67) was predicated on severe austerity in con-sumption, relying on a high degree of political and ideological coercion and mobilisation. To attain its overall goal of economic growth of 41 per cent over the plan period, total investment had to be increased by 137 per cent, while private consumption had to be checked at a minimal in-crease of 18 per cent; this barely covered the projected population increase of 15 per cent during the same period. The Plan was based on an overall strategy reflecting a leading-sector approach which emphasised the build-ing of infrastructure and social overhead capital as a framework within which certain key manufacturing industries could thrive under private enterprise. Of the total planned investment of $2.5 billion (1961 US dollars), approximately 50 per cent was allocated to electric power, transport and communications, another 33 per cent was invested in mining and manu-facturing and 17 per cent went to agriculture, forestry and fisheries (Byun 1983, pp.175–176, EPB 1967). The underlying philosophy of the Park regime was 'guided capitalism' in which 'the principle of free enterprise and respect for the freedom and initiative of private enterprise will be observed'; the government would 'either directly participate or indirectly render guidance to the basic industries and other important fields' (EPB 1967, p.28). Guidance was not limited to macroeconomic or industrial policies: it included all wages as well as retail prices.

The stratification of the financial system immediately after the coup meant that the government was able to regulate the direction of private sector industrial activity towards the developmental path set by the FYEDP, and its output and export targets. Among the measures pushed through were a halving of the value of the won, introduction of an export–import link system under which exporters were permitted to import on favourable terms, accelerated depreciation allowances, an increase in tax incentives to export, and the provision of export finance at concessional interest rates and government underwriting loans (Haggard *et al.* 1991, Suh 1992, Park, S.O. 1991, p.75). In contrast to the Rhee government, the Third Republic mobilised domestic savings to finance the export industrialisation programme. To stimulate savings, in 1965 interest rates were raised from 12 per cent to over 26 per cent. For three years in a row after 1965 savings deposits in commercial banks almost doubled, and the ratio of time and savings deposits to GNP rose from 3.8 per cent in 1965 to 21.7 per cent in 1969 (Suh 1992, pp.11–12).

The above mentioned provisions propelled economic growth at spectacular rates. Average annual expansion of real GNP for the 1963–71 period was 9.5 per cent, more than double the 1954–62 figure. On a per capita basis, real growth for the period was not less than 6.9 per cent, compared with 0.7 per cent for 1954–62. Important structural changes also took place in the economy. The mining and manufacturing sectors increased their share of GNP from 16 per cent in 1962 to 22.5 per cent in 1971, while the share of agriculture, forestry and fisheries decreased from 37 to 26.6 per cent. This shift was also reflected in the sectoral share of employment: in the latter it declined from 63 per cent to 48.4 per cent, while mining and manufacturing increased their joint share from 9 to 14.2 per cent (Suh 1992, pp.13–14). These changes had a negative effect upon the rural areas and worsened the rural–urban consumption differential.

Korea's exports increased by nearly 40 per cent a year – from US$55 million in 1962 to $1.07 billion in 1971 (Kim and Park 1985, Suh 1992). This was spurred by government incentives and by devaluation as well as general expansion of world demand. The remarkable growth in trade was accompanied by a significant change in the composition of export goods: a marked drop in primary products (from 73 per cent to 14 per cent), and a matching rise in industrial products (27 per cent to 86 per cent). However, imports also grew quickly, from $422 million in 1962 to $2.39 billion in 1971, an average annual increase of 21.3 per cent (see Table 2.3). The share of capital goods increasing dramatically from 17 per cent in 1962 to 28.7 per cent by 1971.

The current account deficit increased steadily during 1968–71, reaching 8.4 per cent (Suh 1992, p.15), this due largely to importation of capital and intermediate goods and raw materials needed by manufacturing.

Table 2.3 South Korea: key economic indicators, 1962 and 1971

Indicator	1962	1971	Average annual percentage growth 1962–71
Per capita GNP (US$)	87	288	14.2
GNP (billion won)	3,071	6,962	9.5
Exports (US$m)	55	1,068	39.0
Exports: GNP ratio (per cent)[a]	2.4	11.7	—
Imports (US$m)	422	2,394	21.3
Imports: GNP ratio (per cent)[a]	18.2	26.5	—
Investment rate (per cent)[b]	12.8	25.1	n.a.
Domestic savings rate (per cent)[b]	3.2	14.6	n.a.

Source: *Korea Statistical Yearbook*; Suh (1992), p.14.

Note:
Won are in 1975 constant prices.
a In US dollars.
b Related to prices at specified years.

Though the import substitution programme was sustained, a deepening of the industrial base was needed in order to curtail this dependency.

The disintegration of the vertical organisation of production in the Fordist regimes in the advanced industrialised countries led to a new division of labour which incorporated the peripheral nation-states such as Korea and Taiwan within an international Fordist production network. This new global configuration imposed Taylorisation upon the peripheral nations, transforming limited segments of labour-intensive Fordist mass production to states with high rates of exploitation (Lipietz 1987). This reformulation of accumulation by the core countries served a new regime of international accumulation embracing the Third World and based on super-exploitation through minimising wages and extending the working day (Chou 1994).

In Korea, the surplus rural and urban labour was now to find an outlet in the factories of the export-oriented labour intensive industries. A perception of an inexhaustible supply of labour meant that there was no coherent policy regarding the reproduction of the labour force. Incomes were largely at subsistence level, and working and living conditions in company dormitories were reminiscent of the Victorian workhouse (Ogle 1990). There was a rapid increase in young female migrants to labour intensive industries such as textiles, clothing and footwear, for in agriculture females were less valued than males. Women were favoured supposedly as more dextrous and submissive, and male workers were disinclined to join the manufacturing sector. Almost one third of the total workforce comprised women aged 14 to 24 (Bello and Rosenfeld 1990, Ogle 1990). Average female wages stood at half the male level (Bello and Rosenfeld 1990). Their average working week grew to at least 54 hours (Amsden 1989).[14] Thus, the

Korean economic miracle of the 1960s relied on the super-exploitation of female workers (Ogle 1990, Bello and Rosenfeld 1990).

In the Taylorist period, the state's promotion of capital accumulation, therefore, was at the expense of wages, workers' safety, pensions and job security. Although relatively democratic in form, the state was able to exercise firm control over the unions through coercion and ideological mobilisation. The low wage policy and anti-union legislation were important in attracting foreign direct investment into the Free Export Zones (Ogle 1990). Although labour exploitation was severe, income distribution improved in the 1960s, for the labour intensive industrial strategies increased employment opportunities, and absolute poverty was fast disappearing. While urban income equality was improved, there was a widening of the urban–rural income gap, triggering an increased rate of a rural–urban migration (Suh 1992).

While Korea experienced rapid export-based growth during the 1960s, several factors obliged a change in the direction of industrial development. These included the weakening of comparative advantage due to rapid wage increases and the growing dependency on foreign capital, oil, technology and markets (Cumings 1988, Park 1991). The changing international market for Korean goods reduced the country's ability to service its external debt at a time when recession hit the core countries, especially after the first oil shock. The growth rate for 1971 fell for the first time since 1965, from 9.8 per cent to 7.3 per cent. Korea's balance of payments deteriorated and inflation rose. All this called into question the wisdom of an export-led programme featuring light industries and linked almost entirely to Japanese and American credits and markets (Cumings 1988, p.267). The situation was likened to Korea's former satellite role within Japan's yen bloc (Kuznet 1977, p.85): to many, Korea's dependency problem was now comparable to that of the colonial period (Cumings 1988). Consequently, EOI shifted towards a higher value-added manufacturing; a deepening of the industrial base was essential if dependence on imported intermediate and capital goods was to be reduced.

The Yusin EOI period (1970–79)

Only in the early 1970s did the Korean state seek to escape its dependency through its strong state institutions providing credit to heavy industries, fostering concentration and economies of scale, building the social overhead infrastructure necessary to accommodate the growing economy, and repressing any opposition to ascension of the technological ladder. The shift in the industrial trajectory in the beginning of the 1970s came up against internal and external opposition. By the early 1970s, a potential mass base for a political opposition had come into being. This included the growing urban working and middle classes who opposed the repression of the labour force and the restriction on wages and consumption, the business interests hurt by the export-led programme, and regional interests such as the rural Southwest that had been left out of much of the development of the 1960s. It was from this regional base that Kim Dae Jung[15] emerged and mounted a strong challenge to Park's rule. His platform was to criticise the export-led strategies and especially the newly developing dependency on Japan. The growing political opposition at the general election coincided with the first year (1971) of weak growth in the economy, thus challenging the legitimacy of the EOI programme (Cumings 1988, p.266).

Opposition to deepening of the industrial structure came from Korea's American overseers. They rejected the plans for heavy industrialisation as they threatened the extant international division of labour and would lead to problems of surplus capacity in world markets. At the same time, a new American administration pursued neo-protectionist rather than liberal trade policies and called into question the position of both South Korea and Taiwan within the hegemonic American security system in Northeast Asia. Cumings argues that rather than internal pressures from Kim Dae Jung, it was the opposition of the American administration to deepening the increasing dependency relationships spawned by the light industrial base of EOI and the changing international economic and political climate that led to a political authoritarian regime. The new order was termed the *Yusin* regime of Korean-style democracy.[16] This took as its purpose the forging of a more self-reliant political and economic development path. The Korean state was anything but democratic, but by using the *Yusin* formulation, Park tried to disguise his authoritarianism and centralisation of power. Thus 'Park seemed to be more nationalistic at the precise time that he was being more undemocratic' (Cumings 1988, pp.267–268).

The adoption of the more authoritarian *Yusin* system spelled out a new mode of social regulation, with all the features of a corporatist state.[17] Its instruments were a complex of financial and tax incentives to entice heavy industrial development which starved the rest of the industrial sector of bank loans.

Heavy industrialisation, the state and the emergence of chaebol in the 1970s

The development of heavy and chemical industrial sector and the simultaneous emergence of chaebol as the major form of economic power in the 1970s resulted from the particular industrial strategy of the Park government. This resembled the pattern of heavy industrialisation during the Japanese colonial period in the 1930s, when the Japanese state encouraged *zaibatsu* capital in the heavy and chemical industrialisation of Korea. The similarity in strategy may not be a simple coincidence,[18] and marks a contrast to the direction taken by the Taiwan state in the deepening of the industrial base.[19] The privileged access to funds and loans on favourable rates since the 1970s led to spectacular growth. But by the mid-1990s the chaebols had accrued debts five times their assets, which in due course led to spectacular crisis.

Two main objectives underlay the government's drive to develop a powerful heavy and chemical industrial sector: creation of new strategic export industries and promotion of the import substitution of intermediate and capital goods. Thus, the ISI phase in the 1970s was also part of Korea's export-led development, in which steel, automobiles, shipbuilding and petrochemical industries were favoured (Suh 1992, Cumings 1988). Gold (1986) calls this phase 'export-oriented import substitution'. The development of the heavy and chemical industries not only needed large amounts of capital, but also demanded high levels of management expertise. Only the chaebol groups were capable of meeting these requirements. In return for taking on high risk ventures, the chaebols were offered subsidised interest rates (negative in real terms), preferential credit allocation, tax incentives and exemptions, and licence to operate in the lucrative domestic market where they enjoyed a quasi-monopolistic positioning. The government encouraged large projects with attendant scale economies, and a new National Investment Fund channelled employee pensions and private savings to meet investment requirements (Suh 1992). Heavy foreign capital borrowing, underwritten by the government, became inevitable. Thus, the large firms at the forefront of Korea's heavy and chemical industrialisation were able to make huge profits from negative real interest rates, from state protection against international competition, from rent seeking activities and diversification into protected and lucrative markets. The consolidation of Korea's huge conglomerates was clearly founded on state-nurtured market distortions.

The Heavy and Chemical Industry Development Plan (HCIDP), announced in 1973, revamped those incentive schemes which had previously been devised individually for each industry. The plan established a single framework of integrated tax incentives, as well as loans at special rates for all industries considered strategic. The result was extensive new infrastructure. Beneficiaries included oil refining, petro-chemicals, shipbuilding, heavy machinery, electronics, iron and steel, non-ferrous metals, power-generation, chemical fertilisers, as well as the defence and aviation sectors (Rhee 1987, Suh 1992).

The HCIDP promoted two incentive schemes as the main vehicles to encourage industrial investment: preferential taxation was accorded to investments in fixed capital and R&D in strategic industries; tariff deduction and tariff 'drawback'[20] reduced the tax payments on intermediate goods and raw materials for manufacture for export. The tariff drawback system encouraged import-substituting industries by inducing exporters to use domestically supplied intermediate inputs (Rhee 1987, pp.44–46). In addition, preferential allocation of low interest loans, both domestic and foreign, made investment in the heavy and chemical industries extremely profitable, particularly as real interest rates were negative throughout the period. The chaebol were able to borrow extensively for investment in strategic industries and in addition gain loans for other industries within their groups. The state offered licences to operate in new domestic markets as a sweetener for undertaking risky ventures. The chaebol groups continued to increase their debt ratio rapidly until 1980 when high interest rates and other changes in the government's industrial policies slowed the pace (Rhee 1987, pp.16–17). Table 2.4 shows the extent of preferential treatment given to strategic industries through interest rates. The HCIDP was complemented by extensive infrastructure development in transport and communications. Industrial estates were constructed, and existing port facilities improved (Rhee 1987, Park 1986). These developments were especially marked in the Southeast region (see Chapter 3). This phase continued to stress export orientation, the shift being merely in the industrial trajectory: there was now less support to labour intensive industries (Suh 1992).

Labour repression was particularly severe in this period in labour intensive and capital intensive sectors alike. February 1974 saw one thousand women workers stage a mass sit-in at the Bando Trading Company. In September of that same year 2,500 workers occupied the Hyundai ship-

Table 2.4 Financial trends

	1972	1974	1976	1978	1979	1980	1981	1982
Inflation rate (WPI)	13.8	42.1	12.2	11.6	18.8	38.9	20.4	4.7
Interest rates								
General bank	—	15.5	18.0	19.0	19.0	20.0	17.0	10.0
KDB[1] facility investment	11.0	10.0	12.5	14.0	15.0	21.0	18.5	13.0
Export finance	6.0	9.0	7.5	8.5	9.0	15.0	15.0	11.0
Curb market	39.0	40.6	40.5	41.2	42.4	44.9	35.3	30.6
LIBOR rate[2]	6.0	10.1	5.1	12.1	15.0	18.1	14.0	9.3
Benefits of loans[3]								
General bank	—	25.1	22.5	22.2	23.4	24.9	18.3	20.6
Export finance	33.0	31.6	33.0	32.7	33.4	29.9	30.3	19.6
Real interest rates[4]								
General bank	—	−26.6	5.8	7.4	0.2	−18.9	−3.4	5.3
Export finance	−7.8	−33.1	−4.7	−3.1	−9.8	−23.9	−5.4	6.3

Source: cited in Rhee (1987), p.49.

Notes:
1 Korea Development Bank.
2 London Interbank.
3 Curb market interest rate minus interest rate of the loan concerned.
4 Interest rate for loans minus Wholesale Price Index (WPI).

yard, and early in 1980, miners took control of the town of Sabuk, later known as the Sabuk Uprising. These and other industrial action such as the Chonggye Garment Workers Union's struggle faced the legal, ideological and coercive forces of the state (Bello and Rosenfeld 1990, p.36). Wages, nonetheless, continued to rise, with average increases in the 1970s of 27 per cent annually (Suh 1992). But the beneficiaries were largely the white collar and skilled male workers in larger firms in strategic industries. The unskilled and mainly female workforce suffered deteriorating conditions due to intensifying competitive tendencies in the non-strategic industrial sectors (Bello and Rosenfeld 1990, Amsden 1990, Suh 1992). Labour strategy was designed with the impact upon the strategic industries in mind. While there was some compromise with unions in the heavy and chemical industries, labour in other sectors was almost always dealt with coercively.

The implementation of HCIDP with its labour repression during the 1970s allowed Korea to reduce its reliance on the importation of intermediate goods, especially from Japan. Figure 2.2 shows the decline in the rate of imports during the 1970s. The rate of GNP growth in the mid-1970s was strong: during the 1972–76 period it averaged 9.7 per cent annually, reaching highs of 14.1 per cent in 1973 and 1976 (Hwang 1985, p.12). After 1977, which recorded a 12.1 per cent rate, structural problems inherent to the industrial strategy brought a gradual slowdown. The further concentration of capital in the chaebol groups, dominating as they did the heavy and chemical sectors, was therefore, an ineluctable process.

The most crucial advantage of firms in the strategic industries lay in access to domestic and foreign financing at preferential rates. Table 2.4 shows that huge profits could be derived from loans at the special interest rates for export financing which were negative in real terms during most of the 1970s. These subsidised interest rates, of course, represented a huge

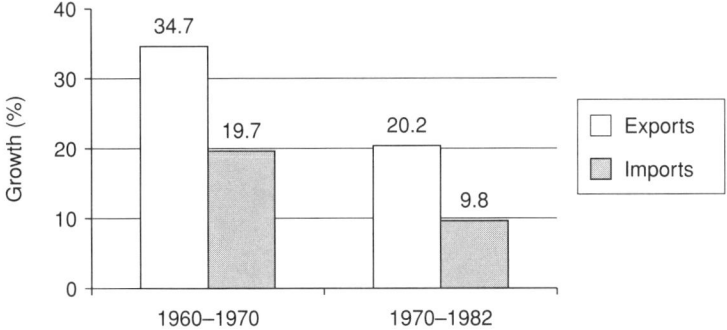

Figure 2.2 Annual growth of merchandise trade.

Source: EPB, various publications, adapted from Steinberg (1989) p.144.

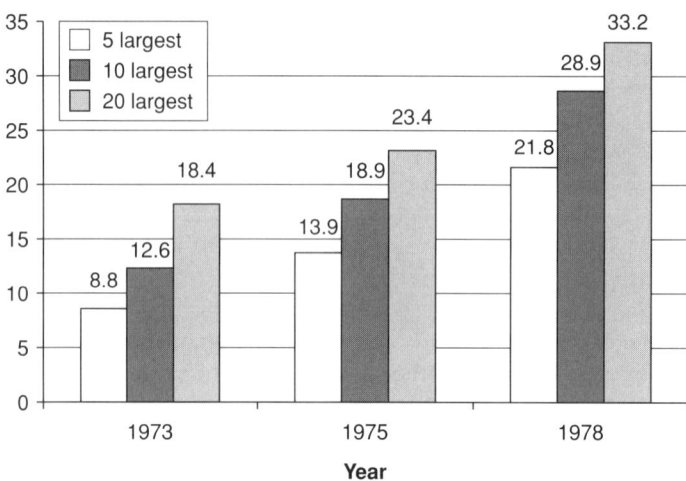

Figure 2.3 Contribution to gross domestic production in the manufacturing sector
     by chaebol groups (in percentage).

Source: Derived from data in Sakong (1980), p.6.

burden on the government's current account. The tax and tariff incentives were used to further reduce financial burdens on chaebol investing in plant facilities, and importing raw materials, and technology and even foreign technical staff. The tariff drawback system encouraged exporters to use intermediate goods produced domestically by the chaebol, offering their products a guaranteed market. The granting of licences to expand into additional lucrative sectors allowed the chaebol groups to rapidly diversify. As can be seen in Figure 2.3, the share of GDP in manufacturing by the top twenty chaebol groups was over 33 per cent by 1978 (Amsden 1989, Sakong 1980, p.6).

There were three crucial ways in which the Park government influenced the pattern of social equity in Korea: corporatist control of labour organisations, inflationary financing and generally regressive tax policies (Koo 1984, p.1032).

Agricultural backwardness, Saemaul Undong *and corporatist regulation*

The backward state of Korea's agriculture was not remedied by the land reform in the 1950s, and agricultural productivity and rural poverty worsened in the 1960s. By the end of the 1960s the poverty was in a 'shared and equalised state' (Steinberg 1989, p.145). While the average rural family owned below subsistence land – 2.2 acres – 40 per cent of all rural families owned less than 1.24 acres (Boyer and Ahn 1991). Urban incomes, as low as rural ones in 1963, rose rapidly by comparison in the 1960s and 1970s. By 1969 rural household income was just 56 per cent of that of urban working class households (Suh 1992). During the First FYEDP (1962–66), overall economic growth stood at 7.8 per cent, but growth in agriculture was 5.3 per cent; during the Second FYEDP (1967–71) the figures were 10.5 per cent and 2.5 per cent respectively (Boyer and Ahn 1991, p.32). But the growing dissatisfaction of the rural areas was echoed in the towns and cities, where the rapid increase in rural–urban migration was causing severe pressure on housing and employment. These problems, and the sharp increase in grain import prices after the first oil shock, stirred support for rural development and self-sufficiency in major food grains (Hwang and Choi 1988, Suh 1992).

The Park government's response to its waning legitimacy due to urban–rural income disparities was the inauguration of Integrated Rural Development (IRD). The state's concerted efforts directed at rural transformation in the 1970s comprised four elements: rural mobilisation by local government under the strong hierarchical control of the Ministry of Home Affairs, provision of rural credit through 'co-operatives' and the policy of buying high and selling low through the Grain Management Fund, and a nationwide 'guidance' system concerned with technical improvements in agricultural production. Finally, the New Village Movement (*Saemaul Undong*) was set up, and this soon became the backbone of the IRD (Steinberg 1989, Bello and Rosenfeld 1990, Boyer and Ahn 1991). With the central government at the apex, the system of rural development was hierarchical and top-down. An important agency for rural mobilisation was the Agricultural Co-operative Federation, closely tied to the state through its funding process. This organisation monopolised 97 per cent of all institutional credit to the agricultural sector and was the major agent for the purchase of rice and for the distribution of fertilisers (Steinberg 1989).

So as to tackle the rural–urban income differential and raise productivity, the government boosted price support for the major grain crops, particularly rice and barley, provided subsidies for fertilisers and farm machinery, sought to improve the credit system, and introduced a high-yielding rice named the *Tong-il*. From 1972 to 1975, total government investment in, and loans to, agriculture amounted to 1.46 trillion won, very nearly double what had been provided in the 1967–71 period. In 1970 the Grain Management Fund was established to subsidise both the farmers and urban consumers through relatively high government prices and low market prices (Bello and Rosenfeld 1990, Suh 1992). This was designed both to pacify growing dissent in the rural areas, and to maintain capital accumulation and the export drive by keeping living costs as low as possible for the industrial workforce. Price support was increased to induce higher production during the self-sufficiency drive after the sharp increase in grain import prices following the first oil shock in 1971. However, the Grain Management Fund and the Fertiliser Fund were jointly responsible for 37 per cent of the total growth of money supply during 1976–78, thus contributing to inflationary pressures (Suh 1992). These measures were also a major cause of the chronic budgetary deficit.

Together with the price support for rice, the 'guidance' system was put in place to raise agricultural productivity. Various technical modernisation measures were introduced: small paddies were consolidated into larger ones which could be worked by machinery, while PVC greenhouses were introduced to produce fruit and vegetables off-season.

These efforts brought significant improvements in rural conditions. By 1974, average rural household income was fast catching up with that of the urban working class, and indeed parity was reached by 1976. However, this increase was soon offset by the rising cost of production due to increasing dependence on ever more costly chemical inputs. The *Tong-il* variety demanded high levels of fertiliser, pesticide and herbicide (Bello and Rosenfeld 1990, Steinberg 1989, p.149). Application of fertilisers increased from 162 kg per hectare in 1970 to 299 kg in 1980. Use of pesticide rose even faster, by over 330 per cent between 1974 and 1976 (Bello and Rosenfeld 1990, p.83). The high chemical input required by growing *Tong-il* left producers with escalating costs and uncertain profit margins; – 'in just one year, 1978, the 100 per cent rise in outlays for fertilisers and other chemicals was the highest increase registered in all categories of expenditure of the Korean farming household' (Suh 1992, p.83).

It was no coincidence that the introduction of *Tong-il* rice coincided with the heavy and chemical industrialisation: fertilisers and pesticides were promoted as strategic goods (Rhee 1987, Suh 1992) and they also provided a firm basis for capital accumulation by the chaebol groups. Structural dependency led to increasing household indebtedness: between 1972 and 1978, a period that marked the height of the *Tong-il* campaign, average liabilities per farm household skyrocketed nearly eight-fold (Bello and Rosenfeld 1990). Paradoxically, rural indebtedness had initially been created in the 1950s land reform, which gave most farmers less land than they actually required for subsistence. It intensified in the 1970s through the introduction of the new rice variety and chemical inputs. The problem was to worsen in the 1980s when subsidies to the agricultural sector were dramatically reduced. The dependence on chemical inputs also led to toxification of soils, and increased sickness amongst farmworkers. Though by 1985 *Tong-il* rice was largely abandoned by most farmers due to its susceptibility to disease and unpopularity with urban consumers, chemical inputs did not decline. The shortage of agricultural labour, and the need to increase output to finance debt, meant that the use of pesticides and herbicides proliferated (Bello and Rosenfeld 1990).

The *Saemaul Undong* introduced in 1971 was a comprehensive rural community development programme with its main focus being the improvement of rural life. However, it is argued that the *Saemaul* ideology was used to dismantle traditional values, seen as barriers to rural modernisation. As such, it constituted a hegemonic project aimed at mobilising society behind the state. Although top-down in its approach, it required a veneer of co-operation, participation and limited democracy at the grass-roots level (Suh 1992, p.16). In 1972, after the successful conclusion[21] to the first year programme of Village Environmental Improvement, which included reforestation of terrain, broadening village access roads, repairing and improving village dikes, preparation and maintenance of ponds, ditches and gutters and constructing community wells, the second phase of the programme was extended only to those villages judged to have good results, – the correct '*Saemaul spirit*'. The range of projects widened from general environmental improvements to home improvements (roofs, bathrooms, kitchens) and beautification and conservation of village environs. Support was also given for village infrastructure projects such as installation of a public telephone and methane gas systems (Bello and Rosenfeld 1990, Boyer and Ahn 1990, Steinberg 1989).

In 1973, *Saemaul Undong* was expanded to encompass urban areas, work-places and schools, taking on the mantle of a national people's movement for social enhancement. The ideological indoctrination of the *Saemaul* spirit was supposed to instil modern values, and breakdown rural–urban cleav-ages and class barriers. In reality it was used as a means of expanding the hegemonic bloc. Although participating organisations and areas pro-liferated and the whole populace became the target for self-sacrificing involvement and indoctrination, the 1980s brought destabilisation and ulti-mately, the demise of the movement (Boyer and Ahn 1991). This was linked to the decline of the government's credibility due to corruption in the implementation programme.

Although the rural development programmes initially seemed successful, they failed to create a prosperous or sustainable agriculture. The growth of indebtedness due to dependence on artificial inputs and inflationary financing through the Grain Management Fund combined to cancel out any positive effects, and in the ensuing years rural underdevelopment increased (Boyer and Ahn 1991, Steinberg 1989). The self-sufficiency goal of *Yusin* had necessitated the extensive exploitation of the agricultural sector to prop up the EOI regime.

Exhaustion of the extensive accumulation regime and political destabilisation

Though state intervention in industrial and rural development led to re-markable growth in exports and in agricultural output, inherent structural problems started to manifest themselves in the latter half of the 1970s. Combined with a deteriorating world economic environment, this led finally to the collapse of Korea's extensive accumulation regime. Due to negative real interest rates, by the late 1970s private investment in strategic sectors was leading to excess capacity and by 1980 plants were being utilised at extremely low capacity (Rhee 1987). The rate of growth in output per unit input slowed considerably, from 4.9 per cent during 1963–73 to only 1.6 per cent during 1972–82. The rapid expansion of the manufacturing and construction sector subsequently led to overheating in the labour market, which caused real manufacturing wages to grow by 110 per cent between 1974 and 1979 (Suh 1992, p.20). In contrast to the favoured sectors, light manufacturing was squeezed by low bank credits, rising wages and increased competition from those NICs with lower labour costs. These factors, with expansionary monetary policies, led to high infla-tion rates, in turn causing the appreciation of the exchange rate, making exports and external debt financing more difficult. Together with these internal structural problems, the global economic recession in the late 1970s brought crisis to Korea's extensive accumulation regime. Korea's external debt had grown rapidly, reaching US$20.3 billion in 1979, (a 372 per cent increase since 1973); the state current account deficit rose from zero in 1977 to 6.76 in 1979 and 8.7 per cent in 1980 due to its exten-sive subsidies to both agriculture and heavy industries (Suh 1992). The heavy and chemical industrial structure created a new dependency on imported crude oil and external markets, leaving Korea vulnerable to external shocks.

At the same time, income distribution in the 1970s worsened considerably, reversing the trend towards equity of the 1960s. This was due to sectoral imbalances, and inflation-induced speculative investment by businesses and individuals.

From 1977, remedial measures were introduced to stabilise inflation, wages and the government deficit, but Korea's economy continued to deteriorate. In 1979, commodity exports declined in real terms by 4 per cent and GNP fell to 7 per cent for the first time since the beginnings of industrialisation in the early 1960s (Suh 1992). When international interest rates increased after the second oil shock, the wisdom of heavy foreign borrowing of the 1970s was called into question, which in turn led to a legitimation crisis both for the heavy and chemical industrialisation and for the Park regime itself.

The peripheral Fordist regime (1980–87)

The term peripheral Fordism was first used by Lipietz (1987) to charac-terise a regime of accumulation which assembles and exports Fordist con-sumer goods under an authoritarian state – in short, an attempt to emulate the Fordist accumulation system in the absence of a monopolistic MSR (Tickell and Peck 1992b). This captures the essence of Korea's accumu-lation regime during the period 1980 to 1987. The emerging intensive accumulation regime coupled with competitive regulation under the most authoritarian state in postwar Korean history gave rise to increased social inequity, stimulating a powerful pro-democracy movement.

Structural adjustment and emerging intensive accumulation of the early 1980s

The policy direction of the new political and accumulation regime was determined by an increasingly competitive global economic environment. Through the new liberalisation policies, which stressed reduced government intervention in the economy, the market mechanism was promoted to enhance competition, to open domestic markets to foreign goods, and to encourage direct foreign investment (Koo and Kim 1992). However, the Chun government (1980–88) was preoccupied by 'economic prioritism' and anti-communist ideology. The purpose was the maintenance of a state of economic austerity, political regimentation, and thus urgent pursuance of industrial restructuring (Byun 1983, p.171). Conscious of Korea's position in the changing global economic environment, the new regime emphasised competition and improved relations with its trading partners as essential to an intensive phase of accumulation (Suh 1992).

In macroeconomic management, price stabilisation was successfully achieved. Within just three years chronic inflation ceased, with a profound impact on all economic activities. The rampant rate of 38.9 per cent in 1980 fell to 4.7 per cent in 1982 and 0.2 per cent in 1983, as can be seen from the wholesale price index in Table 2.4. As prices stabilised, real interest rates soon reached positive levels – including those covering export financing. This reduced the attraction of rent-seeking activities based on bank loans and induced companies to use internal sources for financing. In the 1980s, the debt-equity ratio in manufacturing sector fell as a result. Thus, the most significant impact of price stabilisation was the eradication of rent-seeking activities (Rhee 1987). Additionally, as part of the strategy, the Korean currency was devalued in 1980, improving the competitiveness of Korean products. Although import liberalisation was pursued after the exchange rate devaluation, as Rhee (1987) states the government continued to protect the domestic market through tax and tariff barriers (p.60).[22]

The new industrial policy called for a rationalisation of industries to deal with the aftermath of the excessive investments of the heavy-chemical industrial drive of the 1970s, and the phasing out of preferential tax treatment and access to credit by large firms operating in the strategic industries (Rhee 1987). Instead, the government endeavoured to support small and medium-size firms to rectify structural imbalances created by the previous discriminatory investment policy. As a result, loans issued to the top thirty chaebol groups declined sharply: their share of total credit, which amounted to 36 per cent in 1986, fell to 30 per cent in 1987 and 23 per cent in May 1988 (Park, C-J. 1991, pp.75–76).

A rationalisation of industrial capacity was in due course introduced in August 1980. As can be seen in Table 2.5, the government took steps to realign investment in five major industries: heavy power-generating equipment, motor vehicles, naval diesel engines, electrical transformers,

Table 2.5 Major steps for investment realignment

Sector	Problem	Measure	Year
Heavy power-generating equipment	Excess capacity and excessive competition.	Reduction in the number of producers from 4 to 1.	1980
Naval diesel engines	Excess capacity (3 producers).	Designation of 2 makers for units of over 6,000 HP and 2 makers for units under 6,000HP.	1980
		KHIC to produce diesel engines of over 6,000 HP.	1983
Electric transformers	Overlapping facility investment by four makers.	Reduction from 4 producers to 2.	1980
Motor vehicles	Inability to achieve economic scale of production with plurality of manufac-turers.	Designation of 1 company for passenger vehicles.	1980
		Designation of 2 companies for passenger vehicles.	1981
		Inauguration of advance notice system regarding production restrictions on specific types of vehicle.	1985
Copper smelting	Excess capacity with a sharp slump in demand for electro-smelted copper.	Korea Mining and Smelting Co. merged with Onsan Copper Smelting Co.	1980

Source: EPB, cited in Rhee (1987), p.28.

and copper smelting. In the case of the oligopolistic market structure in these sectors, voluntary capacity reduction was not feasible. Therefore, the government imposed rationalising procedures aimed at capacity reduction, at mergers, and in some cases at liquidation. Table 2.5 indicates the heavy-handed intervention of the government in the rationalisation of the heavy industries, which greatly strengthened existing monopolistic or oligopolistic tendencies (Rhee 1987, pp.25–29).

Preferential tax and tariff institutions were also reshaped in a reformulation of the earlier approach which had directly supported specific industries perceived to be strategic; now a functional approach was to be utilised which provided incentives to any industries for desired functions such as R&D. During this period, the industries classified as strategic were limited: naphtha cracking, iron and steel, machinery, electronics, shipbuilding and aviation. Preferential tax and tariff measures changed to indirect means. The growing dominance of a functional approach rather than the industry-specific approach reduced distortions in the price mechanism, which had been prevalent in the 1970s. The changes reflected the changing position of the government's investment requirements – from developing basic industrial manufacturing facilities in the 1970s to a more intensive development of new production processes and products in the competitive environment of the 1980s. As the desired heavy-chemical industrial base had been adequately established for basic import-substitution, the distortions in the price mechanism, deliberately created to lure private capital into the new high-risk business areas in the 1970s, were removed. The new situation left less room for rent seeking activities, and encouraged investments which fostered technological innovation and enhancement of industrial structure (Rhee 1987, pp.31–40).

On the other hand, state restructuring of the economy was characterised by, a new market-oriented rationale in Korea's financial institutions; on the other, heavy-handed intervention in the industrial sector was to continue. But the way was now open for intensive accumulation under a competitive MSR. Although the formation of oligopolistic markets was state-initiated, competition between firms was also promoted. The tight control of the domestic market made for limited competition, but this was not the case in the export sector. Firms were encouraged to enhance their marketing, improve product quality, raise their technological level, localise component supply, extend product differentiation and develop overseas markets. Though import liberalisation forced some industries to restructure, in some cases resulting in closures, the net effect was positive in terms of government's objectives of increasing competitiveness (Rhee 1987, pp.65–67). As a part of the liberalisation programme, new industries were also opened up to foreign investment from 1981, culminating in the *1984 Foreign Capital Inducement Law*. These changes meant that 92.5 per cent of the manufacturing industries were open to foreign direct investment, albeit the share of ownership still remaining below 50 per cent in any company (Koo and Kim 1992).

The 1980s saw a new rationalisation of business practices. Rather than enlargement of industrial capacity, emphasis was placed on R&D and technical upgrading. Marketing efforts were reinforced, and production differentiation and new product development became integral to business strategy. Due to the rise in real interest rates and a substantial drop in the benefits derived from borrowing, manufacturing firms tried actively to reduce their debt-equity ratio through internal financing. Ratios rapidly declined in the manufacturing sector as a whole, from almost 5:1 in 1980 to 3.4:1 in 1984. Capital borrowing from overseas was also reduced since interest rates in the international financial markets remained high throughout the 1980s, and the Korean currency had been devalued (Rhee 1987, pp.51–52).

Additionally, efforts to reduce production costs intensified (Rhee 1987, p.70). Amsden (1989) notes that in late industrialising countries the production line tends to be the strategic focus of firms that compete on the basis of borrowed technology (p.5). With intensifying competition in the international market, Korean firms now sought to optimise efficiency by imposing low wages and long working hours. The repression of labour was much more severe during the government of Chun Doo Hwan than at any other point in modern Korean history. With the 'purification' of labour unions in 1980, their federal structure allowed top-down control, while at the same time isolating them in individual company wage bargaining (Koo and Kim 1992, Ogle 1990). The skeletal collective bargaining structure of the Park era was completely dismantled, weakening the position of labour considerably. Combined with high unemployment, the repression of labour brought a longer and more intensive working day. Table 2.6 shows that working hours, which declined during the 1970s, started to increase in the 1980s. During the first half of the decade, wages were frozen in the cause of economic stabilisation (Koo and Kim 1992). The militancy of labour struggles in the late 1980s was an inevitable response.

Rapid export growth, trade surplus and changing accumulation regime

Industrial restructuring and higher growth rates globally ensured that by 1985 the Korean economy was showing a remarkably strong performance. The popularly named 'Three Lows' period – the lowered interest rates of major foreign banks, lowered exchange rates for the US dollar against the Japanese yen, and the lower price for crude oil helped Korean exports to the US market (Koo and Kim 1992).

GNP growth rates were continuously over the 12 per cent level in real terms during 1986–88, while price inflation and unemployment were once again low. In 1986, the economy grew 12.5 per cent, creating over half a million new jobs and reducing unemployment to 3.8 per cent from 4.1 per cent, a year earlier. Consumer prices rose by only 2.8 per cent while wholesale prices actually declined by 1.5 per cent. National savings surged to exceed domestic investment, making a remarkable departure from the

Table 2.6 Average weekly working hours, manufacturing: some comparisons

	1965	1970	1975	1980	1982	1983
Korea	57.0	52.3	50.5	53.1	53.7	54.1
Japan	44.3	43.3	38.8	41.2	40.9	41.1
Singapore	—	48.7	48.4	48.6	48.3	48.1
US	41.2	39.8	39.5	39.7	38.9	40.1
Taiwan	—	—	—	50.9	48.1	48.1
West Germany	—	—	40.4	40.0	39.1	—

Source: International Labour Organisation (ILO) (1983) *Yearbook of Labour Statistics*, cited in Christian Institute for the Study of Justice and Development (1985), p.50.

long and heavy reliance on foreign capital. The rapid economic growth in 1986 was driven by a rebound in the export of manufacturing goods and the continued expansion of productive infrastructure in electricity, gas and water. Real gross fixed capital formation increased by 11 per cent, while the growth in consumption remained around 8 per cent (Koo and Bark 1989, p.3). Domestic consumption was suppressed in favour of the export sector. Here, the main expansionary force was provided by exports of consumer durables (typical Fordist goods) – to North America, Japan and to Europe, returning the Korean economy to its earlier situation of export-led growth. In 1986, exports of goods and services grew by a hefty 26 per cent: textiles and garments, cars, electric/electronic products, steel products and footwear were the chief items (Koo and Bark 1989).

For the second time in history Korea recorded current account surpluses for three consecutive years: $4.6 billion in 1986, $9.8 billion in 1987 and $14.2 billion in 1988. Although this improved the balance of payments situation, government policymakers calculated that the growing trade surplus would have undesirable consequences, both domestically and internationally. Domestic investment was biased towards exports, this obstructing a more even growth of the economy. At the same time the increased money supply brought inflationary pressures and impaired painfully achieved price stability. Korea's trade surpluses were beginning to bring pressures to open domestic markets, as well as protectionist measures against the country's exports, especially in the US. Thus, in 1987, Korean economic planners devised a comprehensive surplus management programme. In the past, it had been believed that export growth and a trade surplus should be welcomed, no matter what the scale. The new programme brought about a comprehensive transformation of the nation's trade, investment and finance policies (Koo and Bark 1989).[23] Thus with the shift from export bias to a more equitable balance between exports and the domestic economy, alongside the preparation for the 1988 Olympic Games, growth of the domestic economy was dramatically boosted. The construction industry was a particular beneficiary.

The unfolding paradigm spelt a change in the accumulation regime. Public and private consumption were allowed to rise, leading to pressure on wages. The accumulation of earnings from export markets started to be displayed as speculative investments in the property market, and in conspicuous consumption on the part of the elite. The façade of self-sacrifice for national development, austere wage and union policies – these were becoming difficult to sustain in the face of the ostentatious display of wealth by the few. By 1987, student protests and labour struggles were giving new impetus to the movement for democracy and social justice. Adjustments to the accumulation regime had engendered social forces which challenged the hegemonic MSR. This was the beginning of the end of peripheral Fordism in Korea.

Capital concentration, social disparities and the exhaustion of the peripheral Fordist paradigm

The ideological hegemony of austerity and self-sacrifice of *Saemaul Undong*, and of general anti-communism had disintegrated in the face of a boom economy and rising consumerism. Pressures for social justice undermined the coercive state, obliging the Presidential candidate of 1988, Roh Tae Woo, to declare political and economic reforms. In due course the changes in the accumulation regime led to the restructuring of the state and the overall mode of Korea's development.

From the early 1980s, the agricultural squeeze was intensified by the scaling down of rural subsidies. The Grain Management Fund[24] and the Fertiliser Fund were reduced, and the population was forced to shoulder a fuller burden of *Saemaul Undong*. The government deficit was reduced, while at the same time pressures mounted from the US to open up domestic agricultural markets. Yet the agricultural sector was already under strain from indebtedness. Cost of production began to exceed purchase prices even during the late 1970s when the government heavily subsidised the agricultural sector. With the reduction of price supports and credits and with low market prices, the problem was bound to worsen (Bello and Rosenfeld 1990, Boyer and Ahn 1991). From parity at the height of the rural development programme in 1975, average rural household income had dropped to around 85 per cent of the urban level by the mid-1980s. Between 1975 and 1985, farm debt rose by a factor of 63 – almost ten times the rate at which rural household income and farm assets increased (Bello and Rosenfeld 1990, pp.85–86). Rural indebtedness jumped 31 per cent in 1988 alone, to a huge 3.1 million won per household. Seriously indebted households rose from 76 per cent of the total in 1971 to 90 per cent in 1983, and to 98 per cent in 1985. Though the government tried to address the problem in 1987 with the provision of one trillion won in loans to allow farmers to refinance their debt with lower bank loans, the effect was temporary since the structural origins remained unaddressed (Boyer and Ahn 1991).

The growth of a new class of tenant farmers was a further cause of social and of regional inequality. The 1950s land reform had almost entirely eradicated tenant farming in Korea. However, it soon made a dramatic return: by 1960, 26.4 per cent of all South Korean farming households were tenant farmers, by 1970 33.5 per cent, up to 46.4 per cent in 1981, and 63.2 per cent in 1984. This approached the level of tenant farming under Japanese colonial rule. Boyer and Ahn show in their 1991 survey that tenant farmers were burdened with exorbitant rents and high production costs, and were more indebted than non-tenant farmers.

By the mid-1980s, Korea's rural development programmes had been exposed as deeply corrupt. This brought to an end almost two decades of 'modernisation' during which the government's objective was to exploit the countryside for its food surpluses, while pacifying the rural population in a quest for political legitimation. The continued widening of the urban –rural income gap[25] and uneven infrastructural development created an alienated rural community. The 1988 farmers' demonstration in front of the National Assembly in Seoul, which turned into a riot, signalled the break-down of the hegemonic MSR in rural Korea (Bello and Rosenfeld 1990).

The social disparities between rural and urban sectors were paralleled by increasing social inequalities within the urban industrial sector. Although the government made token efforts to curb economic domination of the chaebol, during the early 1980s the *conglomerates* were able to make good their losses once the 'purification' campaign was over (Koo and Kim 1992). For Koo (1984), the concentration of capital in chaebol arising from the industrial policies of the 1970s and 1980s was the prime cause of social inequality. Liberalisation of the financial and banking sectors intended to help capital dispersion was manipulated in favour of the chaebol (Bedeski 1994). With the state repression of labour by the state, and improvements in the international market during the 'Three Lows Period',[26] the chaebol were able to greatly enlarge their capital bases. Table 2.7 demonstrates that GNP contribution by the top 10 chaebol groups rose to over 67 per cent in 1984. 'Korea has acquired one of the world's most concentrated economies', wrote Amsden in 1989 (p.121). Even Japan could not now challenge the degree of monopolisation of Korea (Table 2.8).

While the middle band of Korea's population was able to maintain its relative income during the two decades of development, the bottom 40 per cent of the population saw a fall in their share of total income from 19.3 per cent in 1965 to 17.7 per cent in 1985 (Table 2.9). International comparisons show that Korean workers spent more hours working and were paid less than anywhere in the Western industrialised world and the newly industrialising countries (Table 2.10). Working conditions in Korea were also a source of social discord from the mid-1960s on. Between 1964 and 1984, the total number of deaths from industrial accidents was 18,000, with disablement

Table 2.7 Dominance of the top 10 chaebol

Year	Top 10 chaebol percentage sales in GNP
1974	15.1
1977	26.0
1980	48.1
1984	67.4
1987	68.8

Source: Jones and Sakong (1980), p.266; Koo and Kim (1992), p.135.

Note:
Top 10 chaebol are based on total capital assets.

Table 2.8 Top three-firm concentration ratios
for Korea, Japan and Taiwan

Country	Average share (per cent)[a]
Korea (1981)	62.0
Japan (1980)	56.3
Taiwan (1981)	49.2

Source: K.W. Lee, *et al.* (1986) cited in Amsden
(1989), p.122.

Note:
a Average share of top three producers (according
to gross sales) in all manufacturing industries.

at 150,000 and injuries at 1,430,000. Since not all work-places were
covered by Industrial Accident Insurance, these official figures are considerable underestimates. The Ministry of Labour estimated that in 1983
alone, 317,000 workers suffered industrial accidents, with an associated
economic loss of 2.4 per cent of GNP (Christian Institute for Study of Justice
and Development 1987, p.115). The long hours of work, the dangerous
working environment and low wages could only be imposed in the context
of a highly repressive state.

The growing opposition to minority conspicuous consumption was further inflamed by skyrocketing housing costs (see Table 2.11) exacerbated
by the speculative investment strategies of the chaebol groups. According
to the Korea Research Institute for Human Settlements, two thirds of all
land was owned by just 5 per cent of the population (Figure 2.4) (Son 1990,
p.16). Home ownership had become an impossible dream for most Koreans.

With lavish consumption and speculative investment on the one hand,
and worsening wages, working conditions and the rising cost of living on
the other hand, both labour and student activism were directed at both the
state and the chaebol. Since the Kwangju massacre in 1980, the student
and labour movements had taken a radical turn towards a Marxian philosophy, which saw the Korean state as controlled by corporate interests
under US supremacy. Labour activism was strongest in areas of high concentration of workers such as Ulsan, where half-a-million Hyundai workers
were concentrated, in the Masan export zone and the Kurodong industrial

Table 2.9 Household income distribution, 1960–85

Income group	1960	1965	1970	1975	1980	1982	1985
Bottom 40%	—	19.3	19.6	16.8	16.1	18.8	17.7
Top 20%	—	41.8	41.6	45.3	45.4	43.0	43.7
Gini index	0.448	0.344	0.332	0.391	0.389	0.357	—

Source: Koo 1984, p.1030 and Christian Institute for the Study of Justice and Development
(1985), pp.43–44.

Table 2.10 International comparisons of wages in manufacturing, 1983

Country	Average monthly wage (US$)	Hours of work	Wage per hour in won	Differen- tial (Korea = 100)	Conditions
Korea	285	236.1	936	100.0	Including some payment in kind. (companies of more than 10 workers)
Japan	1175	178.0	5,252	546.5	Cash wages only. (companies with more than 30 workers)
Taiwan	318	209	1,211	126.0	Cash wages only. (scale of company – n.a)
Singapore	90.70*	48.10*	1,500	156.1	Cash wages only. (companies of more than 10 workers)

Source: Federation of Korean Trades Unions (1984), p.55.

Note:
Figures with * for Singapore are based on average weekly wage and weekly work hours.

estate in Seoul. The student demonstrations were everywhere, but most volatile in Seoul, where they had high impact and visibility. These pressures prior to the 1987 election led to the capitulation of the Chun regime and the end of the authoritarian mode of regulation.

The breakdown of the dominant MSR was thus initiated by the rapid rise in trade surpluses and a shift in state policies, these boosting domestic consumption though not permitting the working classes their proportionate share. In a situation in which the new bourgeoisie flaunted its wealth, Korea's hegemonic ideology of self-sacrifice for national development was bound to dissolve. The struggle for social justice became widespread, and was especially intense amongst college students. At the same time, the staging of the 1988 Olympics in Seoul brought international condemnation upon the Korean state due to its labour repression and human

Table 2.11 Per annum increases in housing costs, 1987–90

		1987	1988	1989	1990
Nation	Housing price	7.2	13.1	14.6	8.3*
	Rents[1]	19.2	13.8	17.6	17.5*
Seoul	Housing price	2.1	9.1	16.6	9.9*
	Rents[1]	18.0	7.9	23.7	21.9*

Source: Derived from Son (1990), p.19.

Notes:
1 Chonsei rents are those which require a lump sum to be deposited with the landlord, who receives the interest; at the end of the lease the money is returned.
* Increases based on 1st quarter of 1990.

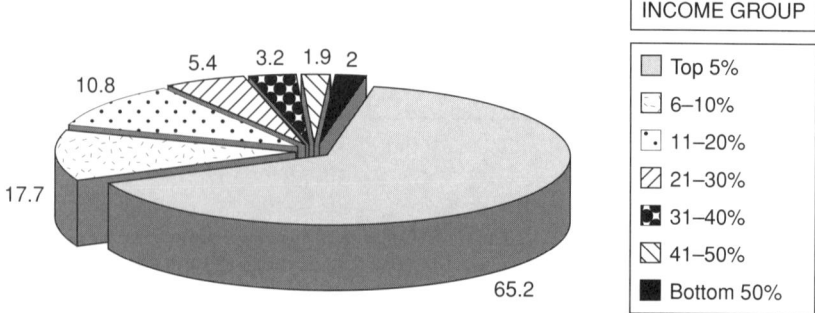

INCOME GROUP

☐ Top 5%
☐ 6–10%
▫ 11–20%
▨ 21–30%
▣ 31–40%
◩ 41–50%
■ Bottom 50%

Figure 2.4 Concentration of private (non-corporate) land ownership, 1988.
Source: KRIHS (1989), derived from Son (1990), p.16.

Notes:
As of June 1988.
Of Korea's total land, individuals own 66.1%, and corporations own 4.1%.

rights abuses. In these circumstances the Chun government was inhibited from deploying the full force of its mighty police. To demonstrate that state reform was at hand, in 1987 presidential candidate Roh Tae Woo distanced himself from Chun by proclaiming his June 29th manifesto for political reform. This marked the end of the peripheral Fordist regime, and the beginnings of neo-Fordism in Korea.

The neo-Fordist period (1988–97)

In terms of our theoretical framework, it is argued that Korea leapfrogged the Fordist accumulation regime with its monopolistic social regulation, moving directly into the post-Fordist era of the global economy. Lipietz (1992) argues that in the wake of the crisis of Fordism, which was a crisis in the productive forces, 'Taylorism' and the national modes of regulation governing the Fordist economy, there arose two types of flexible regimes of accumulation in the core regions: a neo-Fordist regime, which aimed to re-establish the flexibility of market relations as well as capital–labour relations, and a post-Fordist regime, which aimed to overcome the limitations of the Taylorist model by employment deregulation, 'just in time' organisation and strategic co-operation between companies. The Korean mode of development can be described as neo-Fordist, in which mass production and mass consumption patterns were established with the continuation of a competitive mode of social regulation.

Political liberalisation, militant labour struggle and mass consumption

Radical reform of the political superstructure followed the historic June 29th Declaration of Democracy in 1987. As the repression of labour and student demonstrations became less severe, the pent-up discontent of past decades burst into the open. Economically, the most threatening consequence of political liberalisation was the explosion of labour disputes, which increased from over 300 incidents in 1986 to over 3,000 in 1987 (see Table 2.12). Although the number of disputes in 1989, 1990 and 1991 was far below the levels of 1987 and 1988, the intensity of the demonstrations and strikes was more severe. Work stoppages also became longer and more violent. Sectors most affected were automobiles and the labour intensive garment and footwear industries (Koo and Bark 1989). The result was dramatically accelerating wage increases. Through the mid-1980s, annual wage increases were below 10 per cent. After 1987, however, wages rose rapidly, peaking with 1989's increase of 20 per cent. For Asia as a whole, Korean wages in 1990 were second only to Japan's. Working hours also decreased, while working conditions improved slightly (Bedeski 1994). As labour unions became more vocal and with labour legislation in favour of the workers, the unions demanded both higher pay and changes in working practices.

Work stoppages and rapid wage hikes arising from labour disputes along with currency appreciation, seriously eroded the international competitiveness of Korean products after 1989; as Table 2.13 shows, growth in both manufacturing and in exports declined sharply. Industries such as footwear, automobile, iron and steel and marine products were hit hardest.

Table 2.12 Labour disputes, and changes in earnings, urban industrial sector, 1985–96

Year	Number of disputes	Workers involved	Working days lost (1000)	Average monthly earnings in won (% increase)	
1985	265	28,700	64	324,283	(9)
1986	276	46,900	72	350,966	(8)
1987	3,749	1,262,300	6,947	386,536	(10)
1988	1,873	293,500	5,401	446,370	(15.4)
1989	1,616	409,100	6,351	540,611	(21.1)
1990	322	133,900	4,487	642,309	(18.8)
1991	234	175,100	3,271	754,673	(17.5)
1992	235	105,000	1,528	869,284	(15.2)
1993	144	108,600	1,308	886,788	(2.0)
1994	121	104,300	1,484	1,023,390	(15.4)
1995	88	49,700	393	1,124,578	(8.9)
1996	85	79,500	893	1,262,275	(10.9)

Source: NSO (various years).

Note:
All other figures for all industries (mining, manufacturing, services and construction) excluding the agricultural sector.

Table 2.13 Macro-economic and industrial indicators of Korea, 1986–96

Year	GNP growth (%)	Growth in manufacturing (%)	Exports (million US$)	Export growth rate (%)	Imports (million US$)	Import growth rate (%)
1986	12.9	18.3	34,714.5	14.6	31,583.9	1.4
1987	13.0	18.8	47,280.9	36.2	41,019.8	29.9
1988	12.4	13.4	60,696.4	28.4	51,810.6	26.3
1989	6.8	3.7	62,377.2	2.8	61,464.8	18.6
1990	9.3	9.1	65,015.7	4.2	69,843.7	13.6
1991	8.4	8.9	71,870.1	10.5	81,524.9	16.7
1992	4.7	5.1	76,631.5	6.6	81,775.3	0.3
1993	5.8	5.0	82,235.9	7.3	83,800.1	2.5
1994	9.6	10.5	96,013.2	16.8	102,348.2	22.1
1995	7.6	10.8	125,058.0	30.3	135,118.9	32.0
1996	6.9	7.4	129,715.1	3.7	150,339.1	11.3

Source: NSO (1997).

Nonetheless, some sectors managed to achieve robust gains despite the adverse economic conditions. Shipbuilding, electric and electronic products, chemical products and general machinery, all grew by over 10 per cent during the first half of 1989 (Koo and Bark 1989, pp.27–29). See Figure 2.5.

The economic recession in the core countries from the early 1990s and the protectionism of the US and European Community also made matters difficult for Korean exporters. On the other hand, 1988 saw a 10 per cent

Figure 2.5 Comparison of changing rates in exports and imports (percentage increase over previous year).

Source: NSO (various years).

increase in domestic consumption, representing a big surge compared to previous years (Koo and Bark 1989). Between 1988–91 domestic consumption, especially private consumption, continued to increase at an annual average of 10 per cent. The value and composition of imports also underwent rapid change. Imports surged due to the government efforts to reduce tariffs, liberalise trade and appreciate the currency. Koo and Bark (1989) show that increases in imports were mainly to serve domestic consumption, with consumer goods growing relatively faster than capital or intermediate goods (p.30). The increase in domestic consumption due to rising wages from 1987 to 1991 was the main expansionary force and compensated for the slowdown in exports. Thus, Korean manufacturing as a whole was sheltered from the full effects of export decline in global markets.

During the Roh administration (1988–92), the focus of the economy remained the export sector. Existing industries such as semiconductors, shipbuilding and car manufacturing, and new ones such as naphtha cracking were promoted. To restore international competitiveness the government resumed coercive tactics towards the labour unions: in 1990, Roh declared illegal the militant Korean Trade Union Congress (*Chonnohyup*), deploying 300 intelligence agents into over 70 industrial complexes. Large numbers were detained, 140 trades union leaders being jailed indefinitely in early 1991 (Bello and Rosenfeld 1990, p.45). The momentous victory by labour over capital of the late 1980s had thus been short-lived. Although the workers in chaebol firms did see better wages, Korea's export-oriented regime was incapable of extending such improvements to workers in small and medium firms.

Flexiblisation of production and internationalisation of Korean capital

To confront the challenges of an increasingly competitive world economic climate and rising domestic wages and labour disputes in the neo-Fordist period, Korean manufacturing industries sought to flexiblise their production. Flexiblisation through subcontracting and multiple sourcing – particularly in the electronics and automobile industries – was slowly introduced to reduce costs and divide labour unions (Lee, Y-S. 1993). This, however, was insufficient to raise the competitiveness of Korean products in international markets. As one of the highest wage economies in East Asia, but lacking the advanced technologies of the core industrialised countries, Korean capital was forced to look for cheaper labour offshore.

Liberalisation of government regulation of private offshore capital investment allowed some manufacturing industries to find alternative sources of cheap labour. The most labour intensive sectors such as the garments and footwear were the first to locate plants in Southeast Asian countries, the second generation Asian NICs (Bedeski 1994). This trend spread rapidly after 1995 to many other industries (Koo and Bark 1989, *FEER*

1996, 20 June). See Figure 2.6. The relocation of manufacturing plants was aimed not only at exports to Fordist (or post-Fordist) regimes in the core region, but also at expanding markets in the growing economies of Southeast Asia. Korean exports to this region grew steadily, while exports to North American markets stagnated (Koo and Bark 1989). The trade and diplomatic links with mainland China established in the early 1990s, and with some former centrally planned countries, opened new opportunities in offshore locations close to home. An added advantage was their large markets. Simultaneously, investment in the North American and European trade blocs was pushed forward, particularly in Canada, Mexico (*FEER* 1996, 20 June) and the UK (Bedeski 1994).[27]

The scale of Korea's globalisation drive post-1990 was massive. In electronics, Daewoo invested US$1.1 billion in twenty plants, soon generating 60 per cent of its total production outside South Korea. Lucky Goldstar (LG) sank over half-a-billion US dollars in twenty-two factories offshore, while Samsung invested US$200 million in Tijuana, Mexico. Samsung planned to invest a further US$580 million here between 1996 and the turn of the century. These Korean investments in offshore locations were not merely in assembly lines: they aim to replicate miniature versions of their complex, vertically integrated operations (Bedeski 1994, pp.48–49). Affected by rising domestic costs the automobile industries also started to invest heavily in offshore locations. Daewoo Motors sought sites in eastern Europe and the former Soviet Union, and Hyundai was planning to extend its operations to Turkey, Egypt and Botswana (*Financial Times*, 17 June 1996, p.19).

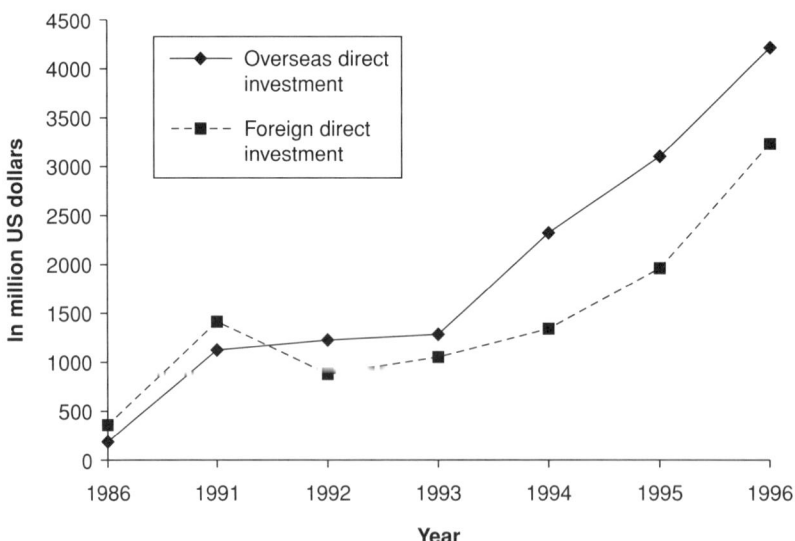

Figure 2.6 Flow of capital in and out of Korea, 1986–96.

Source: NSO (various years).

Changing relationships of capital, state and society

After the late-1980s, the regimes of both Roh and Kim Young Sam tried to re-establish legitimacy by ending two decades of partnership with the chaebol. This strategy included the promotion of small and medium-sized capital to balance the economic power of the conglomerates. The Roh government implemented a number of measures to regulate chaebol speculative activities, diversification, and similar tendencies threatening their uncompetitiveness in international markets (Bedeski 1994, pp.87–88). The state was also intent on pacifying public disquiet. The Roh government introduced indirect instruments of control such as interest rates and tax measures, but it was difficult to accomplish significant reform in the heavily regimented economy. Early in Roh's presidential term, the government ordered banks to grant 35 per cent of all loans to small and middle-sized businesses, in part to deflect growing public resentment against the chaebol. Government measures notwithstanding, small companies were failing to emerge in the manner experimented by Taiwan (Bedeski 1994, pp.84–85). Overall, these measures failed to have an impact due to the recession of the early 1990s and the state–chaebol partnership continued as an attempt to gain recovery through export-led growth. The chaebol maintained their grip, accounting for more than 70 per cent of the Korean economy (Bedeski 1994). Their continuing power was clearly signalled by the candidature of the chairman of Hyundai, Chung Ju Young, in the 1992 presidential election. In contrast to the early days of economic development, when the chaebol were firmly under state direction, by the 1990s they had gained the upper hand in state–capital relations.

Measures to curb chaebol power and promote market mechanism continued with Kim Young Sam (hereafter, Y-S. Kim). After assuming the presidency in 1992, Y-S. Kim pursued liberalisation of the protected domestic markets in an effort to curb monopoly controls.[28] Numerous measures were introduced to open up domestic markets and to curb chaebol power. The *1993 Financial Liberalisation and Market Opening Plan* (known as the 'Blueprint') was aimed at their autarkic practices; it was also intended to address pressures from the US to open up domestic markets and attract foreign capital to Korean stocks. This plan had two major components: deregulation of the banking sector and opening up of portfolio markets to international investors. The regulation on direct investment and foreign ownership of Korean companies remained.

The liberalisation measures were slow to take effect. The partial liberalisation of retail markets led to more foreign goods being available, but at an inflated price due to continuing application of high tariffs. The restriction of foreign ownership of businesses to under 50 per cent necessitated joint ventures with Korean firms, which often led to higher overheads for the foreign partner, thus deterring investment. The deregulation of the banking system was intended to reduce the domination of the loan market by the chaebol; instead, the establishment of merchant banks by them led to easier access to foreign loans – albeit at market prices. The desired creation of a more balanced industrial structure was thwarted by the continued domination of bank lending by the chaebol. As we will examine later, this selective opening up of the financial sector further distorted the Korean economy and exposed it to potential external shocks.

Further restrictions were introduced to curb speculation by the chaebol elite including the implementation of high taxes in real estate transactions. The Y-S. Kim administration in 1994–95 also tried to address illicit wealth accumulation on the part of politicians and government officials by obliging 'real name' transactions[29] in financial dealings and real estate. These measures produced unforeseen side-effects as much capital simply went underground: in fear of taxation and inland revenue investigations, many smuggled cash abroad. The impact of capital retreat from the formal economy was significant enough for the succeeding Kim Dae Jung government to consider repealing the Act. Thus, numerous barriers remained to the untrammelled operation of the market during Korea's neo-Fordist period.

With the intensification of competition in the economy, polarisation of wealth increased and conflicts arose between workers in stable employment and those in the marginal labour market. Although Y-S. Kim strove to eradicate corruption and reduce the domination of the chaebol, social welfare reforms were less emphasised. Expanded housing provision and initiatives in developing social security and health services were almost entirely market-led. As for the quest for economic recovery of 1993, it was very much construction-led. New town schemes were implemented to address the housing shortages in Seoul, which had been increasing during the previous three decades (Byun 1983). In 1980, 56 per cent of households were without their own dwellings, this decreasing slightly to 50.8 per cent by 1993. There was no provision of affordable housing for the urban poor during the 1980s. Even though price controls applied to new apartments, these proved too expensive for residents displaced by re-development projects. Only in 1990 did the government begin to provide affordable rental housing for the urban poor, and at woefully inadequate levels and in locations which were often unsuitable. Although in 1994 housing prices started to stabilise and then fall in Seoul, they remained excessive even for many middle class families. Their main purpose was to stimulate the economy and to stave off a legitimation crisis.

National pension and health insurance schemes were subsidised versions of private schemes, and available only in restricted form. The pension scheme introduced in 1991 benefited only those in full time employment, including the self-employed. This widened the division between those in large companies and the casual labour market. Pension benefits were lost if one's job was lost. The new national health insurance was an extension of private provision, albeit at a lower rate and under state management.

It was not universal and out-of-pocket costs remained high. Rural areas saw more limited provision.

A competitive MSR and a free market ideology institutionalised what amounted to a workfare state. As more manufacturing firms moved their production lines offshore in the 1990s, and the country was opened up to global forces, an increasing proportion of the population fell outside the workfare state.

Exhaustion of the neo-Fordist mode of social regulation

Although the Korean state under the Roh and Y-S. Kim governments (1988–92, 1992–97 respectively) introduced limited social welfare provision, the dominant mode of regulation remained competitive. With the deregulation of offshore investment which allowed capital to restore profit margins, the beginnings of a flexible mode of development were signalled. The regime has been termed neo-Fordist, characterised by accumulation based on mass production and mass consumption, with relatively rigid labour practices in place. Korea's neo-Fordist regime is significantly different to the neo-Fordism of core capitalist economies such as the UK's: a neo-competitive mode of social regulation is in place, as well as flexiblised labour markets and practices.

The neo-Fordist regime in Korea failed to produce a stable period of accumulation. This period saw evasive action by capital in order to restore profits, through migration of manufacturing plants to countries with less rigid labour practices. This was an easier option than confronting the labour unions at home. Both the state and capital embarked on a course of massive investment to upgrade infrastructure and the technological base. The state's infrastructural projects included a new airport at Yeongjongdo and a high speed railway between Seoul and Pusan. Liberalisation of capital markets was intended to attract global capital to the Korean economy. However, the manner in which this policy was implemented made the Korean economy vulnerable to external forces. First, the lack of regulatory mechanisms in the banking sector meant that chaebol-owned merchant banks were able to take on huge international loans to finance parent company expansion. The cross-subsidies between subsidiaries of chaebol groups meant that the banks were making unsecured loans to companies with high debt-equity levels. Second, the government opened up portfolio markets to foreign investment, while keeping foreign direct investment opportunities essentially closed. This attracted speculative and highly mobile international capital to the stock and bond markets. The nature of the portfolio capital meant that, with little regulatory mechanism, the flight of capital in times of economic downturn could lead to extreme currency problems. The liberalisation of the financial sector was to sow the seed for the economic collapse of 1997.

The chaebol aimed to expand manufacturing capacity during a period of global recessionary to prepare themselves for a larger share of the market when the recovery came. However, their grand plan did not materialise. Their over-leveraged operations needed rapid increases in exports: fierce market competition, however, meant that profit margins were small. From early 1997 many Korean businesses, global and domestic players alike, faced dwindling profits and the rising cost of loan repayments. Overseas ventures such as those of Hyundai and LG in the UK (both semiconductors) were particularly hard hit. New competition from Taiwanese chip manufacturers was combined with a sharp decline in the price of DRAM chips due to a world-wide glut. By the late 1990s, many of the Korean overseas investments were not yet fully operational, leaving them with heavy debts and little return. The debt-equity ratio of chaebol returned to the late 1970s levels, averaging over 400 per cent.

The collapse of Kia Motors in 1997 signalled the beginning of the structural crisis. The government handling of this and other companies' bankruptcies contributed to the scale of the crisis. The state stepped in after three months of stalemate between the creditors and Kia management and tried to expedite the turn around of the company. However, instead of speedy resolution of the Kia problem, there emerged a tug-of-war between the state, creditors, management and labour unions. This undermined the confidence of overseas financial institutions and eroded the international credit standing of Korean enterprises. Despite the faltering economy, the state introduced a much watered-down labour law banning corporate layoffs for two years. This left little room for troubled companies to restructure. Following the Kia debacle, a string of high profile conglomerates such as Hanbo, Sammi, Dainong and Jinro also collapsed, creating some 26 trillion won in new bad loans by November 1997 (*FEER*, 20 November 1997, p.16). Thus, the real manifestation of the crisis came from the banking sector which was saddled with mounting bad loans. In response, in October the government unveiled a package of emergency measures, including 4 trillion won in soft loans to banks saddled with the worst debts, and a pledge to honour all international obligations of domestic financial institutions (*FEER*, 30 October 1997, p.58). However, this had little effect on market sentiment. With the IMF raising further doubts regarding Korea's capacity to address its economic problems, traders continued to abandon the Korean currency, which plummeted. The flight of foreign capital contributed to the weakening financial situation in Seoul. To keep the cost of borrowing down, the Bank of Korea maintained support of the won by selling dollars in forward markets. This in turn led to the decline of foreign currency reserves to dangerously low levels. If official sources were to be believed, reserves could now cover just three months of imports (*FEER*, 20 November, 1998, pp.14–16).

There were also powerful exogenous influences at play. The Southeast Asian financial turmoil exacerbated the situation, as Korean banks had loaned extensively to emerging Southeast Asian companies. The collapse of the Thai, Indonesian and Malaysian economies meant that their investments and loans had to be written off. The ensuing devaluation of the crisis-hit Asian economies left Korean products at further price disadvantage. The sliding won and falling stock markets undermined Korea's economy further. Foreign investors accelerated their exodus and domestic players continued to hoard dollars in anticipation of a further depreciation. On 21 November 1997, Korea turned to the International Monetary Fund for emergency help. There was a requirement for servicing of US$60–70 billion in short-term private sector foreign debt that matured in under one year. This proved to be the decisive point of the corrupt chaebol–government alliance that had characterised thirty years of a rapidly growing Korean economy. The Korean won which stood at 891 won to the dollar in June 1997 slid to 1000 won in November, and went into free-fall in December to a record low of 1891 won. This brought the neo-Fordist era to a decisive close.

By mid-December 1997, South Korea was promised US$57 billion in an IMF-led package in return for slashing GDP growth to below 3 per cent (less than half of the 1997 level), holding inflation to 5 per cent, and cutting its current-account deficit to 1 per cent of GDP compared with almost 3 per cent at the beginning of the crisis. The government was also required to produce a balanced budget by cutting spending and raising taxes, while checking inflation by raising interest rates. Other measures demanded by the IMF were to close fourteen troubled financial institutions, write off debts and raise foreign-ownership limits to 50 per cent which effectively gave the green light to take-overs of Korean companies. To make firms more transparent, government was required to oblige all chaebol to publish consolidated statements and curtail cross-subsidiary guarantees (*FEER*, 18 December 1997, p.64).

The collapse of the Korean economy came just weeks before the presidential election. As we have seen many times previously, the crisis in the economy led ineluctably to the reformulation of the state. In this case, the change of presidents was not just a symbolic gesture. Kim Dae Jung came to power on the basis of political alliance with an unlikely partner, Kim Jong Pil, former prime minister in Park Jung Hee's regime. At point of writing, it remains to be seen if the new order can implement the far reaching reforms needed to turn the hierarchical, conservative, political economy of Korea towards a more open and equitable one. Crisis is an opportunity to transform both the accumulation regime and mode of social regulation to achieve political goals. However, under the IMF plans to introduce further competitiveness, the prospects for improvements for social justice seemed poor.

The changes demanded to elevate Korea from its crisis were fundamental. Markets – not government mandarins – were now meant to decide which companies got financing. The chaebol groups were told to cut loss-making divisions instead of relentlessly pursuing expansion and diver-sification. Hope was now invested in the prospects of small and medium-sized companies. Foreign firms could now penetrate every business sphere. Trades unions were told to accede to greater flexibility in the labour market. However, such transformations had little chance of success in the absence of changes in Korea's deeply Confucian society. For example, companies would need to promote managers based on performance rather than on seniority. And the education system, so effective at producing skilled, disciplined workers for the nation's industrial machine, had now to be overhauled to foster initiative and creativity in place of regimentation.

Even as the restructuring process was inaugurated, there were signs that reforms were faltering. Resistance came not only from labour and capital, but from within the state echelons too. Bankrupt businesses con-tinued to operate under an obscure recourse known as *court mediation*,[30] this allowing a financially strapped firm to postpone debt repayments and in some cases even to transact low-interest loans while the management attempted a turn-around. The banks consented to this state of affairs as it averted the immediate slide into receivership, when loans would have to be written off. While healthy companies struggled to repay interest rates exceeding 30 per cent, those in mediation were frequently paying less than 20 per cent. They were also receiving huge loans to keep them afloat even as the banks were clamping down on overall lending. By the end of 1998, most of the bankrupt conglomerates were under court mediation. They included Korea First Bank, Samyang Food, Jinro, New Core, Haitai, Ssangbangwool, Halla Cement, Kia Precision Works and Young Jin Pharmaceutical. At the end of 1997, 201 companies had applied for medi-ation (*FEER*, 5 March 1998, p.55). Essentially, bankrupt firms were now surviving at the expense of healthy ones, many of which were now propelled to the point of bankruptcy. Such deliberate manipulation of the IMF re-covery plan demonstrates the immense difficulty in changing business practices in Korea. The government, of course, continued to propagate its free-market gospel in the absence of an adequate institutional founda-tion. There was, for instance, no mergers-and-acquisitions framework by which to deal with corporate dead-weights such as Kia, the country's larg-est bankrupt chaebol. Instead, the D-J. Kim government obliged relatively healthy conglomerates to 'swap' companies between themselves in similar fashion to that of Chun in the early 1980s. As the *Far Eastern Economic Review* puts it:

> There is no radical shake-up of officials nor dramatic cutting down of the numbers of bureaucrats and functions. There is unwillingness in the abandonment of the Japanese-style economic model of state-led capi-talism that produced South Korea's industrial revolution. To many, it's considered too much. 'You don't change a model like you change

clothes,' says Park Ung Suh, president of the Samsung Economic Research Institute. 'It's who we are.'

(*FEER*, 11 December 1997, p.16)

The resolution of the crisis and creation of a more flexible accumulation regime would require a new consensus upon which a new mode of social regulation might be founded. The Korean state, however, was caught between two pressure systems: on the one hand, greater marketisation was demanded. On the other, the state had to address demands for higher social and infrastructure expenditure. Structural unemployment is, of course, implicit in an economy shifting further towards market orientations. Already by 1999, unemployment rates were nearing 10 per cent, causing high levels of social tension and denying access to medical and other services to many millions. Along with Thailand and Indonesia, Korea has been designated by the World Bank as a crisis case. Loans of US$5 billion were designated for aid to the poorest part of the population (Atinc and Walton 1998). An added factor in the consideration of social stability remains the ever-present threat from North Korea. Thus, it was imperative that a new mode of social regulation be sought which could address the economic, social and national security crises.

Summary

Korea's capitalist industrialisation began with the Japanese occupation. The colonial regime established an exploitative system of social and economic regulation based on a peculiar marriage between state and capital. This provided something of a model for all Korea's post-colonial periods.

The growth of Korea's modern economy has been punctuated by the continual irruption of the political landscape. First came the collapse of Japan's 'Greater East Asia Co-Prosperity Sphere', and later the arbitrary division of the peninsula into Soviet and American occupation zones (Mason *et al.* 1980). The distortion of politics and economics by the combined overlordship of the US occupation forces and the Rhee administration permitted the old hierarchical social order a continued breathing space. Indeed, it was the cornerstone of the new accumulation system, and the source of deep social resentment and political unrest.

The ISI regime between 1948 and 1960 was marked by high levels of corruption, and an economy based on aid maximisation. Once easy substitution had been accomplished, structural factors meant that the ISI was rapidly exhausted. The Rhee and Chang governments' destabilising collusion with certain fractions of capital presaged an EOI regime initiated through a coup d'état. In the 1960s, this regime was characterised by an extensive regime of accumulation and a competitive mode of social regulation. Although such a mode of development raised Korea out of absolute poverty, the country remained incapable of escaping its dependency upon core capitalist economies. Rapid and erratic industrial development created huge social tensions; they also caused stark regional disparities.

To escape from dependency on foreign capital and intermediate inputs for the manufacturing of export goods and on labour intensive low value-added exports, industrialisation founded on the heavy and chemical sectors was then pursued. The extensive accumulation regime based on high capital and technology input was complemented by a corporatist[31] mode of social regulation. The corporatist labour regulation and rural development strategy was able to further the development of Korea's heavy and chemical industries, dominated now by chaebol. Economic performance was spectacular in the mid- to late-1970s. However, the government's industrial strategy encouraged rent seeking on the part of the chaebol; they were to maximise profits through tax and tariff incentives, loans at special rates and through monopolisation of the domestic market. This led to over-capacity in production, and eventually to the exhaustion of the extensive accumulation regime. The structural crisis led to the restructuring of both the mode of development and the state itself.

Economic restructuring produced an intensive accumulation system coupled with a competitive MSR under an authoritarian state – a peripheral Fordist regime. The intensive EOI regime was in response to the changing international economic climate as well as rising labour costs in Korea. The foundation laid during the Park presidency was the basis for the rapid growth of the mid-1980s, this placing Korea firmly amongst the ranks of the most buoyant NICs. As the economy boomed in the mid-1980s, with rising consumption by the middle and upper classes, the authoritarian state experienced an increase in labour disputes and student demonstrations, these challenging its legitimacy. The competitive MSR and the hegemonic ideology of self-sacrifice were under pressure from an inequitable distribution of income and the rising consumerism of the middle classes.

The neo-Fordist phase of Korean development of the 1990s was characterised by a growing tendency towards a flexible accumulation regime with a modified-competitive MSR. This tendency was initiated by the political and economic liberalisation of the Sixth Republic (1988). Militant labour struggles under a more liberal political regime led to the rapid increases in wages, lowering the competitiveness of Korean export goods in overseas markets. The rising costs of export production coincided with a downturn of the global economy, devastating Korean export performance in the late 1980s and early 1990s. But rising wages led to an increase in domestic consumption, which shielded Korean industries from the full effects of the global recession. However, Korean capital as well as foreign TNCs endeavoured to restore profits and improve export activity by locating labour intensive activities in areas of abundant low cost labour, particularly in Southeast Asian countries, in China and in Mexico. The relaxation of state regulations for offshore investment by Korean capital promoted a more flexible mode of development, but did not lead to the re-imposition of market forces in capital–labour relations.

The establishment of a democratic government from 1988 meant a weakening of the state stranglehold over labour unions. Although the state forcefully intervened in labour disputes, its actions were limited to maintaining order rather than intervening overtly on the side of capital. Even in the face of deepening recession the National Assembly, which began to gain power over the executive, was not willing to pass labour laws which would curb the power of unions and the rigidity of working practices. This not only led to falling productivity, but directly led many more firms to seek investment opportunities abroad. This in turn led to a rapid out-flow of foreign currency as well as increasing dependence upon foreign loans. Financial deregulation made foreign loans easier for highly leveraged chaebol groups to bankroll overseas ventures unchecked. Their strategy for capital accumulation continued to be one of enlarging market share rather than profit returns. They thus expanded manufacturing capacity on a global basis in order to prepare themselves for future market penetration. As a consequence, their debt ratios reached almost five times their total assets.

As exports continued to decline while imports rose steadily, the current account balance deteriorated and debt financing became difficult. The Korean won was kept artificially high to service foreign loans and to maintain cheap imports. However, continued expansion of the chaebol overseas, and the state's support of the won, led to severe shortages of US dollar reserves held by the central bank. With foreign loans underwritten by the government, the shortage of US dollars in effect meant national bankruptcy. In addition, the liberalisation of stock and bond markets to foreign capital exposed Korea to greater financial woes: the flight of international capital at the beginning of the crisis led to stock market collapse as well as to a currency crisis. Thus, in November 1997, an unprecedented structural crisis was suddenly precipitated. This crisis stemmed from the inability of the state to modify the mode of regulation within a changing economic environment, particularly that pertaining to labour relations and chaebol accumulation strategy.

The chaebol's accumulation strategy rested on increasing market share through price advantage derived from low wages and scale economies. Instead of increasing productivity through efficiency and flexibility, they chose to pursue a strategy of capacity expansion which was capital intensive. The declining profitability of Korean firms was basically due to continuing reliance on competition that was price-based rather than innovation and technology-based. During the 1990s, Korea's market share and profitability have been steadily squeezed by the Thai, Malaysian, Indonesian and Chinese economies which have greater price-wage advantage. Korea's transition to a higher technology and innovation based accumulation is haphazard. Korea's investment in R&D remained almost the lowest in the league table of industrialised and industrialising countries. According to Henderson (1999), much of Korea's limited private sector investment was concentrated in the electronics industry, a narrow industrial focus. Thus, during the neo-Fordist period, the chaebol strategy, inseparable from the national strategy, remained extensive. See Table 2.14.

By 1998, the IMF was attempting to push through measures which the state had failed to implement over the previous five years. With over US$57 billion in loans, the IMF was in a position to at least extract promises of restructuring, with implications of far greater penetration of global capital into Korean markets. Of the many measures to be implemented, most notable were closure of unprofitable companies within the chaebol groups, flexiblisation of labour relations (that is, permitting companies to lay off workers), restructuring of the banking system, opening up of domestic markets, the possibility of 100 per cent foreign ownership of domestic businesses, unlimited participation of offshore players in the stock market and slimming down of the government and its agencies. All these reforms were now feasible due to the new regime of former dissident leader Kim Dae Jung. President Kim's long association with labour unions and lack of ties with the chaebol were vital factors in the effort to persuade labour unions to accept restructuring. The process faced many obstacles: strikes by militant labour unions opposed to drastic wage cuts and redundancies, businesses struggling to obtain credit under deteriorating economic conditions including high interest rates, and resistance from public and private sector bureaucrats alike. At the point of writing, it is not clear whether these reforms will result in a significant shift in Korea's fundamental trajectory – that is to say, whether a new regime of accumulation and mode of social regulation will coalesce.

The economic change and political restructuring in the postwar period must be understood in terms of a dialectical process. The dominant position of the state in social regulation, and its direct intervention in the formation of the accumulation system did not allow it to overcome structural crises without calling its own legitimacy into question. Due to the inflexibility of the state – its impermeability to economic and political changes – political restructuring was a precondition for economic restructuring. Thus, at every phase, state transformation coincided with economic restructuring. See Figure 2.7.

A central feature of accumulation dynamics in Korea has been the role of the chaebol. The EOI mode of development was based on monopoly capital as the main dynamic force in accumulation, not merely in the manufacturing sector but also in property and finance. The chaebol groups were able to diversify operations into many profitable sectors due to their overwhelming strength and close ties with the state bureaucracy. Due to their unequal access to credit facilities and their speculative ventures, small and medium sized industries were not able to flourish as in the case of Taiwan.

Table 2.14 Phases of Korean regimes of accumulation, regulation and industrial trajectory in the twentieth century

	1945–60	1960–70	1971–79	1980–87	1988–97	1998–
International political economy	Post-war economic boom	Fordism under threat from Third World industralisation	Crisis of Fordism and end of free trade	Flexiblised accumulation and emerging post-Fordism	Intensifying globalisation and emergence of trade blocks	Crisis of neo-liberalism?
Regime of accumulation	Extensive	Extensive (Taylorist)	Extensive (Yusin phase)	Emerging intensive (peripheral Fordist)	Intensive – emerging globalisation (neo-Fordist)	Crisis
Mode of regulation	Corporatist	Competitive	Corporatist	Competitive	Modified-competitive	Super-competitive
Industrial trajectory	Easy ISI	Labour intensive EOI and OEM[1] assembly	Deepening EOISI (heavy and chemical industries)	Capital and technology intensive EOI	High technology-based strategy	High technology-based strategy
Ideology	Nationalism	Democracy and modernisation	Yusin nationalism and modernisation	Anti-communism	Internationalism and democracy	Neo-liberalism and globalisation

Source: Compiled by authors.

Note:
1 Own-name Export Manufacturing.

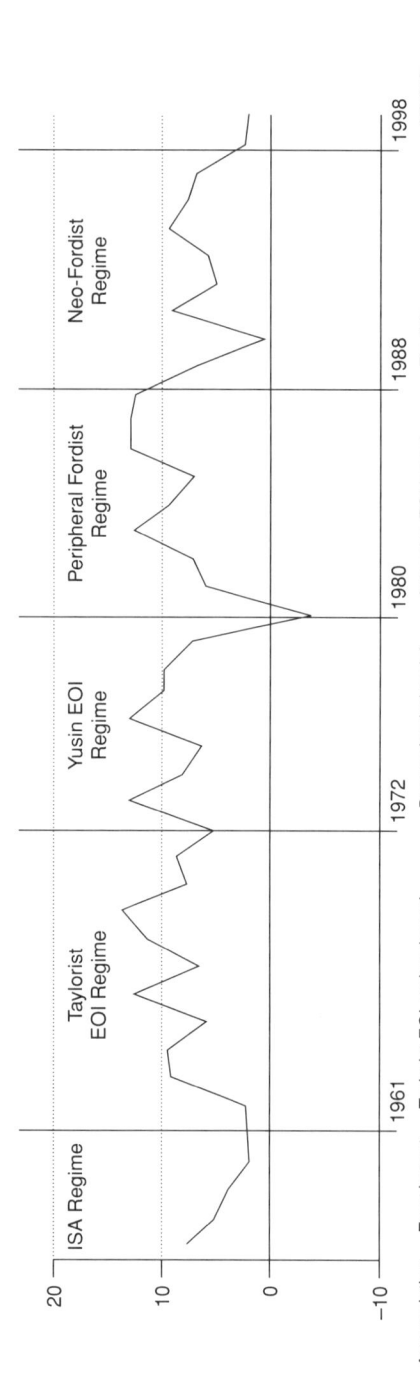

Figure 2.7 GNP growth rate, regime of accumulation and political regulation.

Source: NSO (various years); *FEER,* 8 February 1999.

Capitalist development in South Korea in the postwar period can be divided into five distinct phases. The transition of each accumulation regime to the next was due to the exhaustion of some or all of the structural features in the mode of development, in the accumulation regime, the MSR and industrial trajectory. Especially important has been the role of the state as the guarantor of the accumulation regime and stabiliser of the MSR. The manipulation of the financial sector, repression of labour, the relationship with monopoly capital, separation of production and consumption – these have been the key features of state regulation. However, heavy intervention by the state was not able to avert crises occurring in the accumulation system. As we have seen, the sources of crises came both internally, externally, and related to the structural features of each regime. Recoupling of accumulation regimes and the modes of social regulation were effected through adjustments in the state, particular hegemonic ideologies, the industrial trajectory and various institutional forms such as finance, wage relations and the mode of integration externally.

The deepening of the industrial trajectory and the intensification of accumulation strategies brought Korea rapid economic growth. This incurred, however, severe social and environmental costs. Although general living standards rose dramatically, removing the absolute poverty of the early 1950s, income distribution in Korea worsened over the years. Corruption and speculation only heightened the anger of the alienated classes.

The discrimination of state intervention between production and consumption became a major factor in Korea's growing social and environmental problems. The export-oriented mode of development meant that industrial production was prioritised and social consumption seen as a burden. Thus, the provision of social and physical infrastructure was geared towards education and training, transport and communication networks, power-generation and industrial estate development, all regarded as productive. Sanitation, medical and general welfare provision were largely neglected. Provision of housing in particular was left to private capital, offering an additional means of capital accumulation. Limited public housing and medical schemes appeared only in the 1990s in the wake of democratic reforms.

The state promotion of export-oriented industrialisation also led to the exploitation and relative demise of the agricultural sector. In the 1960s, state bias was towards labour intensive industries in urban areas. In the 1970s, the systematic exploitation of the agricultural sector to promote food production through integrated rural development programmes led to dependence on chemical inputs which, in turn, led to a rural debt crisis. In the 1980s, the rural sector was sacrificed to the need to keep the US market open for Korean exports. In the late 1980s, rural indebtedness reached crisis proportions; official remedial measures proved merely cosmetic.

In addition to general social inequity and rural underdevelopment, the environmental impact of the EOI was extremely burdensome. The deterioration in natural ecosystems caused by industries – as well as by private consumption – became critical. This was a direct consequence of the competitive MSR and the high growth accumulation strategies. The changes in industrial trajectory, accumulation regime and MSR brought about a complex set of environmental problems, ranging from housing to pollution of the natural environment. The intensification of capitalist social relations was responsible for marked spatial differentiation of environmental conditions. Thus, before we turn our attention to the environmental impacts of economic development in Korea, we must examine spatial developments as a manifestation of social interaction with the environment.

3 Spatial strategies and the emergence of uneven development

The previous chapter demonstrated how income distribution, social welfare and rural development were deleteriously affected as the state-dominated MSR and accumulation regime prioritised a rapid accumulation via export-oriented industrialisation. In the present chapter, Korea's spatial transformation (and a highly differentiated environmental landscape) is considered as a function of economic change. The initial section examines the transformation of space in Korea during the colonial period, as a prelude to an analysis of the post World War II period. Subsequently, the processes, determinants and the character of uneven spatial development are discussed.

The process of capitalist accumulation implies particular arrangements of space. The tendency towards spatial convergence and/or differentiation in the capitalist mode of development is often signified by patterns of uneven or combined development (O'Connor 1988, Smith 1984). Here we will investigate this tendency, as well as the influence of state policy on the spatial distribution of industrial activities and population in Korea.

It will be evident that the phases of spatial transformation correspond quite closely with the political-economic periods set out in Chapter 2: at the core lie changes in the mode of social regulation. Korea's spatial development from the beginning of industrialisation is thus presented according to the six phases identified: Japanese colonial, an interim phase, Taylorist, Yusin, peripheral Fordist, and neo-Fordist. Historical precedents to the postwar spatial developments may be observed.

Colonial modernisation

Japanese mercantilist phase

During the Yi Dynasty (1392–1910), Korean society remained remarkably unchanged, as did the spatial configuration of population and economic activities. The growth of a modest number of administrative towns and military garrisons meant only minimal increase in the overall level of urbanisation. The capital, Hansung (present day Seoul), was the largest urban centre. Its population in 1789 was 190,000, some one fifth of the country's total urban population. The second largest city was Kaesung (28,000), while the third was Pyongyang (22,000). Other cities with a population of more than 10,000 were Sangju, Jeonju, Taegu, Chungju, Euiju and Jinju (Hwang and Choi 1988, p.38).

It is of interest to note the hierarchical urban structure of Korea, especially between Seoul and other cities. Seoul was almost seven times larger than the second largest city and larger than the sum of the populations of the second to fourteenth largest urban centres. 'This high degree of primacy reflects three factors: Seoul was the capital city where most of the privileged upper class people lived; it was possible to sustain a large population because of abundant and fertile agricultural land close to Seoul; and Seoul was the nodal centre for all major transportation routes' (Hwang and Choi 1988, p.39). Our review of the history of Korea's spatial development will suggest that the above-mentioned conditions continued to act as centralising forces: indeed, as postwar capitalist development progressed, the primacy of Seoul reappeared.

The Japanese colonial period (1909–45) brought a transformation in patterns of migration or urbanisation inherited from the half-millennium of the Yi dynasty. A crucial factor was the opening of Korea's ports to foreign vessels in 1876. From that point until 1920, urban growth mainly centred around the coastal ports, increasing the number and size of cities. Pusan, Incheon and Nampo developed as major port cities of 20,000–80,000 inhabitants; Hamhung, Mokpo, Haeju, Kunsan, Songrim, Shineuiju and Chongjin grew to within the range 10,000–20,000 inhabitants (Kwon, Y-W. 1991, Hwang and Choi 1988).

The main force for urbanisation was increased trade overseas aided by then-current advances in maritime technology. With Korea's annexation in 1910, the expanding ports were the conduits for agricultural and mineral exports to Japan; they also developed as bases for Japanese immigrants and trading firms. Thus the agglomeration of capital, population and commodities occurred at these coastal cities. The number of Japanese residents in Korea rose from a mere 54 in 1876 to 12,203 in 1895, 42,460 in 1905 and 347,550 in 1920. However, all but one fifth of the in-comers from Japan remained in the ports and in the capital, Seoul (Kwon, Y-W. 1991).

Colonial agricultural policy and spatial development

From the 1920s on, significant changes began to occur in Korea's spatial patterns. The major forces of urban growth were now the extension of the railways, and colonial agricultural policy. Urban development hitherto restricted to port areas, started to spread inland through the construction of the rail network, bringing agglomeration of population and commodities at nodal points of railway system. The project to turn Korea into an agricultural hinterland for Japan required a well articulated rail infra-structure, which in turn brought migrants and urbanisation to the interior. From the opening of the first railway line in 1899 to 1914, major ports (Pusan, Incheon, Shineuiju, Nampo, Kunsan, Mokpo) were linked to Seoul, as well as to the regional capitals of Pyongyang and Daejeon. In order to expedite exports to Japan, major rice growing regions of south and north Korea were penetrated by the rail transportation network. New urban areas served as regional warehousing centres: Jeonju, Kwangju, Sariwon and Jinju. These centres were connected to the major exporting points of Mokpo, Kunsan, Suncheon, Yeosu, Choongmu, Masan and Haeju, which grew to accommodate 20,000–30,000 inhabitants, and Shineuiju, Hamhung, Wonsan, Chongju and Chaeju developed to the 30,000–50,000 range (Kwon, Y-W. 1991, Hwang and Choi 1988, pp.39–40).

Heavy industrialisation phase

As Japan penetrated into Manchuria in the early 1930s, Korea became a base for continental expansion, and urban and industrial transformation intensified. The fast-growing cities in this period were mining and manu-facturing centres in the North (such as Aozi, Haeryeong, Pyongyang, Nampo and Sariwon) and transportation and commercial centres in the South (such as Seoul, Daejeon, Jinju and Masan) (Hwang and Choi 1988, pp.39–40).

In the 1930s, the heavy industrialisation drive was implemented to supply industrial goods for Japan's imperial ventures in Manchuria, China and Southeast Asia. The rail network was extended to incorporate areas of mineral extraction, energy production and heavy manufacturing. With improvements in transportation and job opportunities in the developing industrial sector, urbanisation occurred at an even greater rate. Most of the industrial and urban growth in this period took place in the north-central and northeastern regions of Korea, locus of the bulk of minerals and

Table 3.1 Urbanisation during the colonial period (1000s)

	1910		1926		1935		1941	
	Person	*%*	*Person*	*%*	*Person*	*%*	*Person*	*%*
Total population	12,934	100.0	19,103	100.0	21,891	100.0	24,703	100.0
Number of people in urban areas								
Over 100,000	341	2.6	527	2.8	863	3.9	2,428	9.8
Over 50,000	596	4.6	658	3.4	1,325	6.1	3,163	12.8
Over 20,000	752	5.8	1,378	7.2	1,908	8.7	4,672	18.9

Source: Mills and Song (1979), p.58; *Chosen Sotokufu Tokei Nenpo*, (1910, 1926, 1935, 1941), cited in Mason (1980), p.80.

electricity generation. The north-eastern coastal cities also grew as a result of increasing trade between Japan and its industrialised inland areas. With the application of hydroelectric power, and with plentiful mineral and fishery resources, the north-western region was also incorporated into the new industrial space. It acted as the main transportation artery between the rest of Korea and Manchuria, which led to greater development of the region and its cities. Allied to a rich agriculture, the northwest became a highly productive region. This was reflected by the growth of Shineuiju and Haeju, each to over 100,000 (Kwon, Y-W. 1991).

Although most of the heavy industries were located in the north, the middle and southern parts of the peninsula continued to develop with their agricultural and light manufacturing industries. By 1940, the southern cities of Kwangju, Daejeon, Mokpo, Cheonju, Kunsan, Masan and Jinju entered the 50,000–100,000 size range, while Seoul developed into a city of one million. The growth of Seoul was due to its enhanced role as the centre of administration, communications and indeed, production. Much of the migration during the latter years of colonial period was to large urban areas: the rural population was under pressure from a relentless agricultural squeeze. The appearance of large slums in Seoul, Pusan and other major regional cities in this period testifies to inflows of the poverty-stricken rural dwellers (Kwon, Y-W. 1991). See Table 3.1 and Table 3.2.

Thus, the colonial period saw the intrusion of capitalist social relations in agricultural production, the development of both light and heavy industrial structures and a great increase in the number of urban centres. With the intensification of Korea's industrialisation during 1930–45, most expanded greatly. Indeed, this was the period in which Korea's modern

Table 3.2 Cities and urban population, 1789–1944

Year	Cities	Urban population ('000)	Urbanisation level (%)
1789	3	239	3.3
1907	5	288	2.2
1909	6	380	2.9
1914	7	467	2.9
1920	8	563	3.2
1925	19	1,059	5.7
1930	30	1,606	7.9
1935	41	2,234	10.2
1941	65	4,659	18.9
1944	74	5,067	19.6

Source: Kwon, Y-W. (1977), p.64, cited in Hwang and Choi (1988), p.40.

Notes:
Cities are defined by 'Shi' administrative classification.
'Urban population' is the population of the administratively designated cities.

urban structure was laid down. The colonial strategy of raw material extraction for export imposed a spatially uneven locational structure of economic activities. Most of the new industrial centres were located in the northern and southeastern coastal areas with efficient communications with Japan. The few inland industrial locations were confined to textiles and some basic consumer goods industries (Choe and Song 1984, p.78). The separation of the agricultural south from the relatively well-developed heavy manufacturing of the north also contributed to the economic imbalances of the postwar period.

Interim period: independence, war and the ISI regime (1945–60)

The spatial development of Korea underwent considerable changes after the country's liberation from Japanese rule in 1945. As seen above, during the colonial period there was significant urbanisation and industrialisation throughout the country. The pace of urbanisation in the postwar era was to be even more rapid and concentrated. According to official criteria, by 1990 the urban population constituted 79 per cent of the nation. It is clear that the spatial restructuring of Korea corresponds closely to changes in the mode of development; the uneven development of national space has been integral to this process.

Independence, Korean War and migration

The growth of cities from World War II until 1960 basically reflected the external political situation – the partition of the South and North, the Korean War (1950–53) and postwar rehabilitation. In this period, urbanisation was strongly influenced by the large-scale population dislocation associated with the war (Choe and Song 1984, Chon 1992, Hwang and Choi 1988).

Between 1945 and 1955, the massive flow of refugees was the major factor behind changes in urban size. Independence in 1945 was followed by the first influx of immigrants from China, Manchuria, Japan and the US. Korean labourers and soldiers forcibly mobilised by the Japanese colonial administration made a rapid return, as did other exiles. Alongside this, there was a huge migration from north of the 38th parallel, especially around 1949 when the border was threatened with closure. From 1945 to 1949, South Korea's increase in population due to net migration is estimated to stand at 3.32 million.[1] In this period, Seoul and the other large administrative centres (e.g. Pusan, Taegu, Kwangju and Daejeon), grew rapidly with the influx of refugees and repatriates (Hwang and Choi 1988, pp.40–41). During the turmoil of the Korean War there was a further increase in refugees from the north, and a general migration towards the southeastern regions. In 1955, the population rose to 21.5 million compared to 20.04 million in 1949. Much of the population concentration occurred in South Kyongsang and Kangwon provinces. Especially during the war, Pusan, which was the provisional capital, grew rapidly to contain over a million residents and migrants, and Wonju and Jinhae (military strongholds) developed into cities of 60,000–80,000 inhabitants. While Seoul, Taegu, Masan, Daejeon and Kwangju grew quite rapidly, the smaller cities, originally developed as commercial ports or as agricultural assembly points during the colonial period, grew very slowly or stagnated. Examples include Kunsan, Mokpo, Pohang and Jinju; these received much war damage or were hit hard by the termination of trade with Japan (Hwang and Choi 1988, p.41).

Reconstruction and the ISI regime of accumulation

The 1950s urban and industrial development featured reconstruction and rehabilitation, amelioration of war devastation was in particular centred around Seoul, Incheon and the Southeastern region. The important concentration of light manufacturing industries of Pusan was largely unscathed by the war, but elsewhere production needed to be totally recovered. To restore the primary sector, during the ISI period (1955–62) three major railway routes were opened to link mining areas. The Kangwon mining region, the northeast region of North Chungchong and northern region of North Kyongsang province now became new areas of population settlement and industrialisation. Elsewhere, most of the increase in the number of urban centres was due to the enlargement of city and township boundaries. The postwar baby-boom also contributed to the rapid rise in overall urban population; average annual increase during the 1950s and early 1960s stood at 7.9 per cent (Kwon, Y-W. 1991).

During the Japanese occupation, Pusan had the advantage of being the major Korean port close to Japan. Pusan served as both the major exporting port and the major light manufacturing centre of Korea. During the Korean War, as the only part of South Korea not largely destroyed by the war and occupied by the Communists, South Kyongsang province drew the majority of refugees. Consequently, there was a massive transfer of wealth from the rest of the country. Following the war, the two Kyongsang provinces received the second largest share of infrastructure investment and reconstruction aid from the United Nations Korea Reconstruction Agency. This stood at 17.3 per cent of the total, second only to Seoul's 19.8 per cent (Chon 1992, p.164).

Throughout the 1950s specific locational policy was sparse. The exceptions were the reconstruction of industrial establishments and the building of two new fertiliser plants in Chungju and Naju, and cement works in Munkyong and Danyang. The locational thinking behind these plants (built by the government or with strong government endorsement) was to minimise distribution costs. Locational decisions regarding government and monopolistic enterprises showed a different pattern from those governing small and medium sized private establishments. While competitive private enterprises could hardly dominate national markets, government and monopolistic enterprises like cement and fertiliser industries tended to divide the nation into a few large markets in order to minimise distribution cost (Choe and Song 1984, p.79).

Taylorist accumulation and migration (1961–72)

Efficiency, scale economy and industrial concentration

Following the coup d'état of 1960, Export-Oriented Industrialisation (EOI) based on labour intensive industries was established. Because Korea lacked intermediate industries, at this time most of the raw materials and intermediate goods were imported. For Korea to compete with other budding NICs in labour intensive low value products, it was essential to locate export industries near ports and along the major transportation arteries connected to ports. The location of existing ports thus largely determined the siting of industries.[2] Development of new port infrastructure would have been a huge burden at this early stage of the EOI regime. The ports of Pusan and Incheon, developed during the Japanese colonial period, became the main conduits for the 1960s government-induced industrialisation (Chon 1992, pp.159–163). The main thrust of locational policy in the First Five Year Economic Development Plan (1962–66) was the construction of industrial estates under the provisions of the *Export Industrial Estate Development Promotion Law* 1964 (Kwon, Y-W. 1991, Choe and Song 1984). The first Export Industrial Estate duty free zone was created in the Kuro-dong District of Seoul; others were then set up in Pusan and Incheon. The government provided state-owned land on preferential terms, as well as basic infrastructure such as water supply and access roads. The 1964 Act was not impressive in terms of financial incentives, confining its support to infrastructure provision (Choe and Song 1984, p.79). The industrial agglomeration and population growth of Seoul in the 1960s was partly related to the construction of export industrial estates in Seoul and Incheon (Park, S-O. 1991, p.83).

Transport infrastructure development led to the initial concentration of population and industries in Seoul and other large cities in the 1960s. There was also a shift of emphasis in the mode of transportation. In the First Plan (1962–66), priority was given to modernisation of the rail system; the Second Plan, saw the creation of a national road system, with 655 kilometres of expressways constructed in the 1967–71 period (Richardson and Baek 1988, p.155). In the early 1960s, no fewer than 31 new railways lines were opened, linking many of the mining areas and regional industrial centres.[3] In the late 1960s, implementation of the Second Economic Plan saw the opening of express highways which led to the huge expansion of automobile transportation. From the mid-1960s, the share of passenger transportation by motorised vehicle rose to 80–90 per cent, while that of rail and marine transportation declined to less than 20 per cent. The share of goods moved by road also rose to over 50 per cent (Kwon, Y-W. 1991). Thus, from the 1960s on, road transport played an increasing role in economic development as well as in the concentration of population. There was a corresponding decrease in the use of rail. The rising position of road transportation in the late 1960s had a direct impact on the volume and direction of migration: a long distance coach network provided the stimulus. Those cities at major transport nodes grew quickly: Daejeon, for example, expanded to a city of 900,000 (Kwon, Y-W. 1991). However, due to the lack of job opportunities in the small and medium sized cities, the final destination for migrants was often the two metropolitan cities of Seoul and Pusan. Transport development tended to stimulate both these end-point locations on the national highway system (Richardson and Baek 1988, p.152).

Population concentration in metropolitan cities

Urbanisation in the postwar era has been closely associated with industrialisation. Especially in the 1960s, the rapid growth of urban population was largely in response to the rapid and concentrated growth of labour intensive EOI industries in large urban centres. However, what is notable regarding this period is the high degree of concentration in a few large urban centres, particularly Seoul (Hwang and Choi 1988, p.41). During the 1966–70 period the population of Seoul expanded at a record rate of 9.4 per cent per annum, an absolute growth of 1.7 million equivalent to 77 per cent of the total national population increase. Net migration accounted for more than 80 per cent of Seoul's growth, the capital absorbing 60 per cent of the national figure. Of the in-migrants to Seoul, two-thirds came from rural areas. The main points of origin of migrants to Seoul were Kyonggi, South Chungchong and South Cholla provinces (Hwang and Choi 1988, p.44). The population of Seoul more than doubled from 2.6 million in 1960 to 5.5 million in 1970.

Table 3.3 shows the changes in population distribution in major urban and rural administrative areas. The data reveal that the population shift occurred from the *Myon*[4] (which recorded an absolute decline in population) to the *Shi*,[5] which grew at a rapid pace. However, this rapid urban growth was not equally distributed among all city size classes. For the 1960s, the larger the size of a city, the faster the population growth. On the other hand, small cities and towns, *Eup*[6] grew much more slowly than the large cities, and in many cases more slowly than the national population (Hwang and Choi 1988, p.43). Table 3.4 clearly shows that the rate of migration increased dramatically during the 1966–70 period, and it is

Table 3.3 Population distribution by administrative division, 1960–90

		1960	1970	1980	1985	1990
Eup (rural town)	Number	85	91	169	201	176
	Aggregate Population (%)	2,259 (9.0)	2,850 (9.1)	4,537 (12.1)	4,821 (11.9)	—
	Average pop.	27	31	27	24	—
Myon (rural district)	Number	1,400	1,376	1,256	1,241	1,252
	Aggregate Population (%)	15,734 (63.0)	15,654 (49.8)	11,461 (30.6)	9,188 (22.7)	—
	Average pop.	11	11	9	7	—
Gun[1] (county)	Number	140	140	141	142	137
	Aggregate Population (%)	17,992 (72.0)	18,506 (58.9)	16,002 (42.8)	14,006 (34.6)	11,102 (25.6)
	Average pop.	129	132	113	99	81
Shi (city)	Number	27	32	40	50	70
	Aggregate Population (%)	6,997 (28.0)	12,929 (41.1)	21,434 (57.2)	26,443 (65.4)	32,309 (74.4)
	Average pop.	259	404	535	529	462
National	Total pop. (%)	24,989 (100.0)	31,435 (100.0)	37,436 (100.0)	40,448 (100.0)	43,411 (100.0)

Source: Hwang and Choi (1988), p.42, Seoul Metro. Government, *Comparative Statistics of Major Cities,* (1989, 1990, 1991), National Statistical Office, *Korea Statistical Yearbook,* 1993.

Note:
1 Gun, considered as rural, consists of Eup and Myon.
Population is in thousands; population % is to total population.

related to the size of cities: most rapid for the largest, and slowest for the smallest. This explicitly shows the concentration of population in the larger cities, particularly Seoul and Pusan. Seoul's share of the national population increased from 7.3 per cent in 1955 to 23.8 per cent in 1985, when it accommodated over 9.6 million, with millions more in the Seoul Metropolitan Area (SMA) as a whole.

Rapid urbanisation, particularly in Seoul and Pusan, had a number of related and mutually reinforcing causes. The booming economy based on labour intensive manufacturing industries was heavily concentrated on Seoul, where over 45 per cent of the total increase in national secondary and tertiary employment occurred in the 1966–70 period. The concentration of industries and job opportunities was largely responsible for the swift increase in in-migration. While urban industrial wages were rapidly rising, the subsistence farming stagnated, this creating strong forces of both 'pull' and 'push' (Hwang and Choi 1988, p.44). The dominance of the Seoul economy over the rest of the country was reinforced by the cumulative

Table 3.4 Population increase rate of urban centres by size class, 1960–70, 1970 boundaries

Administrative areas	Annual rate of increase (%)	
	1960–66	1967–70
Seoul (5,536,000)[1]	6.53	9.37
Pusan (1,881,000)[1]	2.90	6.85
Taegu (1,083,000)[1]	5.10	6.12
Other *Shi*;		
500,000–999,999	5.18	5.20
100,000–499,999	3.01	4.85
Under 100,000	2.80	3.02
All *Eup*	2.03	2.01

Source: Cited in Hwang and Choi (1988), p.43.

Note:
1 1970 figures for population of metropolitan cities.

causation of urban growth, concentration of labour and further infrastructural provision which in turn stimulated further industrial concentration and migration (Kwon, W-Y. 1988b, pp.106–108). Significant improvements in the road transportation system enabled migrants to shift to the metropolitan cities readily and cheaply.

However, the rate of in-migration was not matched by the enlargement of employment opportunities. Many rural migrants failed to compete successfully in the urban labour market, swelling the ranks of the urban poor. The metropolitan cities saw a huge growth in squatter settlements, with all their attendant social tensions. Thus, labour intensive industrialisation by the mid-1960s became a barrier to further economic development. The urban land market proved unresponsive, and heightened demand brought prices which inhibited further large-scale development. Rather than a factor for driving down wages, surplus labour in the large cities was increasingly considered a threat to social stability. As a consequence, after 1964 the stemming of population concentration in Seoul became the most pressing issue in spatial policy. The government introduced a battery of strong policy measures which in the event did not take full effect until the 1970s (Kwon, W-Y. 1988b, pp.106–108).[7]

Industrial restructuring and a new spatial order (1972–80)

By the late 1960s, the Park regime faced major economic and social problems that were clearly threatening its legitimacy. On the economic front, the labour intensive EOI strategy of the 1960s was beginning to falter because of alterations in export markets and the rising import costs of intermediate goods. On the social side, industrial developments centred around large cities were widening the income gap between urban and rural households, while the rapid rural–urban migration of the late 1960s had created growing squatter settlements and a large class of urban poor who had little prospect of employment in the formal sector. Economic and social problems were threatening both the preconditions of accumulation and political stability too. In addition, the growing concentration of industries and population in Seoul was leading to urban diseconomies, pollution and deepening concerns over national security.[8] Seoul's dominance in the national urban system had brought a marked interregional inequity and a perception of the city as a separate entity – often dubbed the 'Seoul Republic'. The growing diseconomies of Seoul and Pusan were considered to be a threat to the nation's economic stability (Kwon 1988b, p.108).

In 1972, therefore, the government introduced significant policy changes which aimed to restructure both the economy in general and Korea's spatial configuration. These adjustments sought to reduce import dependence by substitution strategies for intermediate goods, at the same time promoting capital and technology-intensive industries producing export goods for a changing global market. Policies designed to restructure industrial space to the requirements of the new industrial drive involved the provision of infrastructure for decentralisation and spatial expansion. Associated measures sought to implement a population decentralisation policy so as to moderate the urban socio-economic problems which had arisen in the 1960s.

Industrial decentralisation and the state

Measures to deal with growing industrial and population concentration were introduced in 1964, with the Special Measures for the Restriction of Population Growth in the Seoul Metropolitan Area (KRIHS 1984). Various policy options were now considered including the relocation of government offices, the construction of new industrial cities, and restrictions on the expansion of industrial and higher educational facilities in Seoul (Kim and Masser 1990, pp.34–35). Although such spatial policies were not implemented until the 1970s, they had a strong influence on later developments.

The government also introduced the First Comprehensive National Land Development Plan (1972–81), an explicit framework for future physical development and the ironing out of perceived regional disparities (Kwon 1988b). The plan also emphasised 'efficiency maximisation' and 'self-sufficiency' (MoC 1971). Its objectives included population decentralisation from the Seoul region, industrial distribution and infrastructure development. The concept of the 'planning region' was introduced (Kwon 1988b, p.111). The Plan divided the country into eight subregions according to their 'characteristics', to *maximise* their contribution to economic development, rather than to achieve any notion of balanced regional development. It defined five categories of functional zone to enhance the efficiency of land use and management: agricultural, forestry, urban, natural and cultural conservation and continental shelf (MoC 1971, p.14). The zoning of national space and the application of such controls induced further uneven development in terms of industrial location and the composition of the regional economy since it tried to concentrate production in terms of regional characteristics. That is, the southeastern regions were seen as suitable for heavy and chemical industrialisation, while the southwestern regions were designated for agricultural production.

Other important elements of the plan included the continued emphasis upon agglomeration as the most efficient path to development. 'Developed' areas or regions were identified, which had basic levels of infrastructure and skilled labour, and the purpose was then to concentrate industries in such areas. In the 1970s, the state took responsibility for the construction of a large proportion of new industrial estates and infrastructure, and this clearly influenced the location of manufacturing. In conjunction with the industrial redistribution strategy, the Plan offered a framework for physical development by providing public utility and resource development such as reservoirs for water supply and power generation for the new industrial areas (MoC 1971). It also concerned itself with national land conservation issues – for instance, designation of green belts[9] and national parks (Kwon, W-Y. 1988b, pp.111–112).

Under this overall national framework, the state introduced various items of legislation to aid the spatial dispersal of industries and population: the *Industrial Site Development Law* 1973, the *Local Industrial Development Law* (LIDL) 1970, the *Free Export Zone Establishment Law* 1970, and the *Industrial Distribution Law* (IDL) 1977.

The government's sectoral policy of heavy and chemical industrialisation was implemented in conjunction with the 1973 *Industrial Site Development Law*, which was effective in locating industries in Southeastern coastal regions through the provision of large industrial parks. Between 1972 and 1976, 74 per cent of total expenditure on industrial estates for heavy and chemical industries was allocated to the Southeastern region (KRIHS 1982). At this time, these accounted for about 70 per cent of the total area of industrial estates in Korea (Park, S-O. 1991, pp.83–85). Not only did the Southeastern region receive the bulk of the industrial estates, but it also gained the largest share of port and road infrastructure investment outside the Capital region. Korea's largest shipbuilding yard was located at Ulsan, and its largest steel mill at Pohang. Thus, there was a rapid growth of new industrial cities in this region.

Industrial dispersal from Seoul was more difficult and several strong measures were promulgated. Under the 1970 *Free Export Zone Establishment Law*, industrial export estates were built in Masan and Iri to pull foreign investment away from the Capital region. Local industrial development, was promoted by the 1970 LIDL programme through site provision, infrastructure such as access to roads, water and energy supply, as well as tax exemptions and subsidies. In addition, a novel 'standard land price' system was adopted for purchasing sites for industrial use. This system froze the price of land required by the government for public purposes to inhibit land speculation (Kwon 1988b, pp.121–125). During the early 1970s under the LIDL, ten small- to medium-sized industrial estates were developed at Jeonju, Taegu, Chongju, Kwangju, Daejeon, Chunchon, Kumi, Mokpo, Iri and Wonju; over a dozen more were planned. However, the incentives intended to attract plants to these designated areas proved insufficient to overcome the costs of relocation (Park, S-O. 1991, pp.83–85). Many of the local industrial estates remained empty or operated at less than 20 per cent capacity.[10] This caused much financial difficulty to local authorities, and led to a reduction in their social expenditure. The local industrial estates programme largely failed in its aim of dispersing industrial activities and developing the economies of depressed areas (Choe and Song 1984, pp.79–81).

As Table 3.5 shows, the dispersal of industries from Seoul was very slow until 1976 due to the weakness of the decentralisation policies. In order to speed up the process, in 1977 the government introduced its *Industrial Distribution Law*. This was largely modelled on the UK's Industrial Development Certificate scheme introduced in 1947, and also on Japan's *Industrial Relocation Law* of 1972. The legislation divided the country into three areas: (a) a dispersal zone including Seoul and its northern vicinity from which relocation of industrial plants was to be encouraged; (b) a status quo zone, encompassing Pusan, its vicinity and also Seoul's satellite cities, where industrial expansion was to be discouraged; and (c) an inducement zone comprising the rest of the country where industrial development was to be further encouraged (Park, S-O. 1991, pp.83–85).

The policy instruments of the IDL were both stronger and more diversified than those introduced by the LIDL. They offered the same

Table 3.5 Mining and manufacturing GNP by region, 1968–76 (%)

	1968	*1970*	*1972*	*1974*	*1976*
Seoul	28.7	28.9	28.9	26.4	23.5
Pusan	15.0	13.7	14.0	14.1	13.1
Kyonggi	10.0	11.2	15.2	16.5	19.5
Kangwon	7.6	5.7	5.0	4.5	3.6
North Chungchong	3.9	3.8	2.7	2.9	2.9
South Chungchong	6.4	6.8	5.8	4.3	3.9
North Cholla	4.0	3.7	3.0	2.8	2.4
South Cholla	4.2	5.6	5.4	5.5	5.6
North Kyongsang	9.4	8.6	8.0	8.2	10.5
South Kyongsang	10.7	11.7	11.8	14.6	14.9
Chaeju	0.4	0.4	0.2	0.2	0.9
Total	100.0	100.0	100.0	100.0	100.0

Source: Kim (1993), p.23.

range of positive incentives as the LIDL but in addition provided loans for relocating industrial premises. The most significant measures were their powers to issue relocation orders and restrict on-site expansion in the dispersal zone. The Act also gave the government discretionary powers in granting permissions in the location of manufacturing plants and in enforcing specific measures such as plant investment in pollution miti- gating facilities (Kwon 1988b, pp.121–125).[11]

Such controls had a considerable impact on industrial decentralisation from Seoul. For example, in an investigation of the major reasons for locating in Banweol industrial estate (in Kyonggi Province), more than 60 per cent of the surveyed firms had been served with relocation orders to move from zones in which they did not meet legal or anti-pollution requirements (Choe and Song 1984, p.99). The re-zoning of industrial land to other uses, and rising land prices, were responsible for gradually reducing the concentration of manufacturing industries in Seoul. Between 1966 and 1983, Seoul's share of value-added manufacturing output fell from 32 to 16 per cent, this paralleled by its dwindling share of manu- facturing employment (Kwon 1988b, pp.121–125, see Figure 3.5, this volume). Though locational policies had a considerable impact on the level of industrial suburbanisation from Seoul into the adjacent areas of the Capital region, it stimulated only limited dispersal from Seoul to more distant developing areas. Only 2.5 per cent of the plants relocated from Seoul went beyond the Capital region, and thus there was only limited impact on the distribution of industry. Overall, the relatively ungenerous financial incentives of the 1970s' spatial policies failed to provoke any wholesale industrial decentralisation (Park, S-O. 1991, pp.83–85). The concentration of industries in the Capital and Southeastern regions and the limited development of secondary cities such as Daejeon, Kwangju, Chongju and Taegu resulted in 'bi-polar' development – Pusan and Seoul (Chon 1992, Kwon 1988b, Richardson and Hwang 1988). Polarisation reversal was largely limited, (Douglass 1993) due to the centralised economic and political functions of the state and the competitive mode of regulation.[12] Access to, and competition for, loans and other economic and social amenities meant that concentration of economic activities continued to occur in Seoul.

Corporatist regulation, division of labour and new spatial relationships

The decentralisation of manufacturing industries in the 1970s led to a reorganisation in the production processes giving rise to a new division of labour. As had been the case in the core countries, Korean manufacturing capital experienced a vertical disintegration of the Fordist labour process. This disintegration of labour functions heralded the formation of a new spatial structure. The central decision making function, R&D and general administrative and managerial functions remained in the capital or in the large urban centres, while manufacturing and assembly plants moved out to peripheral regional sites. By the late 1970s, distinct spatial patterns could be observed. While the provincial regions of Seoul and Pusan established themselves as the new industrial space, the city of Seoul started to de-industrialise and establish itself as a financial, cultural, administrative and control centre of the nation.

The study by S-O. Park (1986) clearly shows the tendency towards manufacturing decentralisation while corporate headquarters remained in Seoul and Pusan (see Figure 3.1). Park revealed that this trend was led by those chaebol groups involved in heavy and chemical industries. The main reasons for the regionalisation of manufacturing units lay in scale economies, cheaper labour costs and state incentives. On the other hand, the trend towards concentration of headquarter locations was determined by the need to be close to economic agencies of the state which had much control over financial institutions, these mainly found in Seoul (Kim and Masser 1990, pp.19–21). Thus, the extent of the spatial dispersal of industry as a whole was limited. Though the majority of the heavy and chemical industries were located in the Southeast region, the dominant trend of other sectors of industry was to agglomerate in the region south of Seoul (Park, S-O. 1986). By 1982, 85 per cent of the headquarters controlling spatially separated plants were in Seoul.

This new spatial arrangement had social as well as spatial implications. First, the dominance of Seoul over other regions was strengthened. The authority of decision making on investments in new manufacturing plant, facility relocation or expansion, marketing strategies, specialist labour recruitment, investment for R&D and even other general material supplies for plants remained with company headquarters in Seoul. Decision making authority at plant level was negligible (Park, S-O. 1986). The spatial concentration of firms and group headquarters in Seoul meant that control over the Korean space-economy from the capital city remained unchallenged through the period of rapid industrial expansion (Douglass 1993, p.159).

Second, the vertical disintegration of Fordist production processes and the decentralisation of manufacturing could be interpreted as Seoul's economic structure having transformed to a post-industrial stage. By the end of the 1970s, Seoul's economy was dominated by financial, retail, and other services, by international trade, corporate managerial and state administrative functions. Table 3.6 shows that while white-collar managerial jobs increased in the late 1970s, manufacturing blue-collar jobs declined rapidly. It also shows the increasing consumption orientation associated with a growing monied and propertied class based in Seoul. Furthermore, with promotion decisions almost exclusively in the gift of group HQs, and the concentration of social amenities such as high quality education in Seoul, senior and middle managers were (and are) generally reluctant to

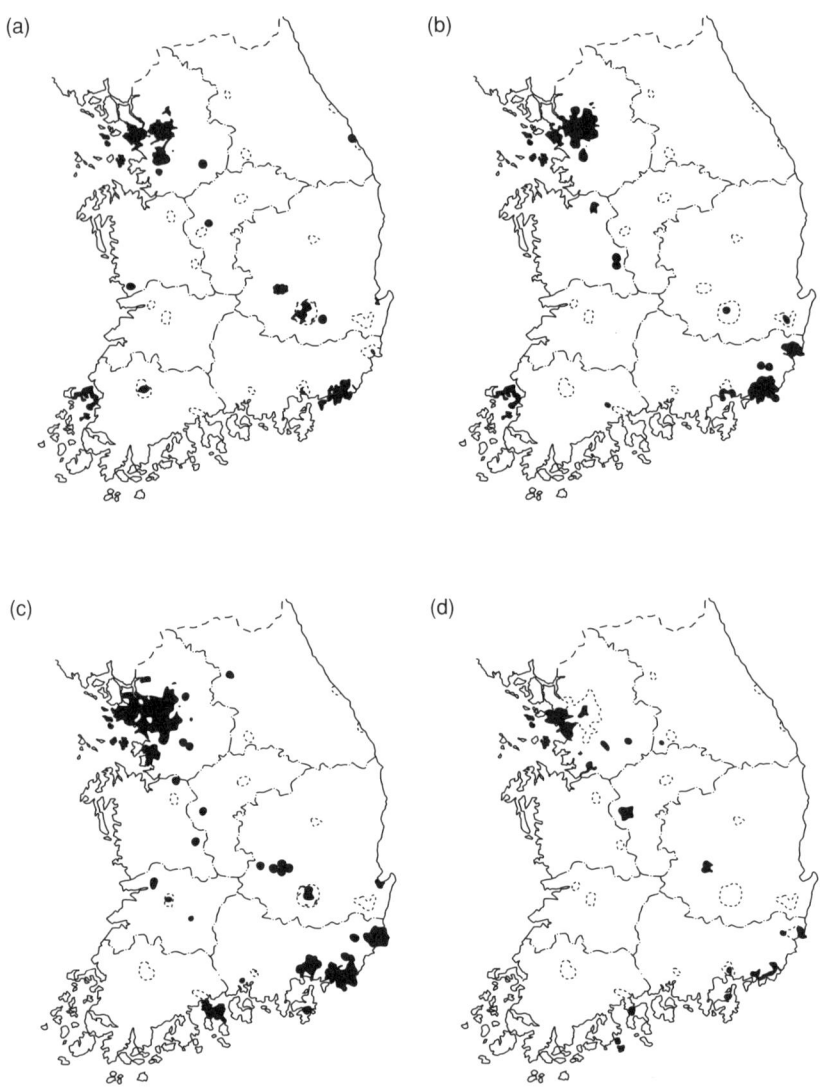

Figure 3.1 Locations of new company HQs, successive periods, 1950s–80s.

Source: Park, S-O. (1986), p.321.

Note:
(a) Before 1960; (b) 1960–69; (c) 1970–79; (d) 1980–84.

reside in peripheral areas. In the case of plants located in the suburbs of
Seoul (Kyonggi Province), most staff commute from Seoul. If the plants
are further away, managers generally live alone in company accommodation, while their families remain in Seoul (Park, S-O. 1986, pp.329–331).

Table 3.6 Seoul: indicators of concentration

Ratio[1]	Indicator	Year	Indicator	Year
<20%	Total population (17.6)	1970	Value added in manufacturing (18.5)	1980
20–29%	Number of manufacturing firms (23.7)	1970	Employees in manufacturing (22.1)	1980
	National wealth (26.3)	1968	Total population (22.3)	1980
	Gross product (26.5)	1970	Number of manufacturing firms (24.8)	1980
	Employees in manufacturing (28.2)	1970	Gross product (29.3)	1980
30–39%	Tax revenue (32.3)	1970	Tax revenue (33.3)	1980
	Retail and wholesale trade volume (32.3)	1970	Mail transaction (33.9)	1980
	Construction workers (32.3)	1971	National tax collection (34.2)	
	Value added in manufacturing (34.7)	1976	National wealth (34.5)	1977
	Mail transaction (38.1)	1970	Retail and wholesale trade volume (36.5)	1979
		1970		
40–80%	Automobiles (49.9)	1970	Construction workers (56.5)	1980
	National tax collection (50.1)	1970	Automobiles (57.9)	1980
	Bank loans (54.4)	1970		
	Bank deposits (63.4)	1970	Bank loans (63.9)	1980
	Managerial jobs (77.0)	1975	Bank deposits (64.9)	1980
>80%			Managerial jobs (81.0)	1980

Source: Kwon (1988b), p.109.

Note:
1 Ratio means Seoul's share in comparison with the national total.

The concentration of control functions, and preference of white-collar workers for a Seoul domicile, have created spatially distinct class divisions between Seoul and Korea's other industrial cities.

Third, the possibility of real regionalisation and decentralisation has now become much more remote, with regional disparities actually growing further. The spatial division of labour and the concentration of corporate head-quarters have also meant that much of the surpluses created in the non-core regions do not return. Rather they find their way to Seoul, further bolstering the capital at the expense of the rest of the nation. The local employment impact in such regions has typically been limited to low level jobs, while forward and backward material linkages within local areas by plants of the chae-bol groups have been negligible. Plants located in the provincial areas may, of course, perform better than the average for all industry in terms of wages, employment scale and employment growth. However, as long as the units located in provincial areas have little autonomy, their contribution to regional development will remain low (Park, S-O. 1986, p.331). The paucity of ties with the localities and the absence of incentives for firms to invest in social and environmental facilities for the local community means that key manufacturing centres like Ulsan, Pohang and Kumi have a legacy of poor environmental quality. They are regarded as 'pollution poles'.

Population distribution and new spatial structure

Industrial decentralisation strategies did create a distribution of population in the 1970s which differed markedly to that of the 1960s. During the 1970s, there were three distinct features: first, with the forced relocation of manufacturing industries from Seoul, the rate of in-migration to Seoul dropped significantly from its peak rate of 9.4 per cent in the late 1960s to 4.4 per cent and 3.9 per cent in the 1970–75 and 1975–80 periods respectively (Hwang and Choi 1988, p.45). There was also a trend towards out-migration from Seoul. In 1979–80 about 3 per cent of the city's households (about 50,000) moved out to the suburban areas, with 25,000 household heads commuting back to Seoul.

Second, the major increases in population occurred in the new industrial spaces of the Capital and Southeast regions. The rapid population growth of counties in Kyonggi seems to correlate with the industrial dispersal from Seoul to its satellite cities. Out of twenty counties with growing population, ten were located within the Capital region, and most of the others were near to large industrial towns in the Southeast region. The population increases occurred in the planned new industrial cities (Changwon, Ulsan, Pohang, Kumi and Ansan) in the Southeast region and the satellite cities around Seoul (Seongnam, Bucheon and Anyang). Cities such as Bucheon and Anyang in the Capital region saw particularly fast population growth rates – at 14.2 per cent and 12.6 per cent respectively. This was due to functional interdependence with Seoul and industrial relocation (Hwang and Choi 1988, p.45). Although other regional centres such as Taegu, Kwangju and Daejeon also experienced substantial growth, they were not able to redress the 'bi-polar' spatial pattern of Korea's urban development (Hwang and Choi 1988, p.47).

Lastly, the peripheral regions which received little industrial development experienced a decline in population. This was in contrast to the 1960s, when even with higher rural–urban migration, high fertility rates ensured positive growth rates. Even Yeocheon industrial town in the Southwest region failed to grow, and indeed became a 'pollution pole' (Kwon 1988b, pp.121–125).

During the Yusin phase of accumulation, the state's sectoral and regional policies created a certain dispersal of industries and population to the provincial cities of the Capital and Southeast regions. The pursuit of H-C industrialisation greatly influenced the development of the Southeast region, while the 1977 *Industrial Distribution Law* was mainly responsible for the suburbanisation of industries in the Capital region. This dispersal of industries to the provincial areas led both to their growth in population and the de-industrialisation of Seoul: the new spatial division of labour reflected the disintegration of Fordist production processes. Restructuring during the 1970s was clearly state-initiated. It was, however, inhibited by the constraints of the pre-existing spatial form of the 1960s. In addition, the mode of social regulation necessitated proximity between business elites and state institutions (Kim and Masser 1990, pp.19–21). The consequence of spatial development in the 1970s was 'bi-polar development', underdevelopment of peripheral regions and spatial differentiation of classes.

With national land use zoning, which segregated rural activities from industrial and urban functions, all this led to the beginnings of a tripartite spatial structure, where each zone was characterised by differing economic functions and by differing class composition.

Peripheral Fordist accumulation and megalopolisation (1980–88)

In 1980, the structural crisis stemming from external shocks and domestic inefficiencies led to the transformation of both the accumulation regime and the MSR. The successor regime was associated with new types of industries related to high-tech and consumer durables: an extensive accumulation regime had now been replaced by an intensive one. The new competitive MSR reinforced the intensive regime of accumulation in order to reduce the dependence of Korean capital on state financial incentives. Reduced protection from international competition meant more competitive labour relations. The state's policy of sectoral bias of the 1970s favouring heavy and chemical industries was now altered to a more 'balanced' industrial policy emphasising domestic and international competitiveness. The Chun regime (1980–88), although pressing competition and a free market philosophy, maintained its control over the financial sector and thus over the economy as a whole. This resulted in a heightened concentration of industrial activities in the Seoul Metropolitan Region, as access to bank loans and capital borrowing depended on the proximity to, and personal relations with, political and bureaucratic power, which remained firmly in Seoul (Kim and Masser 1990). There was an alteration in the basic philosophy regarding spatial strategy, and after 1980, this promoted a rapid agglomeration of industrial activity in the Capital region.

Interregional equity vs. intraregional balance

The growing regional disparities of the 1970s brought in the following decade state strategies aimed at promoting interregional equity while at the same time reducing intraregional bottlenecks. These were competing policies: while the state advocated interregional development through the *Second Ten Year Comprehensive National Physical Development Plan* (1982–91), it also accommodated the growth of the Capital region through a Metropolitan Growth Management Plan, the development of new towns and the improvement of the intraregional transportation system.

The interregional spatial strategy of the peripheral Fordist period relied on the provisions of the Second Ten Year Comprehensive National Physical Development Plan. Its basic goals: (1) inducement of population settlement in regional urban centres, (2) promotion of development potential in all regions, (3) advancement of people's welfare and (4) conservation of the environment (MoC 1982, pp.3–17). The Plan promoted 'growth centres' rather than the 'growth poles' of the 1960s and 1970s, which had been blamed for a dichotomised development pattern. The new strategy intended to establish local 'population dams' to restrict migration to the large cities. Designated growth centres within the Integrated Regional Settlement Areas (IRSA) aimed to reduce regional disparities and encourage people to stay in their own localities. This was to be achieved by enhancing employment opportunities and improving a range of amenities in order to create regional self-sufficiency. In the words of the Ministry of Construction (1982): 'The IRSA is a regional unit which combines a regional central city with its hinterland farming areas in which productive, living and natural environments will be developed on an integrated basis' (p.18). The new strategy was intended to be one of a decentralised concentration providing substantial investment in service infrastructure, and promoting sizeable provincial cities as points of attraction for migrants who would otherwise go to Seoul (MoC 1982, Kwon 1988b, pp.112–113). The country was divided into twenty-eight IRSAs,[13] in three categories according to the particularities of each, including the size of the central city. Identified were five large city IRSAs, seventeen local city IRSAs and six rural town IRSAs (MoC 1982, pp.18–20). Of the twenty-eight IRSAs, only fifteen cities and towns were designated as growth centres, and more than half of these were located in the depressed areas of Kangwon, North Chungchong, and North and South Cholla provinces, all of which had stagnant population growth in the 1970s (Kim and Masser 1990, Kwon 1988b, MoC 1982). See Figure 3.2.

Planning measures for implementing the growth centre policy included:

(i)   incentives for labour intensive manufacturing establishments, for example, the expansion of local industrial estates and tax exemptions;

(ii) provision of sites for universities and research organisations relocated from Seoul;

(iii) improving the transportation network among growth centres and between each growth centre and its hinterland;

(iv) delegation of administrative power to local governments;

(v)   enactment of the Growth Centre Promotion Law to finance its implementation.

(Kwon 1988b, p.114)

To expedite the development of growth centres, rural industrial activities were also fostered under the terms of the *Farm Household Income Source*

Development Law 1983. In addition to incentives available under the IDL, the legislation provided special low interest loans to cover part of the costs of plant operation and facilities. From the mid-1980s, small industrial estates (33,000 to 66,000 m^2) were built in many small cities to provide off-farm jobs for rural people. Eighty rural industrial zones were designated between 1984 and 1988; by mid-1988 twenty-seven had plants in operation (Park 1991, pp.85–86). Around half of these rural industrial estates were concentrated in the North and South Chungchong Provinces, adjoining the Seoul Metropolitan Region (Kim and Masser 1990, p.36). The scheme was thus effective in decentralisation to peripheral regions of labour intensive low value added industries. Regional strategies to alleviate growing diseconomies and to control the industrial and urban developments in the Capital region centred around the Growth Control and Management Plan for the Capital Region (1982–91). This aimed to maintain the green belt, while designating five subregions reflecting different degrees of land use control (special development, restricted development, controlled development, environmental protection and encouraged development). Each of these entailed a different and discriminating implementation of programmes for the region (see Figure 3.3).[14] The basic strategy was to reserve the Special Development and Environmental Protection Subregions as open spaces for future use and for national security purposes, while extensively developing the southwestern part of the Capital region to absorb the population and industries dispersed from other restricted regions (Kwon 1988b, pp.116–117). Other elements included de-concentration of central managerial functions to satellite cities, developing small-scale industrial complexes in the Ahsan Bay area and Banweol in the southwest, establishment of university campus towns and other service centres in the southeast, and construction of a second international airport and an express-way on the west coast (Richardson and Hwang 1988, pp.17 18, Kwon 1988b, p.120).

The Growth Management Plan's promotion of industrial development in the southern part of the Capital region and the accommodation of population in the new towns were not in harmony with the regional decentralisation policies laid out in the National Physical Development Plan. The difficulties of inducing industrial decentralisation to the provincial cities while simultaneously promoting the Capital region were manifest. The macro-economic and sectoral policies in operation meant that agglomeration in the Capital region could not be mitigated without more directional policies. The state's preoccupation with intraregional balance in fact intensified concentration. The resulting suburban concentration of industries and population, therefore, could be attributed to the policy contradictions in the two plans. This trend continued to intensify in the 1990s due to the continuation of the policy structure.

Significant but unanticipated spatial impacts were also inherent in the Five Year Economic Development Plans implemented after 1962. As a

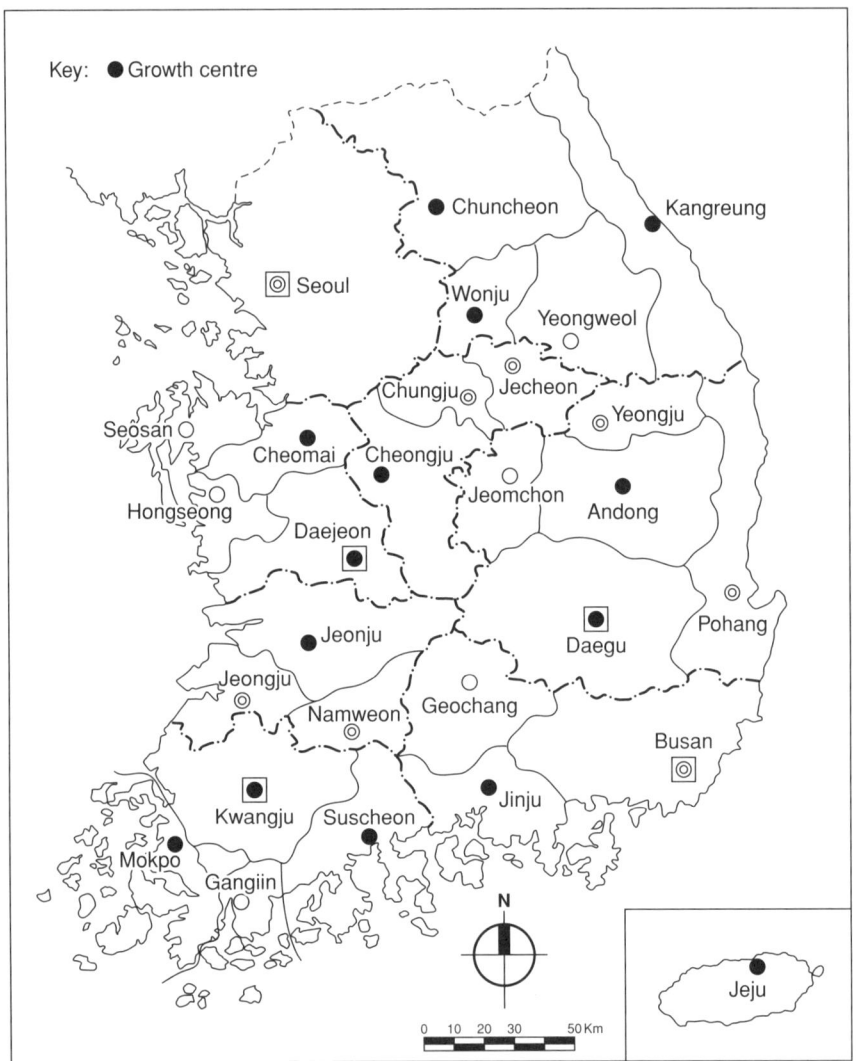

Key: ● Growth centre

Figure 3.2 Growth centres and integrated regional settlement areas.
Source: Kwon (1988b), p.137.

consequence of developments over the preceding two decades, the Sixth
Five-Year Economic and Social Development Plan (1987–91) for the first
time included 'balanced regional development' as one of its policy goals.
The concepts were vague and encompassed much the same aims as other
specifically spatial plans (the Second Comprehensive National Physical
Development Plan and the Growth Management Plan for the Capital
Region). The main strategy of regional balanced development in the Sixth

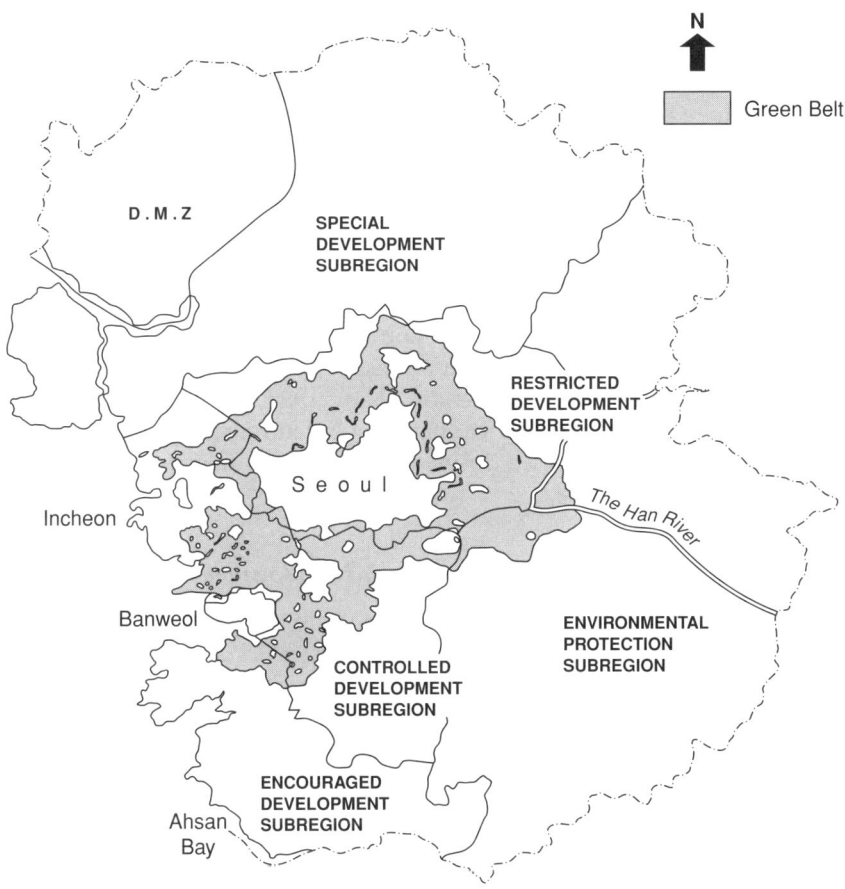

N

Green Belt

D . M . Z

SPECIAL
DEVELOPMENT
SUBREGION

RESTRICTED
DEVELOPMENT
SUBREGION

S e o u l

Incheon

The Han River

Banweol

ENVIRONMENTAL
PROTECTION
SUBREGION

CONTROLLED
DEVELOPMENT
SUBREGION

ENCOURAGED
DEVELOPMENT
Ahsan   SUBREGION
Bay

Figure 3.3 Land-use control in the Growth Control and Management Plan for the
Capital Region, 1982–91.

Source: Kwon (1988b), p.188.

Plan was to be met through the provision of social and physical infrastructure in the small urban and rural areas in the depressed regions. However,
the force of economic factors involving changes in the financial institutions
and the various incentives to promote industrial development caused the
new competitive mode of regulation to countermand the loose decentralisation policies of the Sixth Plan (Richardson and Hwang 1988, pp.14–15).
The government's preoccupation with rapid economic growth meant that
priority was given to the relief of metropolitan diseconomies through
demand-led infrastructure development. This undermined the goal of more
equitable distribution of infrastructure between regions and thus balanced
development which was the express purpose of the Sixth Plan and the

Second Ten Year National Physical Development Plan. Due to the programme being led by demand, the areas with highest demand for transport infrastructure received the highest investment. The 'regional bias'[15] of this plan has been clearly demonstrated in the study done by Kim (1993): Seoul, Incheon and Kyonggi region received 38.9 per cent of total investment, while the Southeast region received 27 per cent. By contrast, the Central region received 9.5 per cent, the Southwest region 13.4 per cent and other regions (Kangwon and Chaeju) saw 3.7 per cent of the national investment (7.5 per cent of the expenditure was invested in non-regional-specific schemes)[16]. Investment priorities were mainly based upon the functional requirements of the regional economic structure, rather than the size of population or region. Regional economic growth disparities were, thus, closely related to investment allocation, as industrial location was closely influenced by infrastructure provision (Kim 1993, p.49). The cycle of greater industrial concentration leading to higher infrastructural investment in the Capital region increased during the 1980s, with the neo-liberal market orientation of the state.

Intensive accumulation and industrial agglomeration in the Capital region

Due to the contradictory goals within spatial strategies and the strength of sectoral policies and competitive regulation, the distribution of industries in the 1980s was strongly biased towards the Capital region. Figure 3.4 shows the distribution of manufacturing employment by regions throughout the rapid industrialisation period, while Figure 3.5 demonstrates the situation within the Capital region. As these two graphs indicate, the labour intensive industrialisation of the 1960s saw a rapid rise in manufacturing jobs in Seoul; in the 1970s' heavy chemical industrialisation period it was the Southeast region which rapidly increased its share of manufacturing employment. The Capital region saw its share decline slightly, but throughout the two decades the peripheral regions, and especially the Southwest region experienced rapid reductions. Figure 3.4 also clearly illustrates the huge gap between the developed regions and the underdeveloped regions in manufacturing employment (and hence their role in overall industrial development). The 1980s saw a reverse trend: the Capital region increased its share of manufacturing employment, while the Southeast region experienced a decline. The peripheral regions continued to be steady but at a very low level. This demonstrates that the 1980s marked the end of the heavy chemical industrial drive based largely on the Southeast region, and there was a clear trend towards industrial concentration in the Capital region. Figure 3.5 shows that industrial concentration occurred in Kyonggi Province rather than in Seoul, which continued its rapid loss of manufacturing employment. The building of the Ahsan industrial complex at the southern edge of the Capital region in the late 1970s, and its operation in the 1980s meant that

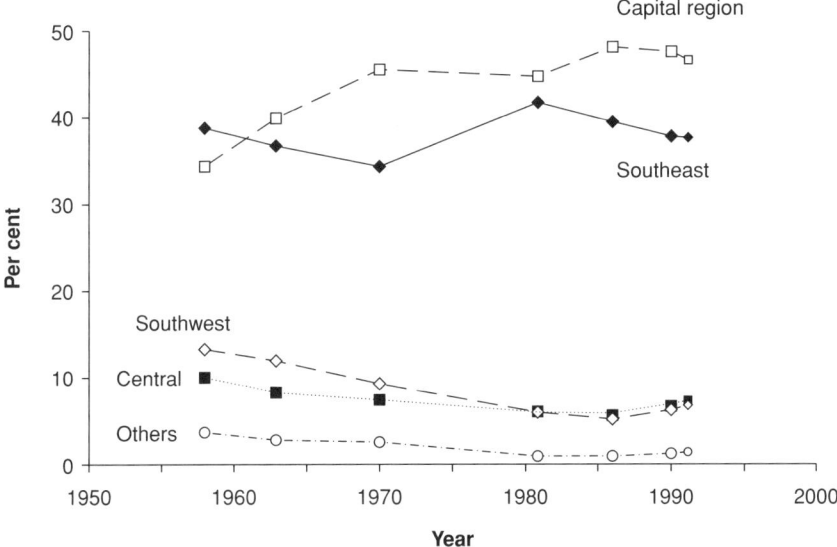

Figure 3.4 Distribution of manufacturing employment by regions, 1958–91.
Source: Data from Park, S-O. (1991), p.83; NSO, (1993).

even the heavy chemical industrial output was dominated by the Capital region.

The high concentration of new industrial activities and employment opportunities in the Seoul Metropolitan Region in the 1980s is shown in Table 3.7. While the peripheral regions such as North and South Cholla Provinces, Kangwon Province and North and South Chungchong Provinces saw the rate of increase of manufacturing workers drop in the 1980–85 period compared to the 1970–80 period, the Capital region had a rate of increase of over 6 per cent in the same period. Over half of the new manufacturing jobs for 1980–85 were in the Capital region, whereas the peripheral areas received only 18 per cent of the new manufacturing jobs. The Southeast region gained slightly compared to the previous period. This confirms the tendency of reconcentration of manufacturing jobs in the Capital region in the peripheral Fordist regime.

The overall spatial distribution of industries showed a marked changed from the situation of the 1960s and 1970s: now, a more spatially differentiated pattern of location between types of industries was emerging. The 1980s saw a trend towards a concentration of precision engineering and high-tech industries in the developed industrialised areas, alongside the dispersal of declining and labour intensive industries to the less developed peripheral regions (Chon 1992, Park, S-O. 1991, Kim and Masser 1990, Douglass 1993).

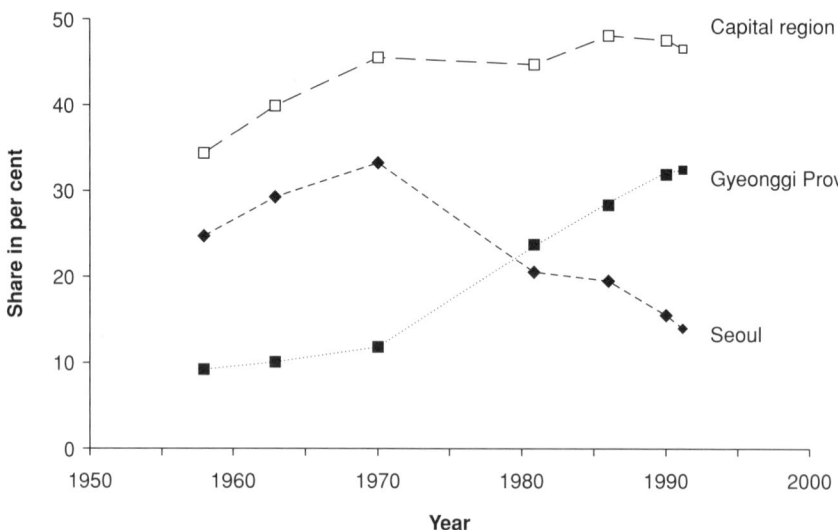

Figure 3.5 Distribution of manufacturing employment in the Capital region and
        Seoul, 1958–91.

Source: Data from Park, S-O. (1991), p.83; NSO (1993).

Notes:
'Capital region' includes Seoul and its metropolitan areas.
'Seoul' represents Seoul city only.
'Kyonggi Province' represents the suburban areas of Seoul only.

   The heavy and chemical sectors were now becoming concentrated in the
Southeast region as well as in the new industrial complexes of the periphery.
South Cholla's share of the chemical industry was significant from the 1970s
on, when the second largest oil refinery and petrochemical complex in
Korea was located in Yeosu (Chon 1992, pp.158–159). Due to the relatively
high level of industrialisation of the Southeast region, land prices increased

Table 3.7 Manufacturing industry employment increase by region

	1970–80	*%*	*1980–85*	*%*
Capital region	650,023	47.3	216,982	53.2
Pusan region[1]	382,070	27.8	117,427	28.8
Other regions	343,207	24.9	73,721	18.0
National	1,375,300	100.0	408,130	100.0

Source: Ministry of Labour, Survey Report on Establishment Labour Conditions (1970, 1980,
1985), cited in Kwon (1988a), p.60.

Notes:
The figures are increases in the number of employees during the period.
The percentage figures are ratio of employment increase between the 3 regions.
1 Pusan region includes Pusan and South Kyongsang Province.

to a level which was not conducive to new ventures. Therefore, large industrial estates started to form in the still underdeveloped southern edge of the Capital region. For example, in 1979 Ahsan Bay industrial complex was located on the border between Kyonggi and South Chungchong Provinces. This large-scale development had an impact on the overall distribution of the heavy and chemical sector.

The 1980s saw a pronounced concentration of the machinery, metals and electronics industries around Seoul and Pusan, this being promoted aggressively from 1973. The two areas accounted for over three-quarters of the total employment in these industries in 1970; during the decentralisation period of 1970–80, the dispersal of these precision industries was limited to the suburban counties of Seoul and Pusan. In 1984, the Seoul-Kyonggi area and the Pusan-Kyongsang area accounted for over 96 per cent of the employment in precision machinery. On the other hand, the share of precision machinery manufacturing employment in North Chungchong, South Chungchong, North and South Cholla and Kangwon provinces remained meagre: 3.8 per cent in 1970, and 3.6 per cent in 1984. Similar patterns were evident in fabricated metal industries, electrical machinery industries and general machinery industries (Chon 1992).

High-technology[17] enterprises have favoured the Capital region above any other region, showing a concentration of over 75 per cent in 1988 (Park 1986, p.23, Kim and Masser 1990, p.34). This is a much higher clustering than for manufacturing industries as a whole (58 per cent in 1988), and arises from a steady accretion starting in the late 1970s and continuing in the 1980s (Park, S-O. 1991).[18] Park remarks that this agglomeration of high-tech industries stimulated the reconcentration of manufacturing in general in the Capital region; in the late 1970s there was some slight industrial dispersal from the Capital region to the rest of the country (p.87). The agglomeration of high-tech industries was due to the concentration of highly skilled labour and R&D activities in the Capital region.[19]

In contrast to the continued concentration of technology intensive industries, labour intensive low value-added manufacturing showed a tendency of slight dispersal towards peripheral regions. Figure 3.6 demonstrates the changing patterns of industrial location and structure. The Capital region experienced a substantial increase in its share of the nation's fabricated metals, machinery, and transportation equipment industries, and decreases in textiles and garments (Park, S-O. 1991, p.85). These moved to less developed regions and away from the port areas, taking advantage of low land values and cheaper labour (Chon 1992).

The concentration of company headquarters in and around Seoul also heightened during the 1980s. By 1985, over three-quarters of large conglomerates and 60 per cent of their branch firms had headquarters in the Seoul Metropolitan Area (Park 1986, p.316, Kim and Masser 1990, p.34). The 1980s, however, saw a trend towards suburbanisation of secondary

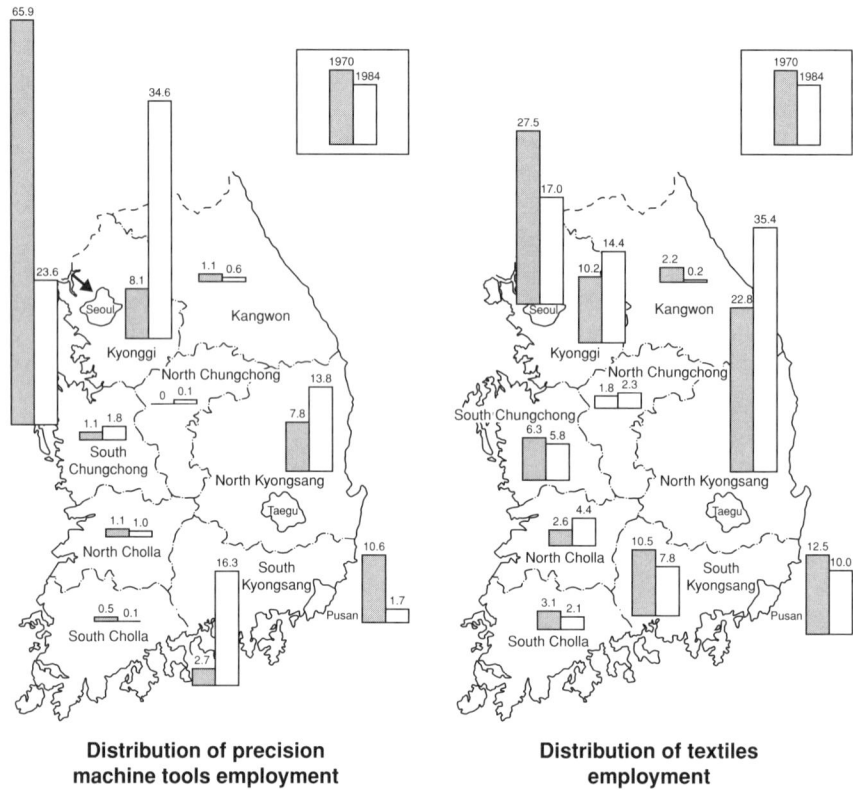

**Distribution of precision
machine tools employment**

**Distribution of textiles
employment**

Figure 3.6 Distribution of employment in the precision machine tools and textile
　　　　industries in Korea, 1970 and 1984.

Source: Lee, C. *et al.* (1988), pp.348 and 353.

clerical and R&D functions to the surrounding districts of Seoul (Table 3.8).
This was partly a result of government policies as well as rising land prices.

　The adoption of an intensive accumulation regime based on a competitive mode of regulation was closely associated with an increased tendency
towards 're-concentration' of industries in the Capital region. In the 1980s,
takeovers, mergers and a high business failure rate resulted in the increasing
centralisation of both capital and industry in Seoul's suburban region. The
structural changes in the accumulation regime caused technology intensive
industries to favour an area where almost all R&D was to be found (Castells
and Hall 1994, p.63). Over the 1981–84 period, most medium-size cities and
rural counties outside the Capital region experienced more plant closures
than new start-ups (Park, 1986). Whereas the share of manufacturing in the
southeastern Pusan-South Kyongsang region remained more or less constant in the 1970s and 1980s, that accruing to the mega-urban region of

Table 3.8 Service sector employment, Seoul and Kyonggi regions, 1981 and 1986 (%)

Year	Wholesale		Banking and financial		Insurance		Real estate		Business services	
	1981	1986	1981	1986	1981	1986	1981	1986	1981	1986
Seoul	53.8	53.3	50.8	49.8	46.5	36.9	64.5	56.5	48.2	52.2
Kyonggi	6.1	7.6	7.9	8.6	8.1	11.4	9.9	16.8	11.3	10.0

Source: EPB (1981, 1986); Korean Federation of Trade and Industry (1990), p.32.

Note:
% figures are of the national total.

Seoul continued to increase at a precipitous pace. Other regions of the country witnessed falling shares (Douglass 1993, p.159). In this respect the Korean experience supports Massey's (1979) view that a hierarchical spatial division of labour reinforces regional inequalities. Massey (1979) also notes that the central metropolis enjoys relative economic advantage as a result of the presence of control functions, research, design and development and managerial and technical strata, while peripheral regions tend to be handicapped by less skilled and less sophisticated production processes and job opportunities (Massey 1979, pp.237–238, Kim and Masser 1990, p.34). Thus, as can be seen in Table 3.9, while the Capital region continued to increase its part of GDP in the 1985–91 period, all other regions show falling shares.

In the peripheral Fordist phase the state paid lip service to problems of balance in spatial development; the dominant market philosophy, however, meant that infrastructure provision was demand-led; mechanisms of dispersal were not applied as determinedly as during the previous regime. Instead the government's position was to 'accommodate' the concentration of industries and population in the Capital region. Thus, the spatial strategies of the 1980s were mainly concerned with the disposition of industrial development within the Capital region. The sustained expansion of the Seoul Metropolitan Region crossed a new threshold in 1988 when its population surpassed that of the combined population of all other provinces outside the Southeast region (Douglass 1993, p.160).

Table 3.9 Regional share of gross domestic product, 1985–91 (%)

	1985	1986	1987	1988	1989	1990	1991
Capital region	42.6	43.5	43.8	44.2	45.1	45.5	45.7
Central region	9.4	9.1	9.0	8.9	8.9	9.0	9.1
Southeastern region	31.8	31.8	31.7	31.4	30.8	30.1	29.8
Southwestern region	11.5	11.2	11.1	11.3	11.0	11.2	11.2
Other regions	4.7	4.4	4.5	4.2	4.2	4.0	4.0
Whole country	100.0	100.0	100.0	100.0	100.0	100.0	100.0

Source: NSO (1993).

Spatial development in the Korea of the 1980s was, therefore, dominated by the concentration of high-tech industries, R&D activities and skilled workers in the Capital region, matched by the dispersal of low value-added labour intensive industries to the less developed regions. The tight control of financial incentives, differential infrastructural investment, the accommodating spatial policies of the state as well as the more intensive and competitive economic environment were the causative factors of concentration. A combination of state policy and competitive mode of regulation reversed the spatial decentralisation of the 1970s.

Globalisation and the neo-Fordist regime (1989–97)

Korea's accumulation regime from the late 1980s on was increasingly intertwined with the global economy. This was marked by growing trade surpluses, the formation of economic blocs such as European Community and North American Trade Association, rising wages in Korea as well as changing regional geopolitics. Under these pressures, the domestic economy began to succumb to foreign capital penetration, while Korean conglomerates started to shift their production offshore, breaching protected markets and exploiting cheaper labour sources. Although strenuous efforts to globalise Korea's economy had to await the demise of the neo-Fordist accumulation regime, the restructuring process had significant impacts on urban and industrial geography.

Two distinct trends showed themselves: the increasing primacy of the Seoul Metropolitan Area (SMA), suburbanisation, and industrial expansion in the Western coastal region.

With the shift in global economic activity to the Asian Pacific region in the early 1990s, the Korean state determined to make Seoul a regional economic hub; indeed, a global mega-city to compete with the 'world cities' of Osaka, Singapore, Hong Kong and Shanghai. To this end, much infrastructural investment was focused on the SMA, enhancing international linkage with global capital. The intensification of infrastructure in the SMA is demonstrated in Table 3.10. A restructuring towards services, information technology and international financial services accentuated the primacy of Seoul in terms of population and capital concentration (Douglass 1993, p.159).

However, the drive to extend Korea's manufacturing capabilities was by no means abandoned. The industrial trajectory of Korea in the late 1980s and 1990s stressed both technologically advanced industries and well established strategic activities such as naphtha cracking (*FEER* 12 July 1990, pp.69–70). The relentless demand for industrial land, stimulated now by the opening up of China, led to the expansion of investment towards peripheral areas, particularly into Western coastal regions (South Chungchong, South and North Cholla provinces) which had previously been zoned for fisheries and agriculture. Huge state investments in land reclamation and

Table 3.10 Infrastructure investment by region, 1992 (unit: billion won, %)

Region	Infrastructure investment	Percentage	Investment per capita
Seoul	1,153.9	11.13	108,729
Incheon	349.2	3.36	192,087
Kyonggi Province	2,413.6	23.29	392,096
Capital region	*3,916.7*	*37.79*	*210,732*
Pusan	310.5	3.00	81,751
Taegu	203.3	1.96	91,205
South Kyongsang Province	127.9	1.23	34,827
North Kyongsang Province	796.9	7.69	278,578
Southeast region	*1,438.6*	*13.88*	*114,536*
Kwangju-South Cholla Province	1,033.5	9.97	283,426
North Cholla Province	463.8	4.47	224,062
Southwest region	*1,497.3*	*14.45*	*261,930*
Daejeon-North Chungchong Province	612.9	5.91	251,264
South Chungchong Province	1,115.2	10.76	553,744
Central region	*1,728.0*	*16.67*	*388,036*
Kangwon Province	480.0	4.63	303,714
Cheju	72.0	0.69	139,913
Other regions	*552.0*	*5.32*	*263,480*
Non-regional	1,231.0	11.88	—
Total	10,363.6	100.00	238,732

Source: NSO (1993), pp.212–213.

Note:
Area by cities and provinces. Subtotal for each region. 'Infrastructure Investment' is defined as investment ear-marked for capital investment for public services in 1992 which include construction of roads, railways, water-supply pipes, airports and seaports, sewage treatment plants, etc.

construction of industrial estates allied with financial incentives to private capital caused South Chungchong and South Cholla provinces to be destinations of particularly high investments (Table 3.10). The figures also reveal that previous investment disparities between developed and underdeveloped regions were no longer so stark. In terms of the per capita figures in particular, the underdeveloped regions were now receiving higher proportions, while the Southeast region received the least. The state's role in opening up new opportunities for manufacturing industries in Korea's underdeveloped regions is thus clear.

Globalisation strategy and primacy of Seoul

The investment in the transportation and communications sector of the 1990s can be expected to have considerable spatial impact. As Table 3.10 shows, the Southwest and Central regions received in the early 1990s relatively high levels of investment. Only the Capital region received a higher share and 'other regions' (Kangwon and Cheju provinces) continued to receive disproportionately smaller shares (in absolute terms).

The transportation sector has played an important role. Already by the early 1970s, investment in the sector accounted almost one quarter of gross domestic capital formation; by 1985 the figure had risen to almost 32 per cent. This massive allocation of capital resources to transportation in each development plan has clearly influenced locational decisions (urban and industrial development along the Seoul–Pusan Highway or the suburbanisation in the SMA) and helped industrial expansion and metropolitan suburbanisation (Richardson and Baek 1988).

In the 1960s, the reliance on existing port facilities in Incheon and Pusan had led to the concentration of industries and population in Seoul and Pusan. As has been noted, the increase in highway investment in the Second Plan had increased the rate of migration to these two end points of a major expressway. In the 1970s, the Capital and Southeast regions were furnished with substantial levels of new port and road networks in order to promote industrial decentralisation, while investment in railways was cut drastically during this period. During the 1980s, in order to alleviate the diseconomies of industrial and population concentration in the Capital region, high levels of investment were put into the intraregional road and subway network. The impact on the suburbanisation of the Capital region was marked: in the 1970s and 1980s, dispersal of population to suburban areas occurred in cities with good transport links with Seoul such as Incheon, Suwon and Bucheon. The expansion of housing estates in the outlying areas within the Seoul boundary could not have been possible without the expansion of the subway network and increased levels of car ownership. Indeed, it was not until the rise of private automobile ownership in the late 1980s and 1990s that there was significant rapid development of satellite cities and new towns (Kwon 1988b, Richardson and Baek 1988).

Between 1990–97, the transportation and communication infrastructure developments were utilised in the promotion of Seoul as a global financial centre and as a means of expanding industrial development into the West Coast region. Two goals were articulated: to relieve Seoul's congestion, and to increase international linkage. Thus, major road building programmes were implemented to reduce congestion in Seoul and its metropolitan area, and a second international airport was constructed at Yeongjongdo to increase air transport capacity.

The Korean government's aim of turning Seoul into a Pacific Asia regional centre (and indeed a global centre) led to a concentrated investment programme to attract international capital. Air traffic was projected to grow at rates of 9.5 per cent for international passengers and 11.9 per cent for international freight (Richardson and Baek 1988, p.162).[20] The demand for international air travel focused on Seoul due to its concentration

of international trade and finance. The major planned project for air transport in the late 1990s was a second international airport at Yeongjongdo[21]
to serve Seoul in addition to Kimpo. This would not only further concentrate air traffic (in 1991 Kimpo airport handled over 90 per cent of all
Korea's 23 million domestic and international air passengers), but would
mean the construction of more roads and rail networks to link the airport
and the cities of the SMA (*FEER* 1992, 10 Sept., p.70). The further concentration of international air transport capacity in Seoul will aggravate
already serious congestion problems, and intensify the disparity between
Seoul and the rest of the country. The domination of Seoul is expected
to increase, therefore, as global capital penetration deepens as a result of
Korea's post-economic crisis political economy.

As a means of linking Pusan to Seoul and the global economy, the
government chose to construct a high-speed rail link in the early 1990s.
This option was selected in place of upgrading Pusan's airport to handle
more international flights. The latter option would have obviated the
need for the expensive and environmentally damaging Yeongjongdo project and the related road construction, thus, reducing the concentration
of transportation networks in Seoul.

From the late 1980s on, large industrial estate projects and port construction went hand in hand. A further related development was the West
Coast Highway intended to relieve the load on the ports of Incheon and
Pusan. The port investment in the 1987–91 period was focused upon the
container and cargo mega-projects of Ahsan and Kunsan. This of course
reflected the changing regional matrix – increasing trade with China and
with the rapidly growing Southeast Asian economies. Ahsan and Kunsan
were seen as the exporting nodes for the ever-concentrating industries in
the Capital and West Coast regions.

In conjunction with the above mentioned development, there was a
trend towards suburbanisation of white collar jobs (and population) into
the satellite cities and new towns in the SMA. Increasing real estate prices
and improvement in transport links and mobility – rising car ownership
– were the main factors (Richardson and Baek 1988, pp.155–159). This
in effect widened the spatial boundary of Seoul's white-collar jobs and
middle class housing displacing manufacturing industries and working class
communities. The development of new towns and satellite cities in the
SMA absorbed much of the population migration to the Capital region
and was able to slow migration into Seoul. Despite industrial expansion to the peripheral regions, the concentration of population into the
Capital region and SMA continued. In 1990, the Capital region accommodated 42.8 per cent of total national population. Migration data for
the 1990s indicate that in the Capital region, Seoul experienced out-
migration while SMA cities witnessed a rapid rise in in-migration due to
suburbanisation and industrialisation. Most of the out-migration continued to be from the underdeveloped rural areas of Kangwon and North

and South Cholla provinces. Other provinces showed a stabilisation of population movement (NSO 1993).

Thus, we have the megalopolisation of Seoul, with the central city and its outlying satellites and new towns merging into a single urban area; only a sliver of green belt area remained. The spatial issue in the 1990s was not one of regional balance but one of disparity between the Capital region and the rest of the nation. In the 1990s, the concentration of finance and trade, control and R&D functions, social and cultural amenities, service industries, political power and indeed consumption in Seoul with high-tech industries almost exclusively in the Capital region meant a clear gulf with the rest of the nation. The dominance of the Capital region also overshadowed the historical rivalry between Kyongsang province and Cholla Province as that receiving investment versus that being neglected.

While industrial expansion has reduced regional disparities outside the SMA, there was a growing disparity between the urban-industrial sector and the rural economy. The agricultural sector of the 1990s was under growing pressures from import liberalisation. Its ability to respond was constrained by the small size of holdings which is a legacy of the land reform in the 1950s. This with the continuous drain of rural labour to the industrial sector, as well as the dependence on expensive chemical inputs, was the cause of structural underdevelopment in agriculture.

Table 3.11 shows that for the 1968–84 period, between regions, rural areas were not dissimilar in GNP values. However, the variation between urban areas was significant. While, in the developed regions, urban areas led the economic growth, in the depressed regions, they tended to show stagnant or even negative growth. This attests to the fact that in depressed regions, it was the lack of development in the urban economy that was responsible for regional disparities. The issue of 'balanced' development

Table 3.11 Urban and rural shares of Korea's GNP by region, 1968–84 (%)

Cities/Regions	1968		1976		1984	
	Urban	Rural	Urban	Rural	Urban	Rural
Seoul	26.5	—	28.2	—	29.1	—
Kyonggi/Incheon	3.7	5.7	7.7	4.9	9.0	6.5
N. Kyongsang/Daegu	4.7	7.2	4.7	6.4	7.5	3.9
S. Kyongsang/Pusan	12.4	5.1	15.8	3.6	15.0	3.8
N. Cholla	2.3	4.3	2.3	2.7	2.1	2.1
S. Cholla	2.6	6.1	1.8	6.8	2.7	4.6
N. Chungchong	1.4	3.0	1.3	1.5	1.3	1.1
S. Chungchong	1.3	7.3	1.6	4.7	2.3	3.5
Kangwon	0.4	4.8	0.4	3.6	1.9	2.1
Chaeju	0.3	1.0	0.3	0.6	0.6	0.4
Total	55.6	44.5	64.2	35.8	71.4	28.6

Source: Kim (1993), p.36.

is not one of rural–urban conflict, but one of regional disparity. It was the weakness of the urban economy in the poorer regions that gave rise to interregional migration flows to the expanding labour markets of the urban/industrial core areas.

Thus, there has been a trend towards spatial differentiation between sectors: an increasing spatial split between business and tertiary activities, and between industrial and agricultural production. The tripartite spatial division of labour which arose with the vertical disintegration of the Fordist labour process in the 1970s established itself in the spatial structure through a continued efficiency-oriented sectoral strategy. This gave rise to a tripartite division: a core consumption zone (CCZ), with a high concentration of business and consumption service industries, a semi-peripheral industrial zone (SIZ), where manufacturing industries dominate the space economy, and a peripheral rural zone (PRZ), where agricultural production and leisure industries predominate.

The 1997 financial crisis marked the end of the neo-Fordist accumulation regime. Prior to 1997, the liberalisation of the economy did not materialise nor did Seoul become a financial centre of world stature. As we have seen in the previous chapter, the continued operation of state-capital tie in business practices, partial opening of markets and the strength of the labour movement contributed to the crisis. The spatial developments for globalisation of Korea are still proceeding. As the post-1997 regime of D-J. Kim removes the old blockages, the influx of global capital is expected to be more significant. It is also expected that the problems already mentioned would intensify as international capital penetration intensifies competition and thus centralisation tendencies.

Summary: uneven spatial development

Historical analysis of spatial development in Korea has revealed the tendency towards spatial differentiation, equalisation and re-differentiation with changing accumulation regimes, MSR and industrial trajectory.

The urban structure of Korea came to reflect Japanese policy aimed at exploiting Korea to meet its own consumption and industrial needs. This settlement pattern in Korea was established in the 1910–45 period. Cities grew as administrative centres for colonial exploitation, as assembly points of agricultural products for export to Japan, and later as production sites for raw materials and cheap manufactured goods for Japanese factories and consumers. The historical legacy of Japanese spatial strategy was important in that it laid the foundation of Korea's urban structure. It was from this base that Korea's postwar economic and spatial strategy evolved.

Postwar spatial development closely reflected the state economic and spatial policies and infrastructural provisions. During the 1950s, the ISI regime of accumulation, the dominance of regional capital and low transportation infrastructure meant that there was a wide distribution of industrial activities. In the 1960s, with the implementation of the labour intensive EOI regime, the state promoted centralisation of labour intensive industries in the large urban centres with existing port facilities and industrial infrastructure – primarily Seoul and Pusan. The competitive MSR and the centralisation of state functions reinforced the concentration tendency of population in the large metropolitan cities. From this arose many urban problems which in turn increased economic bottlenecks. In the 1970s, the state restructured the industrial space in consonance with the restructuring of the regime of accumulation. The state also intervened to redistribute population to the regions by implementing policies with a definite spatial thrust. A series of industrial regulations, incentives and zoning policies were introduced throughout the 1970s, these resulting in a clear bi-polarisation of urban space (regions around Pusan and Seoul). With the re-imposition of a competitive regulation alongside an intensive accumulation regime, the 1980s saw a concentration of capital, industries and population in the Capital region. This process reflected the state's contradictory aims of achieving both balanced interregional and intra-regional development. Two spatial tendencies can be identified: a hierarchical differentiation of industries with the technology intensive sector concentrating in prime industrial areas, and the low-value added labour intensive industries being pushed out to peripheral areas; this has been accompanied by the suburbanisation of population in the SMA. In the 1990s, the state's pursuit of a globalisation strategy, and of industrial decentralisation, reinforced the polarisation between the SMA and the rest of the country. The promotion of Seoul as a world economic centre through massive infrastructure development has increased the concentration of international business functions and capital, widening the gap with other regions. On the other hand, due to changes in global regional geopolitics in the late 1980s and the pressures for industrial expansion in the Capital region, the state implemented huge infrastructural development in the underdeveloped areas adjacent to the Capital region, bringing about the industrialisation of the West Coast region.

All this demonstrates a dual spatial dynamic in Korea's postwar mode of development:

1   A continual concentration and decentralisation of industrial development. However, while the tendency towards concentration has stemmed from the inherent dynamics of accumulation and the state sectoral policies, the decentralisation of industries had to be aided by explicit state intervention;

2   Intraregional suburbanisation of population, particularly in the SMA. This was initiated by the dispersal of industries in the 1970s, and facilitated by the creation of intraregional transport networks.

A summary examination of the spatial dynamic and the resultant spatial structure identifies the following major underlying factors as follows:

- Natural physical characteristics;
- The colonial legacy;
- The dynamics of capital accumulation and the centralisation of capital;
- Centralisation of the state structure and power;
- Unbalanced infrastructural investment and efficiency-oriented spatial and sectoral policies of the state;
- Dependence upon and openness to the global economic system, for example, markets, global capital;
- Technological developments, production processes and the division of labour;
- Social and cultural values.

Particularly important in the spatial allocation of development has been the role played by Seoul. The legacy of Seoul as the seat of government and as the centre for business and social and cultural activities has been a major factor in the centralisation of population and capital and, thus, in uneven spatial development. The strong central economic control of the Korean system is mirrored in the dominant physical weight of the capital city. Seoul managed to increase its hegemony even despite its de-industrialisation. The vertical disintegration of the Fordist production process was necessary to keep corporate headquarters in Seoul while decentralising production lines. As Richardson (1988) argues, the concentration of manufacturing headquarters in Seoul was designed to gain maximum access to government, the prime distributor of scarce resources through various policy instruments including incentive taxes and financial systems (p.99). The division of labour within the company naturally led to the dispersal of the working classes to the semi-periphery. In the 1990s' strategy of 'globalisation' of the Korean economy, Seoul was designated as the lead interface with global capital; its business and physical infrastructure underwent an upgrading process in order to present the necessary image. The concentration of business functions, education facilities, international transport linkages, government offices and financial institutions created a huge gulf with the non-metropolitan regions (Table 3.12). While Seoul enjoyed First World living standards, the rest of Korea existed in very different circumstances.

A key factor has been the state's role in spatial structuration. In the pursuit of an EOI regime and capital accumulation, the Korean government had to mediate between global forces through tariff barriers and financial subsidies. It was also intent on the removal of any spatial barriers to accumulation. It pursued efficiency-oriented spatial policies to promote economies of scale and agglomeration on the one hand, while on the other it pushed for demand-led infrastructural investment to relieve diseconomies.

Table 3.12 Concentration of central managerial functions in Seoul, 1985 (%)

Functions	Large regional centres				
	Seoul	Pusan	Daegu	Kwangju	Daejeon
Population	23.8	8.7	5.0	2.2	2.1
Central government bodies and agencies	83.8	0.9	0.0	0.0	2.4
Manufacturing head offices	69.2	6.3	2.1	0.7	0.9
International trade	96.3	3.2	0.1	0.0	0.0
Higher education	47.2	11.2	9.9	7.0	5.1
Commodity dealing	69.0	9.7	7.8	1.6	3.2
Business information	78.1	3.2	3.6	2.3	4.8
Business finance	47.7	8.0	7.3	4.1	3.9

Source: KRIHS, cited in Kwon (1988a), p.63.

The oscillation between concentration and decentralisation of infrastructural development was governed by the drive for efficiency and rapid growth.

Intraregional policies to relieve the diseconomies of the metropolitan areas represent an implicit policy for concentration of capital and industrial activity and the justification for the continued preferential investment of infrastructure in the developed regions. As capital diminished in the depressed areas, the needs of their declining populations were increasingly marginalised. The emphasis on 'decentralisation' can be seen in terms of a hegemonic project which justified the expansion of industrial space and capital concentration in Seoul, while acknowledging middle class issues such as the high housing and land prices, and traffic congestion. The working classes were, on the whole, marginalised.

A side effect of these state policies was the creation of rural underdevelopment. As we have seen in Chapter 2, the intensive agricultural production introduced in the 1970s brought a cycle of chemical use and indebtedness. The sectoral approach to rural zones led to classic symptoms of underdevelopment. However, this was more a matter of regional disparity than urban–rural differentiation. Both urban and rural areas in the agriculturally designated zones received little industrial or infrastructural investment. As already discussed, Table 3.12 reveals that urban areas in the depressed regions were in stagnant or even negative growth, thus accounting for disparities of the regional scale. The issues of development centre not on rural–urban dichotomy, but on regional differentiation. It is the weakness of the urban economy in the poorer regions that gave rise to interregional migration flows to the expanding labour markets of the urban-industrial areas.

Although these forces shaped the transformation of Korea's space-economy through the restructuring of accumulation regimes and indeed the MSR, developments were also constrained by the spatial form of the previous accumulation regime. Spatial legacies do not simply dissolve: they are the template for the new configuration. The dialectical transformation and sedimentation resulted in the primacy of the SMA, the suburbanisation and regional concentration of manufacturing industries and the regionalisation of urban/rural disparities. The sedimentation of new spatial forms upon old ones resulted in tripartite uneven spatial development.

The uneven economic, social and spatial development in Korea is a function of the state's role in the process of capital accumulation. Mediation between global forces and domestic capital, and the maintenance of social cohesion, have been key elements. It has been achieved by the utilisation of sectoral and spatial policies to restructure industrial space as a means of displacing the tendency towards crisis. Thus Korea's uneven development is a distinct outcome of an EOI regime of accumulation, in which the state suppressed the needs of equitable social development in the interest of capital accumulation.

Combined and uneven development in Korea has caused a differentiation of national space into three distinct zones of development. The size and location of each of these zones have shifted over time. The core consumption, semi-peripheral industrial and peripheral rural zones each have very distinct characteristics of economic structure and class composition. The core consumption zone (CCZ) is characterised by a high level of business and consumption service activities, with relatively sparse manufacturing activities. Social and physical infrastructure in this zone tend to be advanced and elaborate. The social composition of this zone is highly differentiated, with a large proportion of upper and middle class residents, matched by comparable numbers from low income groups; there is only a small concentration of the industrial working class.

The semi-peripheral industrial zone (SIZ) is distinguished by a large manufacturing base and a dearth of other industries. The social composition of this zone follows the economic structure – that is, the industrial working class predominates. The SIZ features a relatively high level of productive infrastructure, with poor social amenities and services. This reflects the lack of consumption capacity as well as the low priority accorded by the state to improving the environment for the working classes. The zone thus suffers from industrial pollution and generally low environmental quality. The character of the peripheral rural zone (PRZ) is one of economic underdevelopment, with a marked neglect of physical or social infrastructure. The government's sectoral emphasis renders the PRZ basically an agricultural production zone. The sparse fixed capital and population do not make it feasible on 'efficiency' grounds to provide social and environmental amenities and services. The low levels of government and private sector investment simply confirm the cycle of underdevelopment. Increasingly, the PRZ areas are intruded upon by the leisure and recreational developments of the CCZ. Natural environments are consumed by golf

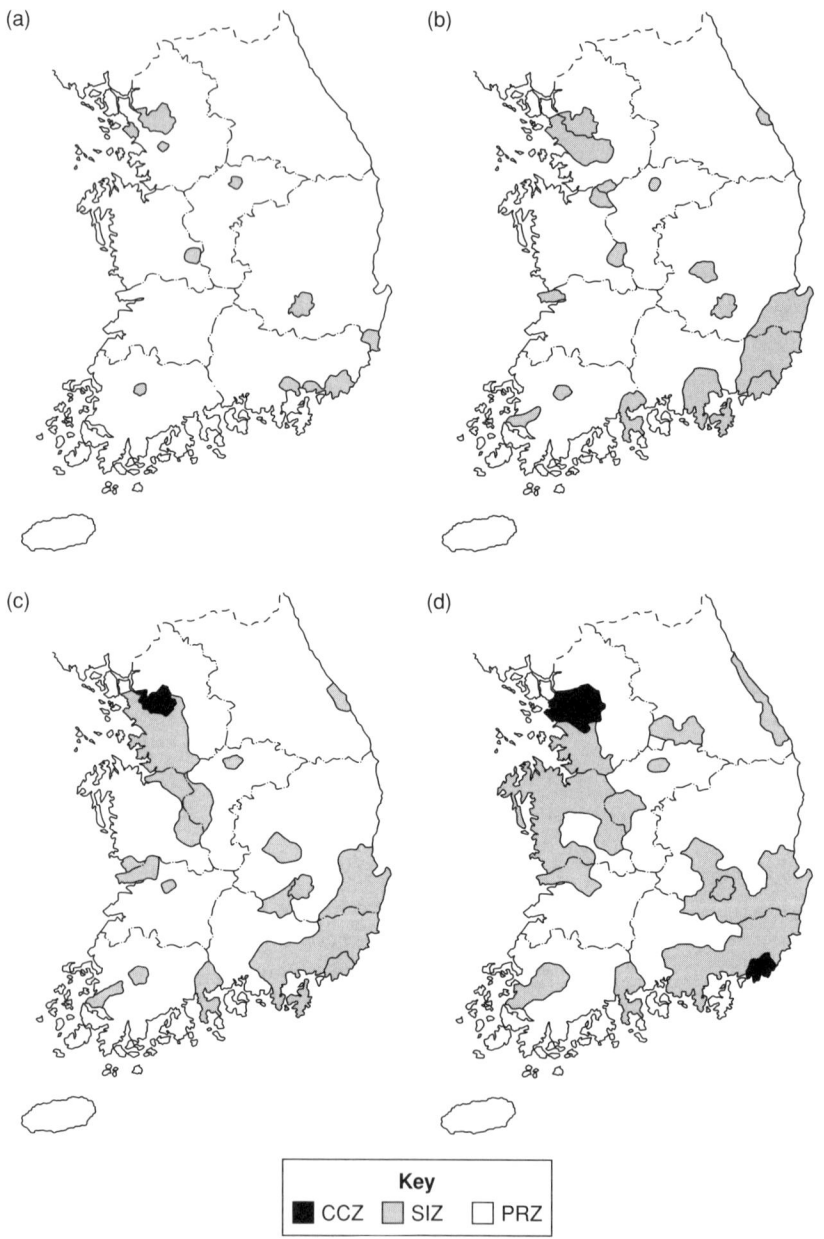

Key
■ CCZ ▨ SIZ □ PRZ

Figure 3.7 Historical development of space in Korea.

Source: Based on MoC (various years) *Ten Year National Comprehensive Physical Development Plans.*

Note:
(a) Taylorist period; (b) Yusin period; (c) peripheral Fordist period; (d) neo-Fordist period.

courses and leisure resorts, bringing low-quality employment opportunities as well as environmental degradation and occasional environmental catastrophe.

These zonal characterisations are to a certain extent conceptual; in reality, a combination of the zones may sometimes exist in one geographical area. Seoul is indeed a prime example of a CCZ, but places like Pusan, Incheon, Taegu and Daejeon are not so clearly defined. These cities tend to display the imprint of both CCZ and SIZ. If we examine the geographical distribution of the three zones, we see that Seoul (and its immediate urban area) and Pusan too, can be classified as CCZs; the remainder of the Capital and Southeast regions are SIZs, as are small pockets of industrialised areas in the Southwest and Central regions. The balance of national territory (with the exception of the above mentioned areas) are PRZs. Figure 3.7 shows the historical transformation and growth of these zones in Korea.

Environmental conditions in Korea are also differentiated by these three zones. The differences in the production–consumption relationship, the level of infrastructural provision and class relationships gives rise to particular environmental conditions in each zone. This differentiation will be looked at in greater depth in the following chapter.

4 Environmental degradation in Korea

A historical overview

The development of society is universally one of utilisation and transformation of nature. The distinction of the capitalist mode of production, in which commodification becomes the supreme end, is that resources are exploited and wastes created at ever more profligate rates. As discussed in Chapter 1, industrial processes, failures of the market, technology, consumption trends and urbanisation are singly or jointly held responsible for environmental problems. The unsustainable use of raw materials, the uncontrolled disposal of waste and the exploitation of labour are governed by both national and supranational modes of social regulation. The regulationist theoretical framework asserts that society and space undergo transformation in continually changing accumulation regimes with their corresponding MSRs. The continual transformation of Korea's environment is a function of the structuration of space within the dynamics of capitalist development.

In the present chapter we review the development of environmental problems in relation to evolving regimes of accumulation and modes of social regulation. Each phase of development, economic and spatial, has produced its characteristic environmental problems. The complex of environmental problems of contemporary Korea reflects a historical accumulation of causes and processes. We consider first the legacy of colonial exploitation, the economic foundation of which produced specific environmental conditions.

By tracing the development of environmental problems, this chapter will also demonstrate that the environmental impacts of economic development have been differentiated over space, giving rise to similar patterns as those discussed in the previous chapter. As one would expect from the concentration of population in Seoul, and of manufacturing in industrial zones, environmental problems in the core consumption zone, semi-peripheral industrial zone and peripheral rural zone tend to be fairly distinct.

Colonial period: exploitation of environmental resources

The environmental condition of Korea before the annexation by the Japanese was very much as it had been over the previous millennium. The agrarian economy had not changed for centuries and urbanisation remained at a low level. Few mountainous areas had been exploited for their natural resources. Lee, K-J. (1993) claims that Korea had retained a high degree of biodiversity for such a small country and this was largely due to its rugged terrain (Lee, K-J. 1993, pp.53–54). It was the annexation of the Korean peninsula as a Japanese colony in 1909 which brought the first major change in the country's economic, social and environmental structure.

The intensive agricultural policies imposed by the Japanese involving chemical fertilisers and pesticides began to affect the fertility of the soil (Korea Catholic Farmers Association and Korea Anti-nuclear Antipollution Peace Research Institute 1990, Park, C-J. 1991). Mineral resources taken for industrial and military purposes severely damaged mountain environments. By the end of the colonial period, Korea's forests were extensively depleted. With the road and rail networks extended in the 1920s, commercial timber production commenced in earnest. Annual harvesting rates stood at 2.5–2.8 million m^3 of timber throughout the colonial period; consequently, the timber accumulation level[1] declined from 49 m^3 per ha in 1939 to 13.9 m^3 per ha in 1945. During their 36 years of occupation the Japanese stripped 72 per cent of the forest in the peninsula (Lee, K-J. 1993 pp.48–50). Rail and road construction and the expansion of urban areas also had a profound effect on the natural environment, resulting in the disappearance of many species of flora and Korea's larger fauna too (Lee, K-J., pp.53–54).

Although some industrialisation took place during the colonial period, it was widely dispersed throughout the peninsula in accordance with raw material and power needs. Recorded evidence of industrial pollution for this period is obviously scant. In the urban areas, overcrowding and the growth of slum areas were closely controlled by Korea's colonial masters: movement of population was restricted, not least for security purposes.

Interim period: war devastation and poverty

Japan's colonial rule came to an abrupt end in 1945. However, any rejoicing at new-found independence was quickly dissolved as the peninsula was divided between Soviet and American blocs. The ensuing Korean War in the early 1950s laid waste to much of the industrial and housing infrastructure of the colonial period; the conflict also had a devastating impact on the natural environment. War devastation and the influx of population from the north created severe housing shortages, imposing huge pressures on the infrastructure of Seoul, Pusan and other large cities. Between 1945 and 1955, South Korea had somehow to cope with an estimated 4.8 million influx of population (Kwon, Y-W. 1991). The threat to public health was acute, and food shortage brought malnutrition to the urban areas in particular. Squatter settlements which appeared during the war continued their uncontrolled expansion. Although a part of the displaced population returned to their rural homes, the émigrés from the North and from overseas remained and were to prove a long-standing problem to many municipalities. Further, with much of the economy destroyed during the war, the UN and later US aid were essential to the survival of much of the population.

The situation for Korea's natural environment was every bit as acute. Perhaps the severest problem of this time was deforestation. The heavy bombardments during the Korean War destroyed much of the country's remaining forest cover. The use of young trees as the only cheap source of fuel as well as commercial logging reduced the timber accumulation level to 4.8 m^3/ha by the late 1950s. The exploitation of natural resources such as timber and coal for both domestic use and export was an imperative in this poverty-stricken post-colonial and postwar era. Deforestation also triggered flooding and landslides during the monsoon season. Only by the 1960s had reforestation become a national priority, with strict policies to protect trees and forests: Korea's timber accumulation rate rose to 27.5 m^3/ha in 1985, while by 1990 it stood at 38.4 m^3/ha. The latter figure, however, was only 78 per cent of that of 1939 (Lee, K-J. 1993, pp.48–50).

As far as the wider political-economic circumstances were concerned, mismanagement and corruption by the new political and economic elite failed to revive the industrial base. Instead, entrepreneurs concentrated on rent seeking and exploitation of primary resources, while the government occupied itself with aid maximisation and political infighting. Unlike postwar European states, reconstruction in Korea clearly benefited only the minority. It was not until the ascendancy of the ensuing regime that economic backwardness and employment for the masses were addressed. However, the poverty that was endemic during this period was the basis for super-exploitative accumulation regimes in following decades.

Taylorist exploitation, migration and the urban environment

The economic and spatial policies of the 1960s which emphasised labour intensive industrial developments in the existing large urban centres gave rise to rapid rural–urban migration. Urban populations expanded greatly, creating even greater pressures on housing and other infrastructure. Most migrants headed for Seoul and Pusan where they anticipated jobs in the manufacturing sector. However, a high proportion lacked suitable skills and had no other recourse but the informal sector. The sudden concentration of industries and population caused the rapid expansion of existing squatter settlements in Seoul and Pusan. The problems of shelter stemming from this period remained as a major issue in subsequent regimes of accumulation.[2]

Population concentration in the burgeoning industrial centres meant appalling living and working conditions for ordinary Koreans. The juxtaposition of industrial and residential functions and the universal use of coal domestically created foul living environments (Byun 1983, pp.209–211). The domestic use of anthracite coal brought high levels of SO_2 as well as widespread incidence of carbon monoxide poisoning. The seemingly inexhaustible supply of labour meant subsistence wages, a lengthening of the working day, and minimal workplace safety. Enterprises routinely provided dormitories as a means of more efficient labour exploitation. Conditions in sectors such as textiles and garments resembled those of industrial revolution England.

Seoul and Pusan experienced especially severe industrial pollution, affecting air quality, as well as the tributaries of Han and Nakdong rivers. It was indeed the severity of pollution in the large population centres which lay behind the central government's initiation in the late 1960s of industrial relocation plans. Although income was rising by the end of this decade, urban environmental quality was rapidly deteriorating. The government and private sector alike were externalising the costs of production to society and to the environment.

Yusin regulation and industrial pollution

Obliged to alleviate economic bottlenecks, to slow down population migration into Seoul and Pusan and to reduce the urban and rural income gap, in the early 1970s the state implemented a new industrial and spatial strategy. Heavy and chemical industrialisation combined with decentralisation policies both worsened and spread Korea's environmental problems (Huh, U-D. 1993, p.18). The HCIDP was underpinned by heavy dependence on fossil fuels.[3] It entailed the production of large quantities of toxic wastes. The spatial policy which centred around the 'concentrated dispersal strategy' through the construction of large industrial estates and cities in the Capital and Southeast regions enlarged the area affected by environmental degradation and at the same time concentrated pollution effects. With many of the industrial estates lacking proper mitigating facilities, the impacts were serious: a decline in crop yield for adjacent farmland, river pollution and consequent deterioration of drinking water quality (Noh 1993, Lee, S-D. 1992), coastal water pollution (Byun 1983, Konghaechubang-undong-yeonhap Yeongu-wiwonhwae 1992), acid rain (Noh 1993) and damage to forests also started to be widespread (Lee, K-J. 1993). This period saw a measurable decline in health of local population (Nishini K. and Noda K. 1991, Yu 1992). Impacts were concentrated in the newly industrialised regions of Kyonggi and South Kyongsang provinces. By the late 1970s the full impact began to be observed, and it was then that the environment became a hot issue. However, the government was unwilling to take regulation seriously. Instead, emphasising the supply side of production, the state concentrated its efforts upon developing physical infrastructure for the more 'efficient' utilisation of environmental resources.

In parallel with heavy and chemical industrialisation, a rural modernisation programme was launched, this spearheaded by the 'green revolution' in rice production. The new process depended on intensive farming, with the liberal application of chemical inputs. Although this raised productivity as well as rural incomes in the 1970s, the degradation of agricultural land and adjustments to subsidies placed Korea's farmers in a vicious cycle of 'agrochemical debt'. Chemical farming exposed rural communities to pesticide poisoning, to periodic plagues of plant pests, while tainting agricultural products with toxic residues.

The raising of the technological trajectory was associated with a corporatist super-exploitation of the environment, particularly as the state became closely associated with the chaebol groups in pursuit of heavy and chemical industrialisation. The chaebol were granted numerous privileges: monopolies in various domestic markets, lower loan interest rates and an implicit licence to pollute. With tight controls on media coverage of environmental issues, the state was able to suppress opposition and prevent it from coalescing into a political force.

In the large population centres, the environmental problems were slowly changing in character. The problems of the 1960s persisted, particularly those related to housing and anthracite use. However, in the late 1970s some areas saw a decline in industrial pollution as the government enforced relocation orders on the worst industries. In general, pollution sources merely shifted their locations to those places away from the public. Even in the 1970s, therefore, marked spatial differentiation of environmental impacts was becoming evident.

Peripheral Fordism and regionalisation of environmental problems

In the early 1980s, industrial restructuring was pressed by the state in order to readjust the inefficient industrial structure to changing world market conditions. A new focus on consumer durables and high technology demanded a raising of the industrial trajectory, within the framework of a competitive mode of social regulation. Through austere economic policies, through repression of labour unions and the political opposition, the state was able to restore rapid economic growth. The latter, however, increased the tendency of spatial concentration of capital, and hence of regional differentiation. This process was complemented by substantial infrastructure development: the overall outcome was a highly uneven spatial configuration. The competitive MSR increased the externalisation of environmental costs by industrial capital. The state, which also took to itself a neo-liberal market philosophy, under-produced environmental and social consumption infrastructure, sowing the seeds of the socio-environmental crisis of the late 1980s.

The government's continued investment in productive infrastructure not only created regional inequities, as we have already seen in the previous chapter, but also effected dramatic changes to the natural environment. Huge investments were put into developing water resources in order to meet rising water consumption.[4] However, supply fell short of demand in the late 1980s,[5] and the government formed plans to construct a further fourteen multi-purpose dams between 1995 and 2010 (Lee, S-D. 1992, p.711). Large-scale infrastructure projects, particularly those relating to water resources were likely to be seriously damaging to natural ecosystems. Reservoir construction ruined both wildlife habitats and rural settlements. These projects reduced river flow and the rivers' natural ability to absorb pollution and sustain a healthy ecosystem (Choi, B-D. 1991a, p.28). See Table 4.1.

Power generation was another part of the productive infrastructure which had great environmental impact. During the 1970–89 period, many coal and oil-fired plants were constructed, electricity consumption increasing 10.6 fold (Choi, B-D. 1991a, pp.28–29).[6] This was due to extravagant consumption by the class of newly affluent. It also reflected relatively low electricity prices[7] and the government's habitual support of provision based on crude demand with no consideration of energy efficiency (*FEER* 1991, 1 August). High levels of energy production and consumption also resulted in high levels of air pollution in Korea's cities: levels due to coal and oil fired power generation were estimated to have increased over five times between the 1970s and the 1990s.[8] The early 1980s saw a change in the government's energy policy: nuclear power plants were brought in and by 1989 they contributed a little over one half of Korea's electricity generation (Choi, B-D. 1991a, pp.28–29). By the late 1990s Korea was planning and

Table 4.1 Electricity production and consumption by source, 1970–89
(unit: 100 million Kwh)

Year	Electricity production				Electricity consumption				
	Hydro	Fossil fuel	Nuclear	Total	Manu-facturing	Domestic	Service	Other	Total
1970	12.2	79.5	—	91.7	49.8	8.0	9.1	10.5	77.4
(%)	(13.3)	(86.7)	(0.0)	(100)	(64.3)	(10.3)	(11.8)	(13.8)	(100.0)
1980	19.8	317.8	34.8	372.4	220.3	53.2	33.3	20.5	327.3
(%)	(5.3)	(85.3)	(9.8)	(100)	(67.4)	(16.3)	(10.2)	(6.1)	(100.0)
1989	45.6	425.5	473.7	944.7	500.5	151.8	115.8	36	821.9
(%)	(4.8)	(45.0)	(50.2)	(100)	(60.9)	(18.5)	(14.1)	(6.5)	(100.0)

Source: EPB (1990), *Major Economic Indicators*, pp.106, 110, cited in Choi, B-D. (1991a), p.29.

building a further series of nuclear plants. However, the government has failed to plan any increase in nuclear waste reprocessing capacity, or seriously to address the key environmental problems associated with nuclear power.

Increased consumption of fossil fuels in industry, power generation, the transport sector and domestic heating meant that throughout the 1980s sulphur dioxide (SO_2) levels in Seoul, Pusan, Ulsan and other major cities exceeded the permitted average annual level of 0.05 ppm for more than 30 per cent of the year (see Figure 4.1 for regional distribution of SO_2 pollution). This belatedly prompted the government to enforce the use of low sulphur oils in industry and in district heating plants. Although the levels of SO_2 declined significantly soon after, by the late 1980s they had returned to earlier levels in the major cities of Seoul, Pusan and Taegu. In 1990, levels of SO_2 reached a dangerous 0.315 ppm in Seoul, 0.382 ppm in Incheon and 0.215 ppm in Pusan (see Table 4.2). The levels of suspended particulates

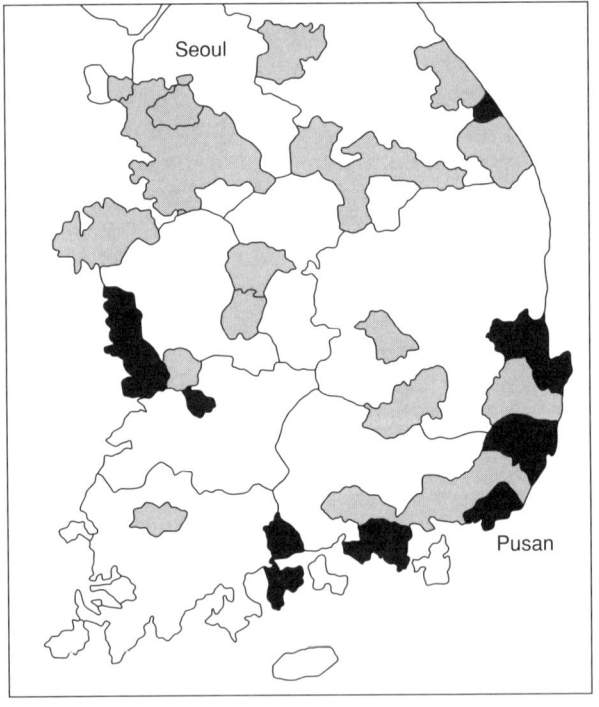

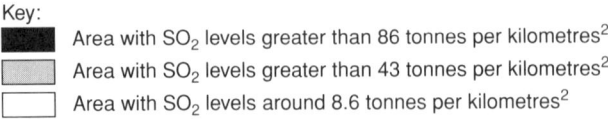

Key:
- ■ Area with SO_2 levels greater than 86 tonnes per kilometres^2
- ▨ Area with SO_2 levels greater than 43 tonnes per kilometres^2
- □ Area with SO_2 levels around 8.6 tonnes per kilometres^2

Figure 4.1 Spatial distribution of SO_2 pollution in Korea, June 1996.
Source: *Chosun Ilbo* 25th July, 1996, p.35.

Table 4.2 Annual sulphur dioxide levels in major cities (unit: ppm)

City		1978	1980	1984	1986	1988	1990	1992	1994	1996
Seoul	Mean	0.082	0.094	0.066	0.054	0.062	0.051	0.035	0.19	0.013
	Max.						0.315	0.178	0.090	0.094
Pusan	Mean	0.048	0.058	0.050	0.042	0.044	0.039	0.033	0.023	0.022
	Max.						0.215	0.129	0.104	0.119
Taegu	Mean	0.033	0.038	0.040	0.043	0.053	0.041	0.040	0.038	0.023
	Max.						0.209	0.179	0.165	0.167
Kwangju	Mean	—	0.009	0.026	0.020	0.019	0.017	0.017	0.013	0.008
	Max.						0.073	0.071	0.058	0.033
Anyang	Mean	—	—	—	—	—	0.051	0.043	0.038	0.020
	Max.						0.266	0.141	0.120	0.061
Ulsan	Mean	0.028	0.053	0.024	0.032	0.028	0.031	0.031	0.030	0.022
	Max.						0.102	0.111	0.122	0.115

Source: MoE (1991), p.52, (1997), pp.143–152.

in Seoul, Incheon, Pusan, Taegu and Ulsan also exceeded the national environmental standard maximum of 150 microgrammes per cubic metre (Noh 1993, pp.4–5). Even though air pollution in Seoul declined slowly in the 1990s, it remained excessive compared with the advanced industrialised countries, especially the maximum levels recorded.

The reconcentration of industries and population in the Capital region in the 1980s caused air pollution peaks in industrial zones such as Suwon, Anyang, Sungnam and Bucheon which were higher than general conditions in the Southeast region industrial cities of Ulsan, Masan and Changwon (Huh 1993, p.16).[9] This stemmed from the higher accumulation of population, industry and automobiles in the Capital region.

The intensification of the accumulation system under Korea's Fordist mode meant that higher consumption levels were beginning to cause problems for the environment. The increase in disposable income of the upper and middle classes in the mid-1980s went mostly into conspicuous consumption heightening social tension among those marginalised from the accumulation process. It was the industrial structure of the 1980s which laid the base for mass consumption in the next phase of development, but with the absence of the required infrastructure to cope with the waste generated. Consumption–related environmental conflicts were to explode in the post-1988 regime.

Neo-Fordist accumulation, megalopolisation and regional disparity

During Korea's neo-Fordist regime (1988–97) two distinct trends emerged: the industrial expansion of the Capital region into the West Coast region and the megalopolisation of Seoul. The large industrial estate development under the Second Comprehensive National Physical Development Plan spread to the Western coastal areas where land prices were lower. However, shallow waters unsuitable for deep water ports made large land reclamation projects in the West Coast region essential before the huge petrochemical industrial complexes in Daesan, Ahsan, Sihwa and Daebul could be developed. Although these industries provided much needed jobs and economic growth, the construction of ports and industrial estates caused much disturbance to the coastal and marine environment, and the large outflow of untreated toxic waste polluted the air, soil, rivers and coastal waters in traditional farming and fishing areas.[10] The rivers and coastal waters near these industrial complexes experienced pollution levels which exceeded BOD of 100 ppm, creating 'dead zones' (Choi 1991a, p.30, Huh 1993).[11]

As industrial developments took shape in the provincial cities of the Capital and Southeast regions, the large metropolitan cities and their suburban areas became further de-industrialised. The changing economic role of cities in the SMA, and the growth of their new middle classes, especially around Seoul, brought heightened consumption-related problems such as solid waste and sewage disposal; air pollution worsened due to spectacular increases in private car ownership. The increasing volume of solid wastes became a key problem for the Seoul metropolitan administration since its main disposal method was landfill sites. Nationally, urban solid wastes averaged 61,000 tonnes per day in 1986, increasing to 84,000 tonnes by 1990, a rise of 7–9 per cent yearly during this period (Noh 1993, p.5, see also Table 4.3 for trend in garbage production). The differences in garbage production between spatial zones reflected consumption power and the distribution of social classes. Solid waste production per capita tended to be highest in large cities like Seoul and Pusan and urban areas in the Capital region. Unsurprisingly, urban areas had higher levels of solid waste production than the rural areas, while industrialised provinces produced far more wastes than underdeveloped provinces. Patterns of output are closely allied to those of the three identified zones. In the 1990s, the incorporation of 'polluters pay principle' in a wide variety of environmental regulations resulted in a significant decline in household waste figures. These are misleading, however, since larger household items were generally disposed of privately. Industrial effluent continued to rise, the

Table 4.3 National household garbage production by year (unit: tonne/day)

	1989	*1990*	*1991*	*1992*	*1993*	*1994*	*1995*
Garbage/person/day (kg)	2.2	2.3	2.3	1.8	1.5	1.3	1.1
Total garbage produced (tonnes/day)	78,021	83,962	92,246	75,096	62,940	58,118	47,774

Source: Sohn (1997); *Korean Economic Year Book*, The Federation of Korean Industries, p.228.

bulk of which were still released into rivers as fines remained lower than the cost of treatment.

The megalopolisation of the SMA aggravated its housing problem (see Table 4.4). From the 1960s on, competition over housing intensified; housing policies favoured the middle classes and of course the profits of property capital. On the face of it, the ratio of housing units to households reached 89.2 per cent by 1996. But such statistics conceal the number of unsold apartments, which rose from some 6,000 units in 1990 to well over 100,000 in 1996 (Sohn 1997, p.221). Also many of the unsold units were in the smaller cities and towns where demand was low. The increase in demand brought suburbanisation of housing developments which encroached on green belt areas. The dense urban development of the Seoul Metropolitan Area was virtually devoid of natural green space and wildlife. Population concentration increased pollution effects: acid rain inevitably became worse and was almost twenty times higher than in areas outside the population centres (Choi 1991a, Noh 1993).

Although statistics show that air and river quality improved from the early 1990s on, physical and social infrastructure remained far from adequate. Traffic congestion in particular became a constant and universal feature of Korean life, while overcrowding on public transport rose to dangerous levels. Open space and recreation facilities were increasingly privatised. Even in Seoul which the government was anxious to promote as a global financial centre, urban environmental quality remained low, particularly outside the CBD.

With rising consumption power and recreational time of the middle classes, peripheral areas were increasingly commodified in the form of golf courses, ski resorts and condominiums. The consequences were deforestation, loss of wildlife, flooding, landslides and destruction of the ecosystem from chemical pesticide run-off.

The neo-Fordist period saw substantial political and economic reform and development. In terms of income, the government could claim that GNP per capita reached the magic target of US$10,000 in 1995. However, in terms of social and environmental infrastructure and amenities, Korea had much catching up to do. The neo-competitive MSR promoted privatisation and free market ideology with the state facilitating its version of economic development rather than providing social consumption goods.

Table 4.4 National housing provision in Korea

	1980	1990	1994	1996
Households ('000)	7,470	10,168	10,939	11,335
Dwellings ('000)	5,319	7,357	9,133	10,113
Dwellings/households	71.2%	72.4%	83.5%	89.2%

Source: Sohn (1997) *Korean Economic Year Book*, The Federation of Korean Industries, p.221.

Thus, public funds were used to promote capital accumulation in chaebol groups, enhancing the economic concentration process. The environmental protection laws of this period came about because of public pressures. However, the implementation of the laws and policies was lopsided: while private individuals and small and medium-sized businesses faced increasing environmental regulation, the activities of chaebol groups were hardly affected. Environmental impact assessments introduced to curb environmentally damaging developments were often used to simply justify their implementation. The environmental regulations of the 1990s created a façade of openness and democratic participation, while in reality they were subsumed in the capital accumulation process.

Summary

Our view of the environmental issues confronting Korea has demonstrated their deepening complexity as industrialisation proceeded. It is also evident that the spatial dynamics of capitalist accumulation were a crucial element in the manifestation of environmental problems through concentration of population and industries in favoured locations.

The historical examination revealed that, as each mode of development deepened its industrial paradigm and intensified its mode of regulation, the environmental problems worsened. The environmental problems of each phase were not resolved during the next phase, but new problems were laid upon old ones. In fact, old problems were intensified in the new phase of accumulation.

Since space is produced by the dialectical interaction of society and the environment, environmental problems are very much a function of spatial development. At global and also local at scales, the agglomeration of industries and population in core areas, and the intensive exploitation of natural resources in peripheral ones create uneven development. Thus, the uneven spatial development of the capitalist accumulation process creates and, at the same time, is a manifestation of differing environmental conditions over space depending on the nature of production and the MSR in play.

The linkages between regimes of accumulation, state development policies and spatial restructuring in Korea have been drawn in previous chapters. The specific development process has resulted in the spatial differentiation and concentration of different production and consumption activities, resulting in *combined development*. The spatial division of labour created three distinct spatial zones: the core consumption zone (CCZ), semi-peripheral industrial zone (SIZ) and peripheral rural zone (PRZ). The consequences of combined development have been uneven economic and social conditions between zones. The most pressing spatial problem is not urban–rural inequity but rather regional inequity since economic growth in urban areas within lagging regions is slower in terms of per capita income than that of rural areas in the same region. Combined development and the resultant regional inequity have been accompanied by serious environmental problems: overall, the consequence has been migration to developed areas.

This chapter has aimed to show two aspects of the evolution of environmental problems in Korea: first, environmental problems have intensified through the development period with the particular industrial trajectory and MSR; second, environmental problems have displayed a similar tendency towards differentiation as had occurred in spatial development. This is not surprising since spatial configuration is an outcome of society's interaction with the physical environment, and the overall picture of private, decentralised actions over the national landscape constitute space itself. Thus, character of local environmental problems depends upon the local socio-economic dynamics prescribed by the spatial zone created under the national accumulation regime and mode of social regulation. Therefore, in order to examine the character of environmental problems in each zone, it is necessary to examine the socio-economic dynamics within each spatial entity. This is undertaken in the next chapter.

5 Environmental problems in the three spatial zones

The historical review of environmental problems of Korea of the previous chapter drew the link between environmental degradation and the intensification of a mode of development through an escalation of the technological trajectory. We have observed that environmental problems became spatially differentiated with geographically uneven development. Korea's environmental problems differ between the three spatial zones identified in Chapter 3. The present chapter examines specific environmental problems of each of those zones, and clarifies the mechanisms by which they are produced.

Socio-environmental problems of the core consumption zone

The core consumption zone (CCZ) may be defined by several factors: an urban centre for social reproduction with high levels of business and consumption services and a low representation of manufacturing industries; concentration of state administrative functions; a relatively high concentration of Korea's middle and upper classes, but with low income groups too, and even a lumpen-proletariat caught up in the large number of low wage service and informal sector activities. The CCZ also demonstrates a high level of consumption. As such, it is a locus of struggles between social groups over the means and conditions of reproduction. The development of the CCZ has been largely confined to Seoul. With the suburbanisation of office work and middle class housing, it has only recently spread to the Seoul Metropolitan Area encompassing the satellite cities of Incheon, Bucheon, Bundang and Kwacheon. Pusan, the second largest city in Korea, may also be considered as part of the CCZ. Other regional cities such as Taegu, Daejeon and Kwangju are regional consumption centres, but these places tend to display characteristics more closely related to the semi-peripheral zones. Thus, for the purpose of this study, the Seoul Metropolitan Area is the focus of environmental problems in the CCZ.

The main environmental problems of the SMA stem from the historical legacy of the capital as the main engine of economic development, and as the repository of politics, culture and administration. The huge concentration of population and capital in the SMA has created a range of severe environmental problems. According to the Seoul Municipal Government (1990a), the top concerns of Seoul's citizenry were all environmental in nature: traffic, housing, urban environment and pollution (p.18). We will first focus on housing, the commodification of which has resulted in the displacement of the urban poor. The environmental implications of mass consumption and the capacity of the physical infrastructure to cope with waste are also matters for analysis, as are the problems associated with the increasing use of the private car. Finally, the totality of the urban and natural environmental quality in the SMA is subjected to evaluation.

Commodification of housing, urban growth and the urban poor

Land and housing are fundamental environmental needs for human reproduction. Increasing commodification renders the housing question a key issue. In Korea's case, housing problems have been exacerbated by high rates of urbanisation, concentrating populations in just a few centres. Pressures on housing have been endemic over the past decades due to the legacy of wholesale destruction of the Korean war. High rates of migration into Seoul and Pusan during the phase of labour intensive EOI of the 1960s greatly worsened the situation. The competitive MSR also tended to reinforce population concentration even after the end of the 1960s industrial strategy of concentrated development. Despite the government's efforts to disperse population from Seoul from the 1970s on, the city grew to be one of the world's largest, having a high and densely packed concentration of national population (see Table 5.1).

Housing shortages have also been very pronounced in other major urban centres such as Pusan and Taegu, as demonstrated in Table 5.2. In the 1960s and 1970s, much of the female urban manufacturing workforce in the Seoul Export Industrial Estate was accommodated in dormitory-style living quarters. They shared their accommodation in shifts – as in a factory line. For others, the private rented sector was the only alternative to living

Table 5.1 Population concentration in major cities: some comparisons

City	Part of national population (%)	Density (person per km²)
Seoul	24.1	18,121
London	13.5	4,039
Taipei	13.4	10,001
Tokyo	9.73	5,430
Paris	3.9	20,445
New York	3.0	9,153

Source: Park, C-J. (1991), p.103; SMG (1993), pp.349–391.

Table 5.2 Housing supply ratio[1], major cities,
         1985

Cities	Housing supply (%)
Seoul	50.6
Pusan	50.9
Taegu	49.1
Incheon	67.3
Kwangju	51.8
National average	69.8

Source: Park, C-J. (1991), p.112.

Note:
1 Housing supply ratio is the ratio of number of
  dwellings to number of households and official definition of households are based on registered married
  couples with or without dependants.

in squatter settlements. Housing supply ratios declined as the years progressed, and overcrowding in sub-standard dwellings was commonplace (see
Table 5.3). Around 60 per cent of Seoul's population were in the private
rented sector. The shortage of affordable rented accommodation led to
many adverse social effects. Family suicides were reported;[1] many others
were reduced to accommodating themselves in polythene greenhouses in
the nearby countryside. Dwellings were usually small and sewerage and
piped water were rarities. Although housing standards rose over the years,
as can be seen in Table 5.3, the gulf between income groups widened over
the three decades of rapid economic growth (Table 5.4). While low-income
group households lived in shared units or tiny apartments with communal
facilities, the small but growing middle class had their sights on large, modern apartments; the upper income groups had luxury houses and villas.

Table 5.3 Housing standards and supply in Korea

Classification	1975	1980	1985	1990
Urbanisation ratio	49.9	58.4	66.7	77.9
Households (1000)	6,376	7,470	8,763	11,361
Dwellings (1000)	4,734	5,319	6,104	7,160
Housing supply ratio (%)	74.4	71.2	69.7	63.0
(urban)	(56.9)	(56.6)	(57.8)	—
(rural)	(91.8)	(91.7)	(92.9)	—
Average size of dwelling (m²)	57.7	68.3	72.6	78.2
Housing area per capita (m²)	7.9	7.9	11.2	13.8
Modernised kitchen[1] (%)	—	18.2	35.1	—
Flush toilet (%)	—	18.4	33.6	—

Source: MoE (1991), p.49.

Note:
1 Modern kitchen is defined as one which has running water and plumbing, and which is
  accommodated within the unit.

Table 5.4 Housing conditions of Korean households by income group, 1985

	Income percentile	Families per unit	Space per household(m²)	Space per capita (m²)	No. of people using toilet
Lower income group	1–3	3	16.5	2	9
Middle income group	4–8	1	66.0	6.4	5
Upper income group	9–10	1	322.7	12.5	1.3

Source: Cited in ACHR (1989b), p.48.

Many of the migrants who came to Seoul during the 1960s and 1970s were unable to obtain jobs and were forced to the squatter settlements which had sprung up on hilltops, in swamps and along open sewers (ACHR 1989b, p.6). The development of slum and squatter areas in this period was very rapid and affected most large cities. The annual rate of growth of squatter settlements in Seoul was 56.6 per cent which was higher than that of Dar-es Salaam (35.7 per cent), Nairobi (22.5 per cent) and Mexico City (12.0 per cent) (United Nations 1976). By the mid-1970s, more than 250 definable squatter areas existed in Seoul (ACHR 1989b).

The growth of squatter developments brought significant environmental impact. In particular, hillside developments resulted in deforestation, leading to landslides during the monsoon season. The lack of sanitation and fresh water and electricity supply posed serious health risks to the poor.

For a lengthy period, the government ignored both the housing and environmental issues of the squatter settlements. In 1966, however, the Seoul Metropolitan Government undertook its first major squatter clearance programme. The three-year project sought to clear 136,000 dwellings containing 230,000 households, while constructing 90,000 public housing units to resettle some of the displaced families. By 1970, some 50 per cent of the targeted squatter settlements were cleared but only 16,000 units of new housing were built. In the event, the squatters were not to be rehoused in the new apartments. Instead, they were forcibly removed to Sungnam New Town, where a proportion received land sites without services. The absence of basic infrastructure such as water supply and sanitation or resources for construction of homes was made worse by the distance from jobs (ACHR 1989a, p.90). Most of the displaced eventually had to resettle in other squatter areas. As Seoul expanded, and especially with the construction of the subway system, by the late 1980s these areas themselves became prime real estate, and their poor inhabitants were once again subject to eviction (ACHR 1989b, p.6).

In the early 1970s, the government was obliged to change its approach by mass demonstrations and riots in the resettled slum areas. The *Housing Improvement Law* (1972), now placed the emphasis on clearing and redeveloping sites, with the intention of providing homeowners whose housing was demolished with apartments on the same site. A series of redevelopment projects implemented during the 1970s did bring a reduction in the number of squatter settlements in Seoul, but in the majority of cases those displaced were not rehoused as promised. Overcrowding thus increased. Residents in such areas were predominantly tenants, who were usually evicted with little or no compensation. Homeowners, in theory, received the right to an apartment on the site: in reality, they usually only received an offer of an apartment at a 'low price' which they could not afford. Many were forced to sell their rights to these apartments to businesses or wealthier households. Between 1960 and 1980, a total of 117 square kilometres of Seoul was redeveloped in this way – around one fifth of the entire city's area (ACHR 1989a, pp.90–91). Between 1982 and 1988 around 250 sites were further designated as redevelopment areas entailing planned eviction of some 3.5 million poor people.[2] Of these, around 100 had been 'redeveloped' by 1988. Housing rights abuses in Korea were found to be amongst the worst in the region. Indeed, the 1987 Berlin Habitat conference listed Korea, along with South Africa, as the country where evictions by force were most brutal and inhuman (ACHR 1989b, pp.1–5).

The case of Mok-dong illustrates the way these redevelopments worked. In 1964, people displaced from six eviction sites in central Seoul were forcibly moved to Mok-dong, which was at that time farmland covering some 400 hectares. In 1968, more evicted people from Yeouido redevelopment were dumped there. This continued during the 1970s, and by the early 1980s Mok-dong became home to around 7,800 families – 2,600 homeowners and 5,200 tenant households evicted from other redevelopment sites. In 1984, Mok-dong was itself subject to redevelopment and 3,200 houses were destroyed. The residents were again forcibly removed. Some 23,000 apartment units were built but their actual sale price was far too high for local people; public agencies registered profits of some US$1,300 million from sales to the middle classes. No compensation or other assistance was provided to the former tenants. The farmers who owned land were paid one-sixth of the market value (ACHR 1989a, p.91).[3]

With increasing vocal opposition by both homeowners and tenants to redevelopment schemes, from the 1980s the state introduced a new model: the 'joint (or co-operative) development' strategy. This measure was designed to defuse popular opposition, demonstrations and sit-ins. In this new programme, responsibility for redevelopment passed to the construction companies. An objective was the incorporation of slum homeowners in the development process, by granting them priority in low-cost purchase of apartments in the new development. However, tenants were excluded from the process even though they usually comprised three-quarters of the residents of such areas. As a document produced by the Urban Poor Institute commented, the only rights enjoyed by tenants were 'to move elsewhere, or resist eviction, get beaten up and then be driven out' (ACHR 1989a, p.91). In fact, the position of the construction companies allowed them to sabotage government intentions. Residents who opposed redevelopment suffered harassment, non-residents were often permitted to purchase units, while violent and sometimes fatal incidents were manufactured by the construction companies in pursuit of their aims.[4]

For most segments of the urban poor, including many landowners, low levels (or in the case of tenants, complete absence) of compensation[5] meant no alternative but to seek accommodation in other low rent areas, that is in other squatter settlements. Even if the difference between their compensation and apartment prices could be afforded, there were other factors preventing resettlement on the same site. New units were expensive to maintain, while jobs which had existed nearby were no longer there. Thus, most displaced owners sold their rights to new units and shifted to other squatter settlements further from the city centre (Chang, S-M. 1991, p.384). By 1989, Seoul's private rented sector still accounted for over 60 per cent of its population; a high proportion occupied old or slum housing areas, to be earmarked for redevelopment in due course. The redevelopment schemes were hugely costly to the many displaced by redevelopment, but hugely rewarding to the construction companies (ACHR 1989a, p.93).

The brutal way in which these redevelopment projects were pursued in the mid-1980s was closely allied to the preparations for the Olympic Games of 1988. Urban redevelopment projects were used to provide the sports stadia, accommodation, hotels and other tourist facilities needed for the event as well as for the government's 'rehabilitation' and 'beautification' projects which were seen as important in enhancing the image of South Korea internationally. This redevelopment programme largely focused on what the government considered 'slums' and unsightly areas which were visible from main roads or near Olympic facilities and hotels. During the spring and summer of 1988, many communities were evicted from such sites, simply because they were visible from the path along which the Olympic torch was to be carried (ACHR 1989a, p.92).

An important reason for the scale of redevelopment was the power of the large construction companies and their need to find more contracts within South Korea as the volume of work overseas decreased. During the 1970s, the rapidly growing chaebol conglomerates started to form huge construction companies by taking over smaller firms. Such companies became the backbone of the chaebol and their mammoth business empires, allowing the accumulation of vast profits through the development of housing schemes in Korea consisting of medium and large-sized apartments (27 to 55 pyeong).[6] Profitable ventures were also undertaken overseas. The international operations of South Korean construction companies, largely in the Middle East, had grown rapidly during the 1960s and 1970s, and by 1981, they ranked among the world's largest contractors. The sudden decline in the Middle East market of the 1980s brought heavily committed firms to the brink of bankruptcy (ACHR 1989a, pp.92–93, 1989b). In an effort to curtail the ripple effect of this crisis on chaebol oligopolies and, indeed, upon the entire economy, the government provided insolvent companies with financial concessions awarding them large contracts in the domestic market (ACHR 1989b, pp.53–54). It was the boom brought by the Olympic Games which was decisive in pulling back the large construction companies from bankruptcy.

Government housing policy all along discriminated in favour of the well-to-do. This is indicated by the changing size of units provided: from 1970 to 1980 the number of new units under 15 pyeong (50 m^2) dropped by 30 per cent while units between 15 and 30 pyeong increased by more than 270 per cent (ACHR 1989b, pp.54–55), see Table 5.5. The return on larger units was disproportionately high. Market prices for units larger than 85 m^2 (26 pyeong) were 16.5 per cent higher (Chang 1991, p.384). This policy allowed two goals to be attained: higher profits for property capital and satisfaction of the demands of the middle classes – the hegemonic bloc.[7] The trend towards larger units was justified in policy terms by the 'housing filtration' argument, whereby it was asserted that the development of medium and large size units permitted the middle and upper classes to ascend to better standards, freeing inferior units for the lower income groups (Ha 1991, 1992). By the 1980s, this notion had lost credibility, for the housing crisis had spread to white-collar workers; they could no longer easily secure mortgages due to spiralling prices.

For Seoul, the severity of the housing crisis was magnified by the sheer scale and rapidity of the process of concentration of capital and population, alongside an absence of effective government policies favouring poorer households (ACHR 1989a, p.93). Housing was certainly not acknowledged as a right and government rental housing was seen as a burden on public expenditure. Under a more democratic regime, however, the growing political constituency of the working classes finally led to the first such housing offered in 1990. Even then, the government designated less than 20 per cent of the 'two million housing unit construction scheme' for public rental housing (Ha 1992, p.254). The number of households living in one room in 1985 was estimated at 2.8 million nationally, 40 per cent being in Seoul. Even then, 20,000 had to make do with polythene greenhouse homes. By 1990, the situation had actually deteriorated: households occupying a single room were 2.9 million nationally, though the part accounted for by Seoul

Table 5.5 Average size of housing units in two districts before and after renewal (m^2)

	Nation	*Sadang District (Joint renewal area)*	*Keumho District (Joint renewal area)*
Before renewal	75.2	49.5–56.1	69.3–82.5
After renewal	75.2	114.5	120.5

Source: Korea Housing Study (1989) *A Study on Housing Problems in Korea*, Korea Housing Bank and MoC (1989) *A Study on Remedies of Urban Redevelopment Program*, cited in Chang, S-M. (1991), p.384.

had reduced to just over 30 per cent because of displacement beyond the municipal boundaries (Seo *et al.* 1993, p.340).

Seoul's new town developments were implemented in the late 1980s as part of the two million housing unit supply policy to relieve the chronic and acute housing crisis, creating dormitory cities without their own employment base. Thus, instead of relieving urban diseconomies, the new town policies heightened population concentration and its attendant problems in the greater Seoul region.

Under immense pressure to meet targets and realise high profits, the construction companies and the public housing authorities built high rise apartments in dense configurations. Shortages of cement and skilled labour combined with the rush for profits resulted in housing being built to low quality. In addition, the living environments of the new towns were marred by deficient public amenities and utilities, particularly water supply, bus services and shops. Unfinished road works were commonplace.

The suburbanisation of housing required the relaxation of zoning restrictions. This was for land that had previously been considered either unsuitable for residential construction, or to be conserved as green space. Special legislation was brought forward to allow the construction of new towns in green belt areas. The most notable development was Kwacheon new town, built as part of the government offices relocation programme. The completion of Kwacheon was followed by numerous new town developments within and beyond the green belt. Although Bundang and Ilsan new towns lie beyond the belt, Pyungchon, Sanbon and Joongdong are well within it.[8] This new town programme was a collaborative venture between the state agencies and the chaebol construction companies.

Thus, in the supposed cause of public interest, the state proceeded to assault much of the natural environment in the SMA green belt, appropriating large amounts of public land for the military as well as for many projects with the character of 'hegemonic'.[9] Park, C-J. (1991) has shown that more than 80 per cent of the abuse of the green belt area was committed by government agencies, in contrast to the violations on the part of residents at merely 15 per cent. The government also encouraged the range of leisure developments in the green belt and National Parks – golf courses, ski resorts and condominiums (*FEER* 1995, 16 Nov).[10] This tolerance shown to capital was not extended to the residents in the green belt. Small private developments such as extensions to houses or farm buildings were met with strict application of the law. The consequences of untrammelled development of golf courses, ski resorts and condominiums was an extensive catalogue of environmental damage, ranging from forest devastation, pesticide, sewage and solid waste pollution to unsustainable levels of water consumption.

The appropriation of the natural environment brought a stark decline in wildlife.[11] In 1990 there were almost 600,000 car trips daily on the suburban highways within the Seoul Metropolitan Area (Figure 5.1), a volume directly

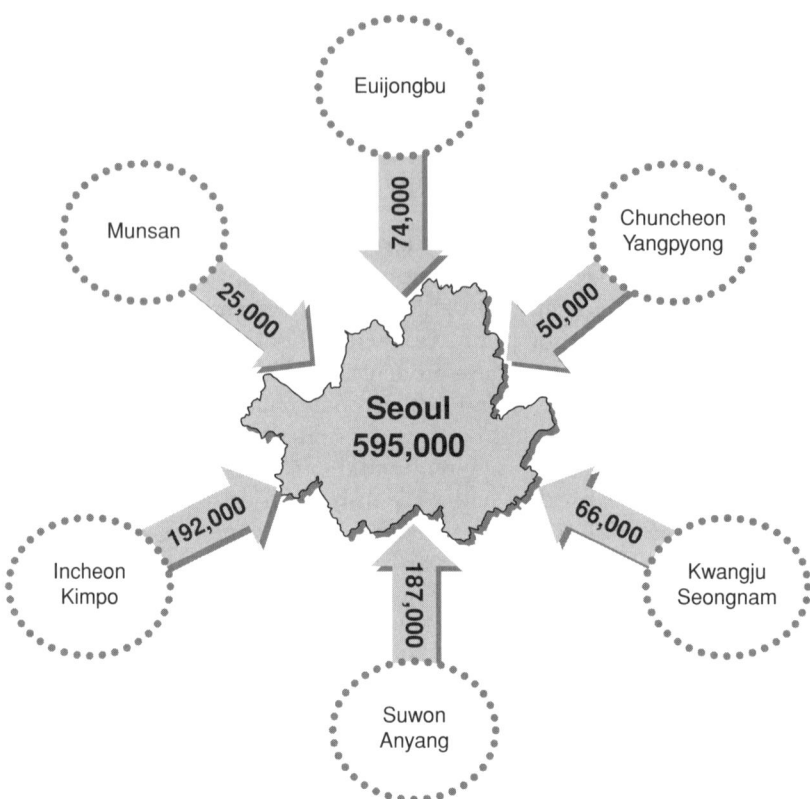

Figure 5.1 Car commuting between Seoul and its satellite cities in 1990.

Source: Derived from Park, C-J. (1991), p.184.

consequent upon the extensive growth of new towns (Park, C-J. 1991, pp.182–185). The vast increase in motor traffic was the main contributor to Korea's acid rain levels (Lee, K-J. 1993).

Following the 1997 financial crisis, the government relaxed green belt restrictions on many of the less environmentally sensitive areas in order to boost the economy through the revival of the construction sector. The creation of more housing in these greenfield peri-urban sites promises to merely exacerbate the range of environmental problems.

Population concentration, mass consumption and the waste problem

With the changes in the dominant MSR of the late 1980s, there was a rapid increase in wages of the middle and working classes and a tendency towards spatial reconcentration of capital and population in the Seoul Metropolitan

Area. Dense private consumption activities meant highly concentrated production of waste. In addition, one of the most serious environmental issues in Korea, as globally, has been the increasing consumption of fossil fuel resources with its consequences both regionally and globally. In its rapid industrialisation drive, Korea has made profligate use of energy. Oil consumption increased dramatically until 1978; thereafter, dependence on petro-carbons declined slightly with the implementation of the nuclear programme (MoE 1991, pp.54–56). Since the 1980s, however, the increased ownership of household durables has greatly increased electricity consumption. Air conditioners, fridge-freezers, washing machines and domestic heating equipment have become commonplace; the power generation industry in its turn became a major source of urban air pollution.

Rapid increases in domestic energy use reflect the structure of government subsidies. Chung (1993) claims that the Korean government has subsidised petroleum prices much more heavily than in Japan or Taiwan (p.69), benefits of which have been enjoyed by the middle classes residing mainly in modern apartment blocks using oil-based heating systems. Lower income groups had to rely upon cheaper but unsubsidised anthracite coal.

Domestic heating has been a key contributor to Seoul's air pollution. Of sulphur dioxide emissions from fixed sources, 32 per cent came from anthracite (mostly home heating and power generation) and 66 per cent from Bunker-C type oil (mostly industries). In terms of carbon monoxide, 41 per cent came from anthracite and 57 per cent from gasoline consumption (OoE 1981, p.11). Seoul's average SO_2 pollution level declined after the implementation of the air quality policy in the 1980s, but the levels of the 1990s still exceeded environmental standards, particularly in the winter months due to the use of high sulphur content fuels for heating purposes.

Oh (1991) clearly demonstrates the interzonal differences in the levels of SO_2 within Seoul (Figure 5.2).[12] The southwest industrial districts such as Munrae and Kuro, and the areas of population concentration to the north of the Han river such as Kilum-dong and Ssangmun-dong showed very much higher levels of air pollution than average – up to 0.130 ppm. Working class residential areas which used more anthracite tended to have higher SO_2 pollution levels. Oh's research revealed that the high SO_2 concentrations corresponded to higher population density rather than to the distribution of offices, hotels and shopping complexes. Thus, the spatial variation in Seoul's air pollution levels, especially in the winter months was mainly accounted for by differences in coal and oil use. The worst affected areas were generally working class and poor districts (Oh 1991, pp.50–51). The high level of sulphur dioxide released from anthracite coal briquettes and Bunker-C oil did, in due course, bring official promotion of cleaner fuel. However, the use of coal briquettes remained prevalent in the 1990s, particularly in poorer districts.[13]

The government's enforcement of low sulphur oil, and liquid nitrogen gas temporarily lowered air pollution in the early 1980s, but it soon

Figure 5.2 Isopotential graph of SO_2 levels in Seoul, 1990.
Source: Cited in Oh (1991), p.38.

continued its upward trend due to the lax regime of government regulation. Permissible emission levels from automobile exhausts were high
in Korea compared to elsewhere (see Table 5.18, p.173), as were levels of
sulphur in petro-carbons (see Table 5.6). Rising coal sulphur content
is demonstrated by the data of Table 5.7: 1973–90 saw a 334 per cent rise
in the SO_2 released per tonne of coal (Park, C-J. 1991). Thus, the decline
in anthracite reliance was offset by higher sulphur contents. The government's regulatory stance can be explained by its support for the ailing coal
industry, as well as pressures from an oil industry which resisted investments
in desulphurising plant.[14]

Air pollution showed higher concentration in districts with greater per-
centages of lower income households, and this in turn has been associated
with the incidents of respiratory illnesses, especially in the younger age
groups. The medical data shows high levels of headaches, and eye, throat
and lung infections (Oh 1991, pp.50–51). Furthermore, Seoul has experienced a localised greenhouse effect – a heat island with increasing acid
rain occurrence (Choi 1991a).

Table 5.6 Permissible levels of sulphur in oil: some comparisons (%)

	Gasoline	*Kerosene*	*Light oil*	*Bunker oil*	*Bunker C*
Korea	0.25	0.5	1	2	4
Japan	0.05	0.05–1	0.5	0.5	0.35
US	0.09	0.08	0.5	—	0.3

Source: Park, C-J. (1991), p.236.

With the rise in mass consumption of the 1980s, the questions of waste disposal and sewage treatment were to take a higher profile. Human wastes now became the single greatest cause of river pollution in the CCZ. Until the 1980s, sewage had been collected separately and transported via tanker-trucks to treatment facilities. In the 1970s, only 71 per cent of night soil collected received basic treatment, and the rest was discharged into the Han River and its tributaries (Byun 1983, SMG 1990a, pp.76–77). The Han river, coursing through the middle of Seoul, has a basin which extends over 27 per cent of the total land area of Korea, encompassing almost half the population. In 1989 contaminated material in terms of biological oxygen demand (BOD) load index constituted as follows: 83 per cent domestic sewage, 10 per cent industrial effluent and 7 per cent livestock farm waste-water. The North Han River contributed 5.2 per cent of contamination, the South Han River 15.5 per cent, the capital's suburbs 28.7 per cent and the Seoul area 50.6 per cent. Thus, nearly 80 per cent of the pollution occurred within Seoul and the suburbs (SMG 1990a, pp.76–77). Although the up-river contamination was modest, it nonetheless badly affected much of the capital's drinking water (Park, C-J. 1991). The Paldang reservoir, the main source, was tainted by untreated sewage from domestic, farms and leisure developments in the seven upstream counties. Around fifty golf courses also contributed to the pollution of the river's tributaries with toxic pesticides and herbicides. The BOD and bacteria levels of the Kyongin-cheon deteriorated to 5.7 ppm in 1988. This tributary was one of many polluting the Paldang reservoir (Park, C-J. 1991, p.240).

Although the quantity of industrial effluent flowing into the Han river was relatively small compared to domestic sewage,[15] with its high concentrations of heavy metals and other toxic substances it posed serious environmental problems. Despite on-site treatment facilities, industrial effluents were often discharged without treatment at night and during rainy seasons

Table 5.7 Sulphur content and SO_2 emission of coal, 1973–90

Year	*1973*	*1982*	*1990*	*90/73*
Sulphur content (%)	0.41	0.6	0.79	193
SO_2 emission per ton (kg)	4.3	10.9	14.3	334

Source: Park, C-J. (1991), p.235.

(Park, C-J. 1991, p.240). The industrial estates around the Yeongdungpo and Kuro districts, located in the heart of Seoul, have posed serious problems for downstream locations. In the 1980s and 1990s, river pollution became worse due to the rapid increases in the use of petrochemical-based detergents from 1.9 kg per capita per year in 1980 to 6 kg in 1990, an increase of more than 300 per cent in just ten years. Korean manufacturers produced detergents with highly toxic substances,[16] long since controlled in the advanced Western countries (Choi 1983, Park, C-J. 1991, p.235).

Since the construction of the first municipal sewage treatment plant at Cheongkye-cheon in 1976, providing primary treatment to 150,000 tonnes of effluent per day (and serving about 1.3 million people), the provision of sewerage and treatment plants seriously lagged behind the rate of population growth (MoE 1991, p.63, Byun 1983). From the late 1980s, as public concern grew over the deterioration of water quality, there was increased investment in mains sewer pipes and treatment plants. However, the limited implementation of the programme left much of the river exposed to continued pollution.[17] Although Seoul received the bulk of national investment, and was able to provide sewerage to 95 per cent of the population, the system still relied on rainwater drains. Nationally, just 31 per cent of the population was covered by 1990 (MoE 1991, p.34). Even when sewage was treated it remained a health hazard because the basic process was unable to remove parasite eggs or adequately break down chemical detergents (Byun 1983). See Table 5.8.

With broken-down residues increasing the level of dissolved cadmium and mercury in the water and raw sewage continuing to be discharged straight into the Han river system, water quality remained well below the environmental minimum. In 1990 the BOD of the Han at Paldang (an upstream location outside the Seoul boundary) and at Kayang downstream were below standard. Kuui, an upstream point and Noryangjin, a midstream point within Seoul were brought within environmental limits, as shown in Table 5.9. However, at both Noryangjin and Kayang pollution levels were still considered serious because of the many water supply intakes below these points. Tributaries of the Han within Seoul, the main receptors of sewage, showed BOD levels of 40–140 ppm; they were breeding grounds for malarial mosquitoes (SMG 1990a, 1990b).[18] Instead of

Table 5.8 Provision of sewage treatment plants, 1981 and 1990

Year	No. of cities with treatment plants	No. of treatment plants	Facility capacity (1000 ton/day)	Percent of population covered by sewerage pipe (%)
1981	3	4	822	18
1990	18	22	5,393	31

Source: MoE (1991), p.63.

Table 5.9 Water quality (BOD) of the Han river

Location	Environmental limit	1982	1985	1987	1988	During Olympics (Oct.1988)
Upstream (Kuui)	Less than 3	1.5	1.7	1.4	1.6	1.1
Midstream (Noryangjin)	Less than 6	5.4	5.9	4.3	4.3	2.2
Downstream (Kayang)	Less than 8	12.8	14.6	7.4	9.9	3.2

Source: SMG (1990a), p.78.

removing these open sewers, the Seoul Government, simply covered them with concrete and made new roads.

A crucial issue arising from river pollution has been that of safe drinking water provision. In the case of Seoul, by the 1990s the city drew water from six points on the Han, two above and three below the areas where large volumes of waste are discharged to the river. Water quality was adequate near the upstream intakes, but was far below standard at crucial downstream intakes. The water quality for urban centres lower down the river like Incheon was even worse. Although water was treated, water-borne diseases continued to be a serious problem due to outdated purification systems (Byun 1983, p.215, Park, C-J. 1991, p.243).[19] The loss of public confidence in tap water brought the rapid growth of the bottled water business, readily affordable only to the middle and upper classes. In the period after 1987 the state did endeavour to ameliorate river pollution by investing in new sewerage facilities. At the same time, environmental standards were lowered to make water quality figures appear more acceptable. The authorities also resorted to the public relations device of banning shampoo and detergent use in public and commercial premises.

As for solid wastes, as Table 5.10 shows, the rate of production was especially high from 1987. This corresponds to the beginning of the neo-Fordist

Table 5.10 Generation of all municipal wastes in Korea

Year	Amount (1000 tonnes)	Rate of increase p.a (%)	Per capita per day (kg)
1984	54,347	—	n.a.
1985	57,518	5.8	n.a.
1986	61,072	6.2	1.99
1987	67,031	9.8	2.09
1988	72,897	9.7	2.17
1989	78,021	7.0	2.22
1990	83,962	7.6	2.32

Source: MoE data, cited in Lee, S-D. (1992), p.713.

Note
n.a. = not available.
The data is an average of all urban centres above 20,000.

Table 5.11 Growth in Seoul's garbage output, 1970–89 (kg/person/day)

Year	1970	1975	1980	1989
Garbage	1.27	1.29	2.51	2.82

Source: cited in Park, C-J. (1991), p.252.

regime and the rapid rise in wages. The increase was 7 per cent annually, and the average waste per person stood at 2.3 kg per day in urban areas and almost 3 kg per day in Seoul. About two-thirds was contributed by coal briquette ash and food wastes, with increasing amounts of plastic packaging (MoE 1991, p.54). The increasing population concentration in the SMA made solid waste disposal a particular issue for the authorities. See Table 5.11.

The figures for 1988 show that the main method of disposal remained landfill sites (Table 5.12). As a result the main solid waste landfill in Nanjido, which is within the Seoul municipal boundary had grown into a mountain 100 metres in height and 2 kilometres in length. This mountain of garbage became the symbol and legacy of unsustainable growth policy of the rapid development period.

Although some of Seoul's garbage was incinerated, unsophisticated plants could not adequately cope with unsorted materials which produce toxins on incineration. Even clinical waste from hospitals was dumped in landfills. In the mid-1990s, the government's efforts to construct more incineration plants met fierce resistance from local residents who feared the environmental effects and the consequences for house prices.

The early 1990s saw the beginning of a new approach to waste management. The government introduced polluter-pays regulations, these imposing full costs for disposal. This encouraged segregation and recycling of aluminium, paper and bottles; but it also increased illegal dumping of larger items such as used tyres. In order to reduce waste at source, in 1995, the state brought in compulsory separation of recyclable items and

Table 5.12 Garbage volume and disposal by method, 1988 (1000 tonne p.a.)

	Total	Landfill	Incineration	Recycling	Uncollected
National	72,897 (100%)	69,248 (95.0%)	1,210 (1.7%)	1,759 (2.4%)	680 (0.9%)
Seoul	28,800	28,548	252	—	—
Self-administered cities	17,141	16,223	1	725	192
Province	26,956	24,477	957	1,034	488

Source: MoC data, cited in Park, C-J. (1991), p.252.

Note:
Self-administered city refers to Pusan, Incheon, Taegu and Daejeon.

devised a 'limited quantity garbage system', by selling standard bags for domestic waste the price of which included the cost of disposal.

The state was keen to shift responsibility for the urban environmental problems to consumers (see Chapter 6). However, levels of waste production were not high if compared to the advanced industrialised countries or even to other NICs. The urban environmental crisis was closely linked to state policy: subsidisation of fossil fuels, promotion of profligate use of energy, alongside neglect of investment in environmental amenities and low standards of regulation. Much of Korea's river pollution could have been avoided through coherent strategy for sewage management; the solid waste disposal problem could also have been largely solved by modern incineration systems. The key priority of the Korean state remained the capital accumulation process, which greater levels of social environmental expenditure would have hindered.

Only in the late 1990s, we have seen concerted efforts by the municipal administration to deal with environmental problems, particularly after the implementation of local autonomy, giving local leaders relative freedom to deal with local issues as against national economic goals.

Mass ownership of automobiles and the environment

In the state-propagated ideology of modernisation, the car has held centre stage as the ultimate consumer item. Rapid increases in automobiles ownership was, therefore, directly linked to a hegemonic ideology. More than elsewhere, the association of the car with wealth became deeply imbedded. Further, the Korean preference is for large capacity, prestige vehicles. Such exhibitionism can perhaps be traced to the dissolution of the traditional Confucian hierarchy and the quest for new identities.

The impact of increased levels of car ownership has been immense, indeed is central to the CCZ's environmental problems. Air pollution, waste oil pollution, disposal of tyres, road congestion, road casualties – these came to Korea in the 1980s in a most extreme form.

Since the early 1980s, the Korean government has of course strongly supported the growth of a domestic auto industry, investing a high proportion of government spending on road building rather than on public transport. Table 5.13 shows the steady growth in dependence on automobile

Table 5.13 Modal split in Seoul's transportation, 1983–88 (% of passengers)

Mode of transportation	1983	1984	1985	1986	1987	1988
Bus	64.3	63.5	58.0	56.7	54.0	50.6
Subway	10.0	10.1	14.0	15.0	15.5	16.8
Taxi	17.0	16.9	16.5	15.8	15.1	16.0
Car and other	8.7	9.5	11.5	12.5	15.4	16.6

Source: SMG (1990a), p.123.

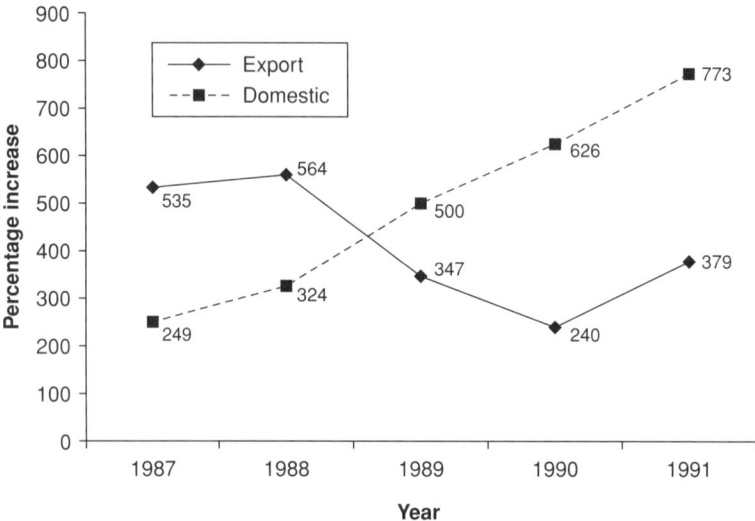

Figure 5.3 Comparison of export and domestic car sales.

Source: Cited in Lee, S-H. (1993), p.448.

transport in urban areas during the 1980s, despite the introduction of the subway system in Seoul. The rise in working class disposable income and the declining export sales of the late 1980s was simultaneous with the rapid increase in private car ownership in Korea (Figure 5.3). Figure 5.4 shows

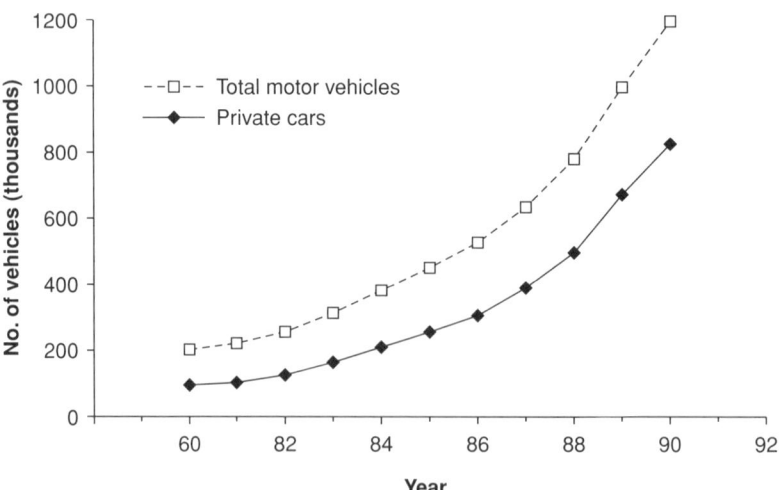

Figure 5.4 Motor vehicle ownership in Seoul, 1978–92.

Source: NSO, *Korea Statistical Yearbook* (various years).

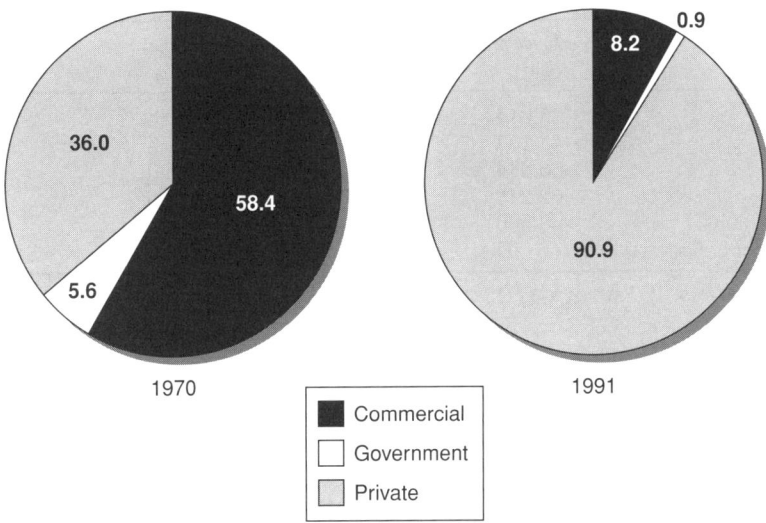

Figure 5.5 Changes in the national composition of cars by user, 1970–91 (%).
Source: Derived from SMG (1993), p.168.

the exponential growth of domestic car registration in Korea, particularly in Seoul, while Figure 5.5 indicates changes in relative ownership structure: in 1970, the private car comprised only 36 per cent of total vehicles, and in 1990, 90.9 per cent. The associated environmental problems have been accentuated by government policy. The road building programme has often produced networks which seem to defy any logic; high density urban development has been matched by lax regulation of the mal-effects such as vehicle emission standards.

Although car ownership has increased rapidly since the mid-1980s, the number of vehicles in Seoul, where the majority were concentrated, was nevertheless low compared with major cities in other nations. In 1990 the ratio of persons per vehicle stood at 9:1,[20] but traffic congestion was amongst the worst internationally.

The state road construction strategy has been dominated by the widening of existing trunk roads. As Table 5.14 shows, total road area increased by 95 per cent between 1970 and 1990, while road length went up by 39 per cent during the same period. Although the state invested more in road construction than in almost any other public project, it was unable to match the rapid rise in private car use (the road ratio increased by 0.53 per cent per annum, while automobiles increased at a rate of almost 30 per cent per annum in the late 1980s). Seoul has one of the highest population densities in the world, but it also has one of the lowest road ratios (road area:total area) and densities (road length:land area) compared to other developed countries (see Figure 5.6 and Table 5.15).

Table 5.14 Proportion of road space to total land area in Seoul

Year	Road area (km²)	Road length (km)	Road ratio (%)
1970	35,014	5,286	9.6
1975	43,107	5,786	11.5
1980	56,244	6,610	15.0
1985	62,248	6,975	16.6
1990	68,600	7,326	18.3
1970–90 increase (%)	95	39	90.6

Source: SMG, (1991); Kwon, W-Y. (1991), p.205.

Note:
Road ratio is ratio of road area:land area.

The government's preoccupation with primary or large roads has meant a neglect of secondary and tertiary road development. Korea has fewer secondary than primary roads whereas in Tokyo, secondary routes are five times the length of the primary roads. Comparing Seoul and Tokyo, primary roads are 10 per cent and 1 per cent of the total road lengths respectively (Park, C-J. 1991, p.187). This demonstrates the Korean government's dependence on trunk or wide arterial roads for urban traffic flow, whereas Tokyo's traffic is largely carried by secondary or tertiary roads. This unbalanced road development has been one of the contributing factors in traffic congestion and parking problems. In Seoul, much of the tertiary roads are so limited that they cannot accommodate vehicular traffic, reducing the road ratio to much lower than the official 18.3 per cent (see Figure

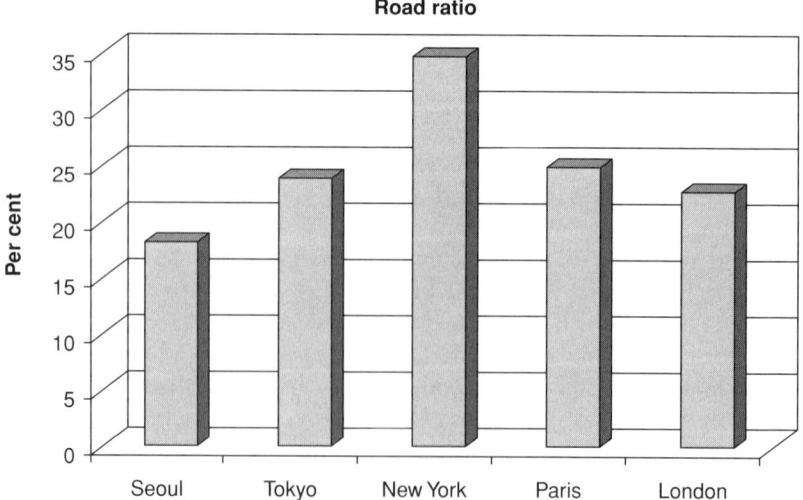

Figure 5.6 Road ratios, some major world cities (%).
Source: Park, C-J. (1991), p.185.

Table 5.15 Some international comparisons of road density (total road length per total land area) (km/km^2)

Korea	Japan	W. Germany	UK	France	Italy	US
0.57	2.91	1.98	1.53	1.46	1.0	0.67

Source: Park, C.-J. (1991), p.186.

Notes:
Data for Korea are for 1989.
Data for other countries are for 1987.

5.6). The lack of service roads for loading and unloading of passengers and goods means that congested roads have to be used. The reliance on trunk roads and urban development based on the 'super-block' system have thus become a major obstacle (Park, C.-J. 1991, pp.187–188). The state's obsession with large roads is no doubt closely linked to its productionist objectives, that is, the interests of big business in the export sector.

Traffic congestion has, in actuality, undermined the efficiency of capital accumulation due to rising diseconomies. The redevelopment of Seoul is tied to ever higher and larger buildings which inherently generate congestion. Inter-urban traffic between Seoul and its new satellites has also seen dramatic increase. Traffic impac`t assessment by local governments has been undertaken, but largely as a formality. Road congestion visibly extends to parking space availability in residential areas and the suburbs. Parking space availability in Seoul's central business area now falls miserably short of demand. Over three-quarters of existing provision, in any case, is restricted to private use. In residential areas acts of extreme violence have been a not uncommon accompaniment of parking conflicts.[21] Private developers routinely minimised road width in order to increase the floor space of developments; entrances to many apartment blocks are barred, even keeping the vehicles of visitors from entering. Korea's nightmare parking problems result from a mix of government strategy (or lack of it) and private sector greed for real estate profits (*Chosun Ilbo* 1995, 19 Sept.).

The parking issue represents just another manifestation of the fragmentation of social cohesion. The competitive nature of social regulation and overall market orientation, thus filters upwards from the productive sphere through to society at large into the very basis of reproduction of civil society. The resolution of the traffic congestion and parking problem in the long term demands a more concerted and co-ordinated effort such as density and height restrictions of new developments, improvement to public transport, enforcement of environmental and traffic impact assessments, road rationalisation, pedestrianisation and small street development. A shift in values towards quality of life rather than efficiency is required.

Spiralling car use in Korea has had severe consequences for public health and the natural environment. Cleaner fuels have meant some considerable per unit reduction in emissions. This has been offset, however, by the increasing volume of motor vehicles: from 1988–91, the contribution of the transportation sector to total emissions rose by 1.3 per cent annually. Other sectors saw a decline or significantly slower rise (Park, C-J. 1991, p.235; MoE 1992, p.486). Lead, hydrocarbons, suspended particulates (TSP) and ozone are recognised as directly harmful to human health, while nitrous oxides, carbon monoxide and sulphur dioxide are sources of acid rain. As we have seen, despite spectacular growth rates, at nine persons per vehicle car ownership in Seoul was still relatively low in 1990. But vehicular contribution to air pollution was substantial: an estimated 57 per cent of carbon monoxide, 30 per cent of nitrous oxides and 41–48 per cent of hydrocarbon loading emanated from automobiles (Byun 1983, p.213, Huh 1993, p.16). Table 5.16 shows a slight improvement in the levels of SO_2 concentration in terms of the national environmental limit of 0.05 parts per million (ppm) in 1991. Nevertheless, such levels would be inadmissible in the US, Hong Kong or even Taiwan, where limits were set at 0.03 ppm; in Singapore, they stood at 0.028 ppm (Yu 1992, p.150).

The seriousness of air pollution in Seoul is well demonstrated by the number of days annually in which the environmental maximum permissible level of 150 microgram/m^3 was exceeded. The World Health Organisation (WHO) recommends that this limit should not be surpassed on more than seven days a year: between 1980 and 1984 Seoul recorded 87 days. With 104 days, Tehran showed a worse performance (Yu 1992, p.149). The assault on public health is heightened by other pollutants such as ozone and hydrocarbons. A particularly carcinogenic substance is benzopyrene, mainly found in vehicle exhaust fumes. Table 5.17 shows the levels in Seoul, alongside comparison with cigarette smoking. The average ambient level in Seoul was equivalent to an individual smoking ten cigarettes per day. Even indoor levels were found to be excessive. The seriousness of Seoul's problem is indicated by an average level at five times that of Tokyo (Park, C-J. 1991, pp.237–238).

Table 5.16 Air pollution in Seoul, 1984–96

Year	Sulphur dioxide (SO_2) Less than 0.05 ppm*	Floating dust (TSP) Less than 150mg/m^2*	Ozone (O_3) Less than 0.030 ppm*
1984	0.061	254	—
1986	0.054	183	0.011
1988	0.062	179	0.009
1990	0.051	150	0.009
1992	0.035	97	0.014
1994	0.019	78	0.014
1996	0.013	85	0.015
During 1988 Olympics	0.015	63	—

Source: SMG (1990, 1997), p.75; Yu (1992), p.150; MoE (1992), *Environmental Yearbook*, p.120.

Note:
* Environmental limit for each category in Korea.

Table 5.17 Benzopyrene levels in Seoul by district, 1985

District	Benzopyrene (mg/ml)	Cigarette equivalent (cigarettes/day)
Cheongjin-dong (commercial)	28,312	20.2
Karibong-dong (industrial)	24,164	17.0
Wonhyo-ro (semi-commercial)	13,895	9.7
Dangsan-dong (semi-industrial)	9,721	6.8
Kuui-dong (residential)	9,416	6.6
Joongang University laboratory (classroom)	4,384	3.1
Average for Seoul	14,972	10.5
Yong-in-gun (rural area outside Seoul)	2,792	1.7

Source: Park, C-J. (1991), p.237.

Table 5.18 compares the laxity of Korea's regulatory regime to those of the US and Japan. Lower emission standards enabled automobile manufacturers to cut production costs, and commercial and private users to save on maintenance. As a major exporter of automobiles to the US, Korea is capable of producing vehicles to equally high standards for the domestic market.

Impacts of acid rain

By the 1980s, acid rain had become an acknowledged problem in the whole of the Seoul Metropolitan Region. For example, 90.6 per cent of the rainfall between August 1985 and May 1986 was classified as acidic (lower than pH 5.6). Of this, almost one-fifth was lower than pH 4.5, and 100 per cent of rain during October and November was considered acidic (Noh 1993, pp.4–5). Table 5.19 shows that in Seoul the problem worsened after 1988: in this de-industrialising city, the rising number of automobiles was increasingly responsible (Choi 1991a).

Already by the 1970s, the damage by acid rain and other forms of air pollution was evident in the forests in and around Seoul. According to Lee (1993), during the four-year period between 1986 and 1990 many common types of oak and pine disappeared. In Changdok Palace located in central Seoul some fourteen sub-species of oak disappeared. The decline in tree density at Namsan mountain in the middle of Seoul was dramatic,

Table 5.18 Permissible automobile emission levels: some comparisons (emission in g/km equivalent)

	Korea	US	Japan
Hydrocarbons	2.8	0.25	0.39
Carbon monoxide	18.0	2.1	2.7
Nitrous oxides	2.5	0.62	0.48

Source: Park, C-J. (1991), p.236.

Table 5.19 Average pH levels of rain in Seoul, 1986–90

Year	1986	1987	1988	1989	1990	Env. standard
pH	4.9	5.2	5.0	4.7	4.8	5.6

Source: SMG (1990) *State of Seoul Environment*, p.42, cited in Park, C-J. (1991), p.238.

with over 75 per cent loss during the period. Many of the relatively young trees planted during the afforestation schemes implemented since 1962 were destroyed before they could mature sufficiently to resist pollution (Lee, K-J. 1993, pp.66–68).

Acid rain damage worsened in the Capital region in the 1990s: Figure 5.7 shows the eastward and southward spread. The latter was the result of increased industrial and population concentration in the Capital region's industrial zone. The eastward spread of acid rain was almost certainly due to the increase in traffic on the Yeongdong Highway (Choi 1991a, Lee, K-J. 1993).

Quality of the urban environment

Korea's urban landscape is one of haphazard juxtaposition of office buildings, slum housing and huge estates of high-rise apartment buildings. Wide

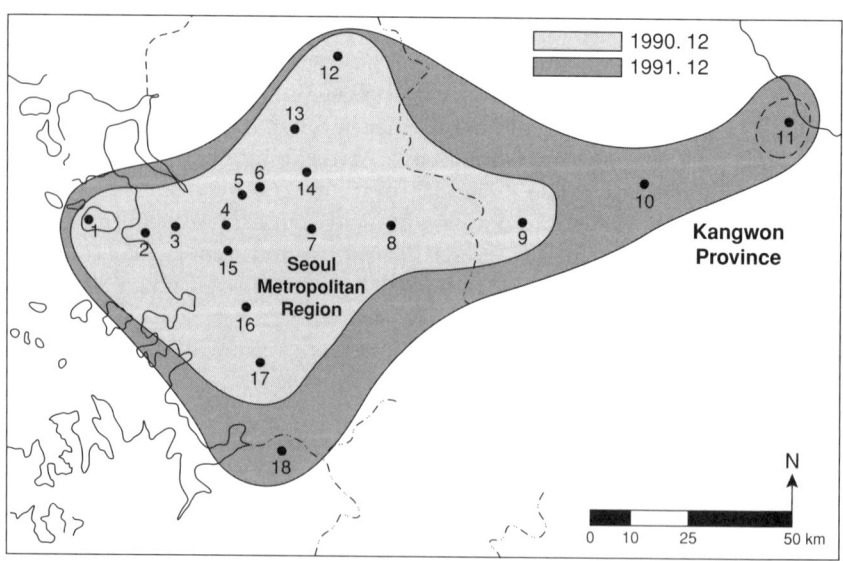

Figure 5.7 Spatial spread of acid rain damage.
Source: Lee, K-J. (1993), p.60.

thoroughfares contrast with narrow streets of the superblocks. The latter underpin Korea's urban redevelopment strategy, as does a gridiron road layout intended to enhance circulation and hence the urban economy. Pedestrians were obliged to navigate the wide interlinking roads by either subterranean footways or overhead footbridges; the less mobile and hand-icapped are at a particular disadvantage in urban Korea. Even in the narrow streets within the superblocks, pedestrians are in constant danger due to the lack of division between pavement and carriageway. Street culture became obsolete. Myong-dong and Daehak-ro are the only parts of Seoul in which partial pedestrianisation has been implemented. However, the popular shopping district of Myong-dong was slowly infiltrated by traffic and the pedestrianised area became unusable.

For non-car users in Seoul and Pusan, the subway was, from the late 1980s, the most popular mode of public transport. However, even here air pollution was found to be extremely high. Table 5.20 details concentrations of TSP, heavy metals and other dangerous and potentially carcinogenic pollutants. Park shows that of the suspended particulate matters, asbestos was also significant (Park, C-J. 1991, p.238). Even in the late 1990s little was done to tackle the TSP levels in the subway system.[22]

A further consequence of Korea's high density development policy has been the low level of green spaces within the urban core of Seoul (see Table 5.21). Woodland declined from 31 per cent (187.8 km²) in 1981 to 26.8 per cent (162.4 km²) by 1988 (Choi 1991a, pp.30–31, Lee, K-J. 1991). In the early 1990s, the total park area in Seoul was 8,470,000 m², but three-quarters was, in fact, part of the Bukhan-san National Park on the fringes of the city, where everyday usage from residential districts was difficult. In 1990 average urban park area per person in Seoul was 0.83 m², when most cities in developed nations exceeded 8.4 m² (Park, C-J. 1991, p.257). See Table 5.21. However, an increasing number of private commercial ventures took advantage of this deficiency. Commercial amusement and leisure parks such as Lotte World, the Yong-in Family Farm

Table 5.20 State of pollution in subway stations in Seoul, 1990–92

Pollutant	1990	1991	1992 (first half)
Suspended particulates (μg/m³)	534	417	441
Sulphur dioxide (ppm)	0.022	0.029	0.029
Nitrogen oxide (ppm)	0.045	0.048	0.055
Carbon monoxide (ppm)	2.8	3.7	3.1
Lead (μg/m³)	0.924	0.633	0.518
Copper (μg/m³)	2.827	1.936	1.676

Source: Lee, S-H. (1993), p.451.

Notes:
The Korean environmental standard for daily level of TSP is 300 microgram/m³ and 150 microgram/m³ for average annual level.
Data from Environmental Health Research Institute, SMG.

Table 5.21 Urban green space: some
international comparisons

City	Park area per person (m²)
Los Angeles	18.9
Washington	40.8
Brasilia	22.1
London	22.8
Paris	8.4
Rome	11.4
Amsterdam	18.6
Stockholm	68.3
Seoul	0.8

Source: SMG data cited in Park, C-J. (1991), p.257.

and the Seoul Grand Park competed for the mass market. One of the largest public spaces in Seoul is now the Olympic Park which, despite being constructed with public money, operates on a fee-paying basis, in line with most leisure sectors in this highly commodified environment.

Korea's well publicised disasters in the built environment are a further consequence of rapid economic development, especially that of Seoul. The ambitious programme of urban development, particularly of housing development in the late 1980s and early 1990s brought shortages of cement and other construction inputs. Substandard materials were consequently widely used and hasty completion schedules meant that many concrete structures were inadequate. State inspection procedures were equally skimped by officials under pressure to meet government targets. This output-driven process led eventually to the disasters of the mid-1990s – the collapse of two bridges in Seoul, the gas explosion at a subway construction site in Taegu. The collapse of Sampoong Department Store in the capital claimed hundreds of lives, planting widespread fear in the urban population. Such are the consequences of a mode of social regulation, characterised by extreme profit maximisation. The dual role of the city as a centre for labour reproduction and capital accumulation lies at the heart of Korea's urban problems. This dichotomous situation has been intense in Seoul's case where high population concentration has been accompanied by extreme reluctance of the state to provide adequate social consumption goods. In every sphere – housing, garbage disposal, waste-water treatment, water supply, transport management, building safety and provision of green space, the state promotion of capital accumulation and the suppression of collective consumption have transformed environmental problems into crises.

Semi-peripheral industrial zone: industrial pollution and the reproduction of labour

As we have seen in Chapter 3, the rapid industrialisation drive since the 1960s charted a particular spatial division of labour. The process concentrated industrial activities in the cities in the Southeast and the Capital region, these semi-peripheral industrial zones interspersed with pockets of agriculture which are home to a large industrial working class. Industries generally have a coastal location or are sited along major rivers. Thus, their development has had a wider environmental impact on natural ecosystems and farmlands (Chung 1992).

Competitive regulation, industrial waste and environmental degradation

The small waterways near residential areas are often the only source of 'general use water'; they have customarily been polluted by nearby industrial zones. Industrial waste-water from heavy chemical industries, particularly harmful due to heavy metals, has adversely affected nearly all the major rivers near the industrial cities (Yu 1992).

Table 5.22 shows the scale of pollution in the major river systems. The majority of discharges were untreated despite waste-water treatment facilities being mandatory for all manufacturing enterprises. Table 5.23 shows the volumes and BOD loadings from the major industrial estates. While the steel and metallurgical production processes in Pohang and Kwangyang produced the largest discharges, BOD loadings were amongst the lowest, as water was mainly re-used for cooling purposes. The chemical industry centres of Ulsan, Onsan and Yeocheon released lower volumes but at much higher BOD loadings. The Taegu estate, a principal centre for the dye industry, and Banweol industrial complex (light industries) also released waste-water with high concentrations of pollutants (Yu 1992, p.153).

Numerous instances have been recorded in which polluted river water has caused considerable damage to crops; an incident occurred, for instance, in the Dalsung-myon and Hwawon-myon areas, where the industrial pollution of the Kumho and Nakdong rivers were found to be responsible. BOD levels on this occasion exceeded 20 ppm (Korea Buddhist Social Education Institute, no date, p.68, Yu 1992, pp.151–152).

Table 5.22 Industrial waste-water released daily by river basin (1000 tonnes/day)

River	Nakdong	Han	Kum	Ansung	Mankyong	Yeongsan	Sabkyo
Volume of pollutants	448	402	152	67	61	36	30

Source: Data published by Ministry of Environment on 28 March 1991; cited in Yu (1992), p.151.

Table 5.23 Waste-water discharge, major industrial estates, 1988

Industrial estates	No. of firms	Major industrial activity	Released waste-water (1000 tonne/ day)	BOD load (kg/day)[1]	Rank[2]
Pohang Steel Estate	26	Steel manufacturing	3,166.4	461	10
Kwangyang	4	Machinery, metals	1,031.4	6	11
Ulsan	151	Heavy chemical	140.2	3,420	2
Onsan	18	Petrochemical	79.8	6,210	1
Taegu Dye Estate	115	Dyeing	59.2	1,194	6
Banwol	237	Light industry	58.7	2,214	3
Kumi	59	Electronics and fibres	42.4	1,101	7
Jeonju	47	Fibres and food	37.6	503	9
Yeocheon	22	Petroleum and chemicals	27.2	1,528	4
Masan Export	49	Electronic products	25.4	1,223	5
Sasang	447	Metals, fibres and chemicals	16.5	1,048	8

Source: MoE (1989) 1988 Report of waste-water treatment facility survey; cited in Choi, B-D., (1991), p.328.

Notes:
1   Pollutant quantity is after waste-water treatment.
2   Rank is by worst polluter in order of BOD loading.

Human health risks posed by industrial effluent have proved extreme in Korea (Chung, T-S. 1992, p.22). In 1984, the National Environmental Research Institute revealed in a survey of Nakdong river that mercury levels increased 700 times (to 36 ppm), and chrome levels by 40 times (to 120 ppm) in the two years from 1982 (Lee, M-H. 1992, pp.243–244). Another source reported that 16.8 per cent of the residents of industrial estates and cities were diagnosed with some degree of heavy metal poisoning (Yu 1992, p.152). In March 1991 the mid-river reservoir of the Nakdong river, supplying drinking water to Taegu and Pusan, was contaminated by chlorophenol, a highly toxic and carcinogenic compound. This incident, which released ten times the maximum level of 0.001 ppm set by WHO raised public health fears and caused an outcry against the environmental practices of the large corporations. Doosan Electronics located in Kumi industrial estate had released the substance when their incineration plant broke down. Even a thirty days' suspension of manufacturing ordered by the environmental agency did not inhibit the company from covertly discharging. The unmasking of this provoked a public boycott of the products of Doosan and its subsidiaries (Lee, M-H. 1992, p.244).

The government's stance towards the control of water pollution had long been passive. Measures remained lax despite public declarations of

Table 5.24 Emissions of sulphur dioxide by source (kilotonnes/year)

Year	Source	Heating	Industry	Transport	Electricity	Total
1978*	Emission	31	555	37	525	1,101
	Share (%)	2.8	50.4	3.3	43.5	100
1990	Emission	336.5	805.6	188.9	279.9	1,611.0
	Share (%)	20.9	50.0	11.7	17.4	100
1991	Emission	314.7	787.2	200.5	295.4	1,597.8
	Share (%)	19.7	49.3	12.5	18.5	100

Source: MoE (1992), p.486, and *data from OoE (1981) cited in Hanguk Konghae Munjae Yeonguso (1983), p.89, modified by authors.

commitment to the environmental protection from the early 1990s on. This is exemplified by the number of categories stipulated in testing water quality. The WHO schedule includes 47 categories; this is largely followed in advanced industrial nations (for example, the UK tests 51 items). Korea, however, limited the number to 29, and even then testing was not necessarily followed by any corrective measures (Yu 1992, p.152).

Air pollution from industrial plants has matched the severity of industrial effluents. Though SO_2 release by industry declined as a proportion of total emissions, air pollution from manufacturing plants remained Korea's single greatest problem. State industrial location policies concentrated pollution in the main industrial areas of the Capital and Southeast regions, and in the new industrial space of the West Coast region. See Table 5.24.

In 1981, SO_2 levels in Seoul recorded a peak of 0.886 ppm or 17.7 times the official limit. Even in 1991 there were peaks of 0.317 ppm in Karibong-dong, and 0.247 ppm in the Kuro area. However, sulphur dioxide pollution was more severe in industrial cities such as Ansan, Anyang, Suwon and Sungnam in the Capital region and the southeastern heavy-chemical industrial cities of Ulsan, Ulju, Masan, Changwon and Pohang (Yu 1992, p.149). Ulsan was particularly badly affected: in the 1970s around 180,000 tonnes of SO_2 were emitted daily, and residents of the Samsan and Dal-dong areas (Taehan Aluminum), Yeocheon-dong (Yeongnam Chemicals), the Yaum-dong area (Chosun Fertiliser) and Bugok-dong (petrochemical industrial estate) were ordered to temporarily move elsewhere when emissions reached danger levels. A survey of the Ministry of Public Health, Social Services and the Southeast Health Institute registered a peak SO_2 reading of 2.87 ppm in the Ulsan Industrial Area in 1978; in the mid-1990s this remained a world record (Korean Buddhist Social Education Institute, no date, pp.49–50, Yu 1992, pp.149–150). The notorious London smog of 1952, showed SO_2 levels at 0.3 ppm. The Capital region's industrial cities experienced worse overall conditions than those of the Southeast region: this was due to higher automobile concentration (Table 5.25).

The impact on plant life sensitive to pollution is a good measurement of levels of toxicity. A study conducted between 1982 and 1992 in Ulsan's

Table 5.25 Sulphur dioxide pollution levels in major cities by region, 1986 (ppm)

Capital region		Southeast region		Other regions	
City	SO$_2$ level	City	SO$_2$ level	City	SO$_2$ level
Seoul	0.054	Taegu	0.043	Cheongju	0.033
Incheon	0.053	Pusan	0.042	Cheonan	0.026
Ansan	0.064	Kumi	0.038	Choongju	0.024
Anyang	0.061	Masan	0.032	Kangrung	0.021
Suwon	0.058	Ulsan	0.032	Yeosu	0.021
Euijongbu	0.057	Changwon	0.032		
Seongnam	0.056	Pohang	0.031		

Source: Data from Choi, B-D. (1991b), p.330.

Notes:
Korean environmental ceiling: less than 0.05 ppm; US, less than 0.03 ppm.
The data are average daily readings over the year.

Gomsol forest adjacent to a heavy chemical industrial estate revealed the impact of Korea's new industrial cities on the surrounding natural environment. Seriously damaged forest areas expanded from a 0.5 km radius from the industrial estate to 1.5 km after five years, and to 2.5 km by 1991.[23] The species of pine tree here is common in the coastal areas of Korea and it is known to be relatively resistant to pollution. Its almost total destruction rendered the Gomsol forest an 'environmentally dead' area. The spread of American red grass was another indicator of deteriorating soil fertility. According to Lee, K-J. (1993), by 1992, it had extended to an adjacent public housing estate almost 5 km away. Such pollution from the industrial estate,[24] causing acidification and soil fertility decline has affected agricultural production around the industrial cities. Table 5.26 demonstrates the

Table 5.26 Decline in fruit production in the Ulsan area, 1961–70

Year	Production per unit area (kg/pyeong)	Percentage (%)	Number of manufacturing plants producing significant air pollution
1961	6.72	111.8	0
1962	6.62	106.9	0
1963	6.19	100.0	1
1964	6.14	99.2	1
1966	6.06	97.9	2
1968	4.12	66.6	5
1970	2.91	47.0	7

Source: Data based on Seoul National University Medical School (1973) *Study on Pollution in Large Industrial Estate*, Seoul National University, p.20. cited in Cho, J-R. (1983), p.95.

Notes:
Data for years 1965, 1967 and 1969 omitted.
1 pyeong = 3.24 m^2.

association between the number of manufacturing establishments and the decline in yield in fruit production locally.

Industrial waste is yet another issue to be considered. By 1988, Korea had some 8,000 registered firms creating significant volumes of industrial wastes, measured at 52,230 tonnes per day overall. Of this, around 4 per cent was classified as 'special' toxic industrial wastes. Sixty-six per cent consisted of inorganic substances produced by mining industries – mainly ash, dust and sludge. Of the 'special' waste produced, around half was treated and disposed of in-house, while the balance was subcontracted to waste management firms (Chung, W-S. 1992, p.21). However, these supposedly specialist companies routinely resorted to illegal disposal methods, partly due to a lack of technical capability (Yu 1992, p.153).

Data for 1990 shows that 55 per cent of industrial waste was recycled, but much of the remainder was either stored or disposed of in a high risk manner (see Figure 5.8). Heavy metals such as cadmium and mercury, difficult to treat, were commonly left in and around the factories leading to health risks to workers as well as to water and soil contamination. For example, approximately 1,100 tonnes of industrial waste was produced daily at Banweol and until 1992, there was no means of proper disposal (Yu 1992, p.154). Only two waste treatment and disposal firms existed in Korea capable of handling special toxic substances, these located in the Southeast region near Ulsan and Onsan (Chung, W-S. 1992, p.21).

Coastal water pollution in the SIZ

Coastal waters are traditionally the lifeblood of local fishing communities. Once Korea's rapid industrialisation commenced, areas near industrial complexes became the dumping ground for industrial wastes. In fact,

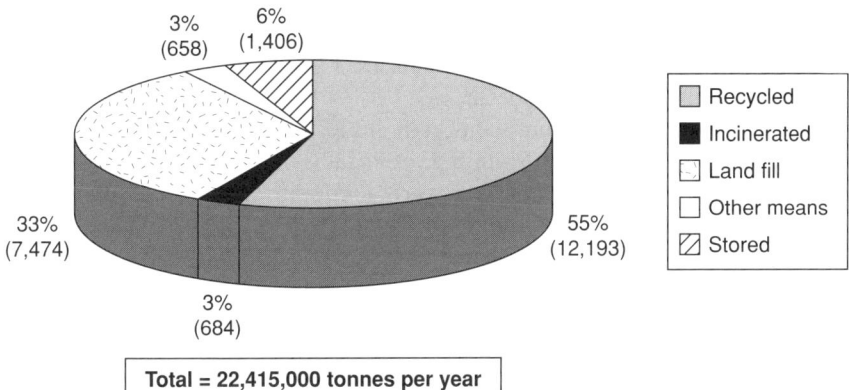

Figure 5.8 Disposal of industrial waste, 1990 (1000 tonnes/year).

Source: Derived from Yu (1992), p.153.

environmental conditions of coastal waters deteriorated in tandem with rising GNP. In addition to industrial discharges (including those from nuclear energy installations), pollution came from agriculture (livestock effluent, pesticide and fertiliser run-off), coastal construction (especially suspended solids from land reclamation) as well as from sewage. Waste from shipping, oil spillages from marine accidents and the impacts of oil exploration have added to the degradation of the coastal environment.

In the official annual survey of 1990[25] large tracts of coastal waters categorised at Grade 3 or below existed near industrial complexes, ports and large coastal settlements such as Sokcho, Pohang, Incheon, Banweol, Mokpo, Pusan, Masan and Ulsan. There were 53 such seriously polluted areas. The more extensive Grade 2 waters were further out to sea; these numbered 80 places. Sixty coastal areas and most of the sea further out from the coast were classified as Grade 1 (Konghaechubang-undong-yeonhap Yeongu-wiwonhwae 1992, p.73).[26] These patterns were reflected by data for chemical oxygen demand (COD), nitrate and phosphate pollution. By contrast, non-industrialised coastal areas like Seosan, Wando, Chungmu and Seokyupo showed reasonably clear conditions, as did areas with good water circulation and superior dispersion of pollutants (ibid.).

A consequence of high COD, nitrate and other pollution has been the epidemic growth of red algae, decimating marine life and destroying fisheries. The first appearance of *jeokjo*, the 'red tide', was in 1963 in the bay of Jindong and until the mid-1970s the occurrence had been limited to a few inland bays for short periods, with little impact on marine life. However, after 1981, *jeokjo* covered an area stretching from Pusan to Jin-hae Bay, with duration of up to two months. Most seriously affected were the coastal waters of Masan between every April and October. After 1983, *jeokjo* spread to most of the south, southeast and even west coasts (the Ulsan, Onsan, Incheon and Kwangyang bays and the mouth of Kum river) (Konghaechubang-undoug-yeonhap Yeongu-wiwonhwae 1992, p.90). In 1995, the epidemic on the south and southeast coasts caused massive destruction of marine ecosystems and fisheries, bringing huge financial losses (*Chosun Ilbo* 1995, 22 September).[27]

Another source of serious coastal pollution has been accidental and deliberate oil spillages from shipping, especially oil tankers. Routine tank-cleaning and accidental leakages were compounded by collisions and sinkings. As trade increased, the numbers of incidents multiplied (see Table 5.27). Large-scale spillages involving oil tankers occurred in 1987 at Ongjin, 1989 at Pohang (sinking of the *Kyongshin*), 1990 at Incheon (the *Korea Hope*) and 1991 at the coast of South Choongchong Province (the *Pacific Friend*) (Konghaechubang-undong-yeonhap Yeongu-wiwonhwae 1992, p.93). In 1995, two serious shipping accidents occurred (the oil tankers, *Sea Prince* and the *No.1 Yong-il-ho*), which highlighted the inadequacies of government agencies in tackling the oil slicks (*Chosun Ilbo* 1995, 27–28 July

Table 5.27 Oil pollution from vessels

Year	Incident (no. of cases)	Total discharge (1000 litre)	Compensation for property damage (million won)	Clean-up cost (million won)
1983	248	361	6,708	2,490
1984	226	201	478	446
1985	166	2,204	5,107	587
1986	158	2,529	916	796
1987	152	482	7,877	1,294
1988	158	1,058	191	610
1989	200	368	173	374
1990	248	2,421	—	—

Source: Lee, S-D. (1992), p.716.

and 22 September). These incidents were proven to be due to a market environment which tempted operators to use unseaworthy vessels and thus externalise their costs. See Figure 5.9.

Working conditions and the reproduction of labour

Neglect of safety gave Korea the world's highest recorded rates of industrial accidents, with an average of five workers killed and another 390 injured daily in the 1980s. The country also came to lead the world in the rate of occupation illnesses, with almost one person in four subject to work-related sickness or injuries; comparable rates for Japan, Taiwan and Singapore were 0.54, 0.63 and 0.85 respectively (Bello and Rosenfeld 1990, p.25). Table 5.28 shows that accidental injury and death in industry constituted the major cause of all accidents (see also Chapter 3). Pneumoconiosis and deafness associated with mining, and heavy metals and chemical poisoning relating to manufacturing are detailed in Table 5.29 (Yu 1992).

As for medical and welfare provision, this was at lower levels in the SIZ industrial cities than in the large cities of the CCZ; this can be

Table 5.28 Accidental injuries and loss of life, 1983

Categories	Number of victims
Car accidents	177,845
Fire	1,351
Industrial accidents	317,000
Coal gas poisoning	172,000

Source: *Maeil Kyungje Shinmun*, 11 June 1985; *Dong-A Ilbo*, 18 Feb. 1984 and 8 Nov 1984; cited in CISJD (1985), p.115.

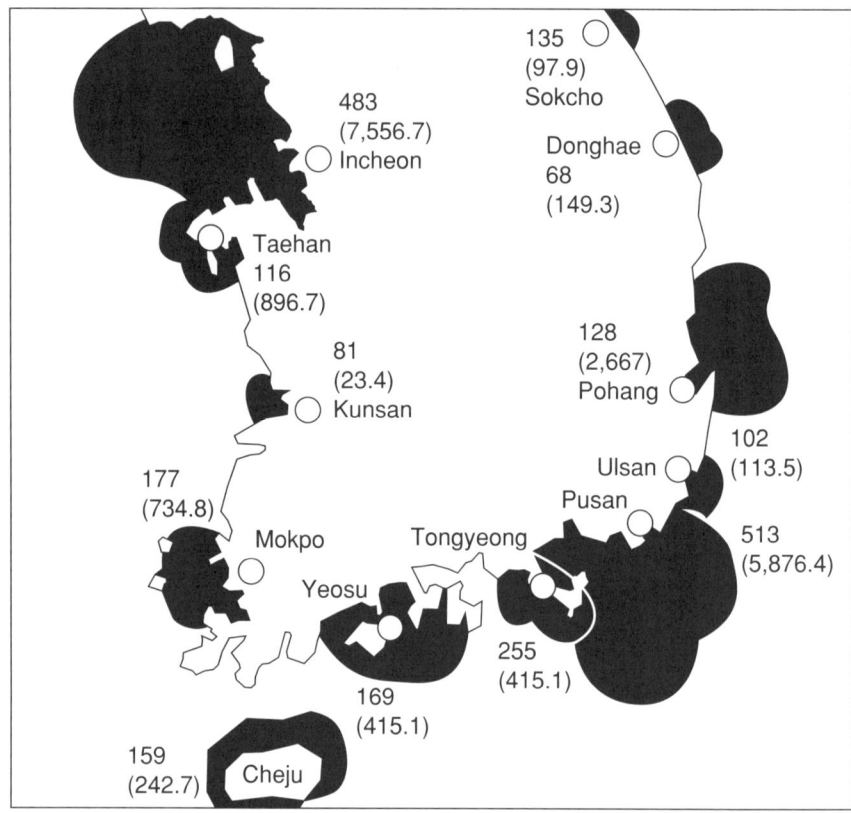

Figure 5.9 Oil spillages by location.
Source: *Munwha Ilbo*, 26 July 1996, p.3.
Note:
Number of oil spillage incidents (quantity in '000s of litres).

explained by the SIZ's lower middle-class concentrations and higher proportion of working class residents. The industrial cities in this zone have been established to serve the central purpose of production. The reproduction of the labour force was therefore largely left to the market.

Table 5.29 Work-related illness by type, 1980s (persons)

Year	Pneumo-coniosis	Deafness	Lead poisoning	Organic substance poisoning	Special chemical poisoning	Other	Total
1981	2,764	1,417	4	6	0	74	4,265
1983	3,894	2,348	61	9	9	24	6,345
1985	3,766	2,889	43	41	14	142	6,895

Source: Cited in Nishina, K. and Noda, K. (1991), p.132.

Table 5.30 Medical and social welfare services in major cities, 1992

	Seoul	Pusan	Incheon	Anyang	Ansan	Pohang	Changwon
Population							
(1000)	10,960	3,890	2,070	540	350	320	390
Hospital	154	69	17	9	2	4	4
No. of beds[1]	29,030	10,525	3,321	1,123	250	1344	305
	(2.65)	(2.70)	(1.60)	(2.10)	(0.71)	(4.2)	(0.95)
Doctors[2]	12,518	3,231	1,038	241	144	306	112
	(876)	(1200)	(1994)	(2241)	(2431)	(1046)	(3482)
Nurses	12,523	3,568	1,395	363	142	444	149
Child welfare	49	26	11	3	—	2	1
institutes[3]	(5726)	(3780)	(797)	(275)	—	(371)	(81)
Institutes for	10	7	2	2	—	2	—
the aged							

Source: SMG (1993), pp.50–51, 88–91, 98–99.

Note:
1 Data in parentheses are numbers of beds per thousand population.
2 Data in parentheses are population per doctor.
3 Data in parentheses are numbers of places for children.

Table 5.30 shows the considerable differences in provision of medical and other services between the CCZ cities (Seoul, Pusan and Incheon) and SIZ cities (Anyang, Ahsan, Pohang and Changwon). In almost all the categories, the industrial cities had lower levels of social infrastructure.

Under the competitive MSR, the private sector was driven to externalise their production costs to the environment and to minimise the cost of reproduction of labour to maintain the rate of capital accumulation. The spatial separation of the SIZ allowed pollution activities and minimisation of labour reproduction to go unchecked.

Peripheral rural zone: the degradation of agriculture and capitalisation of nature

Ecological conditions in Korea's peripheral rural zone are particularly crucial as they directly determine the livelihoods of its inhabitants. We have already considered the effects of industrial pollution on agriculture. Economic activities within the countryside, including agriculture itself as well as leisure developments have also had severe environmental impacts. The PRZ has been treated as the last frontier, the rural community trapped in a cycle of chemical dependency and debt.

Toxic earth: impact of chemical use in rural Korea

The volume of chemical input in the production of rice and other crops increased rapidly after the Korean War; the 1961 to 1964 period alone saw a 320 per cent increase in pesticide use, and toxic mercury-based products constituted 76 per cent of the total. After 1965, the appearance of *mina-mata* illness in Japan and Korea curtailed the use of this chemical. However, harmful chlorine- and phosphate-based pesticides also rose rapidly. For the period 1961 to 1983, the average annual increase in the use of pesticides was 23.6 per cent (KCFA and KAAPRI 1990, p.23).

It was the implementation of rural modernisation and the rice self-sufficiency drive of the 1970s which gave a sustained boost to the use of chemical inputs. Korea's second green revolution which introduced the high productivity *Tong-il* rice, necessitated chemical-intensive farming due to the strain's weak resistance to diseases and pests. Thus, pesticide use shot up from 8,518 tonnes in 1978 to 41,449 tonnes in 1979 (KCFA and KAAPRI 1990, p.24).

Change to the government's grain price policies obliged the farmers to supplement their income from rice with other produce. By the 1980s, pesticide application which had hitherto largely been limited to rice cultivation was extended to corn, barley, fruit and vegetables. Application to crops other than rice rose from around 15,000 tonnes in 1978 to over 25,000 tonnes in 1983. For 1990, average applications in the growing cycle of each crop were 27 for rice, 24 for apples, 17 for cucumbers, and 18 for hops (Lee 1992, p.246). Low grain prices and an ageing workforce meant dependency on pesticides and fertilisers as a means of maintaining productivity (KCFA and KAAPRI 1990, p.25, Lee, M-H. 1992, Nishina and Noda 1991).

Pesticide use in Korea has frequently proved fatal. While the authorities initially tried to deny the existence of pesticide poisoning, the death of the Ko family in 1970 brought the issue into public view (KCFA and KAAPRI 1990, p.26, Chung and Hwang 1983, p.149). Thereafter, there was rising mortality (see Table 5.31). One of the most serious group poisonings occurred in 1982 in Hongseong, South Chungchong province, where 47 people died between January and July. Research conducted by Seoul National University in 1980 revealed that 44 per cent of the rural population in the nine surveyed areas were seriously affected by pesticide poisoning.

The necessity of increasing output was heightened by indebtedness, trapping Korea's farmers in a vicious cycle. Debts mounted in the 1980s due to the reduction in government procurement subsidies, which brought falling returns. The increasing volume of cheap imported American grain

Table 5.31 Deaths due to pesticide poisoning nationwide, 1982–87

Year	1982	1983	1984	1985	1986	1987
Persons	1,186	954	1,135	1,561	1,391	1,400

Source: Nishina and Noda (1991), p.143.

Table 5.32 Some comparisons of fertiliser and pesticide use, 1991 (kg/ha)

	Korea	Japan	US	Philippines
Fertiliser	449	430	94	36
Pesticide	10.9	31.9	3.1	—

Source: Data from Lee, K-J. (1993).

and beef after 1988 struck another blow to the agricultural sector and firmly entangled Korean farmers in the global economy. From the early 1990s, organic farm products were in high demand, but few farmers were able to respond due to labour shortages. In the absence of social welfare infrastructure, and with the alienation of rural opinion in the formulation of crucial policies, the 1990s saw little possibility of halting rural depopulation. See Table 5.32.

Risk to the health of consumers has also come in the form of chemical residues. A survey conducted by the National Health Institute in 1988 in Kyonggi, South Chungchong, North Cholla and North Kyongsang provinces found pesticide levels in eleven types of fruit, vegetables and other crops to be three times the statutory limits. With fruit, most residues could be avoided by peeling the skin. But vegetables, even when washed, retained much of the toxins (Nishina and Noda 1991, pp.147–148).

The use of fertilisers, pesticides and herbicides on golf courses – created for a wealthy urban-based minority – became a major question during the early 1990s. The location of courses upstream of agricultural land and population centres, produces large amounts of chemical run-off (Park, C-J. 1991, p.240).

Table 5.33 shows the extent of fertiliser and pesticide use in golf courses. Over half of fertiliser applied is generally lost in run-off, increasing the COD of rivers (Lee, K-J. 1993, pp.86–87). Pesticide use was relatively small, its effects were more serious. Chemicals with toxicity greater than those used in agriculture have been routinely sprayed. Nishina and Noda (1991) show that of the four golf courses surveyed in Kyonggi province, high levels of organic chlorine (Daconil) were present in the water run-off: 0.1 ppm from Kwanak C.C., 0.68 ppm from Gold, 1.12 ppm from Suwon

Table 5.33 Fertiliser and pesticide use on golf courses, 1991

	Fertiliser	Pesticide
Average per hectare	166.5 kg	10.8 kg
On existing courses	1,015.7 tonnes p.a.	66.1 tonnes p.a.
On new and courses under construction	3,332.8 tonnes p.a.	216.8 tonnes p.a.

Source: Data from Lee, K-J. (1993), p.88, adapted by authors.

and 1.4 ppm from Taekwang; all flow into the Han river. This compound is known to be lethal to wildlife and human beings. Another toxic pesticide (Dacopol) was also found at very high levels of up to 6.59 ppm at Taekwang. A solution at 1.3 ppm would kill off all riverine life (pp.148–149).

Leisure industry, road construction and nature conservation

An additional assault on Korea's peripheral rural zone has come from the rapid increase in leisure developments. These have privatised natural environments, and interrupted public access which itself further contributed to environmental degradation. Benefits to local communities must be set against these severe impacts upon the environment.

The loss of forestland is a measure of these types of development: between 1967 and 1990, it averaged 8,000 hectares per year. The number of golf courses opened or under construction by 1995 totalled 300, incorporating some 25,000 hectares. Six ski resorts were in operation by the early 1990s covering over 1,000 ha and as many were added through the decade. By 1992, there were 65 rural condominiums in operation or under construction, which were built in large estates of high-rise buildings, quite insensitive to local environment (Lee, K-J. 1993, pp.84–85). See Table 5.34.

Surveys show that destruction of some 300,000 *pyeong* for an 18-hole golf course means that 300 to 700 species of plants, hundreds of species of insects, birds, vertebrates, reptiles and micro-organisms would lose their habitats. The sole use of imported bent grass for the majority of playing surfaces has made golf courses devoid of much of their native wildlife. In addition, the use of bent grass requires well-drained soil, causing both high levels of artificial watering and rapid run-off. May generally accounts for little rain, and sprinkler use monopolises scarce local water resources. During the monsoon season (June to September), the result is pesticide-laden run-off flooding of farmlands lower down the valley (Lee, K-J. 1993, pp.86–87).

National parks were first established in 1968 to protect areas of outstanding beauty and for the conservation of environment of national importance.

Table 5.34 Loss of forest area in Korea, 1975–90 (1000 ha)

Year	Total forest area	Yearly decline
1975	6,635	—
1980	6,538	13.52
1985	6,531	1.33
1990	6,476	11.01

Source: Office of Forestry (1991) *Statistic of the Forest Industry*, cited in Lee, K-J. (1993), p.84.

By 1996, there were 66 nature parks at national, provincial and county levels, covering 4.7 per cent of Korea's land area and divided into four main land use groups: nature preservation zones, natural environment zones, settlement zones and collective facility zones. Each were designated with differing degrees of land use controls. Throughout the history of national parks in Korea, recreational functions were put before conservation: first, parks were regarded as a means of local economic development through the promotion of tourism; second, they were under-funded, the authorities choosing to rely on revenue raised through the granting of commercial licences and through entrance fees (Lee, K-J. 1993, pp.88–92).

The impact of road construction to serve rural leisure developments is illustrated as follows: in 1988 as the road between Cheon-un sa, a Buddhist complex, and Banseon in Jiri-san National Park was widened and paved, visitors to the former increased from 50,000 in 1987 to more than 463,000 in 1990. To accommodate the corresponding increases in the number of cars and coaches, a large car park was built at an altitude of over 1,000 metres which necessitated the levelling of a part of the mountain area. The number of visitors using the footpath to the summit rose from 37,800 in 1987 to 263,700 in 1990. The dramatic increase in the number of visitors resulted in the devastation of plant life nearby. In 1991, this area was totally closed for a period of three years (Lee, K-J. 1993, pp.100–101).

Visitors to national parks increased steadily over the years and the damage to the plants and wildlife habitats was substantial.[28] The number of visitors to Mt. Halla National Park in Cheju Island was estimated to be 400,000 in 1990, with over 100,000 ascending the local peak, Baek-rok-dam. By 1990, the total damaged area amounted to about 18 hectares, with costs of restoration put at 30 billion won. Damage from campsites was also severe – they were dubbed 'vegetation free zones'. Lee, K-J. (1993) shows from his research on three national park campsites that most of the damage was in the 3–5 Grade category, meaning almost complete vegetation destruction. In one case, over 90 per cent of the campsite area was categorised at Grade 5, meaning severe soil erosion and widespread destruction of mature tree-cover. Summer peak season concentration of visitors affected the reproduction habits of birdlife, threatening the survival of certain species (Lee, K-J. 1993, pp.103–104).

Social infrastructure and the rural living environment

Korea's rural population, particularly tenant farmers were especially severely exploited during the Japanese colonial times. The post-Korean War period brought redistribution of land. However, the new owner-farmers cultivating small parcels of land remained at subsistence level, as Korea's export-oriented industrialisation strategy required a squeezing of the rural economy. Rural modernisation in the 1970s which aimed at raising productivity to stabilise domestic food prices, and at self-sufficiency in order

Table 5.35 Urban versus rural infrastructure provision, 1984

	Percentage of coverage			Telephones per 100 persons
	Paved roads	Piped water	Sewage treatment	
National	46.3	64.0	8.0	13.8
Large cities	68.1	94.1	17.5	19.0
Small and medium cities	59.2	80.1	0.7	14.3
Rural areas	15.4	19.2	0.0	7.2

Source: Kwon (1988a), p.60.

to obviate grain imports, achieved little in raising the level of social and environmental amenities and services. Basic infrastructure, services and utilities remained far less developed in rural areas than in the large cities of the CCZ or the small and medium cities of the SIZ (Tables 5.35 and 5.36). The lack of higher educational facilities in rural areas has been a particular factor in migration to urban areas, leading to the demise of many rural schools.

Thus, the environmental conditions of Korea's peripheral rural zone have been both intensively and extensively utilised both in agricultural production and by leisure and recreational developments. Although the agricultural sector has not been directly incorporated by large business due to stringent land tenure laws, it has been integrated into the overall accumulation regime via the agrochemical sector. The heavy dependence on agrochemicals supported the rapid development of the Korean chemical industry in the 1960s and 1970s. Korea's rural population has been substantially excluded from economic and social betterment, heightening social and regional tensions (KCFA and KAAPRI 1990, p.24). It is no wonder that the rural population has been rapidly declining, adding to labour shortages in the agricultural sector as well as increasing pressures on urban infrastructure.

Table 5.36 Urban/rural disparities in medical service provision, 1985

	Large cities*	Other cities	Rural areas	Total
Population/doctor	1,310	2,022	7,914	2,039
Medical insurance coverage (%)	62.2	47.8	21.0	100.0
Medical centres (%)	60.3	25.5	14.1	100.0
Population/medical centre	1,880	2,610	7,163	2,814

Source: Kwon (1988a), p.77.

Note:
* Seoul, Pusan, Taegu and Incheon.

Summary

As we have seen in the previous chapter (Chapter 4), the origin of Korea's current environmental problems lies in the heightening of accumulation regimes and the intensification of modes of social regulation during the period of Japanese occupation. The depletion of primary resources such as timber and minerals was the chief characteristic. In the postwar period of rapid export-oriented economic development, the deleterious environmental impacts first took on an urban locus – squalor of squatter settlements, of growing traffic congestion and waste disposal problems arising from rising mass consumption of a more concentrated population. Korea's industrial and rural zones saw severe environmental impacts from chemical pollution. The changes in industrial trajectory of the Yusin period (1970–80) increased the complexity of environmental problems, these clearly reflecting the spatial differentiation of industries. Variation in the economic structure over space created particular mechanisms of environmental degradation: urban consumption centres such as the Seoul Metropolitan Area came to experience as many serious environmental problems as the industrial and rural zones, but of a different nature and origin.

The socio-environmental problems of Korea's core consumption zone reflect the conflict inherent in the reproduction of the labour force. The high consumption demands of the middle and upper classes underlie many environmental as well as social problems, the effects of which disproportionately affected the less politically and economically powerful, whose conditions of reproduction have been continually eroded. The concentration of population in the mega-cities has caused intense competition for land. Under the banner of 'redevelopment', the urban poor have often been physically removed; the beneficiaries have been the new urban affluent and, of course, the property capital. Though overt brutality is no longer routine, this has been the unfailing pattern. Deteriorating environmental quality has often found the lower income groups especially penalised. This is the case with regards to domestic fuel, with poorer classes obliged to use cheaper, high sulphur coal briquettes. Since the late 1980s, private car ownership has become a universal token of affluence; the non-car owning lower income groups, comprising around half Seoul's population in the mid-1990s, had to endure the environmental mal-effects stemming from the conspicuous consumption of the well-off.

The accumulation strategy of Korea's chaebol has been very much urban-centred. In the over-heated economy of the late 1980s, they were encouraged to produce lower quality standards for the domestic market, and the state was willing to turn a blind eye. In the 1990s, this brought disastrous results: collapsing bridges and department stores and calamities in the subway systems were the most notorious outcomes. A competitive mode of social regulation pushed the business sector towards a fairly reckless quest for economic gain.

The scale of environmental impacts upon the semi-peripheral industrial zone was even greater. Environmental problems here were the result of prioritising production at the expense of the social infrastructure. The activities of the heavy and chemical sectors, in particular, led to numerous assaults on the environment, threatening farming and fishing communities as well as urban residents. It was not unusual for whole communities to face temporary evacuation. The coastal areas of the SIZ were amongst the worst to suffer, with oil spillages from tankers adding to the discharges of polluted rivers. As economic growth stimulated demand for more industrial land, the industrial zone spread relentlessly, extending as far as the west coast by the late 1980s. By the mid-1990s, the pollution here was as serious as that along the south and southeast coasts, with red tides a frequent occurrence.

Alongside the increasing pollution of the human and natural environments, collective consumption goods and services such as medical care, sanitation and sewage treatment plants were seriously neglected. The conspicuous absence of middle class communities in the SIZ was due to the low levels of social amenities, particularly education, which the Korean people consider an important factor in deciding where to live. The under-production of social infrastructure and services mirrored the spatial separation of social classes between zones. The state's minimal provision of social amenities meant that labour has to pay the price of an aggressive EOI Strategy.

In the peripheral rural zone, the political and economic exclusion of the rural communities has been entwined with rural environmental degradation. With the demise of rural political power after the land reform, and with rapid urbanisation and industrialisation, the rural economy was squeezed by dwindling state support of agricultural prices and rising cheap imports. The growing dependence on agrochemicals to increase productivity, a consequence of competitive regulation, has had profound and irreversible effects on soil and water quality.

A further source of PRZ environmental degradation was the development of rural leisure facilities implemented in the main by chaebol capital with the backing of state agencies. The heavy use of agrochemicals in these developments was as damaging as their actual creation, while both floods and water shortages ruined the livelihoods of many subsistence farmers. Such developments created low-wage casual employment and siphoned off profits to headquarters usually based in Seoul. Declining subsistence farming, low employment prospects and a poor standard of social, cultural and physical amenities drove the younger generation to the cities, contributing further to the rural malaise.

Though to an extent notional, each of the three zones of this study has experienced environmental impacts of a specific character. Obviously, zones are not entirely self-contained, and problems of one zone impinged on others. Also, coastal waters have been the ultimate receiving ground of pollution from nuclear energy, industrial, agricultural and domestic waste-water. In addition, environmental impacts such as air pollution have not remained localised: for example, that from the Capital region spread east to Kangwon province, while acid rain became a feature of much of the country, causing considerable damage to forestry, natural habitat and agricultural land.

Korea's ever-expanding urban-industrial concentrations have done their best to reduce the whole national territory to a 'production line', reducing the natural environment to pockets of 'managed gardens'. The transmission of environmental problems has become embedded in the exchange process between city and countryside: agricultural commodities produced with high levels of chemical input have become a threat to the health of the urban classes, particularly those further down the social scale.

The accumulation strategy and MSR are central determinants of the production of space and the environment and, ultimately, the multiplicity of environmental problems. In summary, the uneven development of a predominantly competitive MSR and the accumulation regimes based on the EOI has given rise to:

1　The ineluctable megalopolisation of the primate cities of Seoul and Pusan has overwhelmed the urban infrastructure and intensified the competition for scarce resources, particularly land;
2　Rapid growth and spatial concentration of industries and the externalisation of production costs to the environment have concentrated the effects of pollution;
3　In the SIZ and PRZ in particular, the spatial differentiation of classes and the tendency towards zones of production and zones of consumption, has brought a market neglect of social and environmental infrastructure;
4　The state's economic prioritism has also brought lax implementation of industrial pollution controls;
5　The alliance between the state and the chaebol oligopolies meant especially harsh exploitation of agriculture (intensive farming and its associated debt crisis), and of the industrial working classes (poor workplace health and safety, low standards of housing and other social amenities).

6 Mode of social regulation, environmental movement and the state

Korea's environmental problems have multiplied over the decades, from those arising from the pressures of poverty in the 1950s and 1960s, to pollution from intensive industrialisation in the 1970s, and from mass consumption from the late 1980s. By the early 1990s, the accumulation of problems had reached crisis proportions and the environment was a major issue in the political realm. Popular pressure for improved environmental quality has obliged the state to take a more active stance, while at the same time it has continued to press its economic objectives.

This chapter examines responses of the state and society to growing pressures on the environment. Three elements of environmental politics will be considered: the state regulatory framework, the role of environmental groups and the societal impacts in general.

The first section analyses the historical development of Korea's environmental movement, as well as the conjunctural development of state environmental regulation. This historical examination reveals how the changing internal and external political-economic situation during the industrialisation period influenced both the growth of the environmental movement and state environmental policies. An analysis of official environmental regulatory structure and mechanisms of the early 1990s and the social mode of environmental regulation is offered in the ensuing sections; here we focus on how the state has attempted to reconcile its environmental responsibilities with its role as the arbiter of capital accumulation. This imperative is shown to be inimical to environmental preservation and protection.

Historical development of the environmental movement and state regulation

The development of Korea's environmental movement is distinguished by distinct historical phases: these correspond to the development phases of the accumulation regime.[1]

The Taylorist and Yusin period (1960–79)

Korea's first environmental statute was the Pollution Prevention Act of 1963. This was never intended to be a compliance-forcing statute as the state did not acknowledge that serious environmental problems existed. As industrialisation proceeded in the 1960s, pollution incidents increased in number. By the mid-1970s, as pollution became widespread due to heavy and chemical industrialisation, the government responded to growing public concerns by the enactment of the *Environmental Preservation Act* and the *Marine Pollution Prevention Act*, both of December 1977 (Chung, T-S. 1992, p.238). The former act introduced a number of important new features such as the promulgation of general environmental standards, environmental monitoring, emission standards and control, and various administrative sanctions for violations. However, enforcement of the Environmental Preservation Act was overseen merely by a department within the Ministry of Public Health and Social Affairs.[2] The main government environmental policies were focused on the establishment of nature sanctuaries and national parks and the use of zoning in land-use planning to prevent the setting up of factories in locations upstream of major population centres (in the case of Seoul only). Pollution was not directly tackled, either through regulation or investment in waste treatment.

In terms of the environmental movement, this period can be characterised as 'pollution victim centred collective activism'; environmental activism, in fact, dates back to 1966, with the anti-air-pollution demonstrations against the development of Pusan's oil-fired power station. Similar protests erupted in the late 1960s in Ulsan, and in the 1970s in the Yeocheon and Kwangyang industrial areas. Such actions by local residents were limited by their lack of organisation and experience in fighting industries heavily backed by the government: demands restricted to compensation were easily pacified with small pay offs. The early environmental movement was, therefore, mainly one of struggle for compensation for damage to property and health (Kwon, H-S. 1991, p.75). Throughout the 1970s, environmental activism increased in intensity and scope. However, popular activism continued to take the form of anti-pollution demonstrations and were sporadic, localised and short-lived. The weakness of local environmental groups meant that the big business–government nexus was able to marginalise them or simply pacify them with minor compensation deals. The general tendency as far as the state was concerned was firm suppression, as there was a consciousness that any tightening of environmental regulation would slow down economic development. Thus anti-pollution organisations were represented as anti-government (Kim, B-W. 1994, p.214).

The peripheral Fordist period (1980–87)

A number of significant legislative and administrative developments came to the fore in this period. In 1980, under the new political regime, the constitution adopted included a guarantee to the right to live in a clean and healthy environment (Chung, T-S. 1992, p.238). With this formal change, in 1980 the Office of Environment (OoE) was established as a sub-cabinet agency of the Ministry of Public Health and Social Affairs. Though the status of the environment administration was still modest, the creation of a new governmental agency to enforce environmental statutes was in itself a significant development. To overcome administrative difficulties in monitoring pollution activities, the amendment to the 1977 Act in 1986 established six regional agencies of the Office of Environment (Kim, B-W. 1994, Chung, T-S. 1992, p.238).

In 1979, the environmental legislation of 1977 was revised to include Environmental Impact Assessment (EIA) as a further regulatory measure. The 1981 amendment introduced an emission charge system to enforce compliance with emission standards. In 1986, the *Solid Waste Management Act* was introduced to complement several provisions of the Environment Preservation Act and replace the existing *Waste Cleaning Act* (Kim, B-W. 1994). However, the government's prioritising of economic development, the competitive regulation of the 1980s, and the lack of both will and resources to enforce the relevant legislation reduced the legislation to little more than window-dressing. The purpose was essentially one of political legitimation. This situation did little to tackle the worsening pollution problems and environmental degradation.

Despite introducing many changes to environmental administration and regulation, in the 1980s there was little alteration in the government's attitude towards environmental issues, well demonstrated by its handling of industrial disasters. The approach was informed by the aim of damage limitation. With the economic recession of the early 1980s, the state became even more directed towards the promotion of economic growth. As a consequence, well-organised anti-pollution groups were established nationwide whose main object was to support the victims of industrial squalor in Korea. These included the Hanguk Pollution Problem Research Institute (1982), the Anti-pollution Movement Association (1984) and the Anti-pollution Citizens Movement Association (1986). These groups formed alliances with the pro-democracy movement; they emphasised that pollution problems were a result of structural faults in society, and an undemocratic authoritarian government which rested on monopoly capital. Environmental groups were intimidated and suppressed, along with labour unions and the pro-democracy elements. This phase of the environmental movement was termed the 'coalition of democratic and anti-pollution movements' (Kim, B-W. 1994, p.215).

Neo-Fordist period (1988–97)

This period saw further significant changes in the environmental legislation and administration regime: the Office of Environment was elevated
to full ministerial level as the Ministry of Environment (MoE) (Chung,
T-S. 1992).

In the late 1980s, there was also the milestone of the *Long Term Comprehensive Plan for Environmental Preservation* (1987–2001). Although this was
revised and complemented by a medium-term plan (1991–96), the long-
term plan basically stayed in phase as the formula guiding environmental
projects, particularly the designation of 'areas of concern' for intensive
management. The two largest river systems in Korea, the Han and Nakdong, as well as coastal areas adjacent to industrial sites, were selected for
special management. These projects had some success, particularly in the
lowering of water contamination in the Han River. But at the same time
pollution in other river systems increased (Shin 1993).

To strengthen the legislative framework for environmental conservation,
the beginning of the 1990s saw a thorough overhaul of existing environmental legislation, the National Assembly passing a new set of environmental statutes to replace the 1977 Environment Preservation Act. These
were the *Environmental Policy Foundation Act*, the *Air Environment Preservation Act*,
the *Water Environment Preservation Act*, the *Noise and Vibration Control Act*, the
Hazardous Chemical Substances Control Act, and the *Environment Pollution Damage
Dispute Co-ordination Act*. In March 1991, the Solid Waste Management Act
and the Marine Pollution Prevention Act were completely amended (Kim,
B-W. 1994, p.100). Later in 1991, the *Natural Environment Preservation Act* was
introduced. The judiciary also began to tighten the regulatory loopholes in
order to effectively prosecute polluters, while new directives were issued to
raise environmental improvement funds (Chung, T-S. 1992, p.238). Although a complete range of environmental legislation was put into place,
there remained many problems in implementation (MoE 1991, pp.68–70,
Lee, D-G. 1991, p.91, Chung, T-S. 1992, Kim, B-W. 1994, pp.88–101).

With the political liberalisation of June 1987, the environmental movement moved to embrace large numbers of citizens who had hitherto been
inhibited from expressing their grievances. Amongst the wide range of
environmental groups, the most important and perhaps representative was
the *Konghae Chubang Undong Yeonhap* (Pollution Expulsion Coalition Movement) formed in 1988. However, the new NGOs remained impotent in
the face of most of Korea's environmentally damaging developments.

Korea's disparate environmental groups had hitherto been ineffectual.
However, the growing consciousness of environmental concerns in the
world at large eventually led to the formation, for the first time, of nationwide organisations. Commencing in 1993, this process was to bring about
a significant change in the role of the environmental NGOs. For example,
Baedal Hwangyong Club established offices in twelve cities (March 1993),

while the *Hwangyong Undong Yeonhap* (Environmental Movement Coalition) was established through an alliance of eight regional organisations with Konghae Chubang Undong Yeonhap (April 1993). This ushered in a new and more mature stage of the environmental movement which now went beyond the mere reactive and spontaneous (Kim, B-W. 1994, pp.214–216).

Although all the issues of the environment of the 1960s and 1970s prevailed into the 1990s, many had been displaced organisationally and spatially. Working class issues with an environmental connotation such as housing and sanitation were, by the early 1990s, no longer of central concern to the movement. Manifestations of industrial pollution were largely shifted to semi-peripheral areas away from the major population centres. As such, they were less of an immediate issue for most urban citizenry. Instead, more visible and tangible environmental problems such as the deterioration of drinking water, air pollution, degradation of the natural environment, road congestion and solid waste disposal had come to the fore. As the environmental movement gathered mass support, its foci began to reflect middle class preoccupations. This trend, however, did not originate solely from the evolving class structure in Korea; it was also greatly influenced by government propaganda and ideology.

The evolution of Korea's environmental movement (as well as state regulation) was, of course, in direct proportion to the growth of perceived problems. It corresponded also to changing accumulation regimes and the associated modes of social regulation (Table 6.1). After 1988, in particular, state environmental machinery developed rapidly in response to heightened environmental activism which blossomed under a more liberal political environment.

In the 1990s, the emergence of environmental issues in the international political arena was also a spur to the rapid development of environmental regulation in Korea. The high growth export-oriented industrial regime of Korea had been dependent on the importation of raw materials and the export of manufactures; international trends in environmental policy including those regulating trade had, to an extent, to be incorporated by the Korean state, and considerable diplomatic effort was mobilised to this end (Kim, B-W. 1994, pp.149–163). Rising environmental standards in Korea's now-global trading partners (and notably in the US) obliged participation in multilateral initiatives. As the new awareness of the environment began to inform industrial standards, export-oriented Korea was quick to adapt in order to maintain market competitiveness.

In the late 1990s, environmental issues became less politically pressing than the restoration of economic health. Consensus for environmental issues was now eclipsed by productionist imperatives. By once again prioritising economic performance, the new regime under Kim Dae Jung will doubtless witness the return to many of the environmentally deleterious practices of the past.

Table 6.1 The development of environmental policies, institution and responses in Korea

Period	Environmental policy	Environmental administration	Environmental movement	Context
Extensive development period (to 1979)	Pollution Prevention Legislation (1963); Environment Protection Act (1977).	Within Ministry of Health and Social Welfare.	Spontaneous formation of anti-pollution groups in local-ised areas for compensation.	Local environmental problems: Ulsan and Onsan pol-lution damage; expansion of development effects.
Peripheral Fordist period (1980–87)	Constitutional requirement for the protection of the environ-ment.	Establishment of Office of Environment (1980); Comprehensive Long Term Environmental Conservation Plan (1987).	More organised environmental groups allied with pro-democracy and labour move-ment. Character antagonistic and radical.	Expansion of environmental problems: conflict between development and conserva-tion.
Neo-Fordist period (1988–97)	Declaration of Environmental Conservation (1990); National Environmental Policy (1992); Environmental Management Acts.	Upgraded to ministry level (1990). Medium Term Environment Conservation Plan.	Political liberal-isation meant environmental groups became mass movement; national organis-ations through amalgamation.	Environmental problems seen in global context: Rio Summit; 'Green Round'; sustainable development.

Source: Chung (1997), p.233.

Tensions between development and environment within the state apparatus

As chronicled in earlier chapters, the modern Korean state has intervened to differing degrees and with varying effectiveness in the regulation of the economy, social welfare and spatial restructuring. To address the proliferation of environmental mal-effects which rapid industrialisation had engendered, in the early and mid-1990s both the legal framework and the administration of environmental protection were strengthened. Here, we situate these developments in the context of state regulation in general, and within a 'social mode of economic regulation' in particular[3] (Jessop 1994, pp.254–278).

The structure of the Korean environmental management system

Effective protection of the environment has been seriously impeded by the division of environmental responsibilities between a large number of central government ministries and insufficient devolution of power to the local government level. Figure 6.1 represents the structure of environmental administration of the early 1990s; within the central government, environmental functions were scattered amongst fourteen ministries and sub-ministerial agencies and the whole model was heavily biased towards sector II.

The elevation of the Office of Environment to ministerial status in 1990 did not signal a more cohesive management structure. Environmental functions of other central agencies were not transferred automatically to the new Ministry of Environment. Although the aim of the MoE was 'to protect the natural and living environment and prevent the occurrence of pollution' (Kim, B-W. 1994, p.90), its functions were mainly limited to pollution control. Additionally, the MoE administered the Environmental Impact Assessment System, environmental education and research and to a limited degree, the protection of sensitive environments (a function duplicated by the Ministry of Interior and Office of Forestry) (Kim, B-W. 1994, p.90).

This confused matrix was sustained as central fiefdoms were unwilling to give up a part of their responsibilities. Thus, environment-related functions remained divided between the same fourteen ministries and agencies. The Ministry of Science and Technology was responsible for operation and waste management in the nuclear power industry, as well as for nuclear accident response. The Ministry of Interior oversaw nature conservation, the Ministry of Energy and Resources promotion of alternative energy sources, while the Ministry of Construction was responsible for infra-structure including water quality. Public health came under the Ministry

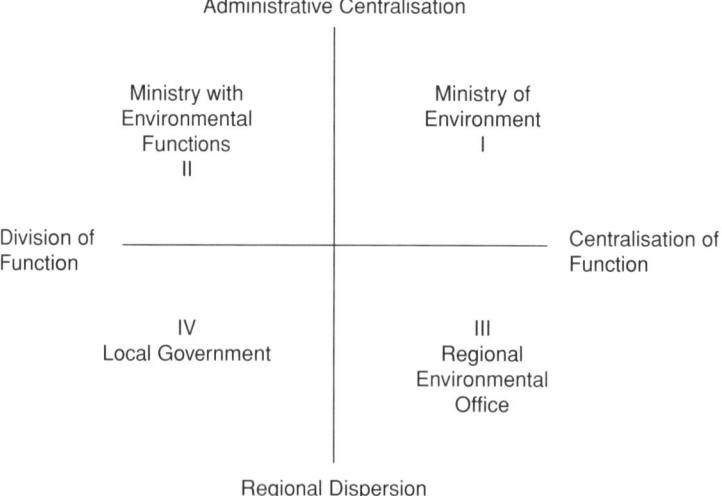

Figure 6.1 Structure of environmental administration.

Source: Kim, B-W. (1994), p.89.

of Health and Social Welfare, while conservation of mountain and forest land lay with the Forestry Administration (Lee, D-G. 1991, pp.91–92, Kim, B-W. 1994).

The frequency of environmental incidents relating to water quality obliged the rationalisation of water quality management in 1991. However, the Ministry of Construction refused to relinquish its water resources and sewerage management responsibilities and, instead, contracted out the administrative and management functions to the MoE without transferring key decision-making controls. This rendered management jurisdiction even more confused (Kim, B-W. 1994, pp.255–256). The reluctance to transfer full responsibility to the MoE was due to the fact that an array of environmental functions brought greater share of government expenditure which could be deployed elsewhere, strengthening the Ministry's position in the bureaucratic power-game.

The division of environmental functions detailed in Table 6.2 contributed to the ineffectiveness of state environmental policies. For example, the Ministry of Construction's role in land-use management and water resources development meant a favouring of infrastructure developments over conservation. The National Parks management, also under the Ministry of Construction, pressed for recreation and leisure developments rather than the conservation of nature (Kim, B-W. 1994). The Ministry of Energy and Resources, in response to growing electricity demand, pursued energy development[4] instead of energy efficiency (*FEER* 1991, pp.54–55).

Korea's environmental administration in an international context

A comparison of jurisdictions of the Ministry of Environment conducted by Kim, B-W. (1994) reveals that the majority of the advanced industrialised countries, especially the European nations, concentrated most environmental functions within one ministry. Enforcement was delegated to local government and autonomous government bodies, as in the case of Her Majesty's Inspectorate of Pollution in the UK. Table 6.3 shows that in the case of Britain and Finland all four main environmental functions, and in the case of Canada three out of four functions, were located in the environmental ministry. Taking the US National Environment Protection Agency (NEPA) and the Japanese Ministry of Environment as models, Korea's central ministry had only one main role (pollution control), although some elements of nature protection came under its aegis in the early 1990s. But Kim stresses in his 1994 study that even in the US, the central role was effectively complemented at the state level in terms of environmental resource management functions as well as the regulation of pollution (Kim, B-W. 1994, pp.85–88). This is in contrast to the central ministerial dominance of the Korean system.

Table 6.2 Division of environmental responsibilities between ministries, 1992

Ministries	Responsibilities
Ministry of Science and Technology	Control of nuclear safety; formation and implementation of radiation protection plan; regulation of transportation and disposal of nuclear waste and radioactive materials.
Ministry of Home Affairs	Protection of nature and the convening of the Committee for Nature Preservation.
(Coastal Police)	Surveillance and policing against coastal pollution.
Ministry of Agriculture, Forestry and Fishery	Anti-pollution plan in the agriculture and fishery sectors; some industrial pollution controls.
(Office of Rural Development)	Testing and management of soil conditions; control in the use of agrochemicals.
(Office of Forestry)	Establishment of forestry plan; regulation of protection of wild flora and hunting; protection of forestry.
(Office of Fishery)	Protection of marine resources and anti-pollution plans.
Ministry of Commerce and Industry	Regulation of import and export of toxic substances and industrial waste; management of industrial waste.
Ministry of Energy and Resources	Supply of low sulphur oil and pollution abatement; R&D of new energy and energy substitutes; safety management of nuclear power stations and recycling of nuclear waste.
Ministry of Construction	Preparation of Comprehensive National Land Development Plan; operation of National Parks; establishment of green belts; preparation of Comprehensive Marine Resources Development Plan; management of river tributaries; planning of water supply and sewerage system; operation of public sewerage system.
Ministry of Labour	Prevention of work-related illness and improvement of the work environment.
Ministry of Transportation (Marine Transport and Ports Authority)	Testing of exhaust fumes; control of noise pollution; location and development of leisure centres; pollution prevention in port areas; management of public waters.
Ministry of Culture	Identification and protection of rare fauna and flora.
Ministry of Health and Social Affairs	Planning and administration for environmental health, e.g. supply and management of drinking water.

Source: Cited in Noh, Y-H. (1993), p.21. (authors' translation; see Kim, B-W. (1994), pp.91–92.

Note:
The names and functions of ministries are those prior to pre-government restructuring in 1995. For example, since 1995, the Ministry of Construction and the Ministry of Transportation have been combined as the Ministry of Construction and Transportation.

Table 6.3 International comparison of environment administration by central ministry, 1992

Country	Pollution regulation	Water resources management	Natural resources management	National and development planning	Comments
UK	Yes	Yes	Yes	Yes	
Finland	Yes	Yes	Yes	Yes	
US	Yes	No	No	No	(Federal Gov't)
Japan	Yes	No	Yes	No	
Canada	Yes	Yes	Yes	No	(Federal Gov't)
Korea	Yes	No	No*	No	(*only in parts)

Source: Cited in Kim, B-W. (1994), p.101; for Canadian data: p. 88.

Financial resources for environmental protection

Environmental protection in Korea has been marked by its poor resource base. Although environmental expenditure increased steadily throughout the 1980s and 1990s, the share of environmental spending in the total government account remained relatively low – in 1990 0.19 per cent of GNP or 1.06 per cent of the total government figure (see Table 6.4 and Figure 6.2). International comparison shows Japan at 0.34 per cent of GNP (2.0 per cent of total government expenditure), the US at 0.57 per cent, Sweden at 1.69 per cent and Switzerland at 1.03 per cent. The meagreness of Korean expenditure is even more evident if we consider that comparable countries invested heavily in environmental infrastructure in the 1960s and 1970s. At that time, they were placing in the region of 2 per cent of GNP in (mainly) the capital investments for environmental protection (Lee, D-G. 1991, p.93, Pearce 1975, pp.138–139). Though in 1995, Korea's environmental expenditure increased to 0.5 per cent of GNP and 2.33 per cent of total government expenditure, it fell far short the levels of Western Europe, the US and Japan.

Problems in local environmental management

Environmental administration at the local government level had many problems, particularly due to the centralisation of power in Seoul. Until 1995 when local authorities gained some autonomy, Korean local government was an extension of the central administration. Environmental regulation in the 1990s was organised through six regional offices under the MoE located in Seoul, Pusan, Kwangju, Taegu, Daejeon and Wonju (MoE 1991, p.71). This was at a time when over seven million tonnes of industrial wastewater were discharged daily from 11,200 point sources; the regional offices and local government agencies were required to periodically inspect

Table 6.4 Environmental expenditure in Korea, 1980–95 (100 million won)

Year	GNP	Gov't expenditure	Environmental expenditure		MoE expenditure		Environmental expenditure ratio		
	(A)	(B)	(C)	(%)[1]	(D)	(%)[1]	(C/A)	(C/B)	(D/C)
1980	368,570	86,478	452	—	121	—	0.03	0.52	
1985	780,884	124,064	877	37.0	421	22.6	0.11	0.71	48.00
1986	839,758	137,965	1,017	16.0	433	2.9	0.11	0.74	42.58
1987	975,317	157,945	1,658	63.0	671	55.0	0.16	1.05	40.47
1988	1,285,920	180,250	2,160	30.3	773	15.2	0.17	1.20	35.79
1989	1,371,400	216,531	1,806	−16.4	645	−16.6	0.13	0.83	35.71
1990	1,782,621	325,369	3,447	39.8	1,172	81.7	0.19	1.06	35.74
1991	2,060,265	313,823	4,570	96.6	2,713	169.8	0.22	1.46	49.04
1992	2,387,046	438,421	5,819	27.3	1,396	48.6	0.24	1.32	23.99
1993	2,655,179	511,879	6,919	18.9	1,887	35.2	0.26	1.35	27.27
1994	3,037,726	644,575	11,232	62.3	4,716	149.9	0.37	1.74	41.98
1995	3,489,790	745,344	17,394	54.8	6,729	42.6	0.50	2.33	38.69

Source: MoE (1992), p.597, (1990), p.596 and (1997), p.464.

Notes:
1   Percentage growth over the previous year.
C/A = Percentage of environmental expenditure to GNP.
C/B = Percentage of environmental expenditure to central government expenditure.
D/C = Percentage of Ministry of Environment expenditure to total environmental expenditure.

effluent control systems (MoE 1991, p.78). However, there were fewer than ten staff in each regional office for this monitoring function. As for the coastal environment, which was divided into eleven zones, each Coastal Police unit had only six to eleven officers per zone. The public agencies were bound to be over-stretched in dealing with large oil spillages (Konghae Chubang-undong-yeonhap Yeongu-wiwonhwae 1992, p.93).

State policy formulation and implementation

The nature of Korea's central bureaucracy has meant that any important environmental measure proposed by the MoE was likely to be diluted or modified as a result of compromise with other ministries at the policy formulation stage (Figure 6.3). Subsequently, a policy had to be approved at the Economic Ministers' Meeting before it could be reviewed by the Committee for Environmental Protection and then endorsed by the President. The role of the President has been pivotal to the bureaucratic process and in the initiation of environmental regulations, which have played softly as far as industrial capital is concerned (Choi 1991b, Chung, T-S. 1992, pp.238–239).

Although no formal channels exist for business involvement in the environmental policy formulation process, influence brought to bear through personal networking is a potent force in Korea. Clearly, selective and

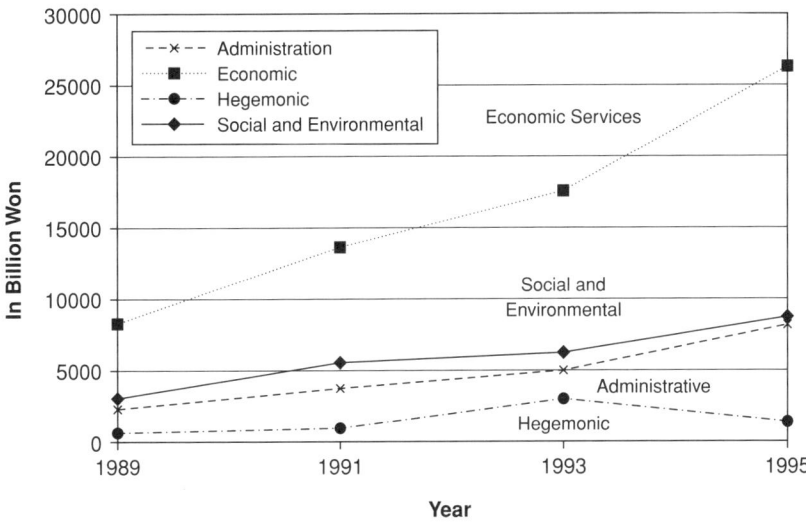

Figure 6.2 Environmental expenditure within government expenditure.

Source: MoE (various years).

Notes:
Hegemonic category includes expenditure on special projects.
Economic category includes infrastructural investment, education and R&D activities.
Social and Environmental category includes social housing, environmental improvement and water purification investment among others.

inequitable access favour capital rather than environmental groups and society at large (Kim, B-W. 1994).

By the mid-1990s, Korea could boast an array of policies, initiatives and regulations for the enhancement of the human and natural environments. Each ministry promulgated its own set of environmental policies and regulations for implementation. Here we will comment on the role of the MoE, as it exemplifies environmental regulation in Korea. Most of the MoE's efforts were directed towards pollution control. From the early 1990s its remit extended to the following areas: air pollution, water quality, waste management, environmental impact assessment, effluent charge, pollution cost charge, waste disposal deposit, garbage limitation, environmental improvement charge and Eco-Mark system (Kim, B-W. 1994, p.132).[5] Although there were other measures employed such as administrative directives to close down polluting firms or even prosecute them in the courts, much of the environmental regulation relied on economic pressures and penalties.

The Effluent Charge System was designed to induce manufacturers to voluntarily invest in pollution mitigating facilities by taxing those businesses which produced pollutants over the permissible quantity or concentrations,

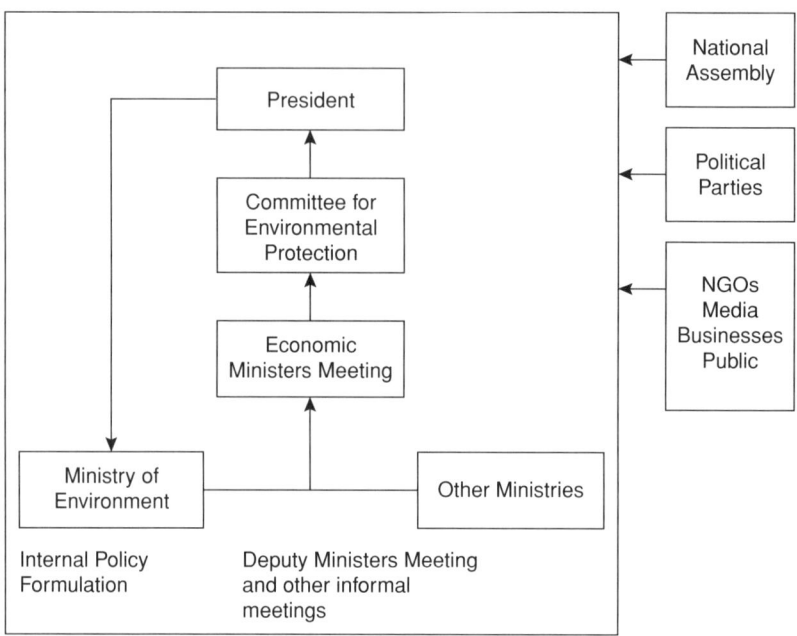

Figure 6.3 Bureaucratic process of environmental policy formulation.
Source: Cited in Chung (1991), p.38.

and by allowing them to voluntarily register prior to waste production. However, the low levels of charges meant that this market-led approach failed to induce reductions in pollutant production or voluntary investment in environmental facilities. Instead, most businesses preferred to pay the penalty and carry on polluting. Penalties were assessed on the basis of concentration of pollutants and did not take account of the quantity discharged (Kim, B-W. 1994, pp.134–135).

Introduced in 1992, the Waste Disposal Deposit System was intended to curb the production and importation of goods which would lead to excessive quantities of waste production. It was also aimed at directing the economy towards energy and resource conservation by ensuring the collection and disposal of waste by private businesses through a deposit system. Covered under this system were products harmful to health, those presenting difficulties in safe disposal or recycling, and those which put too great a burden on public waste disposal systems, such as throw-away products (Kim, B-W. 1994).

A further economic measure was the Environment Improvement Charge System. This capital and revenue-raising tax system for investment in environmental improvement was targeted at producers of pollutants and wastes in 74 location types within urban areas, special environmental areas, coastal zones and nature conservation areas. The tax was levied on businesses, buildings and equipment of greater than specified size and in particular categories.[6] This charge system was not, however, applied to manufacturing plants (Kim, B-W. 1994, pp.135–136). Although the tax was aimed at small and medium-sized businesses, its burden was by and large felt by consumers through increased prices.

One notable non-economic regulatory measure was the Environmental Impact Assessment System. In operation since 1981, it was revised dramatically in the *Environmental Policy Foundation Act* of 1993. The Act aimed 'to conserve and enhance the quality of the environment by assessment prior to the implementation of development plans ... to ensure that environmental impacts of development, subject to Environmental Impact Assessment, were environmentally sensitive and sustainable'. Fifteen types of developments were designated under the EIA system[7] as requiring an Environmental Impact Statement (EIS) by the MoE. Additional provisions included the canvassing of local residents' views (Kim, B-W. 1994, pp.132–133).[8] Other measures were directed at the public at large, for example, the imposition of large fines for littering and spitting in public places, and the banning of the use of shampoo in public bath houses. Thus, Korea's environmental regulation were largely dependent on economic incentives and penalties.

Intra-governmental conflicts were a significant barrier in Korea's environmental protection regime; they occurred at the policy formulation stage and continued throughout the implementation stage. There were occasions when the MoE attempted to implement its pollution regulatory functions but was blocked by other ministries; conflicts also arose when the MoE attempted to enforce EIA regulations on the development functions of other ministries (Kim, B-W. 1994, p.144). Such tensions extended to the Effluent Charge System, when the apparently arbitrary setting of criteria and low level of charges resulted from the pressures from ministries, such as Trade and Industry which were primarily concerned with maintaining competitiveness of Korean firms internationally (Kim, B.W. 1994, p.134).

A further example can be seen in the operation of the Waste Disposal Deposit System. Pressure from business (particularly the packaging industry) caused the Economic Planning Board, Ministry of Trade and Industry and other economic agencies to 'advise' the MoE to reduce its schedule of items as well as the size of deposits. Thus, eleven categories became seven (with 27 types of products), and all charge rates were greatly reduced. However, further intense pressure from the business community eventually brought the number of categories to six, with 19 product types. Plastic packaging and containers, air-conditioners, refrigerators, automobiles/auto parts and other disposable products and large waste items were simply omitted (Kim, B-W. 1994, pp.258–261). Hierarchical interpersonal relationships – often simply ministerial seniority – or the intervention of the

President or Prime Minister with their discretionary powers, usually resolved conflicts in favour of the economic ministries. The Korean state was, after all, one in which economic prioritism reigned.

However, the influence amongst differing industries was uneven. Chung, T-S. (1992) examines cases such as the closed-door procedures for location of plants (Dong Yang Chemical's Kunsan TDI factory) and waste disposal facilities (Anmyon-do nuclear waste treatment plant). Chung clearly demonstrates that official behaviour was biased towards the chaebol. An analysis of the lobbying strategy of the *Jeon Kyong Ryeon* (National Association of Business Executives), a chaebol-dominated group showed, for example, that in 1990 the government was pressed to drop COD measurements in river quality assessment, leaving only BOD criteria. The revised legislation of 1991 did indeed omit the COD criteria as both President and Prime Minister had wielded their discretionary powers (Chung, T-S. 1992, p.241). The main purpose of big business was to conceal the seriousness of river pollution by heavy metals and chemicals, only detectable by COD levels.

The enforcement of environmental legislation was also an arena of ministerial conflict. In the event of a serious pollution incident such conflict routinely revolved around the question of appropriate penalties. During the two-year period January 1990 to December 1991 alone, there were three major pollution incidents of national concern. All three involved intra-governmental conflict, overlaid upon the usual antagonisms between the state and citizen groups (Table 6.5).

One of the most controversial incidents concerned the unlawful discharge of industrial waste-water from the Taegu Dye Industrial Estate and was exposed by the company union branch (April 1991). The Industrial Estate Management had released 20–30,000 tonnes of chemical waste-water daily over a 15-month period, with evidence of state collusion. Exposure by the media led to vocal demands from environmental groups for firm government action. To quote a union spokesman: 'This incident is a prime example of pollution which was due to the close relationship between political parties, capital and the state' (Kim, B-W. 1994, pp.259–262). The MoE ordered the improvement of waste-water treatment facilities to bring pollutant levels from 300 ppm to under COD 100 ppm limit. In addition, production shifts had to be reduced from ten to seven. The Dye Industrial

Table 6.5 Pollution incidents and community conflict, Jan. 1990–Dec. 1991

Incident	Parties involved
Doosan Electronics phenol pollution	MoE, EPB, MoTI, Business Assoc.
Taegu Dye Industrial Estate pollution	MoE, MoTI, business, political parties
Kunsan TDI Factory gas release	MoE, MoTI

Source: Kim, B-W. (1994), p.145.

Estate was thus obliged to invest 3.2 billion won (approx. US$5 million) in waste-water treatment equipment. Levels were brought down to 120-150 ppm by September 1991, and the restoration of ten shifts was demanded. However, the MoE refused to allow normal production since its environmental standards were still not met. The Estate Management complained of government unfairness, since it was prepared to turn a blind eye elsewhere. The lack of compliance to all official directives meant that levels began to rise once again. The MoE's response was to shut down production altogether. However, pressure from the Ministry of Trade and Industry, Economic Planning Board, Ministry of Internal Affairs, and City of Taegu forced a reversal of this decision (*Hangyeorae Shinmun*, 9 Oct. 1991). Now the stipulation was for three-shift production. However, this decision, in its turn, was reversed when the health and social welfare committee of the National Assembly ordered the matter to be taken out of the hands of the local environmental office and be 'politically resolved'. In November 1991, the administrative directive was relaxed and production allowed to resume to seven shifts (Kim, B-W. 1994, p.262).

The application of the EIA system has also been far from free from intra-governmental disputes. Implementation of EIAs has often been formalistic and bureaucratic – lacking in the necessary expertise. Instances of conflict between the MoE and other central agencies have been particularly evident in the various development projects which the government regarded as hegemonic to be forced through at almost any cost.[9] As Table 6.6 shows, the cases of non-compliance with official EIA recommendations are numerous (Chung, p.48, Noh 1993).

Korea's EIA system has without exception come down in favour of development. Eight hundred and fifty Environmental Impact Statements (EIS) were submitted to the MoE between the early 1980s and the early 1990s.

Table 6.6 Non-compliance to environmental impact assessment, 1992

Developers	No. of developments	No. of non-complying developments	Percentage of non-compliance with EIA
Public agencies	201	148	73.6
Office of Railways	5	5	100.0
Local government agencies	116	87	75.0
Land Development Corporation	41	35	85.4
Road Corporation/Housing Corporation	10	8	80.0
Other	29	13	44.8
Private sector	81	56	69.1
Total	282	204	72.4

Source: Cited in Noh (1993), p.29.

Rather than preventing damaging projects from being realised, the system actually gave the green light to many environmentally destructive developments (Lee, K-J. 1993, pp.81–83).[10] Lee, S-D. (1988) also shows that the outcome of the 57 EISs submitted over the four years (1981–84) was mostly positive, with development justified on the grounds of social desirability and the benefits outweighing the costs. There was not one case which condemned the proposed development as unsuitable. As Lee puts it, 'it is not possible to believe that all the major development projects carried out during that period had no or negligible environmental effects' (Lee, S-D. 1988, p.40). Kim, B-W. (1994) comes to a similar judgement, blaming the formalistic application of EIA upon development prioritism, administrative expediency and bureaucratic opportunism (pp.144–145). Broadly, rather than the EIA system ensuring environmental protection, it has been the means by which environmental destruction has been rationalised.

To summarise, Korea's environmental regulation system has been moulded by the following:

1   a division of environmental functions between numerous agencies, with powers centralised in Seoul;
2   a policy formulation process which is largely 'top-down', ignoring public consultation;
3   privileged access to, and influence over, the government by capital (clientelism);
4   a lack of adequate financial and human resources, leading to the formalistic operation of environmental regulations;
5   the overriding discretionary powers held by key government officials;
6   the perversion of the 'polluter pays' principle, to the 'pay as you pollute' principle.

It can be argued that the Korean environmental regulation system is relatively new and time is required for it to become effective. But the government had by the mid-1990s shown little desire to remedy its glaring faults. On the contrary, most policies and regulations tended to shift the burden of environmental costs to consumers in general, to small and medium-sized businesses and above all, to working class communities. In this way pressure on capital would be minimised, especially in the export sector. Indeed, the state administrative structure allowed the interests of capital to be easily incorporated into the regulatory process.

The impact of environmental regulations has been differentiated between spatial zones. Due to their stricter application of environmental regulations in or around large population centres such as Seoul, Taegu and Pusan, environmental quality improved steadily after 1991. On the other hand, loose enforcement of industrial pollution regulations resulted in deteriorating environmental conditions in semi-peripheral industrial and peripheral rural zones.[11] Even with the strengthening of environmental policies, the state pursued its growth priority in other sectors. The state has been shown to be far from neutral in economic development and mediating socio-spatial conflicts arising from environmental problems. To this end, it both employs ideological tools and socialises environmental costs.

Civil society, NGOs and the state hegemony

Here, we posit the ideological process in terms of the concept *social mode of environmental regulation*.[12] Our specific concern is the character of environmental awareness, the place of the environmental movement, and the manner in which state policies coalesce in a hegemonic bloc.[13]

Environmental groups are both opinion forming and awareness raising. In Korea's case they fall into two clear categories – those registered with the Ministry of Environment (implementing state agendas such as environmental education), and the unregistered groups which take their own course, bringing frequent confrontation with the government bureaucracy, particularly the Ministry of Environment (Kim, B-W. 1994, pp.218–219).

Kim's 1994 examination of environmental groups provides further details within the two categories (Table 6.7). Most non-registered environmental groups (NEGs) focused on the exposure of environmental pollution incidents; they fell short of any deep and systematic analysis of the causes of environmental problems. Their practical activities were typically assisting

Table 6.7 Registered and non-registered environmental groups: some comparisons

	Registered groups	*Non-registered groups*
Establishment legitimacy	Legislation, civil law	Popular support
Main activity	State directed activity	Anti-pollution and environmental issues in general
Revenues	State subsidy and other activities	Members subscription and fees
Responsibilities	Accountable to related government agency	Not accountable
Character and role	Moderate reforms, suggesting of legislation reform, etc.	Criticism of regime and legislation, radical agenda, etc.
Scope of activities	Technical development, survey and research	Anti-pollution, anti-government and anti-war activities and research
Central goal of activity	Environmental awareness, education, publicity and lectures	Demonstrations, expose, public meetings, education

Source: Cited in Kim, B-W. (1994), p.219 (authors' translation).

with compensation claims, or mobilising local support for demonstrations. The registered groups (REGs) were very much part of the state environmental management matrix; though criticised for their acquiescence to officialdom, they nonetheless represented wide sections of the public and had the most impact in the formation of popular opinion (pp.222–223).

The close relationship between REGs and the Ministry of Environment extended to their use in propagating hegemonic ideology. In the early 1990s, the heart of their message concerned the impact of mass consumption on the environment. Organisations such as the YWCA and the Consumer Association found themselves singing from the hymn sheet of official environmental propaganda. The ineffectiveness of the NEGs' counter-hegemonic agenda arose in part from lack of resources; it also stemmed from the fragmentation of its various constituent groupings along ideological fault-lines.[14]

Although the activities of environmental groups were no longer illegal by the late 1980s, in the economic recession of the early 1990s there was a resurgence in government activity aimed at curbing the NEGs. A survey conducted by the Environmental Policy Research Institute showed that both REGs and NEGs were greatly dissatisfied with government interference. Almost three-quarters of the surveyed organisations demanded greater representation of NGOs in the relevant government committees (*Hangyorae Shimmun* 7 June 1992). This showed that the state tried to control the activities of environmental groups and the degree to which the views of environmental groups could be reflected in government policy. The usual top down approach to environmental regulation was evident.

Essential to the propagation of the official environmental ideology was the mass media, and also environmental education in schools. The latter focused on problems arising from consumption – domestic waste recycling was a particular focus. It was no coincidence that the dominant environmental agenda was one which would not adversely affect the capital accumulation process. National newspapers participated by staging their own environmental campaigns (for example, *Chosun Ilbo's* 'Save Our Streams Campaign'). These media, owned by or associated with chaebol and hence pro-government, focused too on environmental issues which were not damaging to the interests of capital. The activities they promoted were typically the mobilisation of community groups in cleaning up of parks and mass tree-planting. The media was used to justify state environmental regulations and policies, the whole thrust of which was to privatise environmental responsibilities.

The rise in environmental awareness in Korea was, as we have seen, due to the cumulative effects of environmental incidents and disasters, which brought into being vocal citizens' action groups as well as propaganda campaigns on the part of the government. Various studies of the late 1970s and early 1980s show that environmental awareness among the Korean public remained low, the public attitude towards nature being one of utilitarianism and domination. The rural population manifested rather more negative attitudes towards conservation than the urban population, while the working classes indicated responses more passive than those of the middle or upper classes. Comparisons reveal that Korean environmental awareness of the 1990s was lower than that of the Western industrialised countries. It measured even lower than that of Taiwan in the early 1980s (Yang 1992, pp.97–98). However, as the problems became more pronounced, so did public concern. Yang shows that popular consciousness of the importance of the environment rose from a rank of seven in a listing of most important social issues to third in 1987 and second in 1990 (p.104). This was confirmed in another study undertaken by Seoul National University, in 1984 and 1991 (Shin 1993, p.245). With the rise in environmental concerns, the 1990s saw a change in public attitudes towards economic growth. A high proportion of respondents felt that economic growth should be suppressed or slowed down for the sake of environmental conservation (Yang 1992, p.116). Another survey[15] showed that 85 per cent of Koreans preferred the country's development strategy to be based on ecological or environmental priorities (Lee, D-G. 1991, p.93). This change in attitude is summarised in Table 6.8. The 1970s' attitude of 'nature exploitation and utilitarianism' gave way, by the 1990s to an emphasis on 'environmental protectionism and co-existence' (Yang 1992, p.116). At the same time, the public's esteem for the official environmental regulation and protection efforts steadily declined: in 1992, over 78 per cent of surveyed persons thought that they were seriously lacking compared to 45.5 per cent in 1982 (Shin 1993, p.105). Lee, J-J. (1991, p.11) reports that 80 per cent of his survey respondents considered that government and businesses collusion was largely responsible for pollution of Korea's air and rivers.

Increasing sensitivity of public attitudes towards the environment has been accompanied by a shift in environmental awareness. Until the early

Table 6.8 Survey of opinion on environmental conservation versus economic growth (% of respondents)

Year of survey	Economic growth at the expense of environmental conservation	Favouring limited economic development within environmental capacity	Environmental conservation at the expense of economic growth	Don't know
1982	14.2	69.9	6.6	9.1
1987	6.0	88.7	2.8	2.5
1992	9.9	25.0	35.1	30.0

Source: Cited in Yang (1992), p.106.

Note
MoE (1982, 1987) *Survey of Public Consciousness on Environmental Conservation*, MoE, Seoul; 1992 data based on Yang's own survey.

1980s, consciousness differed with social groups; thereafter such distinctions began to disappear. Now environmental problems affected all classes. One observer suggests that environmental reform did not reflect the interests of a particular class, that is, the impacts of environmental problems and mitigating state policies were socially neutral (Yang 1992). The infiltration of hegemonic ideologies to regulate social behaviour and attitudes was a complementary aspect of state environmental regulation.

Environmental problems were presented as society-wide issues transcending class. However, the increase in environmental concerns on the part of the working classes was directly related to the increased financial burden which environmental legislation imposed on lower income earners. For example, the imposition of market prices for domestic waste disposal hit the lower income groups since the use of anthracite briquettes creates a high volume of waste. More generally, working class consciousness was heightened by the deteriorating conditions of life – housing shortages and polluted air and water.

In the 1990s, the Korean authorities continued to rely on technological developments to solve environmental problems rather than on any radical alterations in social practice. Yang's 1992 survey shows that in answer to the question 'can environmental problems be solved or resolved through science and technology instead of changing the character of society?', over 47 per cent of respondents were in agreement, with 26 per cent disagreeing. In the US, Germany and the UK, the pro-technology responses were 30, 48 and 25 per cent respectively. Although Germany had the highest 'yes' response, 44 per cent of respondents later qualified their views to include some comment on the need for fundamental societal change (Yang 1992, p.106). However, in Korea, public commitment to environmental remedies seemed limited to superficial lifestyle changes. Almost 70 per cent stated that their choice of products has been influenced by environmental friendliness, and a similar proportion was aware of the Eco-Mark system. The remarkable growth of the organic foods company, Pulmuwon,[16] testifies to the growing environmental consciousness of at least the middle classes: the popularisation of organically grown foods, bottled water, green consumer goods and 'eco-apartments' reflected their growing desire to secure their own environmental needs. Such trends have given new impetus to product development and, indeed, to the strategies of capital. On the other hand, the preoccupation with large cars and electrical appliances and conspicuous consumption of energy point up the contradiction in middle class environmental attitudes. Environmental awareness has yet to be translated into broadly collective improvements (Kwon 1990). The exclusion of poorer sections of society has put environmentalism into question.

As Bae, K-H. (1992) concludes, though environmental awareness grew steadily throughout the 1980s and the 1990s, the public consensus was too weak to establish any solid foundation upon which the environmental movement might influence state policies. In its absence, public consciousness could be moulded by government environmental campaigns. This absence of coherent pressures from below could be exploited by the state to justify and legitimise the official mode of environmental regulation.

Traditional attitudes, radicalism and hegemonic ideology

Environmental regulation as a social mode thus became an integral part of the national MSR, stabilising the accumulation regime through the control of social consciousness and action in the environmental context. The shaping of social modes of environmental regulation, as well as the MSR itself, reflects the manipulation of dominant social, political and cultural practices and ideology. An exploration of the underlying traditions of Korea will assist in predicting the future direction of MSR evolution. Prominent amongst the ideological fabric are, Confucianism, anti-communism, economic prioritism and Korean nationalism. Although Confucianism is one of the less explicit creeds of Korea, it is one of the most culturally embedded. Confucianism has long been the force which legitimated the social hierarchy and that of the state bureaucracy too. It underlines the paternalistic attitude of the authorities and the image of the state as a benevolent institution and protector of the national interest. With an emphasis on social conformity and subservience, as well as a strong work ethic coupled with concepts of meritocracy, the modern Korean state has successfully regulated social behaviour to the advantage of the scions of economic power.

Traditional attitudes were routinely mobilised in the face of socio-environmental crises. In the summer of 1991, when peak electricity demand threatened blackouts, the government ordered its offices, large businesses and public institutions to cut electricity use: air-conditioners, lifts, escalators and even lighting were targeted.

> Government planners . . . talk proudly of their jawboning campaigns. These efforts involve the time-worn ritual of calling together businessmen, scholars and citizens' representatives to impress upon them the need to save electricity for the good of the country. There is a strong dose of Confucian austerity in this campaigning. Energy planners solemnly ascribe the surge in the electricity growth to 'the extravagant trend of consumption', in the words of a senior Energy Ministry official.
>
> (*FEER*, 1 August 1991, p.54)

Such ideological manipulation did not mean any permanent eclipse of social discord and resistance. The working classes exploited in the production process, and the rural poor who were systematically alienated

from the fruits of rapid industrialisation, habitually responded by protests and demonstration, particularly in periods of slow economic growth.
When domestic or external pressures were severe enough to call into
question the deeper process of society the state frequently resorted to
other, more emotive means, centring on anti-communist and nationalist
ideologies.[17]

Although during the 1980s the environmental movement had been
closely linked with the pro-democracy and labour movements, the ascendancy of middle class environmental issues in the 1990s brought a certain
passivity through state co-option. The issues of the 1990s were fragmented, and activities focused on the 'environmental' rather than 'socio-
environmental' problems such as housing and the workplace. Even the
unofficial groups failed to systematically tackle issues which impinged on the
working classes. In short, the participation of the middle and educated
classes in the environmental movement deprived it of its radical edge,
diverting it towards the 'softer' issues. From the early 1990s on, environmental groups began distancing themselves from the labour and student
movements: both registered and non-registered environmental NGOs
became increasingly incorporated into the mode of social regulation.

From the late 1980s, the state was intent on consolidation of an ideological context which stabilised the MSR in the face of rising environmental
tensions resulting from political and economic liberalisation. The hegemonic projects initiated within the environmental field were contingent
upon reform of the state machinery, as well as further attention to investment in environmental infrastructure. Rather than adopting an antagonistic
attitude towards the environmental lobby, the state saw the opportunity
to move towards a new mode of environmental and economic regulation.
Its goals were the propagation of a revised environmental ideology, the
delivery of economic growth and enhanced private consumption. The
mode of environmental regulation on the one hand took a distinctly market-
oriented direction; and on the other, the attention of the public was
redirected from industrial pollution issues to the environmental problems
caused by consumption. The state was successful in socialising environmental costs through selective application of environmental regulations.

Various devices of ideological character were mobilised. Prominent were
the pressing of the polluter pays principle and the formula that 'every citizen
is both victim and malefactor of environmental pollution'.[18] These two ideas
were intended to redirect the environmental fire from problems of industrial pollution to those of a more domestic nature. This was intended to
ensure that chaebol-centred economic development policies would be maintained under the aegis of a new environmental ideology (Chung, T-S.
1992, pp.241–242).

It was within this context that the new MSR could be fashioned,
legitimising the state environmental regulations of the 1990s. With the
declaration of these concepts in the environmental section of *The Seventh*

Economic and Social Development Plan (1991), two notable new environmental regulations were introduced in order to reduce waste at source. The first was the 'Limited Garbage Quantity System' which imposed the use of standard bags sold by the local government. Garbage bags had to be purchased at a cost which included disposal charge. Also encouraged was the separation of recyclable materials and the reduction of the total amount of garbage to be disposed of.

A second new measure was the 'Environment Improvement Charge System'. The charge was to be levied on large commercial buildings and facilities as well as on large vehicles carrying such freight as petroleum. The MoE anticipated that it would be able to raise approximately 100 billion won per year – 65 billion from large facilities and 34.2 billion from petroleum transportation vehicles – in order to finance pollution-mitigating facilities, research and the development of environmental technology (*Dong-A Ilbo*, 10 July, 1992). If compared to the total 1991 expenditure of the Ministry of Environment of 85.8 billion won (0.3 per cent of total government expenditure), it is evident that the revenue raised by the new tax system was greater than the Ministry's expenditure. Thus, the state pushed the concept of 'each citizen as a source of pollution' by levying a disproportionately large charge on the service sector, which would be passed on to consumers.

However, in contrast to these new environmental strategies making the public and consumers responsible for their waste, the state was less enthusiastic in applying the polluter pays principle when it came to the conglomerates, particularly in the manufacturing sector – the chief source of pollution. Regulation remained soft, and fines and charges low. The Effluent Charge System was designed to encourage polluters to voluntarily install and operate their own effluent treatment facilities. Instead, it was used by industry to pollute the rivers for a modest fee. Other monetary means of regulating industrial activities also failed to bring about the desired effect due to the low level of fines and charges, and the lack of enforcement mechanisms. The enforcement of environmental regulation was lopsided, and much of the financial burden of environmental improvement and conservation was transferred from industrial capital to society at large by taxing small businesses and the public (Chung, T-S. 1992, pp.239–240).

In the mid-1990s this ideological matrix prompted the state to promote the concept of a 'high tech' scenario for Korea. Korea's future was seen as lying in the development of high technology-based industries for export, with the state subsidising research into new technology. As the government tried to raise the industrial trajectory, and as industries exploited the technological vision in their product sales, there was a cohesive effort to mobilise the society with the notion of creating a 'technotopia' for the twenty-first century. A broad consensus was achieved around the idea that technology coupled with market mechanism could eradicate environmental problems. Thus the mode of environmental regulation extends beyond the mere regulatory mechanisms of the state; the role of ideology and social manipulation is central.

Summary

The conjunctural development of environmental activism and state environmental regulation is closely linked to an intensifying MSR. Specifically, the political and economic liberalism of the late 1980s, which increased the complexity of the environmental issues, and also signalled a new phase of both environmental activism and state responses. Thus, in the late 1980s and 1990s, a comprehensive environmental regulatory mechanism became imperative. The formal response was to legislate and upgrade the administrative machinery, in order to confront the growing problems of the environment. But the government's continued emphasis on economic prioritisation undermined any environmental transformation. The expectations of the population could not be met.

Though much of the Korean population has become environmentally aware, understanding of the route to environmental justice remains shallow. This deficiency was utilised by the state to consolidate a new environmental hegemony conducive to continued capital accumulation and the legitimation of state policies. Two distinct modes of state regulation emerged – legislation and formal policy on the one hand, and social regulation as a function of the hegemonic ideology on the other. It was these two modes of regulation which reinforced the legitimation of the state's environmental as well as economic platform.

The legislative framework was based firmly on the polluter pays principle. Thus, with the exception of the EIA system, all the major environmental regulatory systems demanded the taxing and fining of pollution sources. These regulations were applied to the manufacturing industries. But they were also extended to small and medium-sized tertiary activities and to private individuals too. The official line that 'fifty-five per cent of river pollution is due to domestic households and urban businesses and 45 per cent due to industries', was an attempt to shift responsibility for environmental costs to society at large. Financial means as a form of regulation was intended to oblige polluters to voluntarily reduce waste, or invest in treatment facilities. However, the low levels of charges and fines, particularly for industrial pollution, rendered the regulations ineffectual. Instead, industries now had permission to pollute for a low fee. The de facto situation was 'pay as you pollute'.

In addition to the shifting of environmental costs to society at large, the state started withdrawing public services such as litter bins in urban areas and public parks in order to force people to dispose of their waste within their own garbage disposal allowances. As in all the collective consumption and welfare areas, the government aimed to minimise its spending: environmental expenditure even decreased relatively in the early 1990s. Allocations to the MoE saw even greater reductions during these years as parallel ministries colonised scarce resources. The government introduced tax-raising legislation such as the Environment Improvement Charge System to implement environmental works without diverting funds from economic development projects.

Through its Registered Environmental Groups, the government promoted uncontroversial remedies such as recycling of waste, the cleaning up of nature parks (*Dong-A Ilbo*, 1994, 4 December) and the use of environmentally friendly products. 'Enlightening' the public about the environment, and about the virtues of environmental technology, was an important aspect of the functions of REGs under the MoE. This was designed to deflect 'not-in-my-backyard' attitudes towards government projects, and to conserve energy and resources. REG-led campaigns resembled the *Saemaul Movement* of the 1970s, which was used to regulate social behaviour and attitudes in the modernisation of communities, both rural and urban. The NEGs, which made up the core of the early movement, continued to emphasise environmental justice issues, but they tended to be sidelined by the insistent state-sponsored REG activities.

In terms of hegemonic ideologies, the Korean state was remarkably successful in producing an apparent cross-class consensus regarding environmental issues and policies. In this way, the costs of environmental problems were socialised, while the capital accumulation process was virtually unaffected.

It is agreed that environmental regulation in Korea thus became a vital component in social regulation as a whole, in the realm of both production and consumption. The state was successful in not only socialising the costs of environmental degradation, but simultaneously promoting the notion that environmental problems were mainly consumption-oriented rather than production-related. The spatial separation of industries from population centres was a means of inhibiting the costs of reproduction of the working class, while at the same time sidelining the environmental issues which most impinged upon working class communities. The state environmental administration became structured in a manner in which functions and regulations were not detrimental to economic development. Thus environmental regulation and administration in Korea in the 1990s became not merely window dressing or a means of legitimation, but an active component of the accumulation strategy.

7 EOI mode of development and a sustainable future

It was initially Korea's extraordinary economic performance of the early 1970s which captured the attention of Western commentators. The social and environmental costs of the growth years were less heralded but never far beneath the surface. More latterly, the spectacular collapse of mid-1997 has equally galvanised attention. Not surprisingly, it too has invoked a series of problems of a social and environmental nature. The former have already received considerable publicity; the consequences for the environment are less clear at this point, but there are ominous signs.

The foundations of Korea's postwar economic growth were laid during the Japanese colonial period. Essentially, the accumulation regime during this time had the characteristics of Export-Oriented Industrialisation directed towards the core consumption market of Japan. At first, the export of primary resources such as agricultural produce, timber and minerals was conducted with great efficiency in order to supply the raw materials needed for manufacturing industries in Japan. This type of peripheral exploitation was later replaced by the implanting of an indigenous industrial structure through the establishment of light manufacturing, followed by the introduction of heavy and chemical industries. However, the real legacy of the colonial mode of development to the postwar regime was the means of social, political and economic regulation, the tendencies of capital and the general industrial trajectory. The similarity between the colonial regime and postwar regimes is striking: the structure of the central bureaucracy, the dominance of chaebol monopoly capital almost identical to the *zaibatsu*, the political and economic exclusion of the industrial proletariat, the coercive means of labour suppression and the sequential deepening of the industrial trajectory. At each restructuring, Korea's postwar regimes have ascended the industrial or technological ladder as during the colonial period. Thus, we can see that Korea's relationship with the global, in which Japan was a key element, had a great influence on its development process.

The postwar accumulation regimes in Korea were as much influenced by domestic political economic conditions as by global economic circumstances. The collapse of one regime and the succession of another have been dependent upon the ability of the state to mediate between global economic forces and internal political and economic needs. The extensive accumulation regime based on import substitution industrialisation (ISI) was established soon after the Korean War. National reconstruction was the driving force of the ISI regime, which took advantage of American aid through the processing of primary resources such as sugar, cotton and flour as well as timber and minerals. The autocratic state which rested on the monopolistic activities of capital soon faced a legitimation crisis, as the exhaustion of the ISI regime of accumulation coincided with the destabilisation of the mode of social regulation. This structural crisis not only resulted in the restructuring of the mode of development but also in the transformation of the state and political alliances.

In the early 1960s, an extensive accumulation regime based on labour intensive EOI was established in conjunction with a competitive regulation mode, which took advantage of the growing malfunction of the Fordist economies of the West. As an export-oriented economy, the Korean accumulation regime has been very sensitive to the economic conditions of the major international markets and the changes in the global economic structure. Much of Korea's manufacturing was geared to own-name export manufacturing for American and Japanese companies. This extensive accumulation regime was coupled with a competitive MSR based on labour intensive industrialisation. It was able to stimulate the economy and provide mass employment, but the regime was highly dependent upon external market conditions, and required the super-exploitation of the Korean labour force.

The next major economic restructuring came in the early 1970s, coinciding with the growing political disenchantment of those alienated from the EOI development process within Korea, as well as also with the collapse of Fordist regimes in the Western industrialised countries. With tougher export market conditions for labour intensive low value added products, the corporatist regime based on heavy and chemical industrialisation sought to raise the technological and industrial structure to escape from dependency upon the rising cost of intermediate imports from advanced industrialised countries. Heavy and chemical industrialisation was not a return to an ISI regime, but aimed to promote EOI development by substituting imported intermediate goods with domestic products. Also, the development of the chemical industry coincided with the introduction of intensive farming methods to raise the productivity of the agricultural sector in order to assure self-sufficiency in food supply.

The main problem of the heavy and chemical industrialisation phase was its mode of regulation. On the one hand, this regime brought about a culture of heavy dependence on state subsidy and manipulation of the financial system by monopoly capital; on the other hand, competitive regulation was enforced on other industrial sectors. This resulted in over-capacity and uncompetitiveness of the heavy and chemical industrial sector, while other sectors suffered from a shortage of credit and higher interest rates. The global recession in 1979 brought the Yusin regime to an end.

The dominant Washington-inspired ideology of the free market found resonance during the period of the peripheral Fordist regime (1980–88) which promoted competition and productivity. The restructuring of the industrial system was brought about through active state intervention. However, the reduction in state subsidy and import tariffs forced the chaebols to look for other ways to raise profits. The intensification of production line automation and product development was pursued, while wages were severely restrained, with the state acting coercively in labour disputes. It was this labour repression that sowed the seeds of the collapse of the peripheral Fordist regime in 1988. The chaebol groups had grown rapidly during the corporatist period, maturing into internationally competitive companies and diversifying into more profitable areas such as finance and real estate. The oligopolistic domination of the Korean economy by a handful of conglomerates led to very high concentration of capital. This not only raised social tension between classes but also became one of the main problems of the Korean economic structure: the sparseness of small and medium-sized enterprises. This is in contrast to Taiwan's development process, which was characterised by the strong performance of specialised medium-sized and small firms in a well-established industrial hierarchy. Taiwan's development also contrasts with Korea in terms of the role of Western transnational companies, as foreign investment in Taiwan was the main driving force behind its EOI economy (Chou 1994). But in Korea, national monopoly capital has been the dominant economic force with insignificant foreign investment.

International pressures for political reform and economic liberalisation and rising labour discontent due to poor wealth distribution brought the peripheral Fordist regime to an end, and in the late 1980s ushered in the neo-Fordist regime. This allowed for higher working class consumption, but with a competitive mode of regulation still in force. The gradual opening up of the domestic market to overseas competition and the increase in Korean labour costs intensified the accumulation process. Thus, in the early 1990s the state started to play a greater role in socialising the cost of reproduction of labour by implementing medical insurance and pension schemes in order to reduce the pressure of wage demands. This did not signal the start of a welfare state, but instead a workfare state, where social welfare was purchased individually through a national programme of insurance schemes. Those outside formal employment were excluded from the social safety net. The high charges of a pay-as-you-go medical system excluded the poorer sections of the population. And the new regime did not end the repression of labour by the state. As pressure on wages and the global recession of the early 1990s started to threaten the competitiveness of Korean firms, the state resumed its coercive tactics. The construction of the workfare system on the one hand and the strong-arm tactics in labour management on the other, operated well as a legitimation strategy, where the dominant hegemonic bloc comprising the middle classes feared the loss of their economic stability.

These processes brought deep transformation of society and its spatial configuration. The growth of urban centres was accompanied by industrialisation of much of the countryside. In short, the restructuring of Korea's regime of accumulation was clearly mapped in the changing space economy. Impediments to the accumulation regime were not merely those of the economic cycle: spatial constraints had their part to play. For this reason, emerging conflicts in the accumulation process demanded a restructuring of spatial structure. The old socio-spatial form, however, also constrained the formation of a new spatial-accumulation strategy. Its modification helped to overcome the accumulation blockage, but at the same time intensified existing socio-spatial problems.

Korea's space-environment has, therefore, been subjected to ever-increasing pressures as the accumulation system intensified under state strategies for national territorial development. In the 1960s, the labour intensive export-oriented development was implemented under a spatial strategy of concentration in the two largest cities with good transport infrastructure, Seoul and Pusan. Korea's Taylorist EOI regime was exhausted not only by the dysfunctioning of global Fordism, but also by the spatial barriers to the capital valorisation process. The concentrated spatial strategy stimulated rural–urban in-migration at a phenomenal rate, bringing urban overcrowding, squatter settlement and high urban unemployment as well as rising industrial land prices. Seeking scale economies, in the 1970s the heavy and chemical industries were located in the provincial, purpose-built industrial towns in the Southeast region, creating a new production space. To relieve the overconcentration of population and congestion, the state also implemented a policy of industrial decentralisation. However, the decanting of industries to the provincial areas of Pusan and Seoul did little to relieve migration to the primate city and their satellites. Instead, this was the start of suburbanisation of housing development in the surrounding areas of Pusan and Seoul. Few industries moved to other provinces at this time. The intensive methods introduced into the agricultural sector, and the spatial policies prohibiting industrial activities in rural zones, effectively sowed the seeds for rural underdevelopment and regional inequity. Thus, the country was divided into two functional zones; the industrial urban zone and the rural zone. Geographically, the country took on a bipolar development form, with the Southeast and the Northwest (Capital) regions receiving much of the investment in fixed capital and manufacturing industries as well as population in-migration.

The peripheral Fordist regime of the 1980s introduced a greater degree of market competition, and a new industrial trajectory, intensifying competition at all levels of society. This stimulated the disintegration of production into manufacturing/assembly and control-marketing functions, particularly among the chaebol, thus creating a tripartite spatial structure. The de-industrialising city of Seoul with its concentrated control functions and high level of business services became the core consumption zone (CCZ), the provincial areas of the Southeast and Capital regions with concentrated production functions formed the semi-peripheral industrial zone (SIZ), and the remaining areas of agricultural production constituted the peripheral rural zone (PRZ). De-industrialisation and the rise in the business-service sector of the CCZ turned this zone into a middle and upper income class zone. The SIZ on the other hand, which received high government investments for productive infrastructure to promote efficient industrial and export activities, became the locus of the industrial proletariat; the middle classes were conspicuously absent. Within the expanding SIZ, there was a two-tier development. The emerging high-tech and precision machinery industries were located on the prime industrial sites, whereas the low value-added declining industries were displaced to the peripheral areas of the SIZ. Rising land prices in the industrial zones and falling transport costs were the main factors. Since the 1980s, the PRZ and its population has been increasingly alienated from virtuous development as state subsidies were cut and greater market competition introduced into the agricultural sector. The liberalisation of cheap agricultural imports from the US to secure markets for Korean manufactured goods essentially sacrificed the rural community for the sake of the EOI strategy. Thus, the pursuit of the high growth export-oriented industries, combined with competitive regulation and efficiency-seeking land and resource development strategies, resulted in a highly uneven spatial and social structure.

The division of national space into tripartite zones meant that there existed different social relations and institutional forms within and between these zones. Differences in production activities, in consumption levels and political inclusiveness would suggest quite differing social and environmental conditions. As we have seen in Chapter 5, the dynamics of each zone within the overall national accumulation regime have created distinctive environmental problems. Capital concentration and centralisation towards the CCZ resulted in the overheating of the urban economy, alongside high levels of consumption. One of the most serious problems of this capital and population concentration was the competition over land. The demand for office space as well as middle class housing brought relentless eviction of the urban poor from central areas. However, the huge shortage of land within the city led to the suburbanisation of housing and office developments to the satellite cities. The greenfield sites on the urban periphery have undergone comprehensive commodification, widening the pollution effects. These developments exacerbated pollution of both water systems and of air, the latter due to the new mass ownership of motor vehicles. Korea's neo-Fordist dynamics were soon to overwhelm the available collective consumption infrastructure.

The SIZ, the production core of the Korean EOI regime, received only a minor part of the available capital: the siphoning off of capital to the CCZ resulted in a state of relative underdevelopment, particularly in the consumption field. The CCZ also captured a large part of Korea's managerial classes. With the SIZ largely populated by industrial proletariat, the state–capital nexus was able to treat it merely as a 'production line', with minimal attention to the reproduction needs of labour. Here, the environment became seriously degraded by industrial pollution, capital externalising its production costs to the environment with little opposition from the working classes. Through a competitive mode of regulation, resting on the private provision of environmental needs, the state was able to transfer its environmental responsibilities to capital and to society at large. Monopoly capital was disinclined to voluntarily provide pollution mitigating facilities, while the immature civil society lacked the strength to protect the environment or take responsibility for the supply of environmental goods. Only when environmental disasters brought public outcry did the state act to regulate industries and increase social infrastructure.

The intensification of agriculture through high chemical inputs in the 1970s trapped the farmers in a cycle of debt repayment as the state reduced subsidies, while pushing market-led pricing. Competitive pressures obliged farmers to use increasing quantities of agrochemicals, bringing deteriorating soil fertility. The health problems associated with chemical use were often extreme. Rising affluence of the middle classes brought additional pressures on the PRZ environment in the form of leisure developments: the proliferation of golf courses, in particular, compounded rural problems. Instead of much needed economic growth, the chaebol-dominated leisure industry brought their exploitative practices of casual employment. Surplus capital was again siphoned off to headquarters in the CCZ. State investments both in production and in social infrastructure were conspicuously low.

While each zone had its own environmental problems created by particular production and consumption structures, these could not, of course, be self-contained. Industrial discharges affected water for agricultural use, while industrial and agricultural pollution reduced drinking water quality for the urban population. The cumulative effects of industrial, agricultural and domestic waste water resulted in coastal water pollution, well demonstrated by the *jeokjo* or 'red tide' phenomenon which invaded much of the coastal waters of Korea, destroying huge tracts of marine life including traditional fisheries. Airborne pollution similarly crossed zonal boundaries, acid rain in particular affecting crop yields and causing health problems, even in rural areas.

The uniqueness of the Korean development process lies in the discrimination of state interventions between production and consumption. That is, in order to promote export-oriented economic development the state in Korea played a limited role in maintaining collective consumption demand (at least until 1988), but took full charge of productive infra-structural provision. Discrimination in state intervention is particularly characterised as between differential expenditures in productive infra-structure and social welfare. Expenditure on social investment has been overwhelmingly directed towards production-related programmes. Since the First Five Year Economic Development Plan in 1962, these invest-ments have been directed either to the provision of infrastructure (for example, transportation and communication, power and water supply), or to the improvement of labour productivity (education, science and technology). As in other NICs, in Korea the central state intervened massively in the realm of private production and has indeed constituted a key agency in the promotion of 'productivism'.[1] The delivery of social consumption means has stood in great contrast. Throughout the EOI period, total government expenditure on social consumption, including social modernisation programmes and housing, environmental protection and public health was less than that on 'economic services'.[2] It is hardly surprising that less than one-third of Korea's domestic sewage is subject to primary treatment. Another example of productivism can be seen in the contrast between state intervention in the provision of public housing and in the development of industrial zones, both of which were afflicted by spiralling land prices to levels comparable to those of Tokyo. As noted in Chapter 3, the central government has all along prioritised the provi-sion of industrial estates nationwide, while public housing was, for the most part, neglected. Under a competitive mode of social regulation, the socialisation of collective consumption means is a hindrance to capital in its search for profits. Accordingly, the delivery of social consumption means, such as housing, was overshadowed by activities serving capital accumu-lation. Throughout the postwar period the state met rather less than one-third of its citizens' housing needs, with low-income rental housing virtually non-existent until 1990.[3] We have seen that the inadequate provi-sion of public housing as well as slum redevelopment compelled the vast majority towards 'the second circuit of exploitation' of competitive prop-erty capital. Social tension over housing shortages, particularly in the Seoul metropolitan area was a major source of the state's legitimation crisis. As for the provision of recreational space, its absence in urban areas has been extreme. At the same time, natural green spaces in the urban hinterland have undergone widespread commodification.

Environmental ideology, MSR and accumulation strategy

As we have seen above, the transformation of space and the emergence of environmental problems in Korea have been closely associated with the productivist intervention of the state in the process of national capital formation. The Korean state was not only central to the restructuring of accumulation regimes, but it was also the main vehicle of the mode of social regulation (MSR). It endeavoured to ensure stabilisation in the coupling between the accumulation regime and the MSR through both institutional and ideological interventions. The pervasive feature of the MSR was competition, and this was used to legitimate its economic, social and environmental policies.

Prioritisation of economic growth and the consequent imbalance between productive investment and collective consumption means was politically justified by the notion of 'trickle down'. Both capital concentration in the hands of chaebol and a widening income gap were presented as necessary conditions. Instead of promoting social equity, the Confucian work ethic was promoted as a means to a better living standard. The polarisation of wealth between regions was also presented as unavoidable. Environmental degradation was claimed to be a side-effect that had to be endured if economic growth were to be achieved. The growing working class discontent of the early 1990s saw the pursuit of the workfare state[4] model, in which welfare goods were to be purchased in a nationwide competitive structure. This form is distinct from the pre-1990s welfare systems of Western European countries since it rests upon private pension and protection schemes rather than socialised welfare insurance. Moreover, the national pension scheme introduced in Korea was restricted to those in formal sector employment. The competitive MSR, the absence of well-developed and universal social welfare, and the growing domination of the ideology of free market individualism deepened the fragmentation and polarisation of society and reduced socially-conscious solidarity to the family level.[5] It was also at this level that provision of social and environmental needs was to be met. The prevalent mode of social regulation and rapidly declining public concern for social justice issues, made it impossible to implement a welfare system where the benefit of contributions were socialised in a progressive mode. For example, the provision of clean drinking water was a matter for the individual household to procure from the market rather than from the public realm. The attraction of green products to the middle classes had less to do with environmental justice, and more to do with how they could avoid environmental mal-effects. The outcome is a new and highly profitable area of select environmental technology and services, these confined to the affluent minority.

The prevailing competitive MSR meant that environmental regulation and the state's approach to the provision of social consumption goods was in the same mould and formulated under the same dominant market ideology. Indicative of this mode of regulation was the strategy to privatise environmental costs by introducing measures such as the polluter pays principle. As a means of legitimating state environmental regulations, environmental ideology of the 1990s focused the blame for environmental degradation on the sphere of consumption. The state, naturally, applied the polluter pays principle unequally, lessening the burden on monopoly capital and shifting the costs to society at large. In Chapter 6 we have determined that the financial penalties on industrial pollution discharges were minimal and, indeed, were not strictly enforced, while the environmental improvement taxes on small businesses were high and vigorously applied. Large-scale leisure developments of the conglomerates, often in sensitive natural environments, went ahead with minimal assessment, but small extensions of farmhouses or other such developments in green belts saw the full force of the law. The MSR can thus be seen to regulate social behaviour in favour of the dominant economic development agenda, with environmental ideology creating a social consensus for the mode of environmental protection, designed not to hinder the regime of accumulation.

The study has aimed to reveal the broad features of the Korean development process and its mechanisms of environmental transformation. Korea's capitalist accumulation system reflects continual adjustment towards the changing global economic climate. An accumulation regime based on EOI meant a continuous raising of industrial trajectory in order to meet intensifying global competition. In this context, the state had to regulate wage relations, provide infrastructure, sponsor R&D and protect domestic capital and markets from international penetration. As a late developing country, the state enhanced the preconditions for accumulation by routine intervention in private sector decision-making; this has stabilised the linkage between modes of regulation and regimes of accumulation. The state is an object of regulation as well as an agent: at each crisis, integral to restructuring has been its functional re-configuration. Thus, political transformation has accompanied the transformation of each accumulation system. State strategies promoted rapid capital accumulation at a national level through the vehicles of national monopoly capital known as the chaebol. The competitive regulation of economic activities has induced industrial and property capital to externalise their environmental costs in order to keep production costs as low as possible.

The spatial transformation of Korea was shaped by the state's choice of industrial location policy and selective development of infrastructure. Intervention in spatial development aimed to secure appropriate conditions in order to overcome crisis-ridden capitalist development and prepare for a renewed bout of accumulation. However, the capital concentration tendencies and the functional zoning of industrial space conflicted with the expressed aim of regional equity and population decentralisation. Spatial concentration, dispersal and reconcentration reflect the dialectical relationship between space and the developing accumulation regimes and MSR. Competitive regulation, state involvement in infrastructure development and the industrial location policies, as well as the historical legacy of centralised political, economic and cultural systems in Korea's capital city created an overwhelming concentration of industries and population in the Capital and Southeast regions. Spatial transformation is of vital importance to environmental conditions since the character of the space-economy determines the interaction between society and environment. That is, the 'spatial fix' of capital is manifested in the physical environment (urban development, and the construction of infrastructure and industrial estate).

In Korea, the sedimentation of spatial forms under heightening accumulation regimes has produced a highly uneven and differentiated spatial development, increasing the expropriation of the environment. Uneven spatial development is expressed in wide regional economic and social disparities, and high concentrations of population in industrialised regions and cities, particularly Seoul. A distinct spatial differentiation of production and consumption has also occurred. The efficiency-driven spatial strategies allied with a new division of labour segregated the commerce/control function, manufacturing and agricultural activities into differing zone, thus creating specific environmental problems associated with the particular social relations and regulations of each zone. The causal mechanisms of environmental problems in each zone are as complicated as the historically contingent process of Korean development.

The Korean industrialisation process of the pre-1997 crisis era was one in which the state took a pivotal role in the restructuring of the accumulation regime and in stabilising and shaping the MSR. The disparate intervention between production and consumption spheres has been compounded by spatially uneven investment. The heightening legitimation crisis arising from social polarisation and environmental degradation obliged the state in the early 1990s to promote socio-ecological projects and thus pacify public discontent. Working class agitation forced a rise in wages, which helped to boost domestic consumption at a time of global recession and poor export demand. As for environmental problems, the polluter pays principle, here a hegemonic concept, attempted to shift the blame for the environmental crisis to over-consumption by the masses. Thus, as in other fields, the lop-sided operation of environmental regulation directed the burden of environmental costs disproportionately to society at large rather than towards monopoly capital. In this manner, the state has made use of ideological and institutional weapons to resolve successive crises of legitimation and capital formation. State accumulation strategies have therefore incorporated the spatial, social and environmental spheres; they have by no means been confined to the economic realm. This is not to say that the state is a direct instrument of capital: rather, the imperative of capital accumulation as a means of legitimation and social cohesion has occasioned the broad intervention strategies of the state. The pivotal position of the state (Figure 1.2, Chapter 1) not only allows economic regulation, but it also determines the utilisation of the space/environment dimension in capital accumulation and labour reproduction. The propagation of liberal market-oriented environmental ideology in the 1990s has not been implemented out of concern for the environment, but as a mode of social regulation to reconcile the interests of both capital and labour.

Korea's EOI accumulation strategy is re-examined in terms of sustainable development goals in order to identify constraining factors. In order for any meaning to be bestowed on this exercise, we first briefly recall the tenets of sustainable development.

Principles of sustainable development

The concept of sustainable development was first laid out in the 1980s by the World Commission for Environment and Development. WCED was established to critically re-examine the 'issues of environment and development and to formulate innovative, concrete and realistic proposals to deal with them, and to strengthen international co-operation on environment and development' (WCED 1987, pp.356–357). The overall conclusion was that environmental issues should not be seen as an obstacle but rather as an aspect which needed to be reflected in policies if growth were to be sustained.

'Sustainable development is development which meets the needs of the present without compromising the ability of future generations to meet their own needs' (WCED 1987, p.43). 'Development' is not intended to be confused with growth. Growth is a physical or quantitative expansion of the economic system, while development is a qualitative improvement of wealth and welfare, encompassing cultural, social and economic dimensions. The distributional objective of 'meeting the basic needs of all and extending to all the opportunity to satisfy their aspirations of a better life' (WCED 1987, p.44) obviously deals with issues in a nebulous manner, in a world in which large numbers are unable to feed themselves while an affluent global minority define their needs in terms of luxury goods. 'Meeting the needs of the present generation' means a redistribution of resources both within and between nations and, therefore, is a political, moral and ethical issue. Sustainable development means a movement towards greater social equity for moral and practical reasons. A *cordon sanitaire* cannot be erected around the poor of the south: it is one earth we inhabit and its environmental problems have no borders. When inequalities between classes and nations become too wide, it will bring global political instability which could be far more damaging to both the economy and the environment. The third idea, 'future generations' introduces the concept of intergenerational equity. Humankind is the custodian of the earth over future generations, steering a path which as far as possible benefits both itself and the natural ecosystem. Moughtin (1996) quotes an old North American Indian saying, 'We have not inherited the earth from our parents, we have borrowed it from our children' (p.5). Maintaining the status quo will not achieve any of the above conditions. In summary, the definition from the Brundtland Report implies achieving both inter- and intragenerational equity within a framework of development which does not detrimentally affect the planet's ecological support system.

The WCED specified the following as required by its definition of sustainable development:

- a political system that secures effective citizen participation in decision making;
- an economic system that is able to generate surplus and technical knowledge on a self-reliant and sustainable basis;
- a social system that provides solutions for the tensions arising from disharmonious development;
- a production system that respects the obligation to preserve the ecological base for development;
- a technical system that can search continuously for new solutions;
- an international system that fosters sustainable pattern of trade and finance;
- an administrative system that is flexible and has the capacity for self-correction.

Although these requirements are clear in themselves, we are told little of the means whereby they might be achieved. Sustainable development is, of course, a subjective ideological construct. There are two opposed views on sustainability and the environment: on the one hand, environmental problems are amenable to solution within the present political and economic system, and on the other, there are those who hold that sustainability depends upon the system being fundamentally changed. In reality, sustainable development policies will depend upon the hegemonic ideology of a particular society, and its strategy will vary from place to place and in time. As we have seen in Chapter 6, the hegemonic ideology of Korea is that of the free market, deeply antipathetic to the above listed requirements of a sustainable development trajectory.

The Brundtland Report thus underplays the complex of political, economic and social forces, and its prescriptions remain hollow. The WCED proliferated a massive interest in the notion of sustainable development, while much government-sponsored research utilised the term to justify existing strategies or promoted traditional cultures not conducive to sustainability.

Nonetheless, the main global agencies charged with economic development are obliged to pay lip service to the desirability of sustainable development and the reduction of social inequity. From the mid-1990s, the OECD and the World Bank promoted 'Strategy 21' which aims to reduce extreme poverty by half, while raising social and health care provisions in the world's poorest nations. The stated aim is to put in place national strategies for sustainable development by 2005 to ensure that the current loss of environmental goods is reversed by 2015 (World Bank 1999). But Korea remained one of the over 100 nations lacking any official sustainable development strategy. It is argued that the post-1997 economic and social crisis makes it all the more urgent for Korea to formulate a sustainable and comprehensive development strategy.

Sustaining Korea's EOI regime and sustainable development: a conflict

At the root of environmental degradation lies the accumulation process and a specific mode of social regulation. This takes on institutional forms in terms of regulation (economic and environmental), spatial differentiation, consumption norms and competitive social (wage) relations. Any consideration of sustainable development is inseparable from the arena of social reproduction. However, the conservative efforts to address the development and environment dichotomy through sponsorship of 'sustainable development' strategies represent an attempt to legitimise growth-oriented policies and diffuse political pressures. The sustainable development strategies proposed by the Korean government before the 1997 crisis emphasised the regulation of social and environmental conditions without a corresponding regulation of the economic variables.

To move towards the sustainable development objectives Brundtland would demand profound changes in Korea's mode of development. Particularly, an alteration in the mode of social regulation is of prime importance since this is the mechanism by which social norms and institutional forms can be significantly changed. To address the basic criteria of 'meeting the needs of the current generation without undermining the needs of future generations' would demand a mode of social regulation which allowed long-term strategies for reproducibility of the accumulation regime, allied to collective responsibility in meeting the basic needs of individuals.

Taking the course recommended by Brundtland and setting it against the structural features of Korea's mode of development allows exposure of the inherent contradictions. First, in terms of political system, the WCED calls for *effective citizen participation*. In Korea, the political decision-making was, until the early 1990s, quite inimical to popular demands. Indeed, until 1988 Korea had one of the world's most authoritarian states, with major human rights abuses a regular occurrence. Even after the political liberalisation of the late 1980s and early 1990s, the voices of the working classes, let alone the marginalised, were only listened to when economic necessity dictated. The cultural legacy of Confucianism fused with a technocratic central bureaucracy to confound the democratising process. Confucianism is deeply ingrained in the psyche of Korean society; it bears major responsibility for the ossification of the top-down approach of Korean politics and governance. Since the 1960s, the central government has brought under its aegis a host of economic and social instruments, thereby marginalising the National Assembly. Thus, it was presidential elections that became the focus of 'politics' in Korea. The local government machinery established in the mid-1990s is in its infancy: with limited financial autonomy, devolved power is greatly limited.

Second, sustainable development requires *an economic system that is able to generate surplus and technical knowledge on a self-reliant basis.* Korea's mode of development has been extremely successful in terms of capital accumulation. However, the accumulation strategies of the chaebol (which account for over 70 per cent of national economy) were based on extensive accumulation. That is to say, the chaebol increased their profits through expanding the production base rather than by increasing profitability through innovation, quality and productivity. The chaebol strategies led to an unsustainably high indebtedness. Although economic growth raised the general standard of living, inequity in distribution of wealth became most marked, creating a militant workforce and economically fragile rural communities. From the 1990s, the state introduced some measures to redress the maldistribution of wealth. The new national medical insurance system rested on a pay-as-you-go system, and thus remained beyond the reach of the poorest sections of society. In short, the combination of an EOI regime, which presses down on production costs, and the competitive MSR, which promotes short-term profit motives and externalisation behaviour, constitutes the very antithesis of sustainable development principles.

Third, on the social front, WCED advocates *a system that can resolve tensions arising from disharmonious development.* In the early years of development until the 1980s, the government tried to suppress conspicuous consumption of the wealthy and the newly emerging middle classes in a bid to mobilise the working classes in the interests of 'national development'. When labour resisted, the state routinely resorted to coercive force. With the working class largely excluded from the benefits of economic growth, Korea's labour unions adopted militant tactics. The state often responded most brutally: an example is the treatment meted out to squatters in the ongoing struggle for land and homes.

Fourth, the production system in Korea is far from the ideals advocated by WCED in terms of *respecting the ecological base for development.* As we have already seen in Chapters 4 and 5, the intensity of successive regimes of accumulation degraded the environment and squandered natural resources. The government-inspired differentiated development of Korean space intensified the mal-effects of industrialisation. Prioritisation of economic development and its productive infrastructure went hand in hand with the neglect of social and environmental utilities, this accentuating the exploitation of Korea's socio-environment.

Fifth, the required technical system for sustainable development is that *it should be able to continuously search for new solutions on a self-reliant basis.* The Brundtland Report identified that Third World indebtedness and so called unequal exchange relationship is due to developing countries' reliance upon core industrial nation's technology. In Korea, the technological developments have never been self-sustaining. The chaebol have been occupied in making quick profits by imitative and/or licensed technology, so that the knowledge base has failed to develop towards an innovative cycle. Even in the 1990s, R&D investment levels were amongst the lowest of the industrialised nations (*FEER* 25 Feb. 1999, p.12). Furthermore, investment was largely limited to the leading edge industries such as semiconductors and bio-technology, leaving other Korean sectors, particularly non-engineering industries, in a less competitive state.

Sixth, WCED recommends that *the international system needs to foster sustainable patterns of trade and finance.* We can examine this at two levels. On the one hand, Korea needs to integrate with the global economy in a way by which its trade and finance activities maintain internal sustainable strategies. On the other, Korea would need to engage in international markets in a manner which would not detrimentally affect sustainable development externally. At present, Korean companies operate overseas in a conspicuously unsustainable manner. For example, in the 1990s, they have persisted in logging Indonesia's tropical rain forests in violation of local regulations, with all the consequences for indigenous peoples and fragile ecosystems. This has also been the pattern in Siberia's forests, where lax government controls have allowed Korean logging interests to raze vast areas.

Last, the WCED stresses the need for an administrative system which is *flexible and capable of self correction* in a sustainable society. Korea's state bureaucracy has, as we have seen, played a central role in economic development. However, the repeated crises of the industrialisation process were largely due to the inflexibility of state bureaucratic policies. The unresponsiveness of the state to the changing internal and external economic and political situation necessitated its own transformation at each crisis point. The bureaucratic and top-down approach to governance places the Korean state at variance with the needs of society at large, even conflicting with the needs of certain sectors of the capital.

The competitive free market philosophy combined with a hierarchical social structure emanating from Confucianism reinforces notions of income differentials and social polarisation. The high growth development mode, high disparities in wages and consumption levels increase social instability. Social dysfunctions have been spatialised due to centralised political power in Seoul, this translating into regional antagonisms. The cycle of capital and population concentration in the Capital region has been perpetuated by the competitive MSR underpinned by concentrated political controls. The state's intervention in the economy and in the control of labour has not extended to any moderation of Korea's social fragmentation, this being especially the case from the 1980s with the embracing of neo-liberalism.

The absence of monopolistic MSR in Korea's postwar development process meant that social welfare infrastructure common to most advanced Western industrial nations did not materialise. As with the other NICs, Korea with its late development jumped from a condition of extensive accumulation to post-Fordism. Although rapid economic growth was made possible by skipping over the Fordist mode, there was a serious under-development of institutional arrangements to deal with extreme poverty and environmental problems that are an ineluctable accompaniment of capitalist accumulation under a competitive MSR. With the implementation of popular democracy by the early 1990s, some of the shortfalls in social infrastructure did begin to be addressed. However, these limited moves could not redirect Korea's development towards a sustainable course.

By 1996, it was evident that in the absence of a structural crisis in the mode of development, there was little possibility of sustainable development coming on the agenda. Such a crisis would be needed in order to transform the mode of social regulation which underpinned the hitherto unsustainable process in Korea. In 1997 that crisis did indeed arrive. The reforms which it provoked, however, are not directed towards a sustainable path.

The crisis and future of Korea's mode of development explored

Korea's neo-Fordist regime of accumulation was brought to a grinding halt by the financial crisis of 1997. The first signal of the crisis came with the bankruptcy of the vehicle division of one of the larger chaebol, Kia. The IMF's subsequent denunciation of Korea as structurally unsound and institutionally corrupt hastened the flight of international capital, and a string of chaebol declaring insolvency. This brought the flight of portfolio capital and a collapse of the stock market. The Pacific Asia-wide crisis further compounded Korea's economic problems as Thailand, Malaysia and Indonesia devalued their currencies. In Korea, a contributing factor undoubtedly lay in the policy of the Kim Young Sam government of maintaining a strong won against the US dollar. This bid for popular support was closely tied to the depletion of dollar reserves in the Central Bank. To avert national bankruptcy and to avoid defaulting on international loans, the government appealed to the International Monetary Fund for help.

The post-1992 liberalisation of Korea's capital markets is widely considered to be a cause of the crisis. Foreign capital was attracted into the stock market rather than as direct investments. However, the severity of the financial crisis suggests a far deeper structural basis reaching to the very foundations of the neo-Fordist regime. In the early 1990s the latter was established on the basis of rising wages of militant labour which meant the advent of mass consumption. At first, this shielded the chaebol from the impacts of global recession. However, as the main capitalist economies went into growth, rising wages led to falling profitability. The continued militancy of labour unions and rigidity of labour laws were chief causes of chaebol relocation overseas. Liberalisation of the financial and services market served a dual purpose: first, globalisation of the Korean capital market and second, mediation of the international pressures to open up domestic markets. Deregulation of the financial sector, of course, exposed Korea to external shocks. On the one hand, the chaebol were able to borrow at lower interest on the international markets; most activity involved short horizon loans contracted through subsidiaries. Debt-equity ratios were frequently as high as 5:1. On the other hand, the opening up of stock and bond markets exposed Korea to the possibility of rapid outflow of capital. It was precisely such an event – the outflow of portfolio capital after the collapse of Kia motors – that heralded the financial crisis. In fact, the liberalisation which occurred during the Kim Young Sam presidency (1992–97) was both uneven and inconsistently applied. The façade of the free market was over-laid on the established routines of the state–capital nexus. A purist of neo-liberalism would find, as elsewhere, half-hearted implementation which distorted markets rather than perfecting them. It was, in the main, the burden of debt caused by unfettered expansion of chaebol production which brought the financial system to its knees. High debt ratios were a particular feature of chaebol financing, in which the government encouraged credits without proper security. Korea was now an industri-alised country with all the modern trappings but with cultural practices which seemed little changed since the Choson Dynasty. Collusion between the political elite and the conglomerates, the absence of mechanisms of mediation in industrial relations, rigidity in the labour laws and extensive accumulation strategies based on high capital input to gain market share were the main structural problems. The state, labour and capital pursued a path which was out of line with the rapidly changing global economic conditions.

The IMF's conditions for assistance to Korea demanded nothing less than the total exposure of domestic markets to foreign capital, including the latter's ownership of Korean companies. By 1998, the regime of president Kim Dae Jung had embarked on a general restructuring which invoked a tripartite pact between government, industry and labour. The government pledged to discard many of its bureaucrats and reduce its role in all areas of economy. The labour unions agreed to massive redundan-cies provided that the chaebol introduce transparency and accountability. The chaebol were told to reduce their debt-equity levels to 2:1 by 2001, to consolidate around key operations and sell off loss making peripheral subsidiaries, thus streamlining operations to increase productivity. The IMF demands extended to a complete overhaul of the financial sector, which lay at the core of the crisis.

At the point of writing, the Korean government's efforts towards restruc-turing remain at an early stage. So far, little headway has been made in reducing the bureaucracy, and the chaebol have proved resistant to signifi-cant adjustments in their business strategies. The government endeavoured to apply pressure by removing the ceiling on foreign ownership of Korean companies, giving unprecedented access to those foreign investors with resources sufficient to stay the course. By early 1999, significant foreign take-overs in both manufacturing and financial sectors were coming through. In 1998, mergers and acquisitions in Korea were second only to Japan. Examples of strategic purchases made by overseas interests include the transfer of Halla Pulp & Paper Company to Bowater for US$220 million (*FEER* 25 February 1999). To speed up the restructuring of the chaebol, the Kim Dae Jung government resorted to tactics similar to those of president Chun in the 1980 reordering: the three largest chaebol, Samsung, Hyundai and LG were commanded to 'swap' companies so that businesses were consolidated according to their particular market strengths. Rather than promoting the interests of the more robust firms, the government strategy was to push for monopolistic segmentation of industries. This strategy is aimed at restructuring without huge social and economic costs; ironically, it confounds the neo-liberal official ideology of hitherto.

Obviously a leftist critique would argue that the political and business practices as well as the social mode of regulation demand more than just a simple alteration in the industrial structure.

The underlying structural problems of the Korean neo-Fordist regime

There are in fact a number of similarities behind the regular cycle of crises which Korea has experienced from the 1960s. First, the state-led economic strategies have not been sufficiently responsive to rapidly changing external factors. The 1960 and 1997 crises were marked by inadequacies in state regulation, while the 1970 and 1980 crises were a result of over rigid state control.[6] Both resulted from ineffective governance. When the Korean economy was far smaller and relatively simple in structure, state bureaucrats were able to plan and implement economic and physical development policies to achieve spectacular growth. Today, scale and complexity are far greater and the economy is all the less susceptible to the levers of central control. This was acknowledged in 1992, when the state stood back from domestic markets, allowing them a greater measure of autonomous operation. With hindsight, even the US economist Jeffery Sachs has asserted that the financial market liberalisation in East Asia was implemented in 'just the wrong way' (*FEER* 25 February 1999, p.11).[7] In Korea's case, it was not accompanied by new regulatory mechanisms, which left financial institutions open to abuse by the chaebol. It would seem that each crisis has been caused to some degree by the state's over-promotion of a particular sector. The government's reliance on the chaebol to develop leading sectors of the economy as the main thrust of Korean accumulation tended to create a series of fault lines. The continuation of unsecured financing of chaebol activities and their rampant diversification prior to the 1997 crash was largely due to the government–chaebol pact aimed at achieving growth rates deemed necessary for the legitimation of state authority. The latter was not considered to require the restricting of speculatory activities, particularly in real estate which later became a vital factor in Thai and Malaysian crises. The explicit aim of social cohesion was abandoned in the face of a hegemonic neo-liberal ideology which justified social polarisation as a result of 'natural' competition.

Second, prior to the 1997 crisis, the chaebol groups were seeking to accumulate extensively through expansion of capacity and markets rather than implementing a intensive phase which would require raising productivity and quality as well as business consolidation. These conglomerates, the cornerstone of Korea's economy have remained surprisingly backward in terms of technology and business methods. One post-crisis survey found Korean companies at the bottom the of R&D investment league (*FEER* 25 Feb. 1999, p.12).[8] Acquisition of new technology hitherto depended on licensing from advanced economies, Japan in particular. This left Korean companies trapped in a cycle of price-based competition impeding innovation and new technologies. Quality control is also an aspect of Korean manufacturing which has remained unaddressed due to endemic poor management, low labour skills and conflictual labour relations. As in the government bureaucracy, the company management system is rigidly hierarchical, subordinating individual initiative to a deadening culture of uniformity.

Third, the protection of Korea's domestic economy created an enclave of chaebol uncompetitiveness; it also restricted growth of domestic markets. Absence of market exposure shaped the financial services sector in particular. This is not so much to advocate a neo-liberalist argument as to emphasise the manner in which government-inspired market distortion directly benefited the monopolistic basis of the conglomerates. The government in the 1990s pursued externally-related strategies which under the circumstances were contradictory: on the one hand it attempted to promote the standing of Korea Inc. internationally by gaining membership of the OECD, and playing an active role in such organisations as the Commission for Sustainable Development; on the other hand, it restricted foreign ownership of Korean enterprises, including real estate. The peculiar legacy of Korea's colonial experience resulted in strong xenophobic tendencies. It is difficult to exaggerate the role in postwar regimes of nationalist ideology. An example can be seen in the demolition of the ex-Colonial Government Office building in 1996. The claim was that this act would free the Korean people from the colonial imprint and promote 'national self determination', while ridding Seoul of a building with inauspicious feng shui. This event occurred at a point when Korea's dependency on Japanese capital and technology was particularly overt. In the post-1997 crisis era of globalisation, the type of hegemonic project used in the past is unlikely to be tolerated domestically. When capital market liberalisation was finally thrust on the country by the IMF, it resulted in bargain basement-company sales. Yet the traditional xenophobia is being stoked anew by the bargain basement sell off of Korean companies in the wake of the 1997 crisis and IMF intervention.

Last, labour relations in Korea have been highly adversarial throughout the history of industrialisation. Even the long reign of authoritarian regimes saw wages rise at a greater pace than productivity. This brought high price inflation throughout the postwar era. The political liberalisation of 1988 was, in large part, a victory of the labour unions, and high wage demands were pushed through despite declining productivity. This stimulated off-shore capital flows and the new-found globalisation of Korean capital; it also rendered Korea an unattractive place for foreign direct investment. Until 1985, the government had mobilised the population in the industri-alisation process with the promise of fair distribution of wealth; credence was given to their message partly because of the proximity of the North Korean state. However, in reality it was the upper and middle classes who saw the most rapid rise in living standards, this exacerbating social antagonisms. Working class militancy continued into the democratic era of the Roh and Kim regimes, Korean labour relations machinery proving itself particularly deficient in terms of mediationand arbitration. The rigid positions of confrontation were a key cause of Korean capital's quest for more compliant – and cheaper – production locations offshore.

The neo-liberal ideology propagated by the government was not accom-panied by the operation of an unfettered market. Deregulation in the banking sector was formally implemented, but bank loans were still a func-tion of political pressure. The government's development strategy was still wedded to the notion that chaebol were simply national capital. Thus, the government restricted the foreign ownership of Korean companies to below 50 per cent even after liberalisation.

The entrenched particularities of Korean capitalism present special obstacles to reform in more market-pure directions. The bureaucratic caucus of the state is highly resistant to reduction of its controls over econ-omy and society. Although some government departments were merged in the mid-1990s, this did not reduce state involvement in the economy: it merely rendered it less competent. The family-owned and managed chaebol groups are similarly hostile to changes in their organisational practices towards more 'modern' and transparent forms.

The wage earning classes are so imbedded in their Confucianist mould which ossifies hierarchy that movement towards participation and equity can only be achieved with great difficulty. Class antagonism and mistrust has been ingrained to the extent that dialogue between capital and labour is often one of the deaf. The Korean establishment is dominated by old-boy networks based on family, alumni and other similar associa-tions. Market rationality is often put aside either for favours or simply out of loyalty. This government-business cronyism has also heightened problems of regionalism. Needless to say, the exclusive rigidities of Korean society leave little room for minority groups, for the mentally and physically disabled and those socially stigmatised by unemployment or nature of their work. Thus, there are specific, historically derived, ideological barriers to any fundamental change in Korea's social and economic order.

How can we interpret the current situation and structural problems within our theoretical perspective? We have identified some structural features of Korea's mode of development which have caused the 1997 crisis:

- the effectiveness of the state bureaucracy in economic and social governance;
- the collusion between political and economic leaders through their 'network';
- the absence of acceptable means of arbitration between capital and labour;
- the extensive accumulation strategy adopted by the chaebol, coupled with their inherent weakness in developing technology and promoting quality;
- hierarchical neo-Confucian state bureaucratic and chaebol management systems deaden individual initiative;
- a xenophobic domestic culture which distorts the process of integration in the external economy.

Apart from the chaebol's accumulation strategy, all these issues have their roots in the mode of social regulation, the dysfunctional political, social and ideological regulation which underpins the reproduction of the regime of accumulation. The prime cause of the crisis was the rigidity of the mode of social regulation in Korea's neo-Fordist regime: under intensifying competition and a declining profit rate, social regulatory mechanisms broke down. Korea's neo-Fordist regime was rooted in the mode of social regulation of the pre-globalisation era. In previous regimes where the national economy was largely insular, distortions created by the state were amenable to the mechanisms of the mode of social regulation. From the early 1990s, however, the system was unable to cope with an economy that was increasingly dominated by invisible hands beyond the national boundary. Korea's political, social and ideological spheres failed to adapt to suit the new mode of development. The state failed to restructure the nature of their role in the society and economy which remained schizophrenic, showing a façade of globalisation yet holding on to traditional and nationalistic behaviours. The Korean government underestimated the changes needed in the transition. It failed to construct political and social institutions which would have aided the transition of Korean society. The state itself was so imbedded within the old mode of social regulation that it was unable to implement such changes without itself undergoing structural transformation.

The reform package of 1997 failed to address the fundamental problems of Korea's mode of development – its mode of social regulation. The focus has been on industrial structure and regime of accumulation. However, the real problem lies in the political and social regulatory mechanisms, and these structural issues are hardly addressed by the reforms. Radical changes to the mode of social regulation are essential to an upgrading of industrial trajectory towards the echelon occupied by an average OECD member. And social institutions have to be developed in tandem with economic adjustments.

Social impacts of the post-1997 crisis

Korea's postwar development process had never been characterised by a monopolistic MSR, and this fact is closely associated with the absence of social welfare infrastructure seen in many postwar industrial nations. As with the other NIEs, Korea with its late development leapt from extensive accumulation to post-Fordism. Skipping over the Fordist mode permitted rapid economic growth, but its consequence was the neglect of those institutions common to advanced economies which address poverty, environmental degradations and the like. The collapse of the economy in 1997 provoked a social crisis of unprecedented proportions to break out in Korea. The restructuring of the chaebol meant a rise in unemployment from less than half a million to over two million by the end of 1998 – this in a situation of scant social welfare and unemployment provision. The poverty and misery could be seen in the army of homeless lining the streets and underground stations as well as the large number of children at risk of malnutrition. There are signs that even traditional family support systems were beginning to break down as unemployment became widespread, while healthcare provision proved incapable of offering succour to the majority of those in need. Only 3 per cent of the population was covered by free medical care and livelihood protection schemes. The World Bank's study of social crisis in East Asia following the financial crisis has reported a significant increase in hardship for the poor, due particularly to the high medical costs based on pay-as-you-go medical insurance schemes (Atinc and Walton 1998). In part to bolster Korea's minimal social safety net, the World Bank advanced the Korean government US$5 billion in loans, with a similar sum promised for 1999.

Essential to any comprehensive plan for the South Korean economy would be remediation of environmental problems (and their associated uneven development) inherited from the previous regime of accumulation. The spatial and land-use policy changes since the 1997 crisis have demonstrated a tendency towards deregulation. Particularly significant is the relaxation of restrictions on green belt use, designed to revive the construction and real estate sectors by opening up new opportunities in the Seoul Metropolitan Area where the worst effects of the crisis had been felt.

Unemployment, housing shortages and homelessness have reached new levels.

Korea's regime of accumulation in the twenty-first century

As restructuring progresses into the twenty-first century, a stable period of accumulation might be anticipated. The globalisation process is deepening as the government removes barriers to foreign capital penetration. However, the social structure is a key determinant of whether Korean capital will become a significant global player. A possible scenario is now presented, together with its likely social and environmental implications. The possibility of sustainable development or social welfare statism will also be discussed here.

The future for Korea: a scenario

Korea's recovery process following the 1997 crash is intended to remove the structural obstacles in the economy as well as to transform it to a higher trajectory for future expansion. In fact, each successive crisis raised the industrial trajectory and increased the overall size of the economy. The restructuring plans envisaged that the service sector, particularly the financial and retail sectors, would see major expansion as a consequence of deregulation. The McKinsey Global Institute (1998) showed that these areas have the potential for expansion and the absorption of substantial amounts of surplus labour. By 1999, the opening of domestic markets had begun to bring global capital into the stock and bond markets, as well as the industrial sector. As Korea's economy (particularly financial sector practices) comes closer in line with international standards, more foreign firms are expected to venture into the domestic market.

   As we have seen, the chaebol at least began a process of significant structural change, with strong pressures to make their constituents more independent. As cross-financing within the groups becomes better regulated, non-performing companies within the corporate structure will become less supportable. The rationalisation process is likely to continue in order to reduce debt-equity ratios. It is, however, more difficult to foresee a great change in chaebol accumulation strategies. Tight financial constraints will render increases in R&D spending unlikely. The strengthening of production quality controls is also unlikely since there is little evidence of changes in management philosophy or improvement in labour processes and relations. Domestic capital accumulation will depend upon the replacement by the chaebol of price-based competition by a competition based on innovation and quality. If Korean companies are slow to implement intensive accumulation strategies, their market share is likely to be squeezed by nations with much lower labour costs and rapidly developing technological capacity such as Thailand, Malaysia and China. Korea's labour markets at the turn of the century are rapidly becoming flexible. Swingeing redundancies are paralleled by the introduction by many companies of negotiated contracts rather than the tradition employment-for-life conditions. With labour unions in a disadvantaged position in the capital–labour relationship, there exists little incentive for management to improve channels of communication or arbitration. Thus, if and when the economy picks up, further bouts of labour militancy can be anticipated. With a competitive MSR in operation, it is more likely that foreign capital may have to adapt to Korean methods rather than Korean firms making significant changes in their management regimes. Whatever the mix, wage relations are likely to become more competitive and polarised.

In view of the current interventions, the basic position of the state is unlikely to change significantly. As market forces become more crucial to private sector decision-making, the government will have fewer instruments by which to implement its own economic agenda. However, until the restructuring is more advanced, with markets deregulated, the government will try to maintain a hands-on stance, as it has done in the past. How far the restructuring and the liberalisation of markets is likely to go depends on political imperatives: as long as the reform measures focus on the regime of accumulation rather than the mode of social regulation, the nature of state intervention will not drastically change. To the state, the restructuring process is seen as necessary, but only so far as it is needed to guarantee capital accumulation and thus ensure its continued legitimation.

The reforms in progress by 1999 suggest that a competitive mode of social regulation would remain in force with greater reliance on market mechanisms and individual responsibility for basic welfare. The mode of development would consequently resemble the neo-Fordist regimes of the advanced Western countries, with flexiblised labour relations in all sectors. It can be anticipated that Korea would experience levels of structural unemployment significantly higher than those of the pre-crisis period, even with tertiary sector expansion. There would also be heightened social tension as wage polarisation increases. As in the Western Europe and North America of the 1990s, average wage rises would be tightly linked to inflation, with a small segment of the professional managerial class rewarded disproportionately. The social polarisation is thus likely to intensify, not only between those in and out of work, but between the 'fat-cats' and Korea's semi-skilled workers. Reductions in already poor social expenditure budgets will hasten the pathologies so familiar to the Western city, and atomisation of the traditional extended family will exacerbate these difficulties.

As for the uneven development of South Korea in spatial terms, it is probable that the influx of global capital and the intensification of competition will reinforce the tendency of capital concentration in the Seoul Metropolitan region. A competitive MSR and the flexiblisation of labour will intensify face-to-face contact, which has been identified as the main factor in the megalopolisation of neo-Fordist regimes such as the UK, France and US amongst the Western industrialised countries and Thailand, Malaysia, China and other NICs (Lipietz 1992, Peck and Tickell 1992a). At the present time, Seoul is the only Korean urban centre that has the communication and transport infrastructure and concentration of skilled workforce necessary to accommodate the needs of global capital, particularly in the finance and service sector. Yet further industrial concentration will lead to higher land prices, congestion of communications, as well as other environmental problems. These will be seen more intensely in the Seoul Metropolitan Region. Relative underdevelopment of the provinces would heighten 'regionalisation' of politics. Moreover, the mode of environmental regulation put in place in the pre-crisis 1990s, market competitive and promoting private provision in environmental and social consumption, could not be sustained in the face of flexiblisation of the production process. As polarisation of income and structural unemployment rise, most citizens will not be able to shoulder the burden of environmental degradation or provide privately the required environmental services and goods. Korean society still manifests the social order and value resembling a 'modern' society *vis-à-vis* a post-modern one. The combination of modernist dogma and Confucianist customs produced a rigid social code of conduct and regulation. Any movement towards the breaking down of this stratified social order to become more inclusive and pluralistic would benefit alienated sections of the population. However, the instilling of pluralism can also be seen as on capital's own agenda, as a means of fragmenting working class cohesion. Korea's environmental movement is likely to become even further split between numerous single-issue groups, and all the more ineffectual.

The Korean state's likely function in the more globalised and restructured economy will be to secure the needs of capital by the provision of infrastructure and industrial estates – as indeed it has been in past years. The suppression of labour will also be a natural role. The outcome is easily predicted: Korea's mode of development will at regular intervals move into crisis, recreating the patterns of the previous era. The competitive mode of regulation, and the tenets of the free market hold no remedy for the social and spatial polarisation which further integration into the global economy will bring. In short, the IMF restructuring programme will prove incapable of remedying the underlying causes of the crisis which erupted in 1997: its focus will remain on the economic system rather than the social regulatory mechanism.

Possibility of sustainable development in the twenty-first century

The onset of the financial crisis has exposed the paucity of Korea's social welfare system. Existing social policies resting heavily on market provision were put in place against the backdrop of full employment, rising income and high savings and relatively strong community ties; they took little account of downside risks (Atinc and Walton 1998, p.3). The vulnerability of the poor and unemployed during the late 1990s' crisis is exemplified by the personal costs of medical care which increased four fold over the twelve months to 1998. Furthermore, in 1996, Livelihood Protection covered just 3.3 per cent of the population and the government's medical aid scheme reached 3.8 per cent. The US$5 billion World Bank loan intended for social programmes (which came on-stream in 1999) will go only part of the way to supporting the rapidly increasing ranks of the unemployed and their dependants. Korea is culturally and ethnically homogeneous, and there is a strong layer of common values, including those of social equity. This goal will become more elusive as income polarisation increases. However, government economic and institutional reforms are largely limited to raising economic efficiency and restoring neo-liberal market operation. The World Bank stresses that social issues should be incorporated in the restructuring policies: 'Yet it is vital that the economic and institutional reforms being designed in the crisis countries serve to mend and repair the social fabric . . . and support equitable growth when the recovery occurs. Separating economic policy making and social development is a recipe for failure' (Atinc and Walton 1998, p.1).

The state cannot afford to allow social tensions to develop unchecked. A spirit of 'natural' cohesion in Korea has been important due to the ever-present military threat from North Korea. Indeed, it can be agreed that the sustained rise in average wages after the early 1960s was, to a degree, occasioned by the ideological response to the military pressure from the North. The post-crisis elite consensus is that any significant increase in social unrest may trigger an invasion from the North. Thus, the Korean state is likely to construct short-term compromises with labour, as in the past. This is far more likely than any far-reaching changes to the mode of social regulation.

In view of the complex societal problems facing Korea, the state will need to move towards new frameworks designed to maintain social cohesion and curtail support for the North Korean regime. Simple anticommunist ideology is longer sufficient. As the nature of Korean capital changes in a transnational direction, the state is likely to balance economic growth against social cohesion. The concept of national accumulation will no longer apply. Therefore, political commitment to social development is likely to be a more powerful vote-garnering manoeuvre than economic growth-oriented policies.

If social impacts due to the new mode of development become severe enough to threaten social stability and hence the capital accumulation process, the Korean state will come under pressure to implement progressive taxation as well as a slightly more extended welfare system. Even a means tested welfare system is a more desirable outcome than the present workfare system where only those in work benefit. Establishment of a partial welfare state would be the first real step towards a more equitable society. More important for the current establishment, such a direction might be the only means of sustaining (and sustainably developing) the territory of South Korea. Thus, the existence of North Korea might just be the pivotal condition which provokes a qualitative shift in the nature of South Korean society. A move in the direction of welfare statism would push Korea's social mode of regulation towards a monopolistic form which would increase the opportunity for sustainable development strategies to be pursued as the inevitable crises unfold.

Summary

This book has focused upon the close association between Korea's economic transformation and the production of spatial differentiation and environmental problems. It has demonstrated that Korea's development has been marked by cyclical crises rather than by the often projected image of unbroken and stable growth. Korea's political economic experiment in optimising rapid growth at each phase of restructuring is characterised by an overarching mode of social regulation that was competitive in nature throughout most of the 'development' period.

The state which intervened massively in the development process promoted efficiency in industrial and spatial developments. Korea's rapid economic growth was due to state planning mechanisms which prioritised productive rather than social infrastructure. However, the regular occurrence of economic crisis stemmed from both the rigidity of state planning mechanisms and the rigidity of the social order, reflecting the inability of the MSR to continually adjust to changing internal and external forces.

The socio-environmental consequences were the reflection of the state strategies in economic and spatial development as well as the result of the chaebol-dominated capitalist accumulation regime. Our analysis has showed that due to an efficiency-driven state spatial strategy, Korea is differentiated into three distinct spatial typologies with different economic bases: the CCZ dominated by service and consumption activities, the SIZ dominated by manufacturing production and the PRZ with its agricultural and leisure industries. The social relations in each zones resulted in a differentiation of social classes. As a consequence, the state was able to marginalise the demands of working class and rural communities in the semi-peripheral and peripheral regions.

The 1997 structural crisis was a crisis of mode of social regulation, particularly resulting from Korea's rigid social practices and the prevailing relations of production. The regime of accumulation based on a strategy of global integration demanded significant changes in the mode of social regulation, but Korea Inc. continued to cling to the old MSR which was increasingly out of sympathy with the global environment. Particularly, the deep-rooted xenophobic tendencies from the country's peculiar nationalist ideology and rigid social mores based on Confucianism stood in contradiction to the flexible nature of a 'global' MSR. The Korean state is a newcomer to the 'deregulation' paradigm, and the mistakes made in liberalising the financial sector resulted in the overall crisis.

Korea's globalisation project in the 1990s was, at best, an experiment to deal with its internal problems of falling rate of profit. In recent research, Beaverstock *et al.* (1999) shows that Seoul was no more a global capital centre than Moscow. Korea's restructuring will need to address this problem, not only in terms of economic form and relations, but in its cultural and ideological basis too, particularly its social hierarchy and exclusionary politics, xenophobic tendencies and racial prejudice. The current reform package, however, only addresses the problems in the regime of accumulation, particularly the inefficiencies in the banking sector and the chaebol groups. The restructuring may bring Korea away from the brink, but its structural weaknesses will remain largely untouched.

An alternative reform strategy would have directed its energies to the heart of the problem – the mode of social regulation which encompasses ideologies, social relations and 'politics'. The economic structure is being opened up to global capital penetration as the IMF has demanded, but the traditional political, social and business culture of Korea is becoming more entrenched. Intensifying competition in all areas of socio-economic life will clash with these forms, increasing social tension as social differentiation and alienation is institutionalised. Particularly, the army of the under-class – the long-term unemployed, casualised labour and members of the informal sector will become ever more marginalised from the new workfare state.

Through the regulationist framework, the study has revealed the unique process of environmental transformation associated with the political, economic, social and spatial changes in Korea within the changing global economic order. It has been shown that environmental degradation has been due to the complex interrelationship of many of these causal factors under a singular systemic framework driven by the accumulation regime and the predominantly competitive mode of social regulation. Our framework can be loosely translated to the global scale as a means of understanding the highly differentiated environmental problems in the world today. The wide gulf between developing and industrialised nations in the perception of environmental problems is a symptom of the poor understanding of capitalist spatial dynamics and the uneven spatial development it produces.

The naivety of current debates about sustainable development strategies arises due to the lack of analysis of the regulatory processes. As far as a more deep-rooted reformist perspective is concerned, it is the mode of social regulation which would have to be the main target of change. International efforts to promote a sustainable development mode are the first step only. What is needed is a change in the mode of social regulation at the level of the nation-state and internationally. Effective political and ideological consensus has to be reconstructed around a sustainable mode of development.

In the Korean case, the intensive regime based on EOI coupled with a competitive MSR has little chance of being reconciled with social and environmental justice. Sustainable economic and environmental development can only occur with a de-coupling of the present intensive accumulation regime from Korea's competitive MSR. The 1997 crisis was an opportunity to establish a more equitable economic system for the long term. However, in the event the limitations of the reform package reduce the opportunity to significantly change the mode of development towards any welfare statism, which in the authors' view represents the only sustainable development strategy for Korea. It is envisaged that greater social inequity and environmental damage will occur under the emerging mode of development, and another crisis is again lurking in the not too distant future.

Appendices

Table A1.1 Urbanisation and economic growth: major indicators

		1960	*1970*	*1980*	*1985*	*1990*
Total population	('000)	24,989	31,435	37,407	40,448	43,411
Urban population	('000)	6,999	12,986	21,434	26,442	32,308
Ratio (%)	(I)	28.0	41.1	57.2	65.4	74.4
	(II)	35.8	49.8	66.7	74.0	79.6
Primacy index	(I)	2.10	2.86	2.65	2.74	2.79
	(II)	1.09	1.53	1.43	1.39	1.35[a]
Economic structure						
Total employment ('000)		7,036	10,153	12,682	14,970	18,036
Primary		65.7	50.8	37.8	27.1	18.7
Secondary		7.5	15.2	22.8	24.2	26.9
Tertiary		26.8	34.0	39.4	48.7	54.4
Total production						
(Billion won)		247	2,724	37,820	67,071	131,502
(Million US dollars)		2,331	7,951	62,233	83,214	163,152
Primary		34.1	26.5	14.2	13.6	10.5
Secondary		14.0	22.3	29.7	29.9	33.0
Tertiary		51.9	51.2	56.1	56.6	56.5
Per capita GNP (1000 won)		10	85	976	1,610	4,007
(US dollars)		94	248	1,605	1,998	5,659
Export (million $)		32	835	17,505	30,283	65,016
Import (million $)		240	1,984	22,292	31,135	69,843

Source: EPB (1970, 1985) *Major Economic Indicators*; Hwang and Choi (1988), p.54; NSO (1993).

Notes:
1 Urbanisation Rate (I) is based on Shi; (II) is based on Shi and Eup with population over 20,000.
2 Primacy index (I) is p1/p2, (II) is Davis Index.
3 1990 data added to Appendix table 1 in Hwang and Choi (1988), p.54.
4 (a) Data from Kwon, W-Y. (1991), p.185.

Table A1.2 Export shares of Korea's ten largest export categories, 1970–86 (%)

	1970	1980	1986
Textiles	40.8	29.5	25.2
Electronics	3.5	10.6	19.1
Steel products	1.6	10.5	7.2
Footwear	2.1	5.0	6.1
Ships	0.0	6.7	5.2
Automobile/parts	0.0	2.6	4.8
Machinery	1.1	2.7	3.0
Synthetic resins	1.3	2.9	2.7
Toys/dolls	0.1	1.6	2.1
Metal products	1.5	2.7	1.8
Total percentage of all export	52.0	74.8	77.2

Source: Korea Trade Association, Export Statistics, cited in Steinberg (1989) p.144.

Table A1.3 Structure of manufacturing industry: 1970, 1977 and 1982

Year		Monopoly	Duopoly	Oligopoly	Competitive	Total
1970	No. of commodities	442	279	495	276	1,492
	(% share)	(29.6)	(18.2)	(33.2)	(18.5)	(100)
	Shipments[a]	110	204	439	498	1,252
	(% share)	(8.8)	(16.3)	(35.1)	(39.8)	(100)
1977	No. of commodities	667	425	674	343	2,219
	(% share)	(31.6)	(20.1)	(32.0)	(16.3)	(100)
	Shipments[a]	2,264	1,536	4,716	5,404	13,920
	(% share)	(16.3)	(11.0)	(33.9)	(38.8)	(100)
1982	No. of commodities	533	251	1,071	405	2,260
	(% share)	(23.6)	(11.1)	(47.4)	(17.9)	(100)
	Shipments[a]	5,649	3,275	24,967	15,481	49,372
	(% share)	(11.4)	(6.6)	(50.6)	(31.4)	(100)

Source: Compiled from the Census of Manufacturing database, Economic Planning Board, by K.U. Lee *et al.* (1986), cited in Amsden (1989), p.121.

Notes:
a Billion won.
Concentration ratios (CR):
　　Monopoly (one-firm CR accounts for a market share of more than 80%).
　　Duopoly (two-firm CR accounts for a market share of more than 80%).
　　Oligopoly (three-firm CR accounts for a market share of more than 60%).
　　Competitive (three-firm CR accounts for a market share of less than 60%).

Table A1.4 Combined sales of top ten chaebols, as percent of GNP,[a] 1974–84

Groups	1974	1976	1978	1980	1981	1982	1983	1984
1	4.9	4.7	6.9	8.3	10.5	10.4	11.8	12.0
3	9.0	11.3	16.9	23.9	27.6	27.4	30.5	35.8
5	11.6	14.5	22.9	35.0	41.3	42.2	46.7	52.4
9	14.7	19.3	28.9	46.0	53.3	55.1	59.8	64.8
10	15.1	19.8	30.1	48.1	55.7	57.6	62.4	67.4

Source: Adapted from Seok Ki Kim (1987), cited in Amsden, A. (1989), p.116.

Note:

a (Aggregate net sales of the largest ten groups/GNP) × 100 for each year.

Table A1.5 Comparative growth rates of farm household income and debt, 1975–85

	1975	1980	1981	1982	1983	1984	1985
Income (in 1000 won)	873	2,693	3,688	4,465	5,128	5,549	5,743
Growth rate (%)	—	—	36.9	21.1	14.8	8.2	3.5
Debt (in 1000 won)	33	338	437	830	1,285	1,784	2,024

Source: Park, Chan-Hee, 1987, 'The reality of the Four Trillion Won Farm Household Debt', *Chosun*, March, cited in Bello and Rosenfeld (1990), p.87.

Table A2.1 Increases in urban centres, urban population and the ratio of urbanised population, 1949–85

Period	Increase in the no. of urban centres	Increase in urban population	Increase in the ratio of urban population to total population
1949–1955	0	10,523,767	5.5
1955–1960	29	2,519,062	6.0
1960–1966	22	3,463,213	6.8
1966–1970	3	3,082,279	7.6
1970–1975	27	4,858,597	8.5
1975–1980	−4	4,631,803	8.1
1980–1985	19	5,107,025	7.7

Source: Kwon, Y-W. (1991), p.72; partial.

Table A2.2 Urbanisation and industrialisation

Year	Urbanisation level (A)	Industrialisation level (B)	Difference (A-B)
1966	42.1	42.1	0.0
1970	49.8	49.6	0.2
1980	66.7	66.0	0.7
1985	73.8	75.1	−1.3

Source: EPB (1986) *Major Statistics of Korean Economy*, cited in Kwon (1988b), p.107.

Note:
The industrialisation level means the ratio of manufacturing and service sector employment to national total employment.

Table A2.3 Urbanisation in Korea and population concentration in Seoul

Year	Total pop. (in 1000 persons)	Urbanisation level (%)	Percentage of concentration in Seoul	Davis Primacy Index
1960	24,989	35.8	9.8	1.09
1970	31,434	49.8	17.6	1.53
1975	34,707	58.4	19.9	1.51
1980	37,436	66.7	22.3	1.43
1985	40,467	73.8	23.8	1.39
1990	43,520	79.6	24.4	1.35

Source: EPB (various years) *Population and Housing Census*, cited in Kwon, W-Y. (1991), p.185.

Table A2.4 Regional shares of service sector GRP, 1968–76

	1968	1970	1972	1974	1976
Seoul	43.1	41.2	26.5	44.5	44.0
Pusan	9.8	9.9	12.1	9.8	10.1
Kyonggi	7.5	7.8	10.2	7.7	8.1
Kangwon	4.2	4.4	5.2	3.7	3.6
North Chungchong	2.9	3.1	3.8	2.6	2.6
South Chungchong	5.3	5.4	6.5	4.9	4.6
North Cholla	4.2	4.3	5.6	3.9	4.0
South Cholla	6.3	6.9	8.3	6.2	6.6
North Kyongsang	9.4	9.6	11.9	9.1	9.0
South Kyongsang	6.5	6.5	8.3	6.6	6.4
Chaeju	0.9	0.9	1.6	0.9	0.9
Total	100.0	100.0	100.0	100.0	100.0
Total amount	2,551	3,189	3,677	4,388	5,244

Source: Kim, Y-J. (1993), p.24.

Note:
GRP based on 1975 constant prices (unit; billion won).

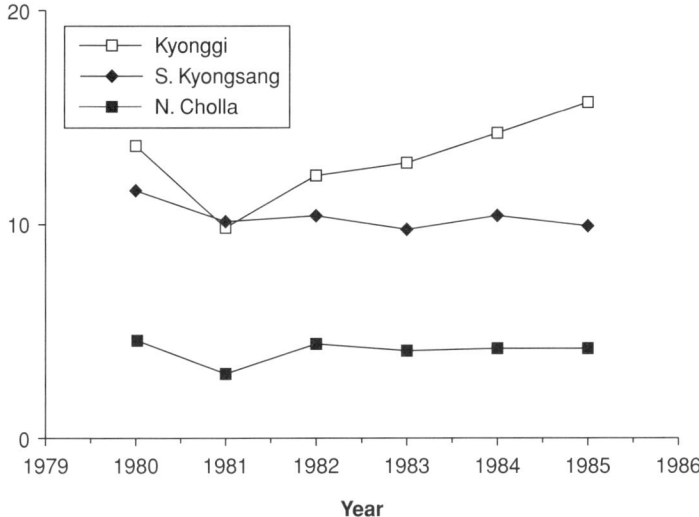

Figure A2.1 Three-region comparison of the construction, electricity and water
production share of GNP, 1980–85.

Source: Cited in Kim, Y-J (1993), p.32.

Table A2.5 Share of infrastructure investment by major cities and provinces

Region	Cities	1965	1975	1985
SMR	Seoul	69.06	49.57	43.10
	Incheon	4.06	2.02	4.80
Southeast	Pusan	13.31	7.21	21.87
Region	Taegu	2.64	9.34	5.07
	Pohang	0.37	1.21	0.88
	Ulsan	0.42	0.75	1.10
	Masan	0.35	1.10	1.05
	Changwon	—	—	0.58
	Kumi	—	—	0.28
	Sub-total	90.21	71.20	78.73
N. Cholla	Jeonju	1.17	1.22	0.88
Province	Iri	0.42	0.82	0.54
	Kunsan	0.44	15.83(0.63)[3]	0.35
	Namwon	—	—	0.05
	Jeongju	—	—	0.15
	Sub-total	2.03	17.87(2.67)[3]	1.97
Other regions	Daejeon/others	7.76	10.93	19.30
	Total	100.0	100.0	100.0
	Total expenditure in billion won	4.5	106.5	1686.3

Source: Cited in Kim (1993), p.50, corrected for errors and inconsistencies.

Notes:
1 Construction expenditure at each year current price.
2 The collective consumption goods included in the figure are roads, sewerage, port facility, dams, works to river banks, piped water provision, bridge construction, urban planning costs, land adjustment costs, and the construction of public housing, market places and parks.
3 The large share of infrastructural investment in Kunsan in 1975 was due to the concentrated efforts to re-construct a water mains system. This was an unusual amount of investment peculiar to that year, and cannot be taken as showing the normal trend. The figures in the brackets represent the normal figures after subtracting the water works investment.

Table A2.6 Distribution of manufacturing employment and population, Seoul and Kyonggi Province, 1973–91

		1973	1978	1983	1991
Manufacturing employment					
Seoul	(%)	70.6	52.3	45.7	30.4
Kyonggi	(%)	29.4	47.7	54.3	69.6
Total	(%)	100.0	100.0	100.0	100.0
Number		580,844	1,031,328	1,019,413	1,367,700
Population					
Seoul	(%)	63.2	63.7	62.3	57.1
Kyonggi	(%)	36.8	36.3	37.7	42.9
Total	(%)	100.0	100.0	100.0	100.0
Number		9,959,396	12,274,866	14,782,854	18,586,128

Source: EPB (1983) *Mining and Manufacturing Census*, Seoul and Gyeonggi (1984) *Statisitical Year-books*, NSO (1993) *Korea Statistical Yearbook*, cited in Kwon (1988b), p.115 (adapted).

Notes:
Manufacturing establishments with 5 or more employees.
Population data for 1991 is based on 1990 census data.

Table A2.7 Regional distribution of the manufacturing industry, 1984

	Industrial site (1000 m²)	Number of firms	Number of workers ('000)	Value of shipments (billion won)	Fixed capital investment (billion won)
Whole country	237,588	43,483	2,540	71,359.8	3,968
	(100.0)	(100.0)	(100.0)	(100.0)	(100.0)
Capital region	74,075	22,653	1,129	28,472.2	1,641
	(31.2)	(52.1)	(46.1)	(39.8)	(41.4)
Central region	18,299	2,847	151	4,115.8	228
	(7.7)	(6.5)	(6.2)	(5.8)	(5.7)
Southwestern region	26,064	4,186	139	6,817.9	185
	(11.0)	(9.7)	(5.6)	(9.6)	(4.6)
Southeastern region	114,147	12,480	1,057	30,405.3	1,724
	(48.0)	(28.7)	(39.0)	(42.6)	(43.5)
Other region	5,003	1,317	74	1,548.8	190
	(2.1)	(3.0)	(3.1)	(2.2)	(4.8)

Source: EPB (1984) *Census of Mining and Manufacturing Industry*; cited in Kwon (1988a), p.72.

Table A2.8 Growth management strategies and programmes for subregions of the Capital region

Subregion	Major cities and towns	Location	Growth management strategies and programmes
I. Restricted development subregion	Seoul, Euijongbu, Kuri, Wondang	Core areas and inner ring with radius of 15 km, located north and south of the Han River	Dispersal, decongestion and decentralisation 1. Denial of new factory construction 2. Relocation of pollution-generating manufacturing plants 3. Dispersal of population and control of inmigration 4. Selective dispersal of educational facilities
II. Controlled development subregion	Incheon, Suwon, Anyang, Banwol	Suburban areas South of Seoul ring with radius of 35 km, and Suwon as the subregion's centre	Control of population growth and avoidance of urban sprawl 1. Limitations on new factory construction 2. Accommodation of some of the displaced industries from Seoul 3. Suspension of disorderly land use practices 4. Managing density development with the aid of the green belt
III. Encouraged development subregion	Pyeontack, Anjung, Ahseong	Southern part of the outer ring with radius of 70 km, new growth potential for peripheral development	Intensive and extensive development 1. New town development such as campus towns 2. Expansion of existing cities and towns as growth centres 3. Development of industrial estates in Ahsan Bay
IV. Environmental protection subregion	Gapyeong, Yangpyeong, Yeoju	The fringe areas of the outer ring located in the basin of upstream Han River	Preservation, conservation and protection 1. Prevention of pollution in the upper Han River basin to maintain water quality 2. Water resources development 3. Natural resources preservation and promotion of recreational activities 4. Promotion of dairy and vegetable farming including industrial crop
V. Special development subregion	Gangwha, Munsan, Dongducheon, Pocheon	The fringe areas of the outer ring located north of Seoul and south of DMZ	Reserved for future development 1. Buffer for national defense 2. Limited development of agro-industries 3. Conservation of forestry and other natural resources 4. Promotion of truck farming and livestock farming

Source: Korea Research Institute for Human Settlements (1982).

Table A3.1 Population, households and housing stock in cities and rural areas

	Unit		1960	1970	1980
Country as a whole	Population	(1000)	24,989	30,882	38,124
	Households[1]	(1000)	4,018	5,375	7,331
	Number of housing units	(1000)	3,464	4,360	5,463
	Housing supply ratio[2]	(%)	86.2	81.1	74.5
Urban areas (cities as administratively designated)	Population	(1000)	6,997	12,710	21,826
	Households[1]	(1000)	1,131	2,264	4,197
	Number of housing units	(1000)	783	1,398	2,542
	Housing supply ratio[2]	(%)	69.2	61.7	60.6
Rural areas (*Gun*)	Population	(1000)	17,992	18,172	16,298
	Households[1]	(1000)	2,887	3,111	3,134
	Number of housing units	(1000)	2,681	2,962	2,921
	Housing supply ratio[2]	(%)	92.0	95.2	93.2

Source: MoC (1982), p.69.

Notes:
1 Indicates the households that would require a separate living quarter on their own. The figure excludes one-member households and legally undefined, quasi-households.
2 Calculated on the basis of one-household-one-unit assumption; i.e. total number of housing units/total number of households × 100.

Table A3.2 Selected government developments within green belt areas

Development	Place	Area
Reunification Training Centre	Mt Bukhan	16,000 pyeong
Army Barracks	Naegokdong, Seochogu	56,000 pyeong
Korea Highways Corporation	Yangjaedong, Seochogu	68,000 pyeong
Korean Development Institute	Umyondong, Seochogu	—
The 2nd Government Building Complex	Kwacheon	—
Seoul Grand Park	Kwacheon	—
Taenung National Sports Training Centre	Kongrungdong, Nowongu	—

Source: Park, C-J. (1991), p.247.

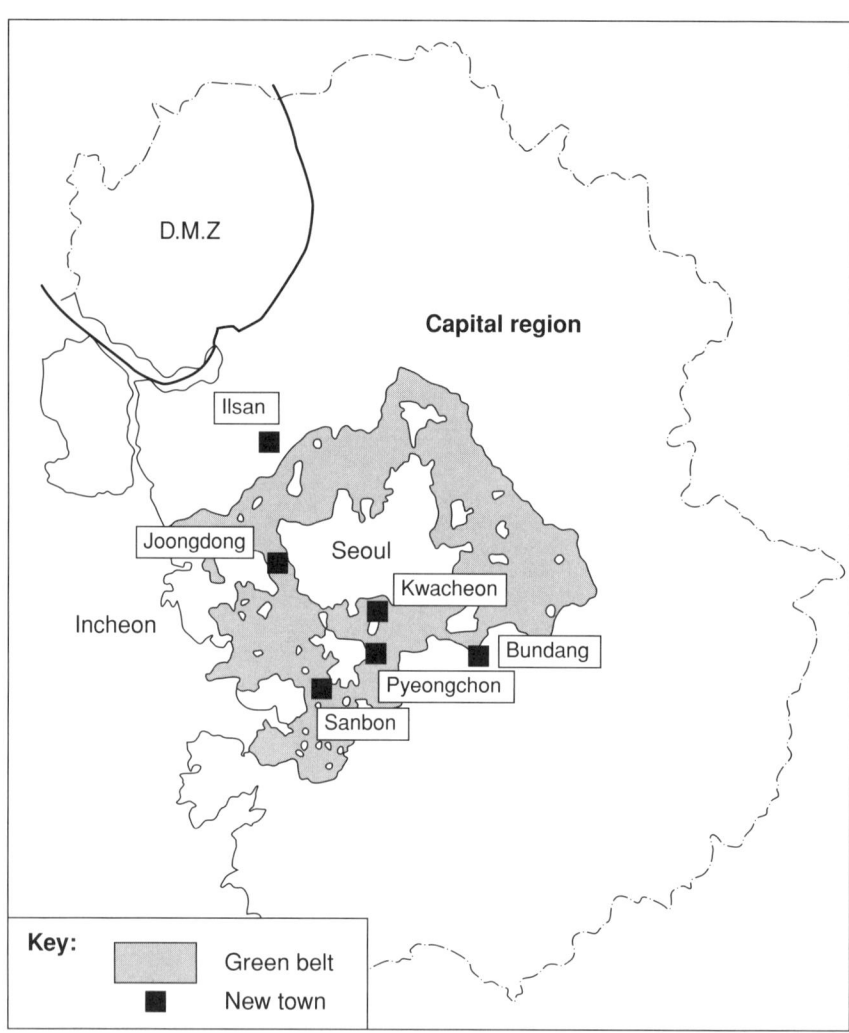

Figure A3.1 Location of new towns in Seoul metropolitan area.

Source: Authors.

Table A3.3 Electricity production and consumption by source, 1970–89 (unit: 100 million Kwh)

Year	Electricity production				Electricity consumption			
	Hydro	*Fossil fuel*	*Nuclear*	*Total*	*Manu-facturing*	*Domestic*	*Service*	*Total*
1970	12.2	79.5	—	91.7	49.8	8.0	9.1	77.4
(%)	(13.3)	(86.7)	(0.0)	(100.0)	(64.3)	(10.3)	(11.8)	(100.0)
1980	19.8	317.8	34.8	372.4	220.3	53.2	33.3	327.3
(%)	(5.3)	(85.3)	(9.8)	(100.0)	(67.4)	(16.3)	(10.2)	(100.0)
1989	45.6	425.5	473.7	944.7	500.5	151.8	115.8	821.9
(%)	(4.8)	(45.0)	(50.2)	(100.0)	(60.9)	(18.5)	(14.1)	(100.0)

Source: EPB (1990) *Major Economic Indicators*, pp. 106, 110, cited in Choi, B-D. (1991a), p.29.

Table A3.4 Volume of pollutants by sector, 1990

Pollutant		*Heating*	*Industry*	*Transport*	*Electricity*	*Total*
SO_2	Nation	337,160	736,805	132,651	239,194	1,445,810
	Seoul	104,120	31,853	11,878	3,358	151,810
	Composition[1]	23%	51%	9%	17%	100.0%
TSP	Nation	105,877	136,000	35,731	108,003	385,612
	Seoul	35,230	2,053	7,087	218	44,587
	Composition[1]	28%	35%	9%	28%	100.0%
CO	Nation	911,538	36,288	574,747	7,061	1,529,634
	Seoul	307,860	3,250	7,087	371	482,449
	Composition[1]	60%	2%	38%	0%	100.0%
NO_x	Nation	53,359	70,280	933,069	68,842	1,121,550
	Seoul	16,501	7,898	187,647	7,276	219,331
	Composition[1]	5%	6%	83%	6%	100.0%
HC	Nation	26,384	37,184	114,687	12,933	199,190
	Seoul	8,811	494	29,337	72	38,714
	Composition[1]	14%	19%	60%	7%	100.0%

Source: MoE data, cited in Chung, H-J. (1993), p.65.

Note:
1 Composition is sectoral composition of national total.

Table A3.5 Seoul: air pollution, 1965–80 (unit: 1,000 ton/year)

Year	Total pollutant*	Sulphur dioxide	Nitrous oxides	Carbon monoxide	Hydro-carbons
1965	140.7	26.4	18.0	66.6	9.6
1970	347.4	94.4	50.1	141.4	26.5
1975	530.1	135.9	79.6	215.9	56.0
1980	618.4	156.9	81.9	260.3	71.3

Source: Seoul City Government (1981) *The Report of Seoul City Administration*, p.372.

Notes:
* Figures based on the amount of fuel consumption; the tonnage for the four pollutants do not add up to the total because certain pollutants, notably particulates and aerosols, have been omitted from the detail.

Table A3.6 Changes in the TSP levels, selected Seoul subway stations (microgram/m^3)

Line	Station	1988	1989
1	City Hall	481	459
	Seoul Rail Station	311	525
	Dongdaemun	689	710
2	City Hall	480	443
	Uljiro 3 ga	455	462
	Dongdaemun Stadium	551	799
	Gyodae	598	455
	Sadang	314	531
4	Seoul Rail Station	244	418
	Dongdaemun	389	362

Source: *Joongang Ilbo*, (21 Sept. 1990), cited in Park, C-J. (1991), p.238.

Note:
Korean environmental standard for daily level of TSP is 300 microgram/m^3 and 150 microgram/m^3 for average annual level.

Table A3.7 Consumption patterns of domestic fuel in Seoul (unit: 1,000 tons)

		1986	1987	1988	1989
Total no. of households		2,428,000	2,518,000	2,658,000	2,816,000
Heating	Anthracite coal	2,074 (85.4)	2,117 (84.1)	2,076 (78.1)	1,962 (69.7)
	Oil	334 (13.7)	351 (13.9)	501 (18.8)	696 (24.7)
	Gas	20 (0.9)	50 (2.1)	81 (3.1)	158 (5.6)
Cooking	Anthracite coal	677 (27.9)	545 (21.6)	447 (16.8)	280 (9.9)
	Oil	338 (13.9)	278 (11.1)	255 (9.6)	212 (7.5)
	Gas	1,413 (58.2)	1,695 (67.3)	1,965 (73.6)	2,324 (82.6)

Source: Cited in Oh (1991), p.43.

Table A3.8 Acid precipitation in major cities in Korea (unit: pH)

Cities	1985	1986	1987	1988	1989	1990	1991
Seoul	5.5	5.3	5.1	5.7	5.6	5.0	5.4
Pusan	5.1	5.2	5.4	5.2	5.2	5.2	5.1
Taegu	5.4	5.4	5.3	5.6	5.3	5.7	5.9
Kwangju	6.1	6.1	5.8	5.7	5.7	5.5	5.5
Daejeon	5.7	5.4	5.5	5.7	5.8	5.4	5.6
Ulsan	5.0	5.2	4.9	5.1	5.6	5.6	5.7

Source: MoE (1992), *Korea Environmental Yearbook*, p.121; Lee, S-D. (1992), p.717.

Table A3.9 Environmental standards for air pollution: some international comparisons

	Sulphur dioxide (ppm)			TSP ($\mu g/m^3$)		
	1 hour max.	Daily max.	Yearly max.	1 hour max.	Daily max.	Yearly max.
Korea	—	0.15	0.05	—	300	150
US	0.5 (3 hr)	0.14	0.03	—	150	50
Canada	0.34	0.11	0.02	—	120	70
Taiwan	0.25	0.1	0.03	250	—	130
Japan	0.1	0.04	—	200	100	—
WHO	—	0.052	0.022	—	230	90

Source: Cited in Park, C-J. (1991), p.237.

Table A3.10 Water quality of major rivers, selected years

River	Places	Env. standard		1989	1990	1992
		Grade	ppm			
Han	Ui-am	II	< 3.0	1.2	1.3	1.7
	Chungju	II	< 3.0	1.3	1.1	1.2
	Paldang	I	< 1.0	1.2	1.0	1.3
	Noryangjin	III	< 6.0	3.6	3.4	4.4
	Kayang	IV	< 8.0	6.4	4.7	5.2
Nakdong	Andong	I	< 1.0	0.8	1.0	1.3
	Koryong	III	< 6.0	13.9	5.4	6.6
	Namji	II	< 3.0	4.7	3.2	4.7
	Mulgum	II	< 3.0	3.7	3.0	4.0
	Kupo	II	< 3.0	3.9	3.3	4.1
Kum	Okcheon	I	< 1.0	1.4	1.5	1.7
	Daecheong	I	< 1.0	1.6	1.7	1.9
	Cheongwon	III	< 6.0	2.6	3.1	3.5
	Kongju	II	< 3.0	3.0	3.2	4.0
	Puyo	II	< 3.0	3.5	4.5	3.8
Yeongsan	Damyang	I	< 1.0	1.8	1.2	1.7
	Kwangju	II	< 3.0	3.9	3.4	4.1
	Naju	II	< 3.0	6.2	6.7	6.7
	Yeongsan lake	II	< 3.0	1.3	1.2	2.4

Source: MoE data, recompiled from Chun, S-H. (1993), pp.127, 132, 133, 134, and Lee, M-H. (1992), p.12.

Note:
The seriousness of river pollution can be seen in the high levels of BOD in up- and mid-stream locations. Ui-am and Chungju locations in Han river should have lower than 1 ppm BOD level and the water standard should be set at that level instead of 3 ppm. The river water quallity standard at Koryong and Cheongweon which are mid-stream locations should be set at lower than 3 ppm instead of the current 6 ppm. The government has lowered the water quality standard to make the pollution at these locations more acceptable.

Table A3.11 Water supply and consumption by source, 1980–91
(unit: 10 million m³)

	1980		1989		1991*	
Production						
River	1,282	(73.3)	1,750	(63.4)	1,830	(60.5)
Under ground	136	(7.8)	160	(5.8)	174	(5.8)
Reservoir	331	(18.9)	850	(30.8)	1,020	(33.7)
Total	1,750	(100.0)	2,760	(100.0)	3,024	(100.0)
Consumption						
Domestic	230	(13.6)	510	(17.6)	567	(17.9)
Industrial	72	(4.3)	260	(8.8)	291	(9.2)
Agricultural	1,081	(64.0)	1,280	(43.5)	1,348	(42.5)
Others	305	(18.1)	890	(30.3)	971	(30.6)
Total	1,688	(100.0)	2,940	(100.0)	3,170	(100.0)
Surplus	62		−180		−153	

Source: Cited in Choi (1991b), p.28 (re-tabulated).

Note:
* 1991 data is an estimated projection.

Table A3.12 State of sewage pipe installation in Korea, 1989 (unit: km)

Total		Rain pipes		Sewage pipes		Remarks
Planned length	*Installed length*	*Planned length*	*Installed length*	*Planned length*	*Installed length*	
70,750 (100%)	37,532 (53%)	49,141 (100%)	34,475 (73%)	21,339 (100%)	3,057 (14%)	Target year of planned length is 2001

Source: MoE (1991), p. 63.

Table A3.13 Capacities of sewage treatment plants, Seoul

Name of plant	Year of foundation	Capacity (1000m³/day)	Treatment method	Output water after primary treatment	Quality after secondary treatment
Pukpu	1975	400	Active sludge	70	
Chungnang	1979	1,000	Digestion	20	
Anyang	85–88	2,000	Concentration and digestion	140	20
Tancheon		500 (600 by 1991)	Secondary treatment		
Nanji		1,000	Concentration and digestion	140	20
Total		4,400			

Source: SMG (1990a), pp.88–89, 118.

Table A3.14 Road construction and increase in automobiles in Seoul by year

Year	Road length (km)	Road area (km²)	Road ratio (%)	Investment (million Won)	Number of automobiles	Annual increase in automobiles* (%)
1984	6,843	59,960	16.01	229,895	377,220	—
1985	6,975	62,248	16.62	281,397	445,807	18
1986	7,058	93,758	17.02	121,254	521,521	17
1987	7,137	64,744	17.29	101,400	601,561	15
1988	7,250	66,734	17.82	180,200	778,940	29
1989	7,322	67,682	18.77	161,500	991,270	27

Source: SMG (1990) *Seoul Sijeong* (Seoul Metropolitan Administration), p.126.

Note:
* Data for annual increase in automobile numbers has been recalculated.

Table A3.15 Average daily travel distance of automobiles: some international comparisons, 1981

Country	Average travel distance per vehicle per day (km)
Korea	109.5
US	45.2
UK	41.4
Denmark	38.1
West Germany	32.6
Japan	24.1
Spain	18.6

Source: Chung, H-J. (1993), p.67.

Table A3.16 Coastal water quality by coastal region, 1990

	No. of coast areas	No. of monitoring points	Class 1	Class 2	Class 3	Comments
West coast	7	49	25	13	11	From Incheon to Mokpo
South coast	13	98	25	47	26	From Cheju Island to Pusan
East coast	8	52	16	20	16	Sokcho to Onsan
Total	28	199	66	80	53	

Source: Konghaechubang-undong-yeonhap Yeongu-wiwonhwae (1992), p.71.

Table A3.17 The chemical composition of soil condition in Ulsan area, by damaged area

Area	Year	pH	Organic composition (%)	Ca^{++} (m.e./100g)	Mg^{++} (m.e./100g)
Severely damaged area (up to 0.5 km)	1982	4.00	1.41	1.30	0.83
	1987	4.10	2.70	0.30	0.15
	1991	4.65	2.60	0.71	0.24
Medium affected area (1.5–2.0 km)	1982	4.20	3.46	2.51	0.49
	1987	4.42	1.93	0.35	0.35
	1991	4.26	1.51	0.33	0.12
Lightly damaged area (2–3.5 km)	1982	4.60	6.83	2.58	1.30
	1987	4.80	1.70	0.78	0.55
	1991	4.85	1.16	1.43	0.48

Source: Lee, K-J. (1993), p.81.

Note:
m.e. = million electrons.

Table A3.18 Environmental standards for coastal water quality

Category	Grade 1	Grade 2	Grade 3
COD (mg/l)	< 1	< 2	< 4
pH	7.8–8.3	6.5–8.5	6.5–8.5
Suspended solids (SS) (mg/l)	< 10	< 25	—
Nitrate compounds (mg/l)	< 0.05	< 0.1	< 0.2
Phosphate (mg/l)	< 0.007	< 0.015	< 0.03

Source: Konghaechubang-undong-yeonhap Yeongu-wiwonhwae (1992), p.74.

Table A3.19 Nature parks in Korea

	National park	Provincial park	County park	Total
No. of parks	20	20	26	66
Land area (km²)	3,786.75	732.48	232.06	4,751.29
Sea area (km²)	2,653.70	—	3.77	2,657.47
Total (km²)	6,440.45	732.48	235.83	7,408.76
Percentage of total park area	86.9	9.9	3.2	100.0
Percentage of total land area	3.8	0.7	0.2	4.7

Source: Based on Ministry of Construction working document; cited in Lee, K-J. (1993), p.89.

Table A4.1 Surveyed demands of Seoul population, 1990

Area of Concern	Needs	Percentage
Roads and transportation	Construction of roads and subway Adjustment of bus traffic signals Control of illegal parking	40.1
Housing and construction	Construction of rental housing Lifting of redevelopment plan	15.7
Health and environment	Street cleaning, pollution control Control of moral decadence	11.5
Public safety and security	Enforcement of crime control Establishment of new police sub-stations	9.5
Water and sewerage	Complaints on water supply Adjustment of fares Installation of sewer	8.9
Commerce and finance	Lifting of the integrated billing system Consumer protection	2.8
Others	Establishment of new schools Installation of public phones	11.5

Source: SMG (1990), p.18.

Table A4.2 International comparison of ratio of environmental investment to
GNP (unit: %)

Japan	*Sweden*	*UK*	*US*	*Switzerland*	*Korea*
0.34	1.69	3.74	0.57	1.03	0.16

Source: OECD (1985).

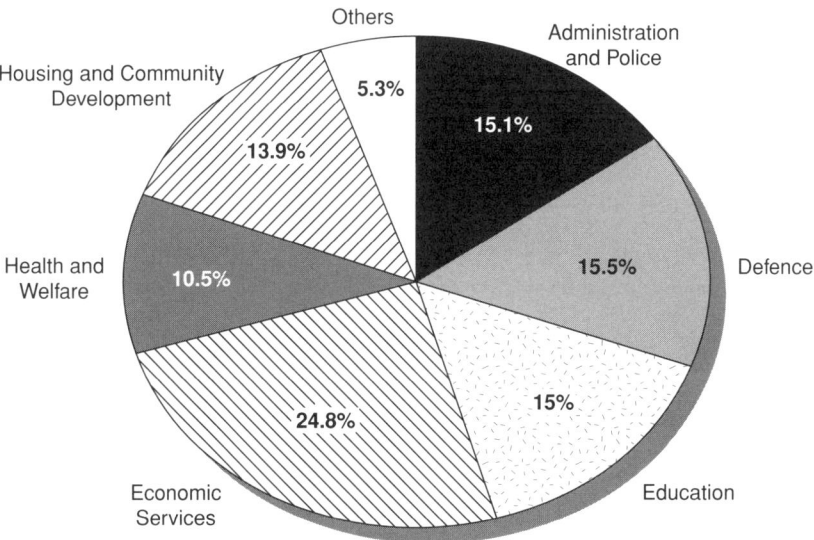

Figure A4.1 Composition of general government expenditure, 1991.
Source: NSO (1993) *Korea Statistical Yearbook*, p.350.

Notes

Introduction

1 Aglietta, M. (1976) *Regulation et crises du capitalisme*, Paris, Calmann-Levy, published in English in 1979, see reference.
2 The official name was the UN Conference on the Human Environment. For detailed discussion on the preparation and outcome of the conference, see McCormick (1989).
3 See also UN (1975).
4 This national unit has been chosen for its unique qualifications: its status as one of the most successful NICs in the prominent Pacific Asian region, its maturity in economic structure, its unique political, institutional and cultural inheritance and practices, its physical size (most East Asian NICs are too small for sub-national geographical analysis; Thailand was not considered due to its relatively early stages of capitalist development). Korea also has prominent social and environmental conditions.

1 A new framework for environmental analysis

1 Environmentalism is often confused with green politics or 'greenness'. Environmentalism is a 'collage of values and views of the world, a general patterning of predispositions, being first and foremost a social movement, though one with political overtones. Being Green is a subset of environmentalism'. Green politics is a particular view among many in the environmentalist debate. There are those in the environmental discussion, who hold the view that technology will save us from the impending doom: the technocentrists. So if 'Green is about creating the conditions that will channel the tide; environmentalism is about the many cross-currents within the complex patterns of tidal forces that constitute modern social values'; see O'Riordan, T. (1989) 'The Challenge for Environmentalism' in N. Thrift (ed.) *New Models in Geography*, vol. 1, Unwin-Hyman, London, p.80.
2 According to Cole, Cameron and Edwards (1983) there are just three schools of thought in the development of economies, which are the subjective preference (SP) theory of value, deriving from political economists such as Malthus, Jevons and Adam Smith, the cost of production (COP) theory, owing much to Ricardo, J.S. Mills and Keynes, and the labour theory of value or abstract labour (AL) theory (Pepper's term), which derives from Marx, drawing on some of Ricardo's ideas. See Pepper (1993), pp.37–43 for more information.
3 See Schmidt, A. (1971) for the debate on human/nature relationship in Marx's writings.

4 In classic Marxist literature, external nature is the natural environment excluding humankind; first nature is nature which is considered natural and includes human beings when they are considered as being imbedded in nature. As human sources became more and more separated from their natural surroundings and began to transform nature into useful forms, there began a distinction between nature and human-produced environments. 'Second nature' is a complex idea which encompasses all physical and non-material creation by humankind including human beings themselves as they become ever more socialised.

5 See Smith and O'Keefe (1980), p.34 for detailed description of 'relations with nature'.

6 See Meadows (1972) *The Limits to Growth; A Report for the Club of Rome's Project on the Predicament of Mankind*, Pan, London. Meadows shows that exponential consumption of non-renewable resources of the contemporary capitalist economy is the most serious environmental problem, though his claim that these resources could quickly be depleted has been much criticised.

7 The condition of production has also been expressed by Carlo Carboni as 'social reproductive conditions'. However O'Connor confines himself to the discussion of crisis tendencies in the process of the production and circulation of capital, rather than social reproduction as a whole. The latter should not be restricted to the production process since a large proportion of what constitutes the conditions of production cannot be separated from the reproduction process – see Harvey (1985a) in *Urbanisation of Capital*.

8 The term 'overaccumulation' is used by Harvey (1985b), a concept which is similar to the crisis of overproduction of capital. This can be conceptualised in a closed system where too much capital is produced in relation to the opportunities to employ that capital. Such is the case when the market becomes saturated and there is no reason for further investment until consumption is stimulated.

9 Castells (1977), see pp.437–471.

10 The combined development term was first used by Trotsky to extend the concept of uneven development to encompass a more complex phenomenon, that of a country experiencing development and underdevelopment in a single space, most often in relatively backward countries or late developing countries. See Mandel (1983).

11 See Marx (1977) p.80, and Engels (1978) p.328; they characterise the state as the means of class exploitation by capital.

12 State monopoly capitalism was the term used in the Soviet bloc, as well as by orthodox Western communist parties loyal to Moscow, in explanation of the formations in the advanced capitalist system (Jessop 1982, p.32, Dunleavy and O'Leary 1987, p.240).

13 See Jessop (1990b).

14 For capitalism to be sustained, the state must ensure certain conditions such as the legal and monetary systems necessary to facilitate the production and exchange of commodities and the accumulation of capital. The state is required also to secure the reproduction of wage labour to the extent that this cannot be done through market forces, and to ensure its subordination to capital in the labour process. This leads to intervention in union activities, education and social welfare. The capital logic school also takes competing capital into account – hence the state will have to secure provision of those use values which are necessary to capital accumulation but the private production of which proves unprofitable. Last, since the total social capital is also divided into different national capitals, the state has to promote the interests of its national capital as well as to co-operate with other states in securing the conditions necessary for continued capital accumulation on a world scale (Altvater 1973).

15 Extensive accumulation is that which increases capital accumulation by expanding the production basis – for example, with further investment in the means of production, rather than raising through productivity.

16 Intensive accumulation is that which is formed on increasing capital accumulation without expanding the production base. Rather, it relies on increasing productivity or the production of higher value-added commodities.

17 This is Marx' categorisation of industries. Department I corresponds to the capital goods sector (shipbuilding, steel, coal, chemicals, etc.) and Department II corresponds to the consumer goods sector.

18 The term 'Fordism' refers to the accumulation system which establishes the link between mass production and mass consumption by increasing working class wages, with corresponding increases in productivity.

19 Amin (1994) categorises three theories or models of transition: the regulation approach, the neo-Schumpeterian approach and the flexible specialisation approach.

20 Lipietz (1992) chooses London and Paris as European megalopolises, rapidly growing to the scale of Los Angeles, São Paulo and Mexico City.

2 Economic development, state strategies and social change in Korea

1 The term *Yusin* expresses the concept of 'self reliance', and dates to the Park period of the 1970s. This term is seen to be appropriate since it represents the dominant character of the MSR during the 1970s.

2 Peripheral Fordism is characterised by an authoritarian state, an economy dominated by export of Fordist products to core countries, labour repression and low wages (Tickell and Peck 1992b, p.202).

3 The idea of the neo-Fordist regime is that of Lipietz (1992), in which he describes a regime of accumulation, which uses a competitive or corporatist mode of social regulation in a flexible accumulation regime.

4 Between 1910 and 1941, agricultural output increased at an average annual rate of 2.3 per cent (Amsden 1989, p.54).

5 The chaebol conglomerates mainly encompass construction, electronics, automobiles, leisure, retailing and shipbuilding.

6 The Japanese *zaibatsu* form of conglomerate dominated the Korean economy by the early 1940s. By 1941, six zaibatsu groups accounted for 70 per cent of Japanese investment in Korea (Amsden 1989, p.34).

7 See Jones and Sakong (1980), pp.26–28 (particularly Table 5 for Korean employment structure). Outside government, there were 1,900 Korean technicians and engineers in manufacturing, 1,300 in mining and 2,600 in service sector (1944).

8 This term describes the nature of individual psychology in Japanese and Korean society: the group is emphasised over the individual, and individuals conform to social norms dictated by the hegemonic group (see Cumings 1981).

9 See Mason *et al.* (1980), p.88 for detailed breakdown by industries in Table 10.

10 This is the abbreviated name of *Choson nodong chohap chonguk pyonggui-hoe*, the largest labour organisation in the South until 1946. It operated in most of the Japanese-owned plants. Although reformist in essence, in the Korean context it was seen to be revolutionary and was the object of widespread suppression. See Cumings (1981) for further information.

11 Bruce Cumings (1981) suggests that the KDP was the party of the capitalists and collaborators. The KCP (Korean Communist Party) represented the proletariat, but the Peoples Party or the KPR (Korean People's Republic) was a mass united front grouping representing workers, farmers, small bourgeoisie and landlords. It excluded only the reactionary and pro-Japanese elements.

Cumings also claims that the KPG (Korean Provisional Government) in Chungking had little grassroots support.

12 Although Amsden claims that American pressures placed the Korean state on a developmentalist path, this is disputable. It may be true that American policies forced the Korean state to adopt a particular direction in economic strategy, but the main source of heavy intervention in the economy came from the internal political need for legitimacy (Haggard *et al.* 1991, Bedeski 1994).

13 The research institutes covered most of the social and economic sectors: the Korea Development Institute (KDI) and the Korea Institute for Industrial Economics and Technology (KIET), under the Ministry of Trade and Industry; the Korea Research Institute for Human Settlements (KRIHS) – the Ministry of Construction; the Korea Rural Economic Institute (KREI) – the Ministry of Agriculture and Fisheries; the Korea Institute of Population and Health (KIPH) and Korea Women's Development Institute (KWDI), under the Ministry of Health and Social Affairs; also, the Korea Education Development Institute (KEDI), under the Ministry of Education. The Korean government also actively supported many research institutes in the field of science and technology. (Suh 1992, p.13).

14 With overtime, actual working hours were much higher (Ogle 1990, Bello and Rosenfeld 1990).

15 Kim Dae Jung was a leading opponent of the military government from the 1960s. Born in Cholla province, his support base is mainly in Cholla provinces; he has led the *Minjung* Party representing the so-called 'ordinary people' of Korea.

16 *Yusin* ideology should not be confused with North Korea's *juche* (self-reliance), although Cumings (1988) claims that the concept of *Yusin* was borrowed from the North (see pp.267–268).

17 The essence of corporatism as an economic system is private ownership and state control (Pahl and Winkler 1974, p.73).

18 It is President Park, who had a key role in the formulation of economic policies, was influenced by his education and military training in Japanese institutions, and thus had an inclination towards the Japanese model of economic development.

19 Chou (1994) shows that Taiwan's heavy and chemical industrialisation was largely achieved by attracting TNCs in foreign direct investment; they formed an important element of Taiwanese industrial structure.

20 The tariff drawback system, which allows industries to claim back tariff paid on imports of primary and intermediate goods when the manufactured products are exported, replaced the existing 'pre-exemption' system, which allowed exemptions from tariffs on imported goods.

21 After the first year of the *Saemaul* programme, which began modestly with government assistance of a mere US$11 million for the 33,267 villages, the results were beyond official expectations. They were said to have yielded improvements valued at US$32.6 million, or three times the government investment (Boyer and Ahn 1991).

22 Rhee (1987) shows that the policy reforms of the early 1980s had the effect of import substitution bias. The effective rate of protection rose significantly during this period from 43.1% in 1978 to 48.9% in 1982, whereas the export subsidy ratio dropped from 7.6% in 1978 to 6.4% in 1982, due to price stabilisation (Rhee 1987, p.60).

23 First, more foreign currency-loans were made available to businesses for imports of capital goods, equipment and raw materials. Second, market opening was accelerated to increase imports and to allow greater market access for foreign goods. The import surveillance list was drastically shortened, and indeed

abolished in 1988. Provisions in the numerous special laws that had restricted imports were substantially relaxed. Third, the government undertook measures to restrain exports of low value-added products which increased Korea's export volume, without providing substantial benefits for the national economy. Fourth, public sector investment was expanded to promote a more balanced growth of the economy. Investment in collective consumption goods (roads, sewers, water supply, housing and medical services) was increased as was investment for agro-industrial complexes and science and technology (Koo and Bark 1989, Rhee 1987).

24 Due to pressures from the IMF and the urban electorate, from the early 1980s subsidies were reduced. The tactics used were subtle in order to hide reversal of policy. See Bello and Rosenfeld (1990), p.87.

25 In the 1980s, there was a new dimension to the agricultural sector. It has been described as a 'sacrificial lamb' to ensure the continued viability of the EOI regime, through opening up of the domestic market to mainly US agricultural surpluses, in exchange for keeping the American market open for Korean manufactured goods (Bello and Rosenfeld 1990).

26 The 'Three Lows' refer to low interest rates, low petroleum prices and a low exchange rate of US dollars against the Japanese yen.

27 In 1996, Lucky-Goldstar electronics established a manufacturing base in South Wales and Hyundai electronics announced plans to build one in Scotland's silicon glen.

28 The liberalisation of domestic markets stemmed both from pressures from Korea's trading partners, notably the US and the desire by the Korean government to become a member of the OECD.

29 Prior to the implementation of 'real name transaction' regulation shares and real estate could be bought or sold under fictitious names, thus avoiding tax payments at higher levels. This measure was to close tax loopholes, but instead created other practices such as 'borrowing' names of close friends or family.

30 Court mediation differs from receivership in that management continues to operate; companies under receivership are run by court-appointed administrators. This Act was designed to protect small and medium-sized businesses, which are often squeezed in the market by chaebol.

31 'Corporatist mode of social regulation' describes an MSR used by a totalitarian state or dictatorship to manipulate institutional forms, in order to direct the national economy in a particular direction. Unlike other periods of development, sources of competition were removed, and most essential services and amenities nationalised. Yet this did not extend to the sphere of private consumption, and thus it cannot be described as monopolistic. Even during the more oppressive dictatorship of the succeeding Chun regime the accumulation system was more competitive in character.

3   Spatial strategies and the emergence of uneven development

1 While accuracy of data is questionable, official sources give the population of South Korea to be 20.04 million in 1949. The total increase in population of South Korea between 1944–49 was 4.16 million. The increase in population due to migration from the north and from overseas was 3.32 million, and the balance natural increase (Kwon, Y-W. 1991, p.79).

2 Korea's major exporting ports are highly concentrated on the east and southeast coasts of Korea due to the availability of deep coastal waters. On the west coast, Seoul's Incheon port was the only major cargo and container exporting port. Although Mukho, Pohang, Ulsan, Masan and Kwangyang, developed during the

colonial period, existed on the southeast and east coasts, these ports were not fully utilised until the 1970s' heavy chemical drive (Chon 1992, p.159).

3 Industrial lines included the No.3 Fertiliser line, No.4 Fertiliser line, Cheonju Industrial Estate line, Pohang Industrial Estate line, etc. Double tracking of existing main lines such as the Seoul–Incheon Dual railway line, and the building of lines to the mining areas of the Taebaek Mountain range (Kwon, Y-W. 1991).

4 *Myon* are rural administrative districts and centres.

5 *Shi* are administratively designated cities.

6 *Eup* are officially designated towns, normally centres of counties.

7 One of the policy measures was the relocation of secondary government functions out of Seoul. However, this was only implemented in 1983 with the construction of Kwacheon New Town and the '2nd Government Office Complex'. Its effectiveness in reducing migration into Seoul was seen in the reduction of congestion in the Seoul's CBD. Another policy was the introduction of the Resident Tax in 1973 as a control measure to slow down the inflow of people to Seoul. This poll tax was initially applied only to metropolitan residents, but it was subsequently adopted in other cities. This happened because the Ministry of Home Affairs accepted its value as an irresistible revenue source for local government. Even though the tax rate was higher in Seoul, the difference was not wide enough to affect individual household location decisions (Kwon 1988b, pp.130–131).

8 Rapid population growth resulted in many severe urban problems: traffic congestion, land speculation, housing shortages, pollution, which threatened the capital accumulation process as well as raising social tensions. National security concerns centred on 'anti-communism', with the threat seen as both external as well as internal. The agglomeration of population and industries within range of North Korean artillery was recognised as highly risky. Additionally, the spatial concentration of low-income groups was believed to increase the risks of mass social unrest (MoC 1971, Kwon 1988b, p.108).

9 In order to control urban sprawl, to prevent the merging of urban areas, and to discourage emerging speculation on urban fringe land, the first green belt (143.4 km^2) was established around Seoul in 1971. Later, 13 other major urban areas adopted this same measure of land use control. As of 1984, a total of 5,397 km^2 were designated as green belts, i.e. 5.4 per cent of Korea's total land area (Kwon 1988b, pp.126–127).

10 See Choe and Song (1984) pp.79–81 for detailed information on local industrial estate development. See also the table on p.80. Many of the unsuccessful estates were in the depressed areas.

11 One important problem of implementation stemmed from the need to determine which manufacturing industries would be required to move out of the dispersal zone. First, the government issued relocation orders to establishments in non-conforming land uses according to city zoning ordinances. Second, several polluting industries as defined by the *Environmental Conservation Act* (1977) were forced to move to Banweol, a new industrial town located 35 km southwest of Seoul. Third, exceptions were made for selected urban service industries such as printing and for food manufacturers producing items of daily urban consumption (Kwon 1988b).

12 Although this phase of development is characterised by 'corporatist MSR', the label applies most closely to the chaebol groups and strategic industries; other sectors were subject to competitive regulation.

13 The IRSA was demarcated at a scale appropriate for planning and development on the basis of geographical features, spatial homogeneity of river basins,

functional linkage of transportation and communication, and socio-economic interdependency considering the peculiar characters and development status of a given region (Kwon 1988b).

14 See Appendix Table A2.8.

15 Regional bias thesis by Kim (1993) is based on the urban bias theory of under-development by Lipton (1976).

16 For biased infrastructure investment over the years (1965–85), see Appendix Table A2.5.

17 The definition of high-technology industries referred to here consists of semi-conductors, new plastics and optics, telecommunication equipment and other high-tech parts manufacturing. These are distinct from the relatively simple and conventional manufacturing processes and industries such as metal fabrication, car manufacturing and even computer assembly.

18 Capital region's share of the whole nation's shipping value was about 66 per cent for high-tech industries and 44 per cent in total manufacturing, indicating that high-tech industries were far more concentrated in the Capital region than was manufacturing as a whole (Park, C-J. 1991).

19 By 1990, no fewer than 464 out of 674 enterprise research institutes were in the Capital region, as well as 13 out of 24 government institutions, 39 out of 40 research associations, and 47 out of the 104 universities and colleges (Anon 1990, Castells and Hall 1994, p.63).

20 Another source states that the average annual growth rate for domestic traffic was expected to slow to 9.2% in the 1990s from 22.3% in the 1980–90 period. Average annual growth of international traffic was forecast to drop to 10.8% from 12.7% (*FEER*, 10 September 1992, p.70).

21 In December 1990, the decision was taken to build the new airport at Yeong-jongdo, about 50 km from Seoul, near the port of Incheon. Costing an estimated 3.5 trillion won, the airport's first phase with one runway and an annual capacity of 27 million passengers was to be ready in 1997, according to 1992 plans. By year 2020, the airport should have its fourth and final runway and will be capable of handling 100 million passengers a year (*FEER*, 10 September 1992, p.70).

4 Environmental degradation in Korea: a historical overview

1 The timber accumulation level is the volume of mature trees which can be used as timber resource per hectare.

2 See Chapter 5 regarding the struggle over housing rights. The continued central-isation of capital and social and economic functions has led to one of the greatest concentrations of population, which perpetuated the housing crisis.

3 With the implementation of an energy intensive and petrochemical-based higher industrial trajectory, the increased use of energy was an inevitable outcome. Even in the government's view energy was used 'inefficiently and profligately' (MoE 1991, p.54). During the period between 1970 to 1989, there was more than four-fold increase in energy consumption. This raised Korea's dependence on overseas energy sources. During the same period, energy imports increased 7.2 times, thus increasing dependency from 47.5% in 1970 to 82.7% in 1989. This external dependency has also been due to changes in the composition of energy type and source, i.e. the reduction in domestic coal use, the increase in imported oil/gas use and the implementation of a nuclear energy programme (Choi 1991a, p.29).

4 Water consumption rose from 16,880 million m^3 in 1980 to 29,400 million m^3 in 1989, a rise of 74.2% (Choi 1991a, p.29).

5 Due to a more than doubling of domestic and a tripling of industrial and 'other' water uses, there was a shortage of 1,800 million m^3 in 1989 (where as in 1980 there was a surplus of 620 million m^3).

6 Although industry continued to consume the bulk of electricity, (approximately 60% of total in 1989) domestic and service sector consumption was also on a rapidly rising curve (Choi, B-D. 1991a, pp.28–29).

7 Low electricity prices stoked surging demand. From 1985 to 1990, electricity prices fell almost 26 per cent even though consumer prices rose 30 per cent. Although The World Bank (1992) claims that Korea was charging the full market price in 1987 (p.69), subsequently the government pushed utility prices down. Political pressures were exerted as the Korea Electric Power Co. (Kepco) was widely seen to be making super-profits (*FEER*, 1 August 1993).

8 See Table 5.28 in Chapter 5.

9 See Table 5.29 in Chapter 5.

10 See Hanguk Gonghae Munjae Yeonguso (1986).

11 Of 67 industrial estates (1988), only 23 were served by waste-water treatment plants; 20 had no plans to have plants built and the rest were in the planning stages.

5 Environmental problems in the three spatial zones

1 On 10 April 1990, the Sung Ok Urm family committed joint suicide after being evicted (Park, C-J. 1991, p.111).

2 The government, however, has refuted ACHR claims by excluding tenants from their figures. Although tenants make up 60 per cent of the squatter population their rights have never been recognised (ACHR 1989b, p.5).

3 See Urban Poor Institute (1988), *Information Packet on the Urban Poor in Korea*, Seoul; Catholic Institute for International Relations (no date) *Disposable People: Forced Evictions in South Korea*, CIIR, London.

4 See the example of Sang-Kye Dong Redevelopment in ACHR (1989a, 1989b).

5 In cases where the land was privately owned, until 1987 landowners were paid only 10–15 per cent of the land value. Only from the beginning of 1988 were some payments close to the market value (ACHR 1989b, p.5).

6 1 pyeong = 3.3 m^2 or 36 ft^2.

7 As stated in Chapter 2, the reference is to those sections of the population who are not only subject to, but also maintain, a hegemonic ideology. In the case of Korea, it is the middle and skilled working classes which serve as the 'hegemonic bloc'.

8 See Appendix Figure A3.1 for locations of new towns and the green belt.

9 See Appendix Table A3.2.

10 Korea's largest ski and golf resort was created in Dogyu National Park (*FEER* 1995, 16th November).

11 Most of the new towns were without sewage treatment plants at the time of initial commissioning. Coal or oil fired power stations were, however, constructed in the new towns. Their use of high sulphur content fossil fuels without de-sulphurisation equipment contributed to the SMA's pollution problem (*Chosun Ilbo* 1996, 25 July, p.35).

12 Oh (1991) 'Air Pollution and Spatial Structure of Seoul' *Jiyeok Hwangyong*, 9 (Dec), pp.18–51.

13 Oh (1991) shows that even in 1989 anthracite was used in over 69 per cent of households in Seoul for heating purposes. The use of oil increased rapidly from 13.7 per cent of households in 1986 to almost 25 per cent in 1989. For cooking, the use of coal and oil has declined rapidly, giving 'city gas', an over 80 per cent share.

14 Petro-chemical companies delayed the introduction of de-sulphurising equipment (*Chosun Ilbo* 25 July 1996, p.35).

15 In 1989 the total amount of waste-water produced within Seoul was 3,400,000 tonnes per day, of which 3,320,000 tonnes was sewage and 80,000 tonnes was industrial waste-water (SMG 1990a, pp.76–77).

16 Korean chemical companies use high toxicity substances, often containing phosphate salts at ten times the concentration used elsewhere (Choi 1983, p.143–144, Park, C-J. 1991, p.261).

17 In 1976, the first municipal sewage treatment plant, was constructed at Cheongkye-cheon with a treatment capacity of 150,000 tonnes per day; in 1981, four more treatment plants were introduced in three cities, treating 822,000 tonnes per day. By the end of 1990, sewerage was available to 31 per cent of Korea's population. Eighteen cities had sewage treatment plants with a total daily capacity of 5,393,000 tonnes (MoE 1991, pp.62–63). In 1991, 38 per cent of urban population was served by mains sewerage. The rest of the raw sewage went directly into the river system. (For further details by region, see MoE (1992), p.517–518).

18 See SMG (1990b), p.105. During the 1981–86 period, pollution levels of the tributaries were BOD 40–120 ppm, making them little more than open sewers. One of the worst affected was the Cheongye-cheon, where the BOD level increased from 90 ppm in 1981 to over 140 ppm in 1986 (p.105).

19 The foam from detergents interfered with water treatment processes. The outdated water purification systems and the use of high chlorination levels also resulted in high levels of harmful THM in drinking water (Park, C-J. 1991, p.243).

20 Based on statistics from NSO (1993), p.37 and p.284, and SMG (1991), p.170.

21 On 3rd September 1995, a resident of Daejo-dong hung himself from a tree by his home, due to a parking dispute. On 18 September, a 25-year-old knifed his neighbours in an argument over parking in Kunja-dong, Seoul. These types of incidents have been most serious in multi-occupancy and high density housing areas such as Wangsip-ri, Sangdo-dong, Dapsip-ri and Bulgwang-dong *(Chosun Ilbo,* 19 September 1995).

22 A Korean-Australian firm had sought a government contract to remove the asbestos in the subway stations and tunnels, but nothing came of this, due to the official view that there was negligible risk to health (interview with the president of the firm, Mr. Choi Bong-gil, April 1994).

23 The severely damaged area has seen almost total destruction of the forest. The only trees left standing in any number were less than 1.5m tall, due to the protection afforded by American red grass, which is a good indicator of soil and ecosystem damage as it grows only in infertile and damaged environments (Lee, K-J. 1993, pp.77–80).

24 See Appendix, Table A3.17 for soil condition in Ulsan's Gomsol forest.

25 Coastal water quality has been monitored by the MoE at 199 points, four times yearly, to determine the state of the coastal environment (Konghaechubang-undong-yeonhap Yeongu-wiwonhwae 1992).

26 The Korean coastal water quality has been categorised into 3 Grades (see Appendix, Table A3.18). See Konghaechubang-undong-yeonhap Yeongu-wiwonhwae (1992): map 5–1 on p.73, which shows that most of the coastal industrial areas and ports have Grade 3 water quality and surrounding bays and coastal areas have Grade 2. The other coastal seas are of Grade 1 standard.

27 The *jeokjo* of the summer of 1995 occurred on the south and southeast coasts and to a lesser degree in ports on the west coast, bringing an estimated 10 billion won damage to fisheries in South Kyongsang Province alone. On 21 September, over a quarter of a million fish died in Yeocheon and Wando fisheries, South

Cholla Province. The explosion of algae took on a different character, the plankton both depleting oxygen and releasing toxins, which killed other marine life (*Chosun Ilbo*, 22 September 1995).

28 See Kim, J-W. (1994) for further information on National Parks. In 1992, the highest concentration of visitors per km^2 was found in Seoul's Bukhan-san NP (an average 99,000 person per km^2), Naejang-san NP in South Cholla Province (17,000 persons/km^2) and Gearyong-san NP, South Chungchong Province (31,000 persons/km^2).

6 Mode of social regulation, environmental movement and the state

1 Kim, B-W. (1994) divides the development of environmental groups into four stages. Here, we have merged the last two stages since the focus is the conjunctural development of environmental groups and the accumulation regime.

2 In 1967, a pollution section, which was the forerunner of the Office of Environment, was set up in environmental health section of the Public Health Department within the Ministry of Public Health and Social Affairs. (Kim, B-W. 1994, p.90).

3 Jessop (1994) points out that the term 'social mode of economic regulation' is more fitting than variants such as 'social mode of regulation' because it identifies both the manner of regulation and its object (p.278).

4 The government announced in 1991 that it planned to spend 46 trillion won (approx. US$60 billion) through to 2006 to build dozens of power stations. Revised plans called for nine nuclear units to be built by the turn of the century and another nine through to 2006. In the mid-1990s, there were nine units in service in South Korea, producing about half the country's electricity. Energy planners are more comfortable working out how to build power plants and how to enforce a cult of austerity for South Koreans than finding ways to cut demand without sacrificing comfort (*FEER*, 1 August 1991, pp.54–55).

5 Eco-Mark is a logo given to manufactured goods which are seen to be environmentally friendly and which comply to environmental standards set by the Ministry.

6 Restaurants (over 48 pyeong), public baths and swimming pools (over 44 pycong), hotels and other tourist accommodation (over 73 pyeong), cinemas, wedding halls, art galleries, department stores and other public and cultural facilities (over 82 pyeong), bus and rail stations (over 115 pyeong), hospitals and other medical institutions (over 115 pyeong), banks and other commercial and clerical offices (over 300 pyeong), and equipment such as trucks, articulated lorries and industrial transportation equipment were subject to this regulation.

7 The 15 types of developments: urban (general), industrial estate including operation, energy, housing, road and highway, marine resources, ports, railway, recreation and sports, river utilisation, landfill and reclamation, tourist resort, mountain areas, special planning district and waste disposal facilities (Kim, B-W. 1994, pp.132–133).

8 The Minister of Environment had the power to order a change of plans to comply with environmental requirements. In the implementation and operational stages, the ministry could halt the development or prosecute a developer not complying with EIA recommendations. The maximum penalty was up to five years imprisonment and/or a 5 million won fine, if plans were breached during construction (Kim, B-W. 1994, pp.132–133).

9 In the case of EIA for the Ilsan line of SMA electric railway, the Ministry of Environment requested the Ministry of Transport and Office of Railway to halt

construction until the EIA was completed. The Office of Railway argued that the construction work for the Ilsan line had begun December 1990 before the EIA legislation came into effect. But the Ministry of Environment was able to successfully exert pressure. In this instance, it was politically expedient to comply with the MoE's demands since the public needed reassurance. However, the MoE's requirements that readjustments be made to development plans were largely ignored (Chung 1991, Kim, B-W. 1994, Noh 1993).

10 An example of how EIA was used to justify environmentally unsound developments is that of a recreational park in the north Incheon area. The total development area was 450,000 pyeong, and included a youth centre, swimming pool, camp site and car parking. The problem was that the development was approved because the woodland was Grade 6 rather than Grade 9 or 10, the only forest land considered environmentally important. However, as much of Korea's forests were replanted three decades earlier after the Korean War, there were very few in the Grade 9 or 10 categories. Although this woodland was only Grade 6, it was a habitat for a diverse fauna and flora, and indeed was one of the few places around Incheon which sustained any wildlife. However, the development went ahead without even a preliminary site investigation, relying on the Grade system for its justification (Lee, K-J. 1993, pp.81–82).

11 Shin (1993) gives the example of the improving water quality of the Han and Nakdong rivers, which flow through Seoul, and Taegu and Pusan respectively, while other major river systems such as the Keum river have deteriorated (p.249). Also he shows that the higher proportion of the residents in industrial cities (93.9%) compared to the national average (77.5%) considered that pollution problems were 'somewhat' or 'very' serious, suggesting that environmental problems were significantly worse in semi-peripheral industrial zones (pp.244–245).

12 The social mode of environmental regulation is the regulation of the environment through social practices and norms. This implies the construction of a social norm through a hegemonic ideology, to bring about a dominant attitude or consensus towards an acceptable mode of production, reproduction and consumption of the environment and its resources.

13 The hegemonic bloc is defined as the dominant section of civil society which supports the hegemonic ideology (see Chapter 2).

14 Kim, B-W. (1994) notes that there are wide differences in ideology in Korean NEGs, ranging from Gaia to eco-socialism (p.215).

15 See 21st Century Committee (1991), *Survey of Public Awareness for the Twenty-first Century*, April, Government of ROK.

16 Pulmuwon is an organic foods company which started small in the mid-1980s, growing to multimillion won status; as such it is often cited as an example of a 'business miracle'.

17 The labour and pro-democracy (student) movements were branded communist organisations and nationalist feelings were whipped up against US pressures to open up domestic markets to American cigarettes, beef and other consumer products.

18 See Environment Section in MoC (1991) *The Seventh Economic and Social Development Plan*, MoC, Seoul.

7   EOI mode of development and a sustainable future

1 Term used by Chou (1994) which originated in Lipietz (1989b).

2 This term is used to describe all expenditure which is used to aid economic growth in all sectors like transportation and communication, roads, electricity and water developments as used in the Korea Statistical Yearbook (1993). Figure A4.1 in the Appendix shows that the hegemonic projects and productive expenditure

(police, education and economic services) of 1991 accounted for 70.4 per cent of the total general government expenditure while expenditure on social consumption means stood at 24.4 per cent (including environmental expenditure).

3   Although the state constructed 'public housing', it was sold at subsidised rate. However, the urban poor were unable to afford it. The real need for rented accommodation for the urban poor was not met. Even when, in 1990, public rental housing was first constructed, the quantity was very small.

4   The term has been borrowed from Jessop (1992).

5   Phrase owed to Chou (1994).

6   The 1960 economic crisis was due to the lack of economic strategies to remove bottlenecks and the 1997 crisis was largely due to the deregulation of many sectors of the economy without adequate alternative measures, resulting in crisis of inadequate state regulation. On the other hand, the 1970 and 1980 crises were due to government dictated industrial policies favouring leading sector industries such as textiles and OEM assembly in the 1960s, and heavy and chemical industries in the 1970s.

7   Sachs claims that financial markets were opened in the wrong way, where restrictions were kept on long-term capital inflows (such as foreign ownership of domestic banks) while short-term inflows (into stock markets) were encouraged. (*FEER* 25 February 1999, p.11).

8   R&D spending of Korea's private sector ranked 44th out of 53 industrialised nations, whereas even Malaysia (31st), Thailand (36th) and Taiwan (38th) are ranked higher (World Economic Forum, 1998).

Bibliography

Adams, W.P. (1990) *Green Development: Environment and Sustainability in the Third World*, Routledge, London.

Aglietta, M. (1979) *A Theory of Capitalist Regulation: The American Experience*, New Left Books, London.

Altvater, E. (1973) 'Some Problems of State Interventionism', *Kapitalistate*, 10, pp. 76–83 and pp. 96–108.

Amin, A. (1994) 'Post-Fordism: Models, Fantasies and Phantoms of Transition', in A. Amin (ed.) *Post-Fordism, A Reader*, Blackwell, Oxford, pp.1–39.

Amsden, A. (1989) *Asia's Next Giant: South Korea and Late Industrialisation*, Oxford University Press, Oxford.

—— (1990) 'Third World Industrialisation: "Global Fordism" or a New Model', *New Left Review*, 182, p.24.

Anon (1990) *Proceedings of the Korea–UK International Symposium on High Tech Centers and Urban Development*, Daejon, South Korea, mimeo.

Archibugi, F. and Nijkamp, P. (eds) (1989) *Economy and Ecology: Towards a Sustainable Development*, Kluwers Academics, Dordrecht.

Asian Coalition for Housing Rights (ACHR) (1989a) 'Evictions in Seoul, South Korea', *Environment and Urbanisation*, vol.1, April, pp.89–94.

—— (1989b) *Battle For Housing Rights in Korea*, ACHR, Bangkok.

Atinc, T.M. and Walton, M. (1998) 'Social Consequences of the East Asian Financial Crisis: Responding to the Global Financial Crisis', Asia Development Forum, March, Manila, World Bank.

Atkinson, T. (1992) 'What Chance Bioregionalism?' *Green Line*, 100, pp.8–9.

Bae, K-H. (1992) 'Change in Public Consciousness towards Environmental Conservation', mimeo. (in Korean).

Balassa, B. (1981) *The Newly Industrialising Countries in the World Economy*, Pergamon, New York.

Beaverstock, J., Smith, R. and Taylor, P. (1999) 'Roster of World Cities', *Cities*, 16 (6), pp.445–458 (also available as Research Bulletin 5, Globalisation and World Cities Study and Network, Dept. of Geography, Loughborough University, http://lboro.ac.uk/gy/research/gawc/rb/rb5.html).

Bedeski, R.E. (1994) *The Transformation of South Korea: Reform and Reconstruction in the Sixth Republic under Roh Tae Woo 1987–1992*, Routledge, London.

Bello, W. and Rosenfeld, S. (1990) *Dragons in Distress: Asia's Miracle Economies in Crisis*, Penguin, London.

Bertramsen, B., Peter, J., Thomsen, F. and Torfing, J. (1991) *State, Economy and Society*, Unwin Hyman, London.

Boddy, R. and Crotty, J. (1974) 'Class Conflict, Keynesian Policy and the Business Cycle', *Monthly Review*, 26 October, pp.1–17.

—— (1975) 'Class Conflict and Macro-policy: the Political Business Cycle', *Review of Radical Political Economy*, 7, (1), pp.1–19.

Bonefield, W. (1987) 'Reformulation of State Theory', *Capital and State*, 33, pp.96–127.

—— (1993) 'Crisis of theory: Bob Jessop's theory of capitalist reproduction', *Capital and Class*, 50, pp.22–47.

Bonefield, W. and Holloway, J. (eds) (1991) *Post-Fordism and Social Form*, Macmillan, London.

Bottomore, T. (1983) *A Dictionary of Marxist Thought*, Blackwell, Oxford.

Boyer, R. (1990a) *The Regulation School: A Critical Introduction*, Columbia University Press, New York.

—— (1990b) 'Regulation', in J. Eatwell, M. Milgate, and P. Newman (eds) *Marxian Economics*, Macmillan Reference Books, pp.331–335.

Boyer, W. and Ahn, B-M. (1991) *Rural Development in South Korea: A Sociopolitical Analysis*, Associated University Presses, London.

Bradby, B. (1980) 'The Destruction of Natural Economy', in H. Wolpe (ed.) *The Articulation of Modes of Porduction*, Routledge and Kegan Paul, London, pp.93–127.

Brenner, R. and Glick, M. (1992) 'The Regulation Approach: Theory and History', *New Left Review*, 192, pp.45–119.

Brown, L.B. (1993) *State of the World 1993*, Earthscan, London.

Byun, D. (1983) *Development and Environment in Less Developed Countries: with special emphasis on the economic growth policy vs. environmental problems in Korea*, Ph.D. Thesis, University of New York, Buffalo, NY.

Capra, F. (1982) *The Turning Point*, Wildwood House, London.

Carley, M. and Christie, I. (1992) *Managing Sustainable Development*, Earthscan, London.

Castells, M. (1977) *The Urban Question*, Edward Arnold, London.

—— (1992) 'Four Asian Tigers With a Dragon Head: a comparative analysis of the state, economy and society in the Asian Pacific Rim', in J. Henderson, and R.P. Appelbaum (eds) *States and Development in The Asian Pacific Rim*, Sage, London, pp.33–70.

Castells, M. and Hall, P. (1994) *Technopoles of the World: The Making of Twenty-First Century Industrial Complexes*, Routledge, London.

Catholic Institute for International Relations (no date) *Disposable People: Forced Evictions in South Korea*, CIIR, London.

Chang, S-M. (1991) 'Republic of Korea', in Asian Development Bank and Economic Development Institute (ed.) *The Urban Poor and Basic Infrastructure Services in Asia and the Pacific*, A Regional Seminar, 22–28 Jan, pp.367–399.

Chen, E.K.Y. (1979) *Hyper-growth in Asian economies: A comparative study of Hong Kong, Japan, Korea, Singapore and Taiwan*, Macmillan, London.

Cherry, G.E. (1988) *Cities and Plans*, Edward Arnold, London.

Cho, J-R. (1983) 'The state and character of Korean Pollution Problem', in Hanguk Konghae Munjae Yeonguso (ed.) *Nae Tang-i Jukerganda (My Land is Dying)*, Ilweol Seogak, Seoul (in Korean).

Choe, S-C. and Song, B-N. (1984) 'An Evaluation of Industrial Location for Urban Deconcentration in Seoul Region', *Hwangyong Nonchong*, 14, pp.73–116.

Choi, B-D. (1991a) 'National Land Development Policy and Resource-Environment Problems', *Hyundai-Sahwoe*, vol. 39, Dec., pp.12–35 (in Korean).

—— (1991b) *Space and Environment of Korea*, Hangilsa, Seoul (in Korean).

Choi, Y. (1983) 'Detergent Pollution', in Hanguk Konghae Munjae Yeonguso (ed.) *Nae Tang-i Jukerganda (My Land is Dying)*, Ilweol Chongseo, Seoul (in Korean).

Chon, S. (1992) 'Political Economy of Regional Development in Korea', in Henderson, J. and Appelbaum, R.P., *States and Development in The Asian Pacific Rim*, Sage, London.

Chou, T.L. (1994) *Capitalist Development, Regulation and Space in Postwar Taiwan*, Ph.D. Thesis, University of Liverpool.

Christian Institute for Study of Justice and Development (1987) *Statistics on Social Justice in Korea*, CISJD, Seoul.

Chun, S-H. (1993) 'The state of Water Pollution and Solution', in Y-H. Noh (ed.) *Hwangyong Bogoseo*, Baedal Hwangyong, Daejeon (in Korean).

Chung, H-J. (1993) 'New 5 Year Economic Plan and Policies for Urban Environmental Pollution Mitigation', *Doshi Munjae*, 296, July, pp.56–75. (in Korean).

Chung, J-K. (1991) 'Study of conflict over policy formulation process of environmental regulation', *Hyundai Sahwoe*, 39, Dec., pp.36–52 (in Korean).

Chung, J-K. and Hwang, E-B. (1983) 'Deadly Farming Methods, Site of Pesticide Pollution', in Hanguk Konghae Munjae Yeonguso (ed.) *Nae Tang-i Jukerganda (My Land is Dying)*, Ilweol Seogak, Seoul (in Korean).

Chung, J-Y. (1997) Capitalist Development, State and Environment in Postwar Korea: A Regulationist Approach, Ph.D. thesis, University of Liverpool.

Chung, T-S. (1992) 'Environmental Policies and Ideology of the State', *Kyongjaewa Sahwoe*, 15, Sept., pp.226–245 (in Korean).

Chung, W-S. (1992) 'The state of environmental problems and approach', *Kyung Hee Graduate School*, vol. 11, pp.3–35 (in Korean).

Clark, S. (1988) 'Overaccumulation, Class Struggle and the Regulation Approach', *Capital and Class*, 2, pp.1–31.

Cole, D. (1980) 'Foreign Assistance and Korean Development', in Cole, Lim and Kuznet (eds) *The Korean Economy; Issues of Development*, Institute of East Asian Studies, University of California, Berkeley.

Cole, D. and Lyman, P. (1971) *Korean Development*, Harvard University Press, Cambridge, MA.

Cole, D. and Park, Y.C. (1979) 'Financial Development in Korea 1945–1978', *KDI Working Paper*, no. 7904, Seoul, Korea.

Cole, K., Cameron, J. and Edwards, C. (1983) *Why Economists Disagree*, Longman, London.

Cooke, P. (1992) *Towards Global Localization: A Case of Britain and France*, UCL Press, London.

Cumings, B. (1981) *The Origins of the Korean War*, Princeton University Press, Princeton, NJ.

—— (1988) 'World System and Authoritarian Regimes in Korea, 1948–1984', in E. Wrinckler and S. Greenhalgh (eds) *The Political Economy of Taiwan*, M.E. Sharpe Inc., New York, pp.249–270.

Desai, M. (1983) 'Capitalism' in T. Bottomore, L. Harris, V.G. Kiernan and R. Miliband (eds) *A Dictionary of Marxist Thought*, Basil Blackwell, Oxford, pp.64–67.

DeVroey, M. (1984) 'A Regulation Approach Interpretation of Contemporary Crisis', in *Capital and Class*, 23, pp.45–66.

—— (1990) 'Theories of Regulation', *Environment and Planning D: Society and Space*, 8, pp.297–321.

Dicken, P. (1993) 'The Growth Economies of Pacific Asia in their Changing Global Context', in C. Dixon, and D. Drakakis-Smith (eds) *Economic and Social Development in Pacific Asia*, Routledge, London, pp.22–42.

Dixon, C. and Drakakis-Smith, D. (1993) 'The Pacific Asia Region', in C. Dixon and D. Drakakis-Smith (eds) *Economic and Social Development in Pacific Asia*, Routledge, London, pp.1–21.

Dobson, A. (1990) *Green Political Thought*, Unwin Hyman, London.

Douglass, M. (1992) 'The political economy of urban poverty and environmental management in Asia: access, empowerment and community based alternatives', *Environment and Urbanization*, vol. 4, no. 2, October.

—— (1993) 'Social, Political and Spatial Dimensions of Korean Industrial Transformation', *Journal of Contemporary Asia*, vol. 23, no. 2.

Drakakis-Smith, D. (1987) *The Third World City*, Methuen, London.

Dunford, M. (1988) *Capital, the State and Regional Development*, Pion, London.

—— (1990) 'Theories of Regulation', *Environment and Planning D: Society and Space*, 8, pp.297–321.

Dunleavy, P. and O'Leary, B. (1987) *Theories of the State*, Macmillan, London.

Eckersley, R. (1992) *Environmentalism and Political Theory*, UCL Press, London.

Economic Planning Board (1967) *Summary of the First Five Year Economic Development Plan 1962–1966*, EPB, Seoul.

Economic Planning Board (various years) *Economic Year Book*, EPB, Seoul.

—— (various years) *Major Economic Indicators*, EPB, Seoul.

Engels, F. (1978) *The Origin of Family, Private Property and the State*, Foreign Languages Press, Peking.

Enzensberger, H.M. (1974) 'A Critique of Political Ecology', *New Left Review*, 84, pp.3–31.

Everest, L. (1986), 'More Bhopals', in *The Nation*, 21 June.

Federation of Korean Trades Unions (1984) *1985 Wage Guide*, Federation of Korea Trade Union.

Florida, R. and Jonas, A. (1991) 'US Urban Policy: The postwar state and capitalist regulation', *Antipode*, 23 (4), pp.349–384.

Foster, J.B. (1988) 'The fetish of Fordism', *Monthly Review*, 39(10), pp.14–33.

Freeman (1987) *Technology Policy and Economic Performance: Lessons from Japan*, Frances Pinter, Oxford.

Froebel, F., Heinrichs, J. and Kreye, O. (1980) *The New International Division of Labour: Structural Unemployment in Industrialised Countries and Industrialisation in Developing Countries*, Cambridge University Press; Editions de la Maison des Sciences de l'Homme, Cambridge.

Gilbert, A. and Gugler, J. (1992) *Cities, Poverty and Development*, Oxford University Press, Oxford.

Glyn, J. and Sutcliffe, B. (1972) *British Capitalism, Workers and the Profit Squeeze*, Penguin, Harmondsworth.

Gold, D., Lo, C. and Wright, E. (1975) 'Recent Developments in Marxist Theories of the Capitalist State', *Monthly Review*, October, pp.30–43, and November, pp.36–51.

Gold, T.B. (1986) *State and Society in the Taiwan Miracle*, M.E. Sharpe, New York.

Goodman, D. and Redclift, M. (eds) (1991) *Environment and Development in Latin America: The Politics of Sustainability*, Manchester University Press, Manchester.

Gough, I. (1975) 'State Expenditure in Advanced Capitalism', *New Left Review*, 92, pp.53–92.

Graham, J. (1992) 'Post-Fordism as politics: the political consequences of narratives on the left', *Environment and Planning, D: Society and Space*, 10, pp.393–410.

Gramsci, A. (1971) *Selection from the Prison Notebooks*, Lawrence and Wishart, London.

Grubb, M. (1993) *The Earth Summit Agreements, A Guide and Assessment*, Earthscan, London.

Grundmann, R. (1991) *Marxism and Ecology*, Clarendon Press, Oxford.

Ha, S-K. (1991) *Theory of Housing Policy*, Parkyeongsa, Seoul.

—— (1992) 'New Understanding of Housing Problem and Policy', in Hanguk Konggan Hwangyong Yeonguhwoe (ed.) *New Understanding of Korean Spatial Environment*, Hanul Chongseo, Seoul (in Korean).

Haggard, S., Kim, B-K. and Moon, C-I. (1991) 'The Transition to Export-led Growth in South Korea: 1954–1966', *The Journal of Asian Studies*, 50(4), November, pp.850–873.

Hahn, S-J. (1992) 'Seoul Daedoshikwon Shindoshi Kaebal-eui Seonggyeok' (The Characteristics of New Town Development in the Seoul Metropolitan Region) in Korean Social History Research Group (ed.) *Regional Problems and Working Class in Korea*, Korean Social History Research Group Paper Compilation 37, pp.61–101, Seoul, Korea (in Korean).

Hanguk Gonghae Munjae Yeonguso (1986) *Pollution Map of Korea*, Ilweol Seogak, Seoul.

Hanguk Konggan Hwangyong Yeonguso (ed.) (1993) *Seoul Yeongu*, Hanul Academy, Seoul (in Korean).

Hanguk Konghae Yeonguso (ed.) (1983) *Nae-tang-i Jookerganda (My Land is Dying)*, Ilweol Seogak, Seoul (in Korean).

Hardoy, J.E. and Satterthwaite, D. (1989) *Squatter Citizen: Life in the Urban Third World*, Earthscan, London.

Harvey, D. (1973) *Social Justice and the City*, Basil Blackwell, London.

—— (1985a) *Urbanisation of Capital*, Page Bros, London.

—— (1985b) *Consciousness and the Urban Experience*, Basil Blackwell, Oxford.

—— (1993) 'The Nature of Environment: the Dialectics of Social and Environmental Change', in *Socialist Register: Real Problems and False Solutions*, The Merlin Press, London, pp.1–51.

—— (1994) *The Environmental Justice*, Paper delivered at Conference on Social Justice and Fin-De-Siecle Urbanism: An Agenda for the New Millennium, 14–15 March, School of Geography, Oxford University, Oxford, mimeo.

Hasan, A. and Azain Ali, A. (1992) 'Environmental problems in Pakistan; their origin and development and the threats that they pose to sustainable development', *Environment and Urbanisation*, 4(1), April, pp.8–21.

Henderson, J. (1993a) 'The Role of the State in the Economic Transformation of East Asia', in C. Dixon, and D. Drakakis-Smith (eds) *Economic and Social Development in Pacific Asia*, Routledge, London.

—— (1993b) 'Against the economic orthodoxy: on the making of the East Asian miracle', in *Economy and Society*, 22(2), May, pp.200–217.

—— (1999) 'The Weakness of Some and the Robustness of Others: Observations on the Governance of the East Asia Economic Crisis', Conference at Leeds Metropolitan University, organised by the Centre for Urban Development and Environmental Management and the Regional Studies Association, 11th March.

Henderson, J. and Appelbaum, R.P. (1992) 'Situating the State in the East Asian Development Process', in J. Henderson, and R.P. Appelbaum (eds) *States and Development in The Asian Pacific Rim*, Sage, London, p.1–26.

Higgins, R. (1980) *The Seventh Enemy*, Pan, London.

Hirsch, J. (1978) 'The State Apparatus and Social Reproduction: Elements of a Theory of the Bourgeois State', in Holloway and Picciotto (eds) *State and Capital: A Marxist Debate*, Edward Arnold, London, pp.57–107.

—— (1983) 'The Fordist Security State and New Social Movement', *Kapitalistate*, 10 (11), pp.75–88.

—— (1991) 'Fordism and Post-Fordism: The Present Social Crisis and its Consequence', in W. Bonefeld, and J. Holloway (eds) *Post-Fordism and Social Form: A Marxist Debate on the Post-Fordist State*, Macmillan.

Ho, S.P.S. (1978) *Economic Development of Taiwan, 1869–1970*, Yale University Press, New Haven, CT.

Holloway, J. and Picciotto, S. (1977) 'Capital, Crisis and the State', *Capital and Class*, 2, pp.76–101.

—— (eds) (1978) *State and Capital: a Marxist Debate*, Edward Arnold, London.

Holmberg, J. (1991) *Defending the Future: A Guide to Sustainable Development*, IIED, London.

Hong, S-H. and Kim, H-S. (1992) *Global City in a Nation of Growth: A Case of Seoul*, paper prepared for 'The International Aspect of Urban Development' Conference in Yokohama, 8–11 Nov., Pacific Rim Council on Urban Development, KRIHS, Seoul.

Hong, S-W. (1988) 'Balancing Equity and Efficiency in Regional Policy', in Richardson and Hwang (eds) *Urban and Regional Policies in Korea and International Experiences*, Korea Research Institute for Human Settlements, Seoul, pp.87–104.

Hong, W. (1978) 'Export Plan and Actual Export Performance in Korea', *Seoul National University Economic Review*, XII (1), December.

Howard, M.C. (ed.) (1993) *Asia's Environmental Crisis*, Westview Press, Oxford.

Hufsmidt, M.M. (1983) *Environment, Nature Systems and Development: An Economic Valuation Guide*, Johns Hopkins University Press, Baltimore.

Huh, U-D. (1993) *A Study on Environmental Problem and Environmental Crime in Korea*, Hanguk Hycungsa Jeongchaek Yeonguwon (Korea Crime Policy Institute), Seoul (in Korean).

Hwang, E-G. (1985) *Investment Priorities and Resource Allocation*, paper presented at the International Forum on Industrialisation and Rural Change, 17–26 September, IEDP, Seoul.

Hwang, M-C. and Choi, J-H. (1988) 'Evolution of the Settlement System in Korea: A Historical Perspective', in H.W. Richardson and M.C. Hwang (eds) *Urban and Regional Policies in Korea and International Experiences*, Korea Research Institute for Human Settlements, Seoul, pp.35–58.

ILT (Investing, Licencing and Trading Conditions Abroad) (1980) *Korea*, Business International Corporation, July.

Jessop, B. (1982) *The Capitalist State*, Martin Robertson, Oxford.

—— (1983) 'Accumulation Strategies, State Forms and Hegemonic Projects', *Kapitalistate*, 10, pp.98–110.

—— (1988) 'Regulation Theory, Post-Fordism and the State: more than a reply to Werner Bonefield', *Capital and Class*, 34, pp.147–68.

—— (1990a) 'Regulation Theory in Retrospect and Prospect', *Economy and Society*, 19, pp.153–216.

—— (1990b) *State Theory: Putting Capitalist States in Their Place*, Polity Press, Cambridge.

—— (1992) *From the Keynesian Welfare to the Schumpterian Workfare State*, Lancaster Regionalism Group, Working Paper 45, September, University of Lancaster, Lancaster.

—— (1994) 'Post-Fordism and the state', in A. Amin (ed.) *Post-Fordism*, Blackwell, Oxford, pp. 251–279.

Johnston, R.J. (1989) *Environmental Problems: Nature, Economy and State*, Blackwell, Oxford.

Jones, L.P. (1975) *Public Enterprise and Economic Development; The Korean Case*, KDI, Seoul.

Jones, L.P. and Sakong, I. (1980) *Government, Business and Entrepreneurship in Economic Development: the Korean Case*, Harvard East Asia Monographs, no. 91, Harvard University Council on East Asian Studies, Cambridge, MA.

Kim, B-W. (1994) *Hanguk-eui Hwangyong Jongchaekkwa Noksaekundong (Environmental Policy and Green Movement in Korea)*, Nanamsinser, Seoul (in Korean).

Kim, J-W. (1994) *Urinara-eui Jayeon Hwangyong Hyeunhwang Bunseok Yeongu (Study of Korea's Natural Environment)*, Korea Environmental Technology Research Institute, Seoul (in Korean).

Kim, K-S. and Park, J-K. (1985) *Sources of Economic Growth in Korea: 1963–1982*, KDI, Seoul.

Kim, S-K. (1987) *Business Concentration and Government Policy: A Study of the Phenomenon of Business Groups in Korea, 1945–1985*, Dissertation, Harvard Business School, Boston.

Kim, W-B. (1992) 'Spatial Division of Classes and Regional Uneven Development', in Hanguk Konggan Hwangyong Yeonguhwoe (ed.) *A New Understanding of Korean Spatial Environment*, Hanul, Seoul, pp.112–138 (in Korean).

Kim, Y-J. (1993) 'Hangook godokyongje-seongjangi-eui Kyeongjejeok Jiyeok Kyokcha' (Regional Economic Disparities of the Rapid Economic Growth in Korea: 1968–85; Analysis and Theoretical Development), in Korean Social History Research Group (ed.) *Regional Problems and Working Class in Korea*, Korean Social History Research Group Paper Compilation, vol. 37, Seoul, pp.11–60 (in Korean).

Kim, Y-W. and Masser, I. (1990) *Industrialization and its Spatial Implications in Korea*, TRP 92, Dept. of Town and Regional Planning, The University of Sheffield, Sheffield.

Konghaechubang-undong-yeonhap Yeongu-wiwonhwae (1992) *Jeonkuk Hwangyongoyeom Hyonhwang (The state of environmental pollution in Korea)*, Konghaechubang-undong-yeonhap (in Korean).

Koo, B-H. and Bark, T. (1989) *Recent Macroeconomic Performance and Industrial Structural Adjustment in Korea*, KDI Working Paper No. 8924, August, KDI, Seoul.

Koo, H. (1984) 'The Political Economy of Income Distribution in South Korea: The Impact of the State's Industrialization Policies', *World Development*, vol. 12, no. 10, pp.1029–1037.

Koo, H. and Kim, E-M. (1992) 'The Developmental State and Capital Accumulation in South Korea', in J. Henderson and R.P. Appelbaum (eds) *States and Development in The Asian Pacific Rim*, Sage, London, pp.121–149.

Korea Catholic Farmers Association and Korea Anti-nuclear Anti-pollution Peace Research Institute (KCFA and KAAPRI) (1990) 'Pesticide pollution problems of our land', *Konghae Daechaek*, no. 138, Feb., pp.22–31 (in Korean).

Korean Buddhist Social Education Institute (no date) *Jiguhwangyongpagwe-wa Saengtege-ui Wigi (Global Environmental Destruction and Crisis of Ecosystem)*, KBSEI, Seoul (in Korean).

Korean Federation of Trade and Industry (1990) *Sudokwon Kaebal Hap-nihwa wihan Sanop-ipji Jeongchaek Bang-an (Industrial Location Policy Direction for the Justification of the Development of Capital Region)*, KFTI, Seoul.

Korea Research Institute for Human Settlements, (KRIHS) (1989) *A Study on Land Taxation*, KRIHS, Seoul.

Kuznets, S. (1977) *Economic Growth and Structure in the Republic of Korea*, Yale University Press, New Haven, CT.

Kwon, H-S. (1991) 'Study of Korean Environmental Movement', *Hyundai Sahwoe*, 39, Dec., pp.75–8 (in Korean).

Kwon, T-H. and Shin, Y-H. (1977) 'On Population Estimates of the Yi Dynasty, 1392–1910', *Dongamoonhwa*, 14, pp.287–330 (in Korean).

Kwon, T-J. (1990) 'Environmental conscience without collective conscience is nothing', *Shin-Dong-A*, March, pp.386–405 (in Korean).

Kwon, W-Y. (1988a) 'Regional Development Policies and Strategies for the Sixth Economic and Social Development Plan (1987–1991)', in Richardson and Hwang (eds) *Urban and Regional Policies in Korea and International Experiences*, Korea Research Institute for Human Settlements, Seoul, pp.59–86.

—— (1988b) 'Population Decentralisation From Seoul and Regional Development Policy', in Richardson and Hwang (eds) *Urban and Regional Policies in Korea and International Experiences*, Korea Research Institute for Human Settlements, Seoul, pp.105–139.

—— (1991) 'Seoul: Mega-City Problems in Korea', International Conference of City and Regional Planning Schools, Department of Asian Universities, Tokyo, Japan, 11–12 November.

Kwon, Y-W. (1991) 'Daedoshiwa Joongsodoshi-eui Seongjang-kwa Jiyeoksah-waekoojo-eui Byunwha' (Growth of cities and changes in the regional-social structure), in Hanguk Jeongsinmunhwa Yeonguwon (ed.) *Hanguk-eui Sahwae-wa Munhwa (Korean Society and Culture), vol. 15; Haebanghu Doshisungjang-kwa JiYeoksahwae-eui Byunhwa (Growth of Cities and Regional-social Change in Post-independence Period)*, Hanguk Jeongsinmunhwa Yeonguwon, Seoul, pp.69–120 (in Korean).

Lee, D-G. (1991) 'Change of Environmental Policies for a Balance between Growth and Preservation', *Hyundai Sahwoe*, 39, Dec., pp.88–102 (in Korean).

Lee, J-J. (1991) 'Hwangyong munjae-wa Hwangyong jeongchaek-eui Gwaje-wa Jeonmang (The projects and prospects for environmental problems and policies)', *Hyundai Sa-whae*, 12, pp.3–11 (in Korean).

Lee, K-J. (1993) 'Namhan Saengtaegae, Ke Silsangkwa Daechaek' (The state and management of South Korean Ecosystem), in Baedal Hwangyong (ed.) *Hwangyong Bogoseo (Report of the Environment)*, Baedal Hwangyong, Seoul, pp.45–110 (in Korean).

Lee, K-S. (1988) 'An Evaluation of Industrial Location Policies for Urban Deconcentration in Korea', in Richardson and Hwang (eds) *Urban and Regional Policies in Korea and International Experiences*, Korea Research Institute for Human Settlements, Seoul, pp.141–150.

Lee, M-H. (1992), 'A Study of the State and Counterplan of Environmental Pollution', in Compilation of Thesis of Pusan Women's University, vol. 13, Dec., pp.231–261, (in Korean).

Lee, S-D. (1988) *Hwangyong Boho Undong-eui Hyangbang (The State of Environmental Protection Movement)*, Daehak Chulpansa, Seoul, (in Korean).

—— (1992) 'Korea's State of Environment and View from Non-Governmental Organisation Sector on the Northeast Asia Environmental Preservation', in *UNCED and Prospect on the Environmental Regime in the Twenty-First Century*, Seoul Symposium 1992, 2–5 Sept., Seoul, Korea.

Lee, S-H. (1993) 'Political Economy of Environmental Crisis in Seoul', in Hanguk Konggan Hwangyong Yeonguhwoe (ed.) *Seoul Yeongu (Seoul Research)*, Seoul, pp.437–463 (in Korean).

Lee, T-I. (1987) 'New Town Planning and Development in Korea', in D.R. Philips (ed.) *New Town in East and SouthEast Asia: Planning and Development*, Oxford University Press, Oxford, pp.109–125.

Lee, Y-S. (1993) 'Industrial Subcontracting and Labor Movement: The Korean Automotive Industry', *Journal of Contemporary Asia*, 23 (1), pp.24–40.

Lefèbvre, H. (1970) *La Revolution urbaine*, Paris.

—— (1976) *The Survival of Capitalism*, Allison & Busby, London.

—— (1991) *Production of Space*, Blackwell, Oxford.

Leff, E. (1993) 'Marxism and the Environmental Question: From the Critical Theory of Production to an Environmental Rationality for Sustainable Development', *Capitalism, Nature, Socialism*, 4(1), March, pp.44–66.

Linge, G. and Hamilton, F. (1981) 'International industrial systems', in F.E. Hamilton and G.J. Linge (eds) *Spatial Analysis, Industry and the Industrial Environment*, vol. 2, *International Industrial Systems*, Wiley, Chichester, pp.1–117.

Lipietz, A. (1984) *L'audace ou l'enlisement: sur les politiques economiques de la gauche*, Maspero, Paris.

—— (1985) 'The World Crisis: the globalisation of the general crisis of Fordism', *IDS Bulletin*, 6(2), pp.6–11.

—— (1986) 'New Tendencies in the International Division of Labour: Regimes of Accumulation and Modes of Regulation', in A. Scott and M. Storper (eds) *Production, Work, Territory*, Allen & Unwin, Boston, pp.16–40.

—— (1987) *Mirages and Miracles: the crises of global Fordism*, New Left Books, London.

—— (1988) 'Reflections on a Tale: The Marxist foundations of the concepts of regulation and accumulation', in *Studies in Political Economy*, 26, pp.7–26.

—— (1989) 'Three Crises: the metamorphoses of capitalism and the labour movement', in M. Gottdiener and N. Komnios (eds) *Capitalist Development and Crisis Theory*, Macmillan, London.

—— (1992) 'A Regulationist Approach to the Future of Urban Ecology', in *Capital, Nature, Socialism*, 3 (3), pp.101–10, September.

Lipton, M. (1976) *Why People Stay Poor: a study of urban bias in world development*, Temple-Smith, London.

Lovering, J. (1991) 'Theorising post-Fordism: why contingency matters – a further response to Scott', *International Journal of Urban and Regional Research*, 15, pp.298–301.

Lucky-Goldstar Economic Research Institute (1992) *Hwangyonggwa Ki-urp*, Lucky-Goldstar Economic Research Inst., Seoul.

Luedde-Neurath, R. (1988) 'State Intervention and Export-Oriented Development in South Korea', in G. White (ed.) *Developmentalist States in East Asia*, Macmillan, London, pp.69–104.

Luxemburg, R. (1951) *The Accumulation of Capital*, Routledge & Kegan Paul, London.

Mandel, E. (1983) 'Uneven Development' in T. Bottomore (ed.) *Dictionary of Marxist Thoughts*, Blackwell, Oxford.

Martin, R. (1994) 'Economic Theory and Human Geography', in D. Gregory, R. Martin and G. Smith (eds) *Human Geography: Society, Space and Social Science*, Macmillan, London, pp.21–53.

Marx, K. (1893) 'Preface' in *A Contribution to the Critique of Political Economy*, Kerr, Chicago, pp.19–23.

—— (1959) *Capital*, vol. 1, Foreign Languages Publishing House, Moscow.

—— (1973) *Grundrisse*, Penguin, Harmondsworth.

—— (1977) *Selected Writing*, edited by D. McLellan, Oxford University Press, Oxford.

Mason, E.S., Perkins, D.H., Kim, K-S., Cole, D.C., Kim, M-J. (1980) *The Economic and Social Modernization of the Republic of Korea*, Harvard University Press (for Council on East Asian Studies), Cambridge, MA.

Massey, D. (1979) 'In What Sense a Regional Problem?' *Regional Studies* 13, pp.233–243.

—— (1984) *Spatial Division of Labour: Social Structures and the Geography of Production*, Macmillan, London.

McCormick, J. (1989) *The Global Environmental Movement, Reclaiming Paradise*, Belhaven Press, London.

McKinsey Global Institute (1998) *McKinsey Report: A Road to Recreate Korea*, Mail Kyeongje Shinmunsa (in Korean).

Meadows, D.H. (1972) *Limits to Growth: A Report for the Club of Rome's Project on the Predicament of Mankind*, Pan, London.

Meadows, D.H., Meadows, D.L. and Randers, J. (1992) *Beyond the Limit: Global Collapse or a Sustainable Development*, Earthscan, London.

Meegan, R. (1988) 'A crisis of mass production?' in J. Allen and D. Massey (eds) *The Economy in Question: Restructuring Britain*, Sage, London.

Miliband, R. (1969) *The State in Capitalist Society*, Weidenfeld and Nicolson, London.

—— (1973) 'Poulantzas and the Capitalist State', *New Left Review*, 138, pp.37–68.

—— (1977) *Marxism and Politics*, Oxford University Press, Oxford.

Mills, E.S. and Song, B-N. (1979) *Urbanization and Urban Problems*, Council on East Asian Studies, Harvard University, Cambridge, MA.

Ministry of Construction (1971) *National Land Development Plan 1972–1981*, MoC, Government of R.O.K., Seoul.

—— (1982) *The Second Comprehensive National Physical Development Plan 1982–1991*, MoC, Government of R.O.K., Seoul.

—— (1991) *The Seventh Economic and Social Development Plan*, MoC, Seoul (in Korean).

Ministry of Environment (1982, 1987) *Survey of Public Consciousness of Environmental Conservation*, MoE, Seoul (in Korean).

—— (1991) *National Report of The Republic of Korea to UNCED 1992*, MoE, Seoul.

—— (various years) *Korea Environmental Yearbook*, MoE, Seoul (in Korean and English).

Mitnick, B.M. (1980) *The Political Economy of Regulation*, Columbia University Press, New York.

Moore Lappe, F. (1977) *Food First: beyond the myth of scarcity*, Boston.

Morishima, M. (1982) *Why has Japan 'succeeded'?*, Cambridge University Press, Cambridge.

Moughtin, C. (1996) *Urban Design: Green Dimensions*, Butterworth Architecture, Boston.

Moulaert, F. and Swyngedouw, E.A. (1989) 'A Regulation Approach to the Geography of Flexible Production Systems', in *Environment and Planning D: Society and Space*, 7, pp.327–345.

—— (1992) 'Accumulation and Organization in Computing and Communication Systems: A Regulationist Approach', in P. Cooke, F. Moulaert and E. Swyngedouw (eds) *Towards Global Localization: The Computing and Telecommunications Industries in Britain and France*, UCL Press, London.

National Statistical Office (various years) *Korea Statistical Yearbook*, NSO, Seoul (in Korean and English).

Nijkamp, P. (1977) *Theory and Application of Environmental Economics*, North-Holland, Amsterdam.

Nishina, K. and Noda, K. (1991) *Hanguk Konghae Report (Korean Pollution Report)*, Kemakowon, Seoul (in Korean).

Noh, Y-H. (1993) 'Hanguk Hwangyong-munjae-wa Hwangyong-jeongchaek' (Korea's Environmental Problems and Policies), in Baedal Hwangyong (ed.) *Hwanggyong Bogoseo (Report of the Environment)*, Baedal Hwangyong, Seoul, pp.3–44 (in Korean).

Nolan, P. (1990) 'Assessing Economic Growth in the Asian NICs', *Journal of Contemporary Asia*, 20(1), pp.41–61.

O'Connor, J. (1988) 'Capitalism, Nature, and Socialism: a theoretical introduction', *Capitalism Nature Socialism*, 1(1), pp.11–38.

—— (1989) 'Uneven and Combined Development and Ecological Crisis: a theoretical introduction', *Race and Class*, 30, pp.1–11.

OECD (1985) *Environmental Policy and Technical Change*, OECD, Paris.

—— (1987) *OECD Environmental Data*, OECD, Paris.

—— (1988) *Transport and Environment*, OECD, Paris.

Offe, C. (1975) 'The Theory of the Capitalist State and the Problem of Policy Formation', in L.N. Lindberg *et al.* (eds), *Stress and Contradiction in Modern Capitalism*, D.H. Heath, Lexington.

Offe, C. and Ronge, V. (1975) 'Theses on the Theory of the State', *New German Critique*, 6, pp.137–147.

Office of Environment (1981) The Report of Air Pollution, OoE, Seoul (in Korean).

Ogle, G.E. (1990) *South Korea; Dissent within the Economic Miracle*, Zed Books, London.

Oh, J-J. (1991) 'Air Pollution and Spatial Structure of Seoul', *Jiyeok Hwangyong*, 9 (Dec), pp.18–51 (in Korean).

O'Riordan, T. (1981) *Environmentalism*, Pion Press, London.

—— (1989) 'The Challenge for Environmentalism', in R. Peet, and N. Thrift (eds) *The New Models in Geography*, vol. 1, Unwin-Hyman, London, pp.78–102.

Pahl, R.E. and Winkler, J.T. (1974) 'The Coming Corporatism', *New Society*, 10 October, pp.72–76.

Park, C-J. (1991) *Seoul, Yidaero Jo-unga, (Seoul, Is It Alright as It Is)*, Nokjin, Seoul (in Korean).

Park, M-S. (1996) *Establishing A Comprehensive Development Plan for the Pusan Economy*, seminar paper delivered at Dept. of Civic Design, University of Liverpool, mimeo.

Park, S-O. (1986) 'Regional Changes in the Industrial System of a Newly Industrialising Country: The Case of Korea', in F.E.I. Hamilton (ed.) *Industrialisation in Developing and Peripheral Regions*, Croom Helm, London, pp.311–334.

—— (1991) 'Government Management of Industrial Change in the Republic of Korea', in Rich and Linge (eds) *The State and The Spatial Management of Industrial Change*, Routledge, London, pp.74–87.

Parsons, H.L. (1977) *Marx and Engel on Ecology*, Greenwood, London.

Pearce, D.W. (1975) *Environmental Economics*, Longman, N.Y.

—— (1989) *Blueprint for a Green Economy*, Earthscan, London.

—— (1990) *Sustainable Development: Economics and Environment in the Third World*, Earthscan, London.

—— (1991) *Blue Print 2: Greening the World Economy*, Earthscan, London.

—— (1993) *Economic Value and the Natural World*, Earthscan, London.

Peet, R. (1991) *Global Capitalism: Theories of Societal Development*, Routledge, London.

Pepper, D. (1991) *Communes and the Green Vision: Counterculture, Lifestyle and the New Age*, Green Print, Basingstoke.

—— (1993) *Eco-socialism: from deep ecology to social justice*, Routledge, London.

Philips, D.R. (ed.) (1987) *New Towns in East and Southeast Asia: Planning and Development*, Oxford University Press, Oxford.

Porritt, J. (1984) *Seeing Green*, Blackwell, Oxford.

Poulantzas, N. (1968) *Political Power and Social Classes*, New Left Books, London.

—— (1976a) *Crisis of Dictatorships*, 2nd edn, New Left Books, London.

—— (1976b) 'The Capitalist State', *New Left Review*, 95, pp.63–83.

Pu, W-H. (1961) 'The History of America Aid to Korea', *Korean Quarterly*, 3 (1), pp.71–96.

Ranis, G. (1989) *The Political Economy of Development Policy Change: A Comparative Study of Taiwan and Korea*, KDI Working Paper No. 8916, KDI, Seoul.

Redclift, M. (1984) *Development and the Environmental Crisis: Red or Green Alternatives?*, Routledge, London.

—— (1987) *Sustainable Development: Exploring the Contradiction*, Routledge, London.

Rhee, S. (1987) *Policy Reforms of the Eighties and Industrial Adjustments in Korean Economy*, KDI Working Paper No. 8708, KDI, Seoul.

Rich, D.C. and Linge, G.J.R. (eds) (1991) *The State and The Spatial Management of Industrial Change*, Routledge, London.

Richardson, H.W. and Baek, C.H. (1988) 'The Transport Sector and Spatial Policy', in H.W. Richardson and M-C. Hwang (eds) *Urban and Regional Policies in Korea and International Experiences*, Korea Research Institute for Human Settlements, Seoul, pp.151–170.

Richardson, H.W. and Hwang, M-C. (1988) 'Introduction', in H.W. Richardson and M-C. Hwang (eds), *Urban and Regional Policies in Korea and International Experiences*, Korea Research Institute for Human Settlements, Seoul, pp.11–32.

Roddick, J. (1988) *The dance of the millions: Latin America and the debt crisis*, Latin America Bureau, London.

Rustin, M. (1989) 'The politics of post-Fordism or, the trouble with "New Times"', *New Left Review*, 175, pp.54–78.

Sakong, I. (1980) 'Economic growth and concentration of economic power', *Korean Development Study*, (Spring), KDI, Seoul, pp.2–13 (in Korean).

Sale, K. (1985) *Dwellers in the Land: the Bioregional Vision*, Sierra Club, San Francisco.

Sano, J. (1977) 'Foreign Capital and Investment in South Korean Development', *Asian Economics*, 23, December.

Saunders, P. (1984) *Urban Politics: A sociological interpretation*, Hutchinson, London.

Sayer, A. (1989a) 'Post-Fordism in Question', *International Journal of Urban and Regional Research*, 13, pp.666–695.

—— (1989b) 'Dualistic Thinking and Rhetoric in Geography', *Area*, 21 (4), pp.301–305.

Sayer, A. and Walker, R. (1992) *The New Social Economy: Reworking the Division of Labour*, Blackwell, Oxford.

Schmidt, A. (1971) *The Concept of Nature in Marx*, New Left Books, London.

Schumacher, E.F. (1973) *Small is Beautiful: Economics as if People Really Mattered*, Abacus, London.

Scott, A.J. and Storper, M. (1989) 'The geographical foundations and social regulation of flexible production complexes', in J. Wolch and H. Dear (eds) *The Power of Geography: How Territory Shapes Social Life*, Unwin Hyman, Winchester, MA.

—— (1990) 'Work organisation and local labour markets in an era of flexible production', *International Labour Review*, 129, pp.573–91.

Seabrook, J. (1985) *Landscape of Distress*, Blackwell, Oxford.

Seo, J-K. (1993) 'Housing Problems and Politics of Housing', in Hanguk Konggan Hwangyong Yeonguhwoe (ed.) *Seoul Yeongu*, Hanul Academy, Seoul, pp.331–357 (in Korean).

Seoul City Government (1981) *The Report of Seoul City Administration*, SCG, Seoul.

Seoul Development Institute (1994) *Sustainable Seoul Development: The City Report on the Environment*, SDI, Seoul.

Seoul Metropolitan Government (1990a) *Seoul Metropolitan Administration 1989*, SMG, Seoul.

—— (1990b) *Seoul City Plan for the 21st Century*, SMG, Seoul.

—— (1993) *Comparative Statistics of Major Cities 1992*, SMG, Seoul.

—— (various years) *Seoul Metropolitan Administration*, SMG, Seoul.

Seoul National University Medical School (1973) *Study on Pollution in Large Industrial Estate*, Seoul National University.

Shin, D-H. (1993) 'Economic Growth and Environmental Problems in South Korea: The Role of the Government', in M.C. Howard (ed.) *Asia's Environmental Crisis*, Westview Press, Boulder and Oxford, pp.235–256.

Smith, N. (1980) 'Symptomatic Silence in Althusser: The Concept of Nature and the Unity of Science', *Science and Society*, 44(1), pp.58–81.

—— (1984) *Uneven Development*, Basil Blackwell, Oxford.

Smith, N. and O'Keefe, P. (1980) 'Geography, Marx and concept of nature', *Antipode*, 12(2), pp.30–39.

Sohn, B. D. (1997) *Korean Economic Year Book*, The Federation of Korean Industries, Seoul

Son, J-Y. (1990) *Analysis of and Reform Proposals for 'The Land Problem' in Korea*, KDI Working Paper No. 9013, KDI, Seoul.

Steinberg, D.I. (1989) *The Republic of Korea; Economic Transformation and Social Change*, Westview Press, London.

Suh, S-M. (1992) 'The Economy in Historical Perspective', in V. Corbo and S-M. Suh (eds) *Structural Adjustment in a Newly Industrialized Country; The Korean Experience*, The Johns Hopkins University Press, London and Baltimore, pp.6–34.

Swyngedouw, E.A. (1988) *Capitalism: Quo Vadis, Reflections on the spatial structure of flexible production and consumption*, paper presented to the International Conference on the Regulation Theory, Barcelona, 16–8 June.

Thomas, C. (1992) *The Environment in International Relations*, The Royal Institute of International Affairs, London.

Thrift, N. (1989) 'New times and new spaces? The perils of transition models', *Environment and Planning D: Society and Space*, 7, pp.127–129.

Tickell, A. and Peck, I. (1992a) *Time, Space and Flexibility: the Social regulation of Uneven Development*, paper presented to the conference of the International Geographical Union Commission on Industrial Change 'Time, Space, Competition and Contemporary Industrial Change', Orlando, August.

—— (1992b) 'Accumulation, Regulation and the Geographies of Post-Fordism: Missing Links in Regulationist Research', *Progress in Human Geography*, 16(2), pp.190–218.

Torfing, J. (1991) 'A Hegemony Approach to Capitalist Regulation', in B. Bertramsen, J. Peter, J. Thomsen and J. Torfing (eds) *State, Economy and Society*, Unwin Hyman, London.

21st Century Committee (1991) *Survey of Public Awareness for the 21st Century*, April, Government of ROK.

Ullrich, O. (1979) *World Standard: in the Blind Alley of the Industrial System*, Ratbuch Verlag, Berlin.

United Nations (1975) *Yearbook of the United Nations 1972*, vol. 26, UN Office of Public Information, New York.

—— (1976) *World Housing Survey*, UN Department of Economic and Social Affairs, New York.

Vincent, A. (1987) *Theories of the State*, Basil Blackwell, Oxford.

Wade, R. (1990) *Governing the market: Economic theory and the role of government in East Asian industrialization*, Princeton University Press, Princeton, NJ.

White, G. (ed.) (1988) *Developmental States in East Asia*, Macmillan Press, London.

White, L. (1967) 'The historical roots of our ecologic crisis', *Science*, 155, pp.1203–1207.

Williams, K., Cutler, T., Williams, J. and Haslam, C. (1987) 'The end of mass production?' *Economy and Society*, 16 (3), pp.405–439.

Williams, K. and Haslam, C. (1991) 'Ford versus Fordism', Department of Economics, University of Wales, Aberystwyth, mimeo.

World Bank (1992) *World Development Report 1992*, Oxford University Press, Oxford.

—— (1999) *Social Policy and Governance, Poverty and Korea*, at http://www.worldbank.org/eapsocial/countries/korea/pov1.htm

World Commission on Environment and Development (WCED) (1987) *Our Common Future*, Oxford University Press, Oxford.

World Economic Forum (1998) *1998 Global Competitiveness Report*, at http://www.weforum.org/reports_pub.nsf/Documents/Home+-+Reports+and+Publications+-+Global+Competitiveness+Report

World Resource Institute (1992) *World Resources 1992–93; A Guide to the Global Environment*, Oxford University Press, New York.

—— (1994) *World Resources 1994–95: A Guide to the Global Environment*, Oxford University Press, New York.

Wrinckler, E.A. (1988) 'Globalist, Statist and Network Paradigms in East Asia', in E.A. Wrinckler and S. Greenhalgh (eds) *The Political Economy of Taiwan*, M.E. Sharpe Inc., New York, pp.270–281.

Wrinckler, E.A. and Greenhalgh, S. (eds) (1988) *The Political Economy of Taiwan*, M.E. Sharpe, New York.

Yaffe, D. (1973) 'The Marxian Theory of Crisis, Capital, and the State', *Economy and Society*, 2(2), pp.186–222.

Yang, J-H. (1992), 'The changing environmental awareness of Korean public and social basis', *Hanguk Sawhoehak (Korean Social Science)*, vol. 26, Winter ed., pp.89–120 (in Korean).

Yim, C-H. and Choi, J-H. (1991) 'Urban Poor, Housing and Basic Infrastructure Services in The Republic of Korea: The Case of Three Cities', in Asian Development Bank and Economic Development Institute (ed.) *The Urban Poor and Basic Infrastructure Services in Asia and the Pacific*, A Regional Seminar, 22–28 Jan., pp.669–713.

Yu, S-M. (1992) 'Hanguk Nodongja-gyegup Saenghwalkwon-eui Hwangyong-munjae' (The environmental problems and the reproduction of Korean Working Classes), *Donghyangkwa jeonmang*, 15, March, pp.143–157 (in Korean).

Index